ITALY AND THE
WIDER WORLD

Why is Italy always in 'crisis'?

Why have Italians spread around the world?
With what effect?

'It would be difficult to imagine a wittier or more stimulating text.'

Paul Preston, *LSE*

R.J.B. Bosworth's lively overview of Italy's role in European and world affairs from 1860 to 1960 highlights the ambiguity of Italy's political, economic and social fortunes in the modern era. In successive chapters he examines Italy's relationship with other countries in formal diplomacy, military matters, trade and finance, imperial policy, emigration, 'high' and 'low' culture and tourism. In dealing with each theme Bosworth asks challenging questions of the existing historiography, offering an original vision of Italy's place in modern history.

Based on deep acquaintance with archival sources and an extensive range of secondary sources, this fresh approach presents vital background to contemporary Italy and will appeal to historians of modern Europe and Italianists alike.

R.J.B. Bosworth is Professor of History at the University of Western Australia. He has published widely on modern Italian political and social history, including emigration history, and on historiography.

ITALY AND THE
WIDER WORLD
1860–1960

R. J. B. Bosworth

London and New York

First published 1996
by Routledge
11 New Fetter Lane, London EC4P 4EE

Simultaneously published in the USA and Canada
by Routledge
29 West 35th Street, New York, NY 10001

© 1996 R. J. B. Bosworth

Typeset in Garamond by
Ponting–Green Publishing Services, Chesham, Bucks
Printed and bound in Great Britain by
T. J. Press (Padstow) Ltd, Padstow, Cornwall

British Library Cataloguing in Publication Data
A catalogue record for this book is available from
the British Library

Library of Congress Cataloging in Publication Data
A catalogue record for this book has been requested

ISBN 0–415–13477–3

for Enrico Serra

CONTENTS

Tables   viii
Preface   ix
Introduction: The problem of Italy and the wider world
1860–1960   1

1 ITALIAN DIPLOMACY AND EUROPEAN
   POWER POLITICS 1860–1922   15

2 ITALIAN DIPLOMACY AND EUROPEAN
   POWER POLITICS 1922–60   36

3 THE ITALIAN MILITARY IN WAR AND PEACE
   1860–1960   57

4 ITALIAN COMMERCE AND THE WIDER
   WORLD 1860–1960   76

5 THE RISE AND FALL OF THE ITALIAN EMPIRE
   1860–1960   94

6 THE RISE AND RISE OF THE EMPIRE OF THE
   ITALIES: EMIGRATION 1860–1960   114

7 CULTURES AND IDEOLOGY FOR EXPORT:
   ITALY AND THE ITALIES 1860–1960   137

8 VISITING ITALY: TOURISM AND LEISURE
   1860–1960   159

Conclusion   182
Notes   188
Index   241

TABLES

6.1	Emigration from Italy 1876–1975	115
6.2	Repatriation to Italy 1905–74	115
6.3	Emigration by gender 1876–1975	118
6.4	Emigration by region 1876–1975	119
6.5	Emigration by destination 1876–1975	128
8.1	Tourists visiting Italy and their means of access 1931–56	176
8.2	Number of tourists to certain countries 1953 and 1956	178
8.3	Hotel and other accommodation in certain regions, 30 June 1957	178

PREFACE

In the sparse literature of my now home state of Western Australia, there are at least two outstanding autobiographies. One is by Albert Facey, a bush worker. It is entitled *A Fortunate Life*.[1] The other is by Emma Ciccotosto, an Italian or Abruzzese immigrant. Her memoir's subtitle is 'a translated life'.[2] I have no intention of competing with either of these writers, but I am a person both fortunate and translated.

I am fortunate that Michael Hurst initially suggested to me the idea of writing this volume. I am fortunate, too, in that I have a host of friendly critics who sacrifice their time to read my prose before publication, and thus help to curb my stylistic solecisms and reduce my factual errors. In the case of this book I am especially indebted to Roger Absalom, Walter Adamson, Ruth Ben-Ghiat, Michal Bosworth, Margot Melia, Ros Pesman, Gino Rizzo, Rob Stuart, Graham White, Shane White and to Janet King. Since I am one of those academic historians who live, at least partially, through the perpetual challenge and unending rewards of teaching, I must also thank Lorenzo Polizzotto, with whom I presently teach a course on 'The Italies in crisis', and the students who have taken this course or others which, over the years, I have taught on Italy. When the world goes right, as it not infrequently does, students teach the teachers.

In order to write it is necessary to have time alone to wrestle with prose and meaning. I was particularly fortunate in commencing the construction of this book while on study leave from the University of Western Australia in 1992. Part of that leave I spent as a Visiting Scholar at St John's College, Cambridge; the rest in Venice – two perfect environments for a writer.

After the writing comes the publication, and here I am fortunate again to be associated with the team at Routledge under Claire L'Enfant. Attempting to be a European historian as an Australian sometimes seems to be an activity done from the periphery, if only in the mind. Routledge, however, treat the world as one and, even before email, thus were already helping to end any perceived 'tyranny of distance'. They do not seem to have minded that, in this book in particular, I have indeed tried to write as an Australian Europeanist.

My good fortune extends further. Spending my life in great part as a historian of modern Italy has been a career choice which I have never regretted. I have enjoyed it all the more because I, a fifth generation Anglo-Saxon Australian, have been brought into repeated contact with Italians both in emigrant communities and in Italy itself, and with such distinguished, and very different, historians as Luigi Goglia, Luisa Passerini, Sergio Romano, Luciano Tosi, Romano Ugolini and Enrico Serra, that doyen of historians of Italy's place in the world, to whom this book is dedicated. Each of these friends has put up with the vagaries of one best defined as the *canguro* of Italian historiography and has courteously directed me through archives or to the most important literature, even when they knew that I, an outsider of outsiders, would see only through a glass darkly.

In this as in other senses I am not only fortunate but also 'translated'. As a historian I perceive myself, in what is a decidedly Aussie image, as a small boy with nose pressed against the window of the sweet shop called Italy. Inside are luscious and garish items in endless variety. But before my eye has measured the exact shape and my mind made out the exact texture of each item, I, after all the *canguro*, move restlessly on to ponder something else. However frequently I visit the shop, I am destined never quite to get inside its doors, never quite to comprehend its 'reality'.

But my 'translation' simultaneously has another side to it. I go to Italy often. In 'Italo-Australia' I regularly fill the role of token Anglo-Saxon on this or that 'community' committee. Italy and the Italies form part of my own identity. I, too, am some sort of 'Italian'. This book is thus a product of an essential 'duplicity', of a doubleness and ambiguity. As an outsider, I have written a history of Italy's relationship with the wider world in the period since national 'unification'. As a person and a historian, I live in a city which is regularly defined as the most isolated in the world. And yet, even in Perth, Italy and the Italies have constantly and insistently visited me, and will, I trust, continue to visit me, so that I can continue my process of imagining both an Italian 'community' and myself.

Richard Bosworth
Perth (WA) 1995

INTRODUCTION: THE PROBLEM OF ITALY AND THE WIDER WORLD 1860–1960

In Perth, Western Australia, 'the most isolated city in the world', Kings Park looks out over the central business district. In this park can be found the unique fauna and flora of Western Australia – raucous parrots, nocturnal marsupials, tortured 'kangaroo paws' and giant gums. On Sundays, the populace gathers there to picnic and to play. But, a young anthropologist has told us, beware what goes on at the wall by the Pioneer Women's Fountain. For there congregate some second- and third-generation Italo-West Australians. Their clothes, their gestures, their style flaunt their version of *italianità*. Males greet each other with dramatic hugs and fervent kisses like football players having scored a goal. Females talk knowingly about the superior sexual mores of 'Marias' (Italian girls) compared with those of 'skippies' (Australian girls). Morality, material goods and ethnicity mingle. The anthropologist's description runs on: 'there were many Fiat cars, many Italian flags and many private number plates sporting Italian names. Most rear vision mirrors dangled crimson garters'. Should non-Italian Australians intrude into this sacred space, they are expelled: 'A group of Australian cyclists passed the wall and one [Italian youth] commented [sarcastically]: "Oh look, the whole family is here". They were quickly booed and jeered and chased off the scene.'[1]

Is this a tale of imperishable *italianità*, of Italian nationality enduring in the harshest climate, of Italy conquering the wider world? – Perhaps. If it is, there is one small problem. The 'Italian' youths speak a version of Australian-English. As likely as not, they know little of their supposed homeland and less of its official language.

This linguistic contradiction is only one conundrum among many. What can be learned of Italy's place in the world from the fact that a Connecticut museum boasts that 'the first American pizza was served' in that state?[2] Or that, in the printing trade of St Petersburg at the turn of the century, the lowest of the low were described as the 'Italians of the craft, alcoholic wrecks who dressed in rags and changed jobs repeatedly in the course of the year'; or that the Russian word for strike, *zabastovka*, derives from the Italian *basta* (enough)?[3] Or even that, for Adolf Hitler, 'despite their weaknesses, the Italians have so many qualities that make us like them'. Their countryside was beautiful, the Führer reflected, their souls musical and artistic and, anyway, 'there's also our own past on Italian soil'. Italy, as a vehicle of history, must always appeal, and he concluded portentously, 'a man who is indifferent to history is a man without hearing, without sight. Such a man can live, of course – but what a life?'[4]

Boccaccio and beggars, Catholicism and Al Capone, Dante and Danakil tribesmen, Ferrari and Florence, Garibaldi and grappa, Machiavelli, Mussolini and the Mafia – an alphabet of contradictory images from Italy's past and Italy's present jostles for attention. Hardly surprisingly, much the same bustling *mélange* of jarring images can be found in the way Italians understand themselves and their place in the world, and in the world's understanding of Italians. Any analyst of the problematic of Italy and the wider world 1860–1960 is thus confronted with an immediate dilemma – there are many Italies to be pondered, both in the scholarship of historians or of other experts and in the popular mind. Indeed, so numerous are these Italies that the most enduring cliché about 'Italy' is that there is no such place. Antonio Gramsci[5] and others have argued that commentators, before talking about 'Italian policy' or 'Italian life', must remind themselves that the history of Northern Italy is not synonymous with that of the South, that urban Italy has seldom held the same ideas and pursued the same interests as rural Italy, and that Italian governments and the Italian bureaucracy ('legal Italy'), whether Liberal, Fascist or liberal democratic Republican, have by no means lived in harmony with the Italian people ('real Italy').

To these fundamental schisms can be added many more. For example, the *Annales'* injunction that geography is the beginning of wisdom in the *longue durée* raises the vexed issue of the physical boundaries of Italy. In the century after the Risorgimento, Italy has not possessed stable political borders. The Veneto was gained in 1866, Rome in 1870, the Trentino and Trieste in the First World War. Istria and pieces of Dalmatia were annexed in 1918–19 but were surrendered to Yugoslavia, or Slovenia and Croatia, at the end of the Second World War, even if, in the 1990s, some 'post-Fascist' nostalgics were hoping that the surrender might not after all be permanent. When Mussolini's regime collapsed the Val di Tenda was lost to France and Italy's possession of the Val d'Aosta was seriously threatened. An empire was briefly constructed in the Horn of Africa (from the 1880s), in Libya and the Dodecanese Islands (1911–12), in Ethiopia (1935–6) and in Albania (1939) and more swiftly lost with the defeat of Fascism in 1940–5. But, until then, certainly Italian politicians and intellectuals, and perhaps the Italian people,[6] their thirst for territorial gain as yet unslaked, talked glibly of 'regaining' Nice or Savoy or Corsica or Fiume or Malta or Tunis or Cyprus or Corfu, and of seizing Djibouti or Yemen or parts of Turkish Asia Minor. Many in both Liberal and Fascist Italy dreamed fitfully of the 'Third Rome' holding sway over a dominion which would somehow replicate or enlarge that of the 'First Rome' of Augustus and Trajan.

These last ambitions are a reminder that 'geography' is as much a construct as is everything else, and that borders are, at least partially, the product of peoples' minds. In the designation of borders, so many rival disciplines and emotions – history, political ideologies, economics, 'languages' and 'dialects',[7] religion and philosophy, family, love, work, age, gender and time – can interfere. Rather than being determined by geopolitics, as Italian diplomatic historians have been accustomed to aver,[8] Italian 'national interests', even more markedly than with those of other states, were manufactured in the eyes of the beholders. It is a commonplace that the gap between 'legal' and 'real' Italy was as wide in dreams of empire as in everything else. 'Legal' Italy, driven by a costly and perhaps irrational desire to mimic an imagined past, played the games of European Great Power politics and sought to seize territory in the *mare nostrum* and its hinterland. The 'real' Italies, by contrast, through emigration laid the bases of the commercial and cultural empires of the future, in New York and Buenos Aires, Kenya and Australia.

Here then are manifest some of the first complications of *paese*, a word which simultaneously signifies home village and nation state and which is at least as plural in its resonances as is that emblematic Russian term *mir*. Students of social history and of emigration have indicated how every Italian *paese* has, in a sense, pursued its own *Weltpolitik*. But, even while it could thus act as a world-ranging 'community', each *paese* simultaneously can be understood as a shell in which the dealings of smaller fractions of the village were negotiated. Parishes, united by reverence for a particular saint or church bell, and families, in alliance or in conflict, on the rise or in decline, established their agreements and sorted out their disagreements in ways that were both intensely parochial and surprisingly worldly-wise. Before the transoceanic emigration which commenced in the 1870s and 1880s, *paesi* had already sent out their sons as soldiers and brigands, clerics ('Southern intellectuals') and seasonal labourers. Even their daughters sometimes contrived to travel, as prostitutes or serving girls, and as brides to living men or to Christ. The world also reached the *paese*, through merchants and itinerant preachers, through musicians and other entertainers, through the tax collectors and military forces of the official state[9] and, of course, through ideas, myths and folk-legends which, from time to time and place to place, would take root like seed borne on the wind.

By the end of the nineteenth century, mass emigration – initially from the North and to Europe, but which soon spread, however unevenly, to all parts of Italy and the world[10] – greatly expanded the borders of the *paese*. The nation state has been in modern times so much the dominant and successful political form that it is hard to conceive of a map of the globe not 'naturally' divided between 'nations', each with its own continuous borders. But, for many Italians, the more obvious and decisive frontiers were not located in a printed atlas but wherever their minds or custom advised. For, as that splendidly ambiguous phrase puts it, '*tutto il mondo è paese*' ('it's a small world' but, literally, 'the whole world is home'). To be more accurate, fragments of the *paese* existed in this German city or that American suburb or town, in this camp-site in Queensland or that sugar plantation in Brazil. Your passport may have stated baldly that you were Italian (or perhaps even that you had 'assimilated' to your new country), but the image of your *paese*'s saint or madonna, a particular pasta sauce, a wine, or special liqueur or *digestivo* from your home village, your most familiar employer or fellow worker, the way you carried yourself, the clothes you wore and your most intimate gestures and phrases, your wife and children (who often remained in Italy), and thus most of your 'culture', marked you as a *paesano*.

The most useful map for any student of modern Italy is not, perhaps, that of the nation state, but rather is one which charts how a multiplicity of *paesi* can be found scattered all over the world and how their values and cultures are transmitted and, consequently, reinvented through letters and ceremonies, voyages of departure and return, and the constant need to guard against the enmity, real or imagined, of the *paesano*'s neighbours. One of the more suggestive pieces of information[11] about Italo-Western Australia is that companies of fishermen, themselves divided by provenance from Molfetta ('the *Pugliesi*') or Capo d'Orlando ('the *Siciliani*'), named for themselves the chief landmarks of the West Australian coast.[12] The naming of their world was, they assumed, still their own task and not that of officialdom. The maps of their working, as well as of their daily, lives were not those which accepted that rational or taylorised ordering of time and space which begins at Greenwich and which is coterminous with the triumphs of the nation state and of capitalism.

But is this too romantic a picture of where the borders of Italy or *paese* might reside in an Italian, or *paesano*, mind? The image so far constructed is that of the *Weltpolitik* of a *paese* at peace and in stasis. But such peace and such stasis never really existed. Instead, every individual's identity and culture were in perpetual movement and could be changed, whether by intention or not, in response to situation, opportunity or threat. In the century from 1860 to 1960, many 'Italians', at different times and places and in different ways, could find themselves caught up in the processes of nationalisation, regionalisation, Catholicisation (or, rather, the 'disciplinisation' of the modern church), Fascist- or other idelog-isation, assimilation or, as varieties of multiculturalism became more popular or widespread, ethnicisation. The family, too, was in flux,[13] as were the ways of being a man or woman or a child. For those who would investigate Italy's place in the world since the Risorgimento, the most basic datum must be that the words 'Italy' and 'Italian' do not have a single or a consistent meaning. From 1860 to 1960, as E.P. Thompson might have said, *italianità* was always a 'happening' and never a 'thing'.

An underlining of such inconstancy is perhaps superfluous for a readership which, for more than a generation, has been so sedulously taught about the fragility and subjectivity of all discourse. And yet the existing historiography of Italy's place in the world rarely acknowledges the ambiguities of Italian identity. Students of the practice of the Italian state and of the processes of Italian society seem to work in circles closed one to the other. In particular, the huge literature on Italian diplomatic history is often posited on the most simplistic historicist assumptions that the task of an historian is to report what actually happened.

Such conventional views survive despite the *Annaliste*, Jacques Le Goff's celebrated declaration at the beginning of the 1970s that all 'political history' was moribund.[14] Le Goff expressed an opinion held by many social historians that the practitioners of diplomatic history were narrow minded and conceptually barren traditionalists, unable to record more than what one clerk wrote to another. Their fondness for 'facts' barely masked a blind loyalty or subservience to their own nation and to its ruling class. Granted prestigious and cushy jobs in their national universities, these historians habitually lied for their countries.

Some of these criticisms were just. Until 1945 and even beyond, the relating of international policy was a matter of especially great importance to the nation state, whether in Italy or elsewhere, and to its rulers. The history of diplomacy and war was by definition the key source of exemplary tales which might be deployed to 'invent tradition', to 'nationalise the masses' and to forge or 'imagine' a national 'community'.[15] In the best of all national worlds, it was accepted, diplomatic historiography should be above party, and a nation's international policy should be esteemed too serious a business to be handed over to anti-national or critical historians. A patriotic historian, like the Fascist Gioacchino Volpe, should write patriotic history, seconding, for example, Italian ambitions on Corsica. He should then be read patriotically – in the Second World War, King Victor Emmanuel believed reports that the islanders had received invading Fascist troops with enthusiasm because, he said, he had consulted Volpe's pages and thus learned what to expect.[16]

Nonetheless, critical historians there had been, especially Marxists, hostile to their nation's existing ruling elite, and other internationalists. And, in the 1960s, these traditions were revived as the writing of diplomatic history was revolutionised, especially in the aftermath of the 'Fischer controversy' in West Germany.[17] Fritz Fischer, and younger generation historians of what came to be called the Bielefeld school, reprogrammed the work of Eckart Kehr to argue that the practice of diplomacy could not necessarily be separated from the daily deeds of domestic politics and society. Rather, they argued, international policy, at least in Germany's case, was often conducted as a diversionary tactic deflecting the menace of revolutionary change at home. Germany was the place of 'social imperialism', where either risking or fomenting a war was seen by the elites as preferable to imposing income tax or yielding to the other dangers of democracy.

Though not all the writings of the Bielefeld school were convincing, the idea that diplomacy and other forms of international policy should be placed in their social and economic context was also widely accepted by Anglo-Saxon scholarship (as it usually had been, though with inconsistent results, by Marxists of many persuasions). In a brilliant article, James Joll identified the 'unspoken assumptions' which inevitably guided one clerk's pen in response to another's.[18] If such latent influences could be brought to the surface, the study of diplomatic history would be connected with the history of labour markets and financial practices, emigration and ideology, tourism and leisure, philosophy and sociology, and power in its fluctuating and manifold political, social and economic forms. Just like other scholars in the discipline, diplomatic historians, should they accept Joll's advice, must aspire to understand the *mentalités* of their own age and of that which they are studying. They, too, must aim to write *histoire totale*.

If there was one country in which these messages were not received, however, it was Italy. Though, since the fall of Fascism, Italy has produced such fine historians as Franco Venturi, Federico Chabod, Rosario Romeo, Carlo Ginzburg and Luisa Passerini, its diplomatic historians have mostly remained confined within the certitudes of the Rankean and nationalist past. In 1950, for example, the conservative Niccolò Rodolico, reviewing Volpe's *Italia moderna* for the liberal Establishment journal, *Nuova Antologia*, remarked how readers would 'follow with lively pleasure this Italian historian, who preserves the ancient faith, and who serves Italy, through studying its modern history'.[19]

Nor were such sentiments merely a last flourish of a world that was being lost. In subsequent decades, popular historians, like the radical-conservative, ex-Fascist, journalist Indro Montanelli, the Republican Party politician and sometime Prime Minister Giovanni Spadolini, and, more subtly, the conservative diplomat and writer Sergio Romano, sought to maintain or restore some sort of identity between the past and contemporary Italian patriotism. These authorities found the 1970s – those years during which right- and left-wing terrorism threatened an Italian state which was also flirting with a final legitimation of the Italian Communist Party (PCI) – especially troubling. As Romano wrote ambiguously, 'Italians only exist because they have existed in history'.[20] But, he also warned, history might not always be a reliable help in times of trouble. Critical readings of the Italian past could destabilise the Italian present: 'If the Risorgimento is a *rivoluzione mancata* and the Resistance a promise betrayed . . . it is not surprising that people [now] utilise the methods of the Risorgimento and the Resistance to complete that revolution or to realise that promise.'[21]

The 1980s, however, were anything but a decade of revolution.[22] Instead, historiographically at least, Renzo De Felice, the increasingly conservative biographer of Mussolini, ushered in something more closely resembling a counter-revolution. By 1990, De Felice could portray Italy's Second World War (1940–3) as a struggle drained of any particular moral significance. Indeed, Mussolini was depicted as a rather unlucky leader, since he had endorsed the war mainly to restrain Hitler at the peace-table.[23] The Italian people were most culpable in their lack of a sense of national community which meant that they could not, in that regard, compete 'morally' with Germans or Japanese.[24] When he addressed himself to the diplomacy of the war, De Felice also transmitted solidly conservative messages. He was absolute, for example, in his commitment to Rankean ideas about the *Primat der Aussenpolitik*: 'Political–diplomatic and military [matters] were those which conditioned internal politics and not vice versa.'[25]

De Felice's *Mussolini* provides the most flagrant example of the move to methodological and political reaction in Italian historiography, but such conservatism is not really a new development. In the 1970s a great number of facile statements were made about the Marxist occupation of the fortresses of Italian culture. In fact, in many areas and especially in diplomatic historiography, conservative traditions remained robust, repelling, as they always had, any attempt to amend their practices or conclusions. Italian students of Italy's place in the world were rarely 'Fischerised' (and, predictably, De Felice reverentially cites the work of arch-conservative, nationalist German historian, Andreas Hillgruber, a violent critic of the whole Bielefeld school).[26]

This surviving narrowness in the definition of foreign affairs is all the more surprising because of the publication in 1951 of Chabod's *Storia della politica estera italiana dal 1870 al 1896*. This work prefigured much of the methodology of the new diplomatic history and was both subtle and wide ranging in its uncovering of 'the entire life of a nation'[27] and in its emphasis on the influence of ideas, myths and ambiguities, of unspoken assumptions and covert structures in framing diplomatic acts. Chabod was especially acute in weighing the burden imposed on United Italy by the myth of Rome. Once the

'Eternal City' had been seized in 1870, he remarked: 'Rome was looked on from every part as something greater than a normal capital.' Possessing it, Italy could not become merely 'a Belgium without coal'.[28] Since 'Italian national sentiment had been the creation of thinkers and writers', and the Risorgimento had had vitality breathed into it by 'the memory of past greatness [and] the expectation of future greatness', United Italy became the special fount of ideas which 'gave life and could kill'.[29]

Chabod had once been a loyal servant of Mussolini. In May 1936, he was overwhelmed with enthusiasm by the news that Addis Ababa had fallen to Fascist arms, hailing the 'victorious and triumphal affirmation of the new, Greater, Italy'.[30] By the end of the war, however, Chabod had risen from the grave of his Fascism to live again as a liberal democrat and patriot. Thereafter, he seemed the embodiment of all that was best and most enlightened in non-Marxist Italian intellectual life. Almost single-handedly in 1945 he saved his home territory, the Val d'Aosta, from French territorial covetousness. His ideas were received with favour in the second post-war International Congress of Historical Sciences, held in Rome in 1955,[31] an event which, in the 'West', absolved Italian historiography from any perception of Fascist contamination. In reviewing this congress, Franco Valsecchi, a fertile writer on Risorgimento diplomatic and political history, was triumphant in his tone. At the earlier congress in Paris in 1950, he stated, the Germans had been absent and the Italians still 'a little disoriented' (literally 'spaesati'). 'Now, here in Rome, there is no trace of the barriers of that time. Doors are open to all. ... We breathe the air of the family home at this Congress, of the great Western family.'[32] Re-entering this familiar world would, in time, engender respect. 'Italian historiography is endeavouring to introduce itself into international circulation. Its level is aligning it in the very first ranks.'[33]

It was Chabod who gave most substance to these aspirations; and, after his early death in 1960, he preserved his reputation as an ornament of liberal scholarship. Spadolini was not the only reader who hailed the *Storia della politica estera* as 'the very peak of lay Italian historiography'.[34] Though De Felice was more candid than some in admitting Chabod's 'national-patriotism',[35] almost all non-Marxist historians continued to regard Chabod as occupying the pinnacle of their profession and to label his history of Liberal foreign policy a profound and important book.[36]

Chabod may have been praised and honoured, but there is little evidence that his work has been critically read or used. The more able and challenging Italian diplomatic historians of the following years, notably Enrico Serra, Brunello Vigezzi, Ennio Di Nolfo and Luciano Tosi,[37] have written at length about 'public opinion'; they have been well aware of the context in which international policy inevitably operates; but they, rather like Chabod himself in his somewhat disorganised books, let alone his Fascist teacher, Volpe, have generally failed to insert a thorough analysis of the decision-making process into these matters of context. Text and context have not always met.

In most recent times, there has been one major attempt to amend this situation. Diplomat turned political scientist Carlo Santoro has published the most valuable brief analysis of Italian foreign policy since national unification. That policy, he says, was always double- or triple-faced: 'in perennial search for a rank rather than a set role, for support rather than independence, affected by perceptions more than reality, forever swinging between excesses of timidity and bravado',[38] Italian diplomacy could never find a settled place. In a curious way, Italy was a 'frontier territory' on either the North–South or the East–West divide. 'Theoretically least of the Great Powers but in hard fact first of the Little Powers, Italy further conditioned its geographical ambivalence through a duality of status which was in turn expressed in a variegated external behaviour.'[39] Liberal, Fascist and even Republican regimes made little difference. Fascism 'did not radically shake the bases of Italian foreign policy', except in so far as it exaggerated Italy's commitment to manipulation and inconstancy. Fascism, says Santoro sagely, constituted

> the Italian political regime which, more than any other, before or since, conducted the policy of a Little Power, [that is] greedy and deliberately disturbing of the international order, without the strategic plans of a Great Power in terms of final objectives, general direction and ultimate capacity for influence or hegemony.[40]

As a political scientist, Santoro is more concerned with building his models than with filling in the detail, but his generalisations will be of great significance in any future historical analysis of the subject.

Nothing in non-Italian writing about Italy's place in the world equals in acuity Santoro's observations. Despite some useful monographs by French, German and Anglo-Saxon historians,[41] the history of post-Renaissance Italy has not assumed a particularly high profile in international scholarship and few non-Italian historians of modern Italy have won much fame for their methodological sophistication or analytical profundity. In the first generation after 1945, there was only one major non-Italian historian of Liberal and Fascist Italy, the Oxbridge radical, Denis Mack Smith.[42]

It was in the 1950s that Mack Smith first made his name, publishing a fine, narrative, 'total political history' of the dealings between Cavour and Garibaldi. Mack Smith followed this monograph with a general study, *Italy: A Modern History* (1959) which, in a revised edition, remains probably the most widely used textbook, in any language, on post-Risorgimento history.[43] Rapidly translated, the *Storia d'Italia* also became, for a time, the most debated work in Italian historiography. Conservative and patriotic historians were outraged by it, all the more because, in the centenary celebrations of Unification (1959–61), they were hoping, as Rosario Romeo put it, that their liberal–nationalist version of history would bind the Italian people together.[44] Mack Smith had meshed the Italian past and present in a different and less patriotically useful way by enunciating a thesis of continuity in which Fascism was the child of Liberal Italy, the 'revelation' of Italian history.

Though Mack Smith was by no means the first to perceive such continuity, his pithy prose gave him a huge popular audience, as also, perhaps, did his stature as a distinguished foreigner delivering himself of a judicious verdict on Italy's past and, by implication, its present. Mack Smith's analysis similarly fitted that debate about continuity in German history which would be inspired by Fischer's *Griff nach der Weltmacht* and A.J.P. Taylor's *The Origins of the Second World War*.[45] For those in the wider world obliged to give a few lectures on Italy as part of a general course in modern European history, the 'Mack Smith thesis' rendered Italian history normal and predictable. Moreover, although Mack Smith was certainly not a Marxist, his work on the Risorgimento seemed easily reconciled with Gramscian views on the *rivoluzione mancata*, and was thus reinforced as the 'myth of Gramsci' became pervasive and influential both inside Italy and in the world beyond.

A decade and a half later, Mack Smith turned his attention more directly to Fascism and to foreign policy, publishing in 1975, at the very apogee of the 'crisis of the Italian crisis', his *Mussolini's Roman Empire*. This brilliantly written and at times riotously funny book is undoubtedly the best-known account of any aspect of Italy's international dealings in the century after the Risorgimento. But, though readable and diverting, *Mussolini's Roman Empire* is neither profound nor entirely consistent. His conclusions, Mack Smith declares, are simple. He will explain 'how Mussolini deliberately and even carefully steered his fascist movement' into brutal imperialisms and fruitless wars[46] and how, as a system of government and political ideology, Fascism was little more than a farce. Apart from Mussolini, Fascists were a sorry and craven lot, lacking honour, honesty and courage. The Duce himself, an 'artist in propaganda',[47] gulled almost all the people all of the time, and thus was able to lead Italy through Corfu, Ethiopia, Spain, Albania and the Axis to a world war against Britain, the USSR and the USA, for which the nation was ludicrously unprepared. This final disaster should be known until the end of time as 'Mussolini's war'.

Paradoxically, what Mack Smith was now saying was something rather like what had been claimed about Nazi Germany before the Fischer affair. Then, to the relief of conservative former fellow-travellers with Nazism, it was concluded that Hitler was the 'accident in the works', who had full responsibility for everything that happened during his regime. Now, Mack Smith, without explanation, was contradicting much of what he had said or implied in his earlier work about those lasting structures which made Fascism the 'revelation' of Italian history, unless Mussolini himself was the single product of past sin, the awaited Anti-Christ. Similarly, though he continued to have a marvellous eye for telling detail and was often adroit in his depiction of the character of Fascist politicians, Mack Smith ignored the most fruitful theoretical aspects of contemporary diplomatic historiography. From *Mussolini's Roman Empire*, a reader learned a meagre amount about the decision-making structure of Fascist Italy and little about the views or influence of industry or church, intellectuals or officialdom. Since, if Mack Smith were to be believed, Mussolini had the whole Italian world in his hands, there was nothing new that needed to be known. There was, however, always room for one more tale about the Duce's pretentiousness, rashness, ignorance and frivolity.

If Mack Smith and De Felice frequently exchanged polemics and scarcely agreed on politics or on the purpose of history as a discipline, their methodologies and the issues which they saw as significant in Fascist Italy were similar. For all Mack Smith's verve and penetration, and for all De Felice's perseverance and archival labour, the two have left modern Italy as the least of the great historiographical powers. In pondering Italy's place in the wider world 1860–1960, a student will need to go beyond their work, to consult other historio-graphies and to ask different questions about Italian politics and society.

This short book is scarcely the appropriate base from which to launch an historiographical revolution. But, in the pages which follow, I shall try to do more than merely describe Italian diplomacy during this or that major international event. Rather, aware of the cautions expressed in the first part of this chapter, I shall try to ask structural questions about how Italy (and the Italies) related to the wider world. I shall wonder whether in diplomacy itself, in military matters, in trade, in colonial affairs, in emigration, in cultural policy, in tourism and leisure, in formal ideology or popular myth, the policy of Italy (and the Italies) was reflective more of change than of continuity. Was Fascism a revolution, and 1922 a great turning-point in Italian history? Was the arrival of liberal capitalist democracy after 1943–5 as much or more of a sundering of assumptions and tradi-tions? Why was it that a nation, whose policies, instructive in their crass brutality and cynicism or exemplary in their manipulativeness and corruption, which was frequently defeated and more often scorned, should nonetheless prosper both in the direct economic sense and in the minds of those who, in so many ways, were influenced by its cultures? Through most of the century under study and in the three decades since 1960, Italy (or perhaps 'Italy') has been 'in crisis'. And yet, amid the troubles of dictatorship or depression, war or ideological battle, most Italians somehow preserved, at least some of the time, an attitude of love and charity towards their neighbours and themselves and thus well embodied what Jonathan Steinberg has so wonderfully defined as the 'banality of good'.[48]

During the last five generations, many brilliant Italian writers, film directors and other artists have sought to portray the character of their times. The portraits have varied – the lush self-indulgence and sexist cruelty of D'Annunzio, the *gallismo* (cock-ism) exposed by Brancati, the more bitter sensuality of Moravia and Visconti, the wry 'idiocy' of Fellini, the almost surreal anger of Malaparte or Sciascia, the cleverness of Calvino, the menacing calm of Bassani. Such a list could and should continue. But in summing up the dilemma of Italy, the Italies and the wider world 1860–1960, one starting-point is provided by the Triestine novelist, 'Italo Svevo' (1861–1928). This writer, real name Ettore Schmitz (his pseudonym means 'Italo-Swabian' and implies that he was half-Italian and half-German), was a not very successful industrialist (and a generous patron of James

Joyce) in turn-of-the-century, Habsburg, Trieste. His family origins, his history, made him in fact part-Italian, part-German, part-Jewish, part-Hungarian, part-Slovene and part many other things. The many parts constituted a richly human person who knew that 'it is the fate of Man to live in mixed tenses', and who superbly expressed this world-view in the novel, *Confessions of Zeno* (*La coscienza di Zeno*) (1923).[49]

Zeno lived an alphabetical dilemma. Granted a name starting with 'z', he obviously needed a wife whose name started with 'a'. He met and married a dutiful girl called Augusta. But then she had a sister called Ada . . . and, through it all, over and over again, Zeno smoked his last cigarette. He knew that smoking brought cancer and death and so, each time he stubbed out that last cigarette, he jotted down the letters l.c. in his diary. Like a good historian, he inscribed this culminating event, the last crisis, on a piece of paper and only dimly worried about what it would mean if this were not, after all, the end. In his sense of humane irony and fruitful failure, Zeno wonderfully reflected what was best in those citizens of Italy and the Italies as, in the last century, they have striven to survive and to live in this dangerous and delightful world, and to avoid that moral death which comes from reaching the last resolution and knowing the answer to all our troubles.

1

ITALIAN DIPLOMACY AND EUROPEAN POWER POLITICS 1860–1922

In 1939, Harold Nicolson, minor English diplomat, politician and littérateur, penned, in a manual which he published on international diplomacy, the classic description of the basic traits of Italian foreign policy. Amid the European powers, he wrote, Italy was *sui generis*:

> The rigidity of French diplomacy stands in striking contrast to the mobile diplomacy of the Italians. The Italian system is derived from the traditions of the Italian states of the Renaissance and is based neither on the sound business concept, nor on power-policy, nor on the logical attainment of certain ends. It is more than opportunist, it is based upon incessant manoeuvre. The aim of Italy's foreign policy is to acquire by negotiation an importance greater than can be supplied by her own physical strength. It is thus the antithesis of the German system, since instead of basing diplomacy on power, she bases power on diplomacy. It is the antithesis of the French system, since instead of striving to secure permanent allies against a permanent enemy, she regards her allies and her enemies as interchangeable. It is the antithesis of the British system [Nicolson went on, with a certain patriotic bias] since it is not durable credit that she seeks for, but immediate advantage. Her conception, moreover, of the Balance of Power is not identical with the British conception; for whereas in Great Britain that doctrine is interpreted as opposition to any country who may seek to dominate Europe, in Italy it is desired as a balance of such equipoise that her own weight can tilt the scale.

These characteristics, Nicolson asserted, could be identified in even the most mundane diplomatic action:

Italian diplomatists make a speciality of the art of negotiation. Their usual method is first to create bad relations with the country with whom they wish to negotiate and then to offer 'good relations'. Before entering upon such negotiations they are careful to provide themselves with three bargaining counters. The first of these is a sense of grievance and hostility which are [sic] artificially provoked among the Italian people. The second is some form of nuisance-value against the country with which Italy is about to negotiate. And the third is a claim for some concession which Italy does not expect to obtain, or really desires, but the abandonment of which will oblige the other country to pay some compensation.

'Italy', Nicolson concluded, 'combines, on the one hand, the pretensions of a Great Power with, on the other, the methods of a Small Power.'[1]

This battery of confident and even peremptory conclusions might be dismissed as a period piece, prompted either by Nicolson's direct experience as a negotiator at Versailles in 1919, or by Fascism and the nearness of the Second World War, were it not for the fact that Nicolson's book has continued to be republished and that echoes of his ideas can be detected in similar books produced at other times and in different places.[2] Machiavellian, fickle, crisis-ridden, untrustworthy, adolescent, a Great Power clinging precariously to first-class status, with relegation an ever-looming possibility – these are the words, phrases and figures of speech which recur in discourse about Italy's part in European power politics between 1860 and 1960.[3] Italians, too, often shared these opinions – Mussolini was only one among many to use the relegation metaphor.[4]

The insecurity of Italy's status could readily prompt an uneasy grandiloquence about the recognition which, in an ideal world, the nation should receive.[5] Already in the 1840s, the Abbé Vincenzo Gioberti had proclaimed the 'moral and civil primacy of the Italians',[6] and, in succeeding generations, many nationalists would reiterate his claim with a greater alacrity, as if they half knew that there was no chance that deeds could defend Italian power and well understood that only words could hide that fact.

Much of the tone, method and intent of Italian diplomacy may have been established in the Risorgimento, if not before, and yet the unification of Italy was, at least formally, very much a revolutionary event. In a few months, ancient dynasties fell and accustomed maps were redrawn. A 'nation state' emerged where none had been before, possessing frontiers which were entirely new. Although only some 2 per cent of the population had the right to vote (and half of them, as loyal Catholics, did not take up their option), the new Italy was to be governed through a liberal, parliamentary constitution. It was true that large parts of the kingdom were almost totally 'pre-modern' in their economy – fields were tilled with wooden ploughs, diseases like cholera could ravage the population[7] when the favoured remedy of regular cannonades failed,[8] railways were rare and even roads were sometimes absent; for some Italians the wheeled cart remained a novelty. Nonetheless, along with its parliament, Italy had also opted for a capitalist economy.

Indeed, Camille de Cavour, the most renowned 'Maker of Modern Italy' and the united state's first Prime Minister, was an almost archetypal new capitalist. The younger son of a Piedmontese *noblesse de robe* family (with a special interest in police duties), Cavour abandoned his destined military career in favour of speculation. He gambled on the new-fangled game of whist (King Charles Albert's acceptance that a Whist Club could open in Turin in 1841 was a telling indication of the royal flirtation with change);[9] he gambled on the stock market; and he would gamble as nervelessly on the tables of diplomacy. He sought to improve the productivity in rice and sugar beet on his estates (and ruthlessly exploited his peasants);[10] he ventured capital on paddle steamers for the north Italian lakes, or on railway schemes; he corresponded with new men in Paris and London and earned a eulogy from Thomas Brassey, the age's greatest transport entrepreneur: 'as a man of business I never met his equal except in Mr. Brassey'.[11] While his luck held, Cavour could achieve great things.

In 1861, then, as its first parliament (though it was called its eighth) met to advise its first king (though his title was Victor Emmanuel II), Italy, for all its fragilities and inconsistencies, seemed to have boarded the locomotive of history. If a great number of Italians did not yet know what 'Italy' meant, perhaps they were Italians in the making; if liberty seemed mockingly absent in most of their lives,[12] liberty could be spread; if the practices of capitalism did not always arrive with the wheeled cart, the process of accumulation could commence and the systems of agrarian capitalism might, in time, foster full-scale industrialisation. As a Fascist historian would proclaim,[13] and as many an optimistic and patriotic speechifier had already surmised, Italy was 'on the march'. The revolution had been a *rivoluzione nazionale*, favoured by the 'best elements' residing in the Italian peninsula. The best elements could teach the less good about nation, government, economy, civil society and international relations.

This sort of Whig optimism[14] in interpreting the Risorgimento, however, has long since gone out of fashion, especially among those who decided that Fascism was the 'revelation' of the history of United Italy and who knew by 1945 that Fascism spelled military and national defeat and humiliation. Rather, as the able sociologist, Paolo Farneti, would notice, most discussion of the travails of United Italy would soon use as its starting-point the belief that something had been missing (*mancata*) in the Risorgimento. For positivists like Gaetano Mosca, Vilfredo Pareto and Luigi Einaudi, Italy was held back by a lack of secularisation; for experts on the South like Francesco Saverio Nitti, Pasquale Villari, Gaetano Salvemini and Guido Dorso, by a lack of integration and, finally for Marxist or Liberal revolutionaries like Antonio Gramsci and Piero Gobetti, in the words which would contest the *rivoluzione nazionale* and which still underpin mainstream historiography, by a lack of genuine, social revolution (*rivoluzione mancata*).[15]

Even among contemporaries of the unification process, there was a common unease about the boasted 'national revolution', its profundity and durability. As the English statesman, Lord Palmerston, mused in November 1860, the unification of Italy was 'miraculous'; 'no one in his senses or in his dreams could have anticipated such continuous success'.[16] Cavour, he and others admired or envied as the man who had broken the bank at Monte Carlo, Vienna, Paris and the rest. But what would happen over real time, and in that real world in which, as an Italian diplomat of the next generation would wisely recall, 'nothing fails like success'?[17] What, especially, would happen in the real world of power politics, that world in which Europeans did not need a Bismarck to instruct them that great decisions were made through blood and iron, or a Clausewitz to argue that war was merely the conduct of diplomacy by other means? 'Miracles' were frowned on in an age of science. Could the miracle of unification last?

Moreover, to return to that metaphor which would become so commonplace in the twentieth century, the Risorgimento had meant Italy's promotion into the league of the Great Powers. But could the country with the smallest population, the least developed economy, the most vulnerable strategic position and the most yawning gap between politics and society, theory and practice, really hold its place?[18] If relegation did not occur this year, would it not come in the next? And, from this eternal threat arose a basic need. At its very birth, Italy was a state which, contrary to the assumptions of some modern social historians, necessarily embraced matters of diplomacy, peace and war. United Italy could only exist while it had a foreign policy.

But which foreign policy? – that was the question which governed much Italian political life until at least 1945. What, in this regard, had Cavour and the other makers of modern Italy bequeathed as an inheritance? For one thing, there was ambition. Italy, though 'made', was as yet incomplete. If, during the first decade of its existence, defeat in war fortuitously brought the new Italy Venice and Rome, there were still other 'Italian' territories to be won. The 'prophet of the nation', Giuseppe Mazzini, of whom it was remarked acutely that, for him, 'people' did not exist, only 'the cause', had detected that God had made Italy the 'best-defined country in Europe'.[19] But, even by 1870, the Deity's full wishes had not yet been met; Istria, the Trentino and Corsica, too, were destined to become parts of Italy. Nice (Nizza) must return.[20] Similarly, Cavour, however great his antipathy towards Mazzini, had his own little list. On it were inscribed Malta, Istria, the Trentino, Trieste and maybe Dalmatia and the Ticino. Seizing them, he liked to suggest, would be the task of the next generation.[21]

Neither in their hearts nor in their 'culture' did the populace of the new state always object when politicians or ideologues maintained that diplomatic advantage needed constantly to be sought. In the mosaic which had once covered the Italian peninsula, little states had always cherished ambitions on their neighbours. When, in 1796, French revolutionary armies occupied much of northern Italy, the Bolognese delegation to Paris coveted Ferrara, that of Ferrara thought Cento should be theirs;[22] the Ligurians resented the Piedmontese opening to the sea at Oneglia and wanted it closed and transferred to them.[23] Nor was this texture of loss and gain absent further down in Italian society. As he invaded Sicily, the Piedmontese *garibaldino*, Giuseppe Cesare Abba, stated a truism that, if one *paese* welcomed the Thousand, the next rejected them out of hatred for the welcomers.[24] For much of the century after 1860, most *paesani* would regard as *forestieri* or outsiders, and thus potentially hostile and aggressive, gullible and exploitable, all those 'Italians' not born within the sound of their village bell.[25] Beyond that ken, in the midst of wayward and unfathomable *forestieri*, it was sensible to travel alert and armed.[26]

Perhaps the Southern bandit, Michele Caruso, taken prisoner by the 'Italian' army of occupation in December 1863, was extreme in his violence and cynicism. But, in a wicked world, many Italians knew what he meant as he remarked on his way to execution: 'Ah, sirs! If I'd known how to read and write I'd have exterminated the human race.'[27] After all, his cynicism was not so much greater than that of the Prime Minister, Urbano Rattazzi, who opined briskly that United Italy, in thus killing bandits, would 'make our school for Africa'.[28] The world, many an Italian perceived, in another wide-spread simile, was like a *carciofo* (an artichoke).[29] Ideally, when hunger came, the *carciofo* should be consumed one leaf at a time, piece by piece. Moreover, once one piece was digested, there were many more available (though Bismarck summed up non-Italian views on such potential feasting by remarking brutally that Liberal Italy had a large appetite but very poor teeth).[30]

Franceso Crispi, that nationalist, sometime terrorist and revolutionary who, by the 1880s and 1890s, had transmogrified himself into a reactionary and imperialist Prime Minister, would then maintain that it had been the vision of Italy as a Great Power which had sustained the leaders of the Risorgimento.[31] He himself pursued policies whose openly aggressive character would not be equalled until the days of the Fascist regime. Crispi increased military expenditure, talked cheerfully of a European conflagration, and alarmed his German or British friends with his suggestions of preventative attacks on his enemies. His policies were ruinous, both for Italy's trade with France, and, more humiliatingly, for colonial ambitions in East Africa.[32] Crispi's lust for territory there was thwarted when, on 1 March 1896, the armies of Ethiopian Emperor Menelik routed Italian forces at Adowa (and killed about the same number of soldiers as had died fighting for Unification in 1859–61) in what has been defined as an unparalleled disaster for a modern army.[33] Crispi, whose private life (he was perhaps a trigamist) and personal finances (King Umberto paid off the more pressing of his debtors) were objects of perennial scandal, went into dishonourable retirement. Classically for someone of his personality and career, Crispi had long identified the nation with himself. Three months before Adowa, he could already be heard muttering that the system to which he had dedicated his youth could not endure. '*In Italy, a parliamentary government simply isn't possible* [sic] .... It won't be I who does anything against parliament, but whoever comes after me will be simply unable to govern with this system.'[34]

Fascist Italian historians were right to see Crispi as a precursor of Mussolini.[35] But, if Crispi flaunted the ambitions of United Italy, most other politicians of the Liberal era balanced a longing for eventual power with a timorous common sense which taught that, at least in the short run, diplomatic passivity and international harmony were the best policies. In the aftermath of the 'miracle' of unification, the preservation of what had by then become the status quo headed the national agenda.

The world, the Italian elite readily understood, was a dangerous place. The peasants who, in 1860, composed the great majority of the population were certainly unpredictable and perhaps menacing. Until they were nationalised, who could tell when they would unbridle their natural perfidy and violence in another *jacquerie*?[36] And, in the 1890s, the arrival of socialism, with its professed commitment to both internationalism and revolution, only made things worse. Foreigners, their eyes made starry by viewing art, or eating peaches, or being warmed by the sun, or satiated by sexual indulgence, might reiterate that 'the *people* ... are the charm of Italy'.[37] But many an Italian intellectual and politician feared instead that the people were the bane of Italy; in their present condition, the less that was done to stir them up the better. Until at least 1922, Italy, to the dismay of some new nationalists,[38] remained a country very different from that Germany in which pressure groups of the nationalist, navalist and imperialist right so rapidly identified a genuine popular base. Imperial Germany, in its triumphant rise from being the last arrived of the Great Powers to occupying the centre of the world stage, may have been applauded by considerable sections of its populace. In the foreign policy of Liberal Italy, by contrast, 'public opinion' (except in very restricted definition) played a minimal role.

If the threat of domestic change counselled a fabian approach to international ambition and opportunity, there were many additional reasons for present inaction. Liberal Italy had been united against a sea of enemies. Furthermore such enemies, even as they became old men, did not forget. For the first three or four decades after the Risorgimento, one of the most malevolent foes of the new regime seemed to be the Vatican. As Domenico Farini, the great political diarist of the 1890s, noted, 'priests are a nest of vipers'. Although Pope Leo XIII (1878-1903) might appear, to credulous eyes, to be a dear old man, actually, he was a deadly menace to Italy. 'The Pope', Farini warned, 'cannot recognise and will never accept the Italian state as it is presently constituted.'[39] Catholics would slyly pray for international broils in which Italy could be undone and some form of the Temporal Power restored. Though, by 1914, there were plenty of indications of a *ralliement* between the Italian church and state, many still feared the Vatican's likely claims in any post-war settlement. If a counter-factual history of the First World War, in which Germany and Austria-Hungary won, were to be imagined, Italy may well have found Rome stripped from its charge. Certainly it is hard to believe that, in the event of the Central Powers' victory, the Vatican would not again have sought its Eternal City. King Victor Emmanuel III (1900–46) was not the only Italian with a long memory who believed that, of all the evils which beset him, and there were many, the papacy was the most malign.[40]

While spectres of domestic revolution or counter-revolution mingled in Italian diplomatists' minds, more evident dangers lurked within the international system. When Italy 'won' in the Risorgimento, the ancient empire of Austria lost. The loss, however, was not total. The Emperor Francis Joseph (1848–1916), who, in a disturbingly commonplace metaphor, knew that Italians were a nation of 'pickpockets and land thieves',[41] continued to govern the Italian city of Trento, the heavily Germanophone but strategically necessary region of the Alto Adige or South Tyrol around the more northerly city of Bolzano (Bozen),[42] and, away to the east, the polyglot city of Trieste, which, in contemporary parlance, everyone agreed was one of the 'keys to the Adriatic'. Irredentists, whether publicly (in the Trento and Trieste Society, established in 1877) or covertly (in the case of almost all the Italian ruling class), claimed that these regions were as yet 'unredeemed' by the new Italy. In redeeming them, as it did eventually in the First World War, Italy was but fighting the Fourth (and last) war of the Risorgimento.[43]

To the issue of irredentism was added, especially as the decades passed, the torbid problem of the Balkans. In that internationally contested and domestically unstable part of the world, Italian policy was inconsistent. Some of the sons of the great Garibaldi spread the gospel of national independence and urged that Serbia or Greece should assume the mantle of the 'Piedmont' of the region; others of more humdrum purpose sought instead economic influence or control;[44] others, still, considered that 'Albania' in particular (there was no state of that name until 1912) should be the foundation stone of the empire of the 'Third Italy'. Did not the remains of a great Roman road run suggestively and 'luminously' out of Durazzo

(Durres)?[45] If the Austrians, already established in Bosnia and Herzegovina, did not get there first, Durazzo or Valona or the island of Saseno could be the citadel from which the legions could sally forth anew. (The Italian military did occupy Saseno in December 1914, finding to their dismay that it possessed no supplies of running water; their occupation later in the war of Valona, in reality a village with less than 10,000 inhabitants, was scarcely more comfortable.[46])

For both irredentists and imperialists, for nationalists of all kinds, it thus seemed that Austria held the position of international public enemy number one. Enmity with Austria was the logical result of any forward Italian policy. And, until 28 August 1916, when Italy officially joined the conflict against Germany, Austria was the only European power against which Liberal Italy declared war. Nonetheless, for most of the time between 1866 and 1915, Italy was not the enemy of Austria-Hungary but rather its ally. In 1882 Italy became a member of the Triple Alliance, a treaty with Austria-Hungary and Germany which thereafter was regularly renewed, the last occasion being in 1912.[47] Conversing with King Umberto in 1892, the diarist Farini summed up Italian policy in this regard as well as anyone (though his obsessive anti-clericalism lent his arguments a somewhat old-fashioned air):

> I believe that the Triple Alliance is indispensable, above all since we are in Rome. The Central Powers represent European conservatism; if we were not with them, the whole Roman Question would surface again for them. To be in Rome, a city of world interests, forbids us from isolating ourselves. We simply must associate ourselves with other powers, and cannot detach ourselves from policies related to great European interests, because [whatever happens] others are [here] with us.[48]

Given Italy's need to deal with an Austria whose political or military leaders, despite the alliance, sometimes envisaged that happy day when Habsburg forces might launch against their ally a sudden and vengeful war,[49] membership of the Triple Alliance constituted the nation's only sensible policy.

If Austria menaced Italy to the north-east and in the Adriatic, to the west lay France, the enigmatic 'Latin sister', or 'step-sister' – the usage of these terms depended on mood or speaker. For Luigi Menabrea, Prime Minister (1867–9), a general and an ambassador, it was all quite simple: 'the French, through their traditional policy, always will be, whatever type of government they have, our enemies'.[50] Others were not so sure, and after a decade of rapprochement, Italy would fight on the French side in the First World War. So what did Menabrea, and other commentators who shared his views, mean?

France presented United Italy a number of potential threats. The deals between Cavour and Napoleon III which, in 1859, had brought a French army to Northern Italy (and with the result that more Frenchmen and Austrians would die in the wars of the Risorgimento than did Italians) had required a pay-off. While Piedmont expanded into Italy, Cavour surrendered Nice (birthplace of that quintessential national and romantic hero, Giuseppe Garibaldi) and Savoy ('cradle' of the Piedmontese/Italian dynasty) to France. Thereafter an Italian 'claim' to Nice and Savoy was not quite forgotten, and, in the 1930s, a respectable historian could be found maintaining that Ciamberì (Chambery) in 1848 and 1860 had been superb in its *italianità*. 'Thank God', this historian concluded in eloquent (and meaningful) echo of his Duce, 'treaties are not eternal'.[51]

But neither Nice nor Savoy, let alone 'Ciamberì' or 'Marsiglia' (as some extreme nationalists deemed the proper 'Italic' name of Marseilles), possessed the rallying power of Trento or Trieste. France's real menace for Liberal Italy lay elsewhere. To a small extent it was ideological – republican France might give too much succour to Italian democrats; Catholic France might too closely befriend the Pope; intellectual France might too arrogantly evince its cultural superiority; and economic–commercial France might too openly dominate Italian finance or too blatantly corrupt the Italian press. But the nub of the Italo-French dispute (and what, in the final analysis, rendered it less significant than Italo-Austrian conflict) was imperial. It began and intensified in the Mediterranean and on what nationalists proclaimed was Italy's 'fourth shore' (that is, the North African littoral). Those politicans or commentators who deemed Italy's essence to be European and pursued a 'Northern' policy saw Austria as Italy's first friend or enemy; those who favoured a 'Southern' policy, a small Italian version of *Weltpolitik* – however much directed at those regions where Italy did not have great commercial or demographic interests and ignoring places like North and South America, where 'Italians' did increasingly live – defined France as the heart of the national problem.

One incident justified this definition. In May 1881, France occupied Tunis and soon after constructed a major naval base at Bizerte (Bizerta).[52] But well before, thousands of (Southern) Italians had already emigrated to Tunisia – in 1881 they were estimated to number 11,000 as against 3,000 French settlers.[53] If any European power had a demographic claim to that territory, it was Italy (far more Italians would continue to live in Tunisia than in the whole Italian empire as it would eventually be constituted). Worse still, Bizerte, in the strategic understanding of the time, menaced Sicily and any naval action threatened in war to detach it from the Italian mainland. (Had not the British fleet already preserved that unruly island in the counter-revolutionary cause during the Napoleonic wars?) France's policy in Egypt, France's policy in Syria, the French presence in Djibouti, French ambitions beyond Lake Chad and in the Fezzan, even France's pretensions to supervise the Catholic or Christian cause in the Holy Places[54] – all could arouse Italian resentment and trepidation. France was public enemy number two.

Thus, until 1918, there smouldered in ambitious Italian minds the thought that, in an ideal war, Italy might find itself on the winning side against both Austria and France. But such a combination persistently failed to occur. Instead, more fearful and more rational Italian diplomatists noticed, as the years passed, that Austria and France each acquired a great and powerful friend and ally. In Austria's case, from 1879, this ally was Germany; in France's, from 1904, though in the ambiguous garb of the Entente Cordiale, it was Britain. Yet these were the two countries which Italians most esteemed, and they were also the nations against which no rational Italian wanted to fight. If Austria and France impinged most directly on Italian diplomacy, Germany and Britain had the greater long-term and structural effect.

As they contemplated this dilemma, diplomatists recognised that Germany stood nearer to the borders of the Italian state and of Italian minds. Italian soldiers envied the strength and discipline of the German army (though Italian strategists ignored the authoritative advice of von Moltke the elder and built fortresses rather than railways).[55] Benedetto Croce, in the two decades before 1914 the most celebrated Italian intellectual, and the historian and philosopher of Italian liberalism, schooled himself in German culture and aspired to match the prestige of the German professor.[56] Italian banking, in reaction to the corruption and incompetence revealed by the Banca Romana scandal of 1892–3, became the client of German financial expertise.[57] More generally, many in the Italian ruling class sensed that the history of Italy and Germany, the two new Great Powers created in the nineteenth century, might run in parallel. Perhaps they blanched a little when German nationalist historian Heinrich von Treitschke proclaimed that the parallel did indeed exist, but, before becoming significant, needed to be tempered by Italian participation in a victorious Mediterranean war.[58] Perhaps they were not quite as peremptory as was post-Second World War conservative historian Rosario Romeo, when he bewailed Liberal Italy's failure to pursue 'a genuinely great national purpose' like that of Imperial Germany.[59] The crassness of Emperor William II was annoying[60] and, just before the First World War, the arrival of too many German tourists and the too unashamedly greedy dumping practices of German industry caused complaint. But, until then, no Italian seriously imagined fighting Germany or directly contesting Germany's national interests. Indeed, Giovanni Giolitti, who had been the dominant political figure in the decade before 1914,[61] tried to delay Italian intervention in the Great War because of his characteristically long-sighted worry of how his country would, in a post-war world, deal even with a defeated Germany which had learned to number Italy among its enemies.

British power manifested itself less directly in Italy, but was, in the final analysis, probably even more influential. Though Italy conserved irredentist claims against the British empire, notably over Malta, and although an Italian North African and eastern Mediterranean empire seemed, at least in retrospect, certain to rub up against British interests in Suez (or in the oil fields of Mesopotamia), until 1922 Italy very rarely assumed anti-British stances. For one thing, Italy remained hopelessly vulnerable to a superior naval power. Italian railways ran right along the coastline of the Adriatic and the Mediterranean. Great cities like Genoa, Naples and Palermo lay wide open to seaborne bombardment or attack. And the acquisition of an empire, notably in Libya (1911–12), made things worse. Italian communications with the 'Fourth Shore' or beyond Suez could only survive on sufferance of the Royal Navy. Moreover, and crucially, Britain, the exporter of coal, held a stranglehold over Italian energy supplies.[62] Before 1914, though there had been increasingly successful experimentation with hydroelectricity, the Italian navy, the Italian railways and many an Italian factory remained dependent on British coal. War against Britain was unthinkable unless an energy substitute could be found.

A whole host of factors thus conditioned and restrained the ambitions of Liberal Italy. As Giolitti, the most able and clear-thinking of the successors of Cavour, saw matters, it was possible to hope that Italy would one day be a real Great Power, but, to that end, Liberal diplomatists needed both to garner national strength and to cherish political prudence. Since wealth was 'now the only exact measure of the power of the nations',[63] and since Italy, despite its marked industrial growth in the Giolittian decade (1903–14), remained poor, peace, not war, should be the nation's present purpose. Indeed, as Agostino Depretis, Prime Minister (1876–8, 1878–9, 1881–7), always maintained, Italy should try as far as possible to circumvent international broils: 'whenever I see an international crisis on the horizon I open my umbrella and wait till it passes'.[64]

In sum, then, Italy, from 1860 to 1914, regularly acted as a force for general peace in Europe (although that did not rule out the seeking of specific advantage) and Italian leaders usually preferred the obfuscation of diplomatic negotiation to the clarity of military decision. Except under Crispi, or perhaps in the Libyan War of 1911–12,[65] Italy, in the final analysis, hoped not to jangle the harmony of the Concert of Europe. For most of the time, fear and common sense held ambition in check and Italian leaders wisely understood that the most fruitful part of valour was discretion.

There was one other corollary of this policy which deserves comment both because of its contemporary significance and because it has occasioned some historical debate. That corollary was the 'dishonesty' of Italian foreign policy – as A.J.P. Taylor claimed, in one of his brilliantly clever footnotes, Liberal Italian diplomatists should be exempted from the dictum, otherwise true of the pre-1914 era, that all those then involved in the making of foreign policy were 'honest according to their moral code'.[66]

It is easy to see such 'dishonesty' or pragmatism as an original sin of the Risorgimento. The Venetian leader, Daniele Manin, told the Piedmontese in 1855: 'Make Italy and I am with you. If not, not.'[67] A little earlier, another nationalist had urged that 'any means is good to obtain the most holy good of our independence'.[68] The special exemplar of (creative) dishonesty was Cavour; as he himself argued provocatively: 'if we did for ourselves what we are doing for Italy we should be real scoundrels'.[69] Denis Mack Smith has taken special pleasure in displaying this side of Cavour and has concluded that contemporaries assumed Cavour was being mendacious even when he spoke the truth.[70]

Many of Cavour's successors followed similar practices. In the decade before 1914, Tommaso Tittoni, a Roman who came from a background of prefectural administration in Naples and papal finance, and Antonino Di San Giuliano, a Sicilian schooled in adapting his noble background to local Catanian and national Italian politics, took turn and turn about as Foreign Minister.[71] Each had a deserved reputation for slipperiness. Di San Giuliano,[72] at the top of his form, took an almost perverse pleasure in brutal dishonesty as he remarked to his interlocutors on the fickleness of international law, the irreligion of the church, the transitoriness of alliances, or, when Italy had actually gained something (the Dodecanese Islands), pursued the argument that, in those circumstances at least, possession was nine-tenths of the law. Throughout the Giolittian era, Italy, the 'ally' of the Triple Alliance and the 'friend' of their enemies in the Triple Entente, to most non-Italians seemed, in the practice of its foreign policy, a case-study in dishonesty.

What contemporaries and some later historians did not understand, however, was that, for most of the time, such 'dishonesty' was far and away the most efficacious policy for Italy. Sidney Sonnino, who was Foreign Minister from 1914 to 1919, and with a personal reputation, perhaps deserved, for honesty in all his dealings, has strong claims to have conducted Italy's least successful foreign policy.[73] While ambition and fear co-mingled at the heart of Italian diplomacy, while Italy, the least of the Great Powers, necessarily pursued multiple policies, the last thing that was needed was too much exposure of the ultimate contradictions in its position. Rather, what Giolitti, Cavour and many another Italian understood was that matters which might, in the final analysis, prove humiliating and disastrous could be useful and advantageous as long as that last stage was not reached. 'Dishonesty', as Taylor implied, was a structural characteristic of Italian foreign policy rather than the result of this or that personal peccadillo.

It is tempting to conclude that the only cost of the dishonesty that was nourished at the root of Liberal Italian foreign policy was a trifling one to that bauble, reputation. But such a conclusion would be inadequate. As the world democratised and Europeans adopted their version of the 'new diplomacy', and as, within Italy, the first generation of those who had made the Risorgimento was replaced by the second, with a third generation waiting in the wings, Cavourian policies lost much of their appeal. Students of Italy's place in the world ought to have understood long before the work of modern semioticians that words matter. When in 1914–15, Italy was confronted by the greatest problem posed since the Risorgimento – whether or not, or when exactly, to enter the First World War – the then Italian leaders, especially Prime Minister (1914–16) Antonio Salandra[74] and his friend and colleague Sonnino, chose war. They reached that decision, however, not so much because they had coolly and accurately appraised where the national interest lay, but because they had been impelled by the words which formed in their mouths and those of their contemporaries. As they said (and Mussolini himself would later use similar language) war gave them the chance to 'enter history'.[75] Now or never Italy must master the past and make the Risorgimento 'real', rather than something perennially lacking (*mancata*). War, they surmised, would at last make an honest power out of Italy.

So far in this chapter I have attempted no general assessment of how the decision-making process of Liberal Italy worked, an omission which will be rectified in the following chapters. But it can be remarked here that assessing decision-making after the Risorgimento is not such a difficult matter. Though not all historians agree,[76] most would maintain that in Italy, until 1914, an adapted version of the traditional system of managing diplomacy survived. The making of Liberal foreign policy rested in the hands of those who had made the Risorgimento. When the Prime Minister was a powerful figure – a Depretis, a Crispi, a Cavour or a Giolitti – then final decisions were usually his. Italy was, however, a monarchy, and the Foreign Ministry or Consulta was symbolically situated across the square from the Royal Palace, the Quirinale, and at some distance from the Prime Minister's office down the hill in the Palazzo Chigi. Ambassadorial appointments were always influenced by the Court, and an aspirant Foreign Minister could scarcely afford to be *persona non grata* there. King Victor Emmanuel II (who died in 1878), a monarch who loved hunting, wenching and (the promise of) war, but had some difficulty distinguishing among these pursuits, had a considerable effect on actual policy (and deployed an assortment of personal agents for his own international ends). But his successors were not so forward – Umberto I (1878–1900), because his dull mind could scarcely master such complicated matters, and Victor Emmanuel III, because of his almost pathological hatred of the limelight.[77]

Foreign Ministers, too, could be influential, the most notable in this respect being Emilio Visconti Venosta, who held office 1863–4, 1866–7, 1869–76, 1896–8 and 1899–1901, and who preferred passivity to activity, and caution to the *bella figura*.[78] Naturally, Prime

Ministers, Foreign Ministers and monarchs all carried in their minds 'webs of significance', sets of 'unspoken assumptions', which they had learned at other times and in other situations. Thus intellectual and journalistic debates,[79] financial options, military and strategic assessments, the practices and beliefs of Freemasonry,[80] domestic political hopes and fears – all could have an impact on their decisions. But, whatever the structures of Italian political and international life, if power means anything at all, the power to make Italian foreign policy up to 1914 was grasped by only a few hands. And, at least in its day to day operation, Italian diplomacy was crafted with some acceptance of a 'primacy of external politics' and of national interests being 'eternal' and above domestic concerns. Giolitti declared grandly that the Italian annexation of Libya was 'a historic fatality'.[81] What he meant was that, although in 1911 there were plenty of internal political pressures, to which he was habitually alert, for an imperial adventure, nonetheless what finally pushed him to send ships and men to Tripoli was the current situation as regards the Concert of Great Powers. In a short-term sense, Giolitti acted more because there were external opportunities (which might prove fleeting) than because of potential domestic advantage (though that should not be gainsaid). By contrast, a 'primacy of internal politics' acted in a more indirect and long-term fashion. Giolitti, like others in Italy's leadership, while aware of the many fragilities and contradictions of the system, maintained that Italy could not avoid participating in the world of Great Power politics, even while he feared that exposure through drastic defeat in that world would undermine and perhaps destroy the Liberal regime. He and his colleagues believed, whether rightly or not, that Italy lay in the heart of Europe and, unlike Sweden or Spain, could not forever ignore European quarrels.

However, during the *intervento* (the ten months gestation from August 1914 to May 1915 of the national decision to enter the war),[82] those certainties, and this system, began to unravel. The *intervento* was as crucial a turning-point in the making of Italian foreign policy as it was in domestic politics. Contrary to the wishes of those honest or misguided conservatives, Salandra and Sonnino, who proudly told each other that 'we two alone' were in charge,[83] decisions of peace and war had now been permitted to become subject to 'public opinion' (that is, subject to the views of the 'third generation' of the Italian ruling elite)[84] as never before. As a result, in the succeeding thirty years, a primacy of internal politics would sometimes outweigh the primacy of external politics in the daily as well as in the structural determination of Italian policy.

The character of this 'public opinion' can be readily enough appreciated by listing those who favoured or opposed Italian entry into the war in the special circumstances of 1915's *primavera di bellezza*. Those against, for one reason or another, and in one fashion or another, included the great majority of the populace and the old political class. The peasantry, with good reason, saw war as the worst of the many evil ways in which government capriciously intruded upon their lives. The industrial working class, which had been growing in number and developing stronger political and industrial structures, rejected the war, though some of the moderate leaders of the Socialist Party, and especially the reformist, Filippo Turati,[85] were patriotically inclined to compromise and favoured a policy of 'neither support nor sabotage'. (By contrast, a significant number of revolutionary and intellectual leaders, including Mussolini himself, saw war as their historic moment and now abandoned official socialism.) Catholicism, both 'popular' ('white' unions and a potential Christian democract politics were also on the rise in the Giolittian era) and elite (in the Vatican of Pope Benedict XV, 1914–22), preferred that Italy stay out of the war. So, too, did the great majority of parliamentarians, with Giolitti at their helm.

Many of the key elements in Italian society were also lukewarm about going to war – King Victor Emmanuel III was not a natural soldier and, at the prospect of war, almost had a nervous breakdown in August–September 1914; Fiat director Giovanni Agnelli[86] realised that there were profits to be made as much from neutrality as from combat, and a number of other industrialists and financiers shared his views. Freemasonry, perhaps the most pervasive social institution of the first two Risorgimento generations, by no means automatically opted for war; even the army command was not rash in advocating entry.

Giolitti, of course, had never actually rejected Italian participation in the war, but he had wanted the conflict to retain a Cavourian purpose. Italy should only enter after it was absolutely clear who was winning, and then on that winning side. Italy should be preparing to deal with the embittered and vengeful losers in a post-war settlement. Italy should remain as ever on the look-out for any leaves of the *carciofo* which might fall its way – quite a lot (*un parecchio*), he had explained in February 1915, could be won from talking to the Central

Powers. 'Quite a lot', he implied, was better than risking, and perhaps losing, all.

However, by the spring of 1915 such logic seemed inapposite and 'corrupt'. Salandra, Sonnino and, much more significantly, a great proportion of the Italian intelligentsia, both real and aspirant,[87] most sons and some daughters of Liberal fathers, sensed that time was running out for Italy or for themselves. Stephen Kern has written perceptively about the 'culture of time and space' in *fin de siècle* Europe.[88] His ideas could easily be translated to the Italy of 'Radiant May', a historically redolent month in which once Garibaldi had sailed for Sicily. Italy entered the First World War on 24 May 1915 because those who seemed destined to become the next generation of its political and cultural elite decided that the locomotive of history, boarded in the Risorgimento, was now well behind schedule. The war, and the opportunities it presented, would, they fancied, allow Italian history once more to run on time.

In this assumption, and in their presumption, they were, of course, tragically wrong. A more detailed discussion of the war will be found in Chapter 3. For the moment it suffices to say that participation in the great conflict jolted Italy's relationship with the wider world as never before and left it out of joint for a generation. Again it is worth recalling an A.J.P. Taylor dictum: 'The first war explains the second and, in fact, caused it, in so far as one event causes another.'[89] It is a conclusion which certainly deserves to be borne in mind when historians argue too peremptorily that Mussolini was the 'one man alone' who took Italy into the Second World War.

Italy's First World War was such a characteristically *sui generis* one. Officially Italy was on the winning side and this 'victory' helps to explain why the war continues to have a surprisingly good press there. Rosario Romeo thought it 'the greatest triumph in our history and ... the supreme proof of the political strength of the post-Risorgimento state',[90] and even so left-wing a historian as Lucio Villari was able to assert recently that the Italian contribution to the war was relatively greater than that of any other power.[91] Moreover, whatever the value of its military and economic effort, Italy did achieve its basic war aims. With the acquisition of the Alto Adige, Trieste and Istria, the Italian border with the Germanic (and Slav) world reached the alpine watershed and so, at least while traditional strategic views lingered, Italy was 'secure' as never before. As if to clinch the argument, Austria-Hungary, the great enemy against which the Risorgimento had been fought, disappeared from the map of Europe. Italy had triumphantly liquidated 'public enemy number one'. But, as Italian hyper-patriots were soon saying, this victory was 'mutilated'. Certainly it was hollow. Why? In what sense did Italy lose the First World War?

As so often in these pages, the answer to these questions lies not so much in 'what actually happened' but rather in what seemed to happen, what contemporaries perceived as happening. Italy's loss, so much more significant and influential than any victory – indeed, as profound as that of Germany and more profound than that of Russia – was all in the mind.

'Defeat' came in many ways. The military rout at Caporetto in October–November 1917 ensured that foreigners, for all the immense sacrifice of Italian men and materials to the war, would continue to dismiss Italy's military prowess in the most insulting terms. Much more important, however, was the nature of the Italian war effort. Though a liberal-democratic or national revolutionary new generation cheered Italy into the war, formal power had rested in the hands of elderly conservatives like Salandra and Sonnino, or Vittorio Emanuele Orlando, a Giolittian renegade with ties to the Mafia,[92] who was the unlikely and highly uncharismatic 'Prime Minister of Victory', 1917–19. It was Salandra who had tried to define Italian wartime policy in pre-modern dynastic terms as that of *sacro egoismo*, and he, Sonnino and Orlando were peculiarly out of place in the peacemaking world of Wilsonian liberal capitalist 'new diplomacy' (or of Leninist internationalism).[93]

Given, furthermore, that 'victory' had brought to the surface long-standing and grandiose Italian ambitions ranging from a mandate over the Caucasus, to a restoration, or, rather, take-over, of the Venetian empire in Dalmatia and the Aegean Sea, and that the 'honest' Sonnino was incapable of cloaking such ambitions with truthful ideology or lying virtue, Italy became the natural whipping boy of the Versailles conference.[94] A first abyss of humiliation and bathos was reached in May 1919, as Sonnino and Orlando, rather than face further contemptuous rejection of Italian claims, ostentatiously withdrew to Rome, but then had to creep back to Paris when the peacemakers, with a sigh of relief, carried on regardless. A second crisis, with more evident domestic ramifications, occurred from September 1919 when Gabriele D'Annunzio, ornate poet, dauntless war hero and tireless if ageing sexual athlete, stormed into the small northern Adriatic port of Fiume (Rijeka)[95] – this 'city of blood' then had a population of some 30,000. D'Annunzio, who was backed by nationalists of many descriptions, and, while it was in their interests to do so, by Mussolini and his new Fascists, and by sections of Italian business and finance, challenged the government, now headed by the moderate, if somewhat pedantic, Southern reformer, F.S. Nitti,[96] to get him out. Death, said the poet, was preferable to surrender.

For all his high words, D'Annunzio would eventually choose the latter course. Giolitti, who had returned for his fifth and last premiership, and Carlo Sforza, his Foreign Minister,[97] a new liberal who had inherited many of the ideas and methods of Di San Giuliano or Cavour,[98] simply negotiated with the fledgling Kingdom of the Serbs, Croats and Slovenes as though D'Annunzio did not exist. The result was a sensible border settlement in the Treaty of Rapallo of November 1920. However, Giolitti and Sforza failed more generally to resituate Italy into its old policies of fear, common sense and ambition, policies which would enable it to restate some sort of opportunist arbiter role between the Greater Powers of what was in any case a badly war-damaged international system.

In this as in other matters, despite the victory proclaimed at Vittorio Veneto on 4 November 1918, the Liberal regime was unable to repair the gaps between politics and society which had been so exacerbated by the war, and which continued to widen after 1919, as one season of discontent succeeded another.[99]

International failure or humiliation may have speeded the arrival of what the Fascists claimed would be their new, and this time 'real', national revolution, but Liberal Italy actually collapsed from within. Though 'border fascism' sprang to life very early, and would remain an element of his movement, already by 1920 Mussolini was winning more members and more financial backing through squadrist raids on peasant and socialist institutions in the Po Valley, Tuscany and Umbria, and through the consequent reversal there of the poor's recent improvements in pay and conditions, than by asserting the imperishable *italianità* of the Quarnaro, Isonzo and Adige. In office after 1922, Fascists would talk much about foreign policy but do little to prepare Italy militarily for a grab at world power. This combination of policies, this Fascist version of a *Primat der Innenpolitik*, would eventually lead to military defeat and disaster in the Second World War (and to what, with the establishment of the Republic, would soon become a victory for most Italians). When, on 30 October 1922, Mussolini, freshly arrived on an express train from Milan, accepted the prime ministership from the timid, alarmed or relieved Victor Emmanuel III as the prize for the 'March on Rome', the Duce is said to have remarked: 'Sire, I bring you the Italy of Vittorio Veneto'.[100] In so saying, Mussolini spoke more truth than he knew or meant.

2

ITALIAN DIPLOMACY AND EUROPEAN POWER POLITICS 1922–60

On the last day of March 1940, in a Europe still pregnant with anticipation that the 'phoney war' might one day turn real, Benito Mussolini, the Duce of Fascist Italy, sent a memorandum to the constitutional Head of State, King Victor Emmanuel III. The Duce's mind wandered over the dilemmas confronting Italy since 'non-belligerency' had been declared national policy:

> If the war continues, to believe that Italy can stay out until the very end is absurd and impossible. Italy is not relegated to a corner of Europe as Spain is, Italy is not semi-Asiatic like Russia, Italy is not far away ... as Japan and the United States are. Italy, rather, lives right in the middle of the combatants, both by land and by sea. Even if Italy changed its views and passed bag and baggage to the Anglo-French side, it would not avoid an immediate war with Germany. And this war would be one which Italy would have to fight *alone* [*sic*]. Italy cannot remain *neutral* for the duration of the war without abandoning its role [as a Great Power], without disqualifying itself, without reducing itself to a Switzerland times ten.[1]

What, on reflection, is most piquant about Mussolini's words at this moment just before many issues about the Second World War were to be clarified (or so it seemed) is not their 'Fascist' character, their novelty, their ideological faith, their blind commitment to aggression. Rather, Mussolini's thinking had revolved around ideas which would not have been unfamiliar to other Italian minds in similar circumstances in the past. These ideas were also probably not far removed from those of the King, or of the other members of the then ruling elite. What Mussolini's memorandum echoed with was not so much a bloodthirsty Fascist 'revolution', or a fanatical 'totalitarian' commitment to war, as that mixture of ambition and fear delineated in the last chapter as typical of Italian foreign policy after the Risorgimento. If this memorandum may be assumed to be significant then, to adapt a well-known A.J.P. Taylor dictum about Hitler, 'in international affairs there was nothing wrong with Mussolini except that he was an Italian'.[2]

Yet, such a conclusion starkly contradicts the interpretation of Fascism maintained, with such an ostensibly unassailable mountain of evidence, by Renzo De Felice and his followers. The younger generation of De Felicean historians are emphatic in their neo-Rankean commitment to the idea that the Fascist regime can only be assessed 'objectively' 'on its own terms', that it was near to God in its own special way and that Fascism was, indeed, a revolution.[3] For Emilio Gentile, the most able of the new conservatives, Fascism should be defined as 'a mass nationalist movement of a new type – the party as militant organisation [partito-milizia]. [Fascism] arose in a parliamentary democracy with the declared aim of destroying it and replacing it with a "New state" which would be authoritarian, hierarchical and militarised'. 'Fascism', Gentile has continued,

> was the first modern party to carry mythical thought to power. . . . For twenty years Italy was transformed by the PNF into an immense laboratory where, whether willing or not, millions of men and women were involved in the attempt to realise the myth of the totalitarian state in order to create a new race of Italians raised in Fascist integralism, in the idolatry of the *primacy of politics* and in the cult of the will to power as the supreme ideal.[4]

Nor is Gentile alone in making these exaggerated claims. In her recent study of public opinion under the Fascist regime, Simona Colarizi has emphasised the triumph of 'consensus':

> Throughout the twenty year period there were developed and perfected modern techniques of organisation, communication and information which would ensure that Fascism had an always firmer grasp over society, shutting it into a monolithic system which was almost impermeable to external influences.[5]

Both Colarizi and Gentile argue that Fascist Italy was a 'totalitarian state' and thus agree with Dante Germino's classic 1950s 'totalitarianist' thesis that Fascism was 'a political religion, equipped with the machinery necessary to realize its program'.[6]

In the original model of totalitarianism, as developed by Carl Friedrich and Zbigniew Brzezinski, foreign policy represented a key, perhaps the key, factor.[7] Any totalitarian regime would necessarily have war as its ultimate purpose. It could not exist without opting for a military final solution. But what of Italy? For all their confidence about the radicalism and novelty of Fascism, and its totalitarian achievement or intention at home, De Felicean historians have offered little assistance to a student of Italy's place in the world. Rather, though the extent of his writings and the tortuousness of his style makes him a little hard to pin down, De Felice himself has often sounded as though he believes that foreign policy was one area in which Fascist Italy was neither totalitarian nor revolutionary.

In the early volumes of his biography of Mussolini, for example, De Felice declared that Italian diplomacy after 1922 changed less in substance than in style, and was in any case 'cautious and reasonable' most of the time.[8] Whereas Catholic historian Giorgio Rumi had argued that foreign ambitions and imperialism were at the very root of Fascism,[9] De Felice emphasised the absence of a Mussolinian *Mein Kampf* or *Secret Book* and concluded that Fascism lacked an original international programme. Foreign affairs, rather than driving Fascism, were its plaything and were habitually manipulated for domestic purposes.[10] De Felice seemed almost to believe in a Mussolinian *Primat der Innenpolitik*, though he doubtless did not accept the Marxist views of Giampiero Carocci that Fascist foreign policy was erratic because, in that field, an identity of interest between Mussolini and Italian big business was not as all-embracing as it was at home.[11]

During the last decade, nationalism has begun to reassert itself more stridently in Italian historiography and it is natural that it should recur among diplomatic historians, few of whom had ever been won over by Gramscism or had voted for the PCI. So far as the history of Fascist foreign policy is concerned, the most single-minded advocate of this new nationalism is Rosaria Quartararo. In her book, *Roma tra Londra e Berlino*, Quartararo has argued that 'the expansionist aims of Fascist Italy fit into those of Liberal Italy and its old colonial and Mediterranean problems'. But, she continues, 'from 1925 to 1940, the evolution of the regime's foreign policy was absolutely *independent* of its internal policy'. In that regard, Italy was, she says, in the final analysis most influenced by Great Britain and any flirtation with Nazi Germany was merely intended to put 'pressure on England with a view to a general accord'.[12] Rather than one fascist naturally allying with another in the 'brutal friendship'[13] of the Axis, Mussolini was actually a frustrated potential ally of Britain. Fascist Italy pursued the fine Crispian tradition of possessing multiple ambitions and a policy option always held in reserve, but, in these admirable aims, the Duce was thwarted by British arrogance and British aggression. The British refused to appease Italy out of fear of having to share some of their empire: 'The ideological mask – the destruction of the Nazi and Fascist regimes [as ideologically unacceptable] – was too weak, however, to hide the imperialist motives which [by 1940] had driven London to war.'[14]

Though he made frequent use of Quartararo's research and gave it due acknowledgement in his footnotes, De Felice was far too cautious fully to endorse her remarkable theses. He preferred to argue a more realistic line – Fascist policy could be sensible, as it was, for example, in the hands of Dino Grandi (Under-Secretary for Foreign Affairs 1925–9, Foreign Minister 1929–32, Ambassador to London 1932–40), and so long as that protean politician could plot a deal in which Italy would be acknowledged as the *peso determinante* (the balance-tipping weight) of European diplomacy.[15] According to De Felice, even Mussolini did not lack realism and good sense as a maker of foreign policy. Though the decision to enter the war on 10 June 1940 was Mussolini's own,[16] the failure of Italy's diplomacy once the war began was due more to bad luck than to bad judgement. Mussolini's appraisal of the conflict as having its epicentre in the Mediterranean was just and intelligent, the only real problems being Hitler's unappeasable fanaticism about the war to the east, the German readiness to 'betray' their Italian ally and the deficient civic sense of Italian elite and 'middle-class' opinion. In general, De Felice argues, there was nothing especially deplorable about the idea of a *guerra parallela* (a parallel war), even though it sounded like Salandra's failed policy of *sacro egoismo* by any other name.[17] The sorrow and the pity of Italy's Second World War, we now seem to be learning, was merely that a cruel fate would not allow it to be Italy's war (and ensured that Italy lost). Though De Felice would never say so openly, his Mussolini-as-international-statesman is morally indistinguishable from Di San Giuliano and perhaps even from Cavour.

An outsider's bafflement at the current state of the Italian historiography of Fascist foreign policy is enhanced by the De Feliceans' treatment of the work of the American historian (now moved to England), Macgregor Knox. In his *Mussolini Unleashed 1939–41*, the most detailed and scholarly analysis of Italian entry into the Second World War, Knox revamped a 'totalitarianist' interpretation. The war was indeed a *guerra fascista*. The brutality of its conduct, and the 'vigor and extent of [Fascist Italy's] expansionist ambition' should not be underestimated, Knox says. So far as foreign policy was concerned, Fascist Italy and Nazi Germany were comparable regimes: 'Italy's weakness and Germany's strength explain the disparity between the two dictators' performances better than the usually alleged differences between their personalities.'[18] Though Knox was willing to admit major deficiencies in Fascist planning for war – in regard to intelligence matters, for example, he has noted, 'as in most other areas of the Fascist regime, authoritarian anarchy prevailed'[19] – he is convinced that Mussolini had developed his programme of aggression by 1925–6 and thereafter pursued it with malice aforethought.[20] Despite the fact that these theses about Fascism abroad seem easily reconcilable with those alleged by Gentile or Colarizi about Fascism at home, Knox has been singled out for criticism by De Felice himself. According to De Felice, Knox, along with Mack Smith, is one of those 'historical journalists' who oversimplify the past and fail to understand Fascism on its own terms.[21]

With the historiography so beset by polemic and contradiction, a commentator enters with trepidation upon the task of providing a brief summary of the nature of Fascist foreign policy. Nonetheless, with more guidance from the debates about Nazi German policy than from those about Italy, it is easy enough to draft a list of the major questions with which to approach the story of Fascist diplomacy. How 'revolutionary' or 'fascist' was it? Did Fascism indeed mean war, and were the conduct and aim of its foreign policy markedly diverse from those of its Liberal predecessors (or its Republican successors)? Was it 'Mussolini's foreign policy' and 'Mussolini's war', or did the Duce merely carry into practice the views of members of the Fascist Party or other elite groups or, indeed, of the Italian populace at large? How was foreign policy made in Fascist Italy and who contributed most to its making? To whom were all those violent sounding Fascist words directed and what did they really mean?

Before the March on Rome, diplomatic historian Ennio Di Nolfo has concluded, Mussolini possessed no foreign policy worthy of the name,[22] and certainly the Duce's own pronouncements both before and immediately after obtaining power were notable neither for clarity nor consistency. As he editorialised in *Il Popolo d'Italia* as early as 1 January 1919, there was a sense in which 'imperialism is the eternal law',[23] and, Mussolini proclaimed, a Fascist Italy should always be on the lookout for advantage. Rome was fated now as in the past to be 'the leading city of civilisation'. Italy, the 'proletarian nation', should not be squeamish in dealing with semi-savage, 'so-called Albanians'. Britain would have to learn that Italy did not want to live only on its ruins or by selling tourists sorbets in summer – if Italy went along that path it would turn into 'a great international casino'. The Third Italy had 'now grown up and would not tolerate being babied any more'. The Italian people should assume a greater role in the making of foreign policy and the future lay with the 'new' nations, that is, with Germany, Russia and Italy.[24]

This list of prejudices and ambitions was, however, sometimes qualified by caution. Expansionist aims were reasonable, but, in the circumstances of November 1920, Italy needed peace. In February 1921, too, a policy of 'balance and conciliation' between the powers seemed sensible. Having obtained office, Mussolini promised that 'Italian foreign policy ... will finally be a policy of dignity without yieldings or threats'. Fascist Italy expected to be treated by the Great Powers 'like a sister rather than a waitress', but, as he explained to the Chamber of Deputies in February 1923, Fascism did not, however, signify untoward change: 'there is no originality in the bases of [our] foreign policy'.[25]

For all this possible good intent, Fascism did rapidly become embroiled in an international tangle. On 28 August 1923, Mussolini, at a moment when heat and holiday had driven out of Rome his most respectable diplomatic advisers,[26] ordered the occupation of the island of Corfu, using as an excuse the murder of an Italian general who had been working on an international commission trying to draw a satisfactory border between Albania and Greece.[27] The so-called 'Corfu incident' excited brief international alarum, with newspapers recalling the unfortunate precedent in July 1914 of unilateral action by a Great Power against a Balkan state.[28] The disapproval of Britain, still so evidently the supreme Mediterranean naval power, induced a Fascist withdrawal from the island before Greece had met Italy's demands and, amid contemporary inter-nationalist ardour for this first 'test-case' of the new League of Nations, the dispute was sent to arbitration.[29]

In some of the historiography, the Corfu incident has been built up into a major manifestation of the 'real character' of Fascism. The 'moderate, old-fashioned and conciliatory ways'[30] of the Italian Foreign Ministry had been abandoned in favour of peremptory and ill-judged action. An erosion of Liberal tradition had begun which would climax in the invasion of Ethiopia[31] in October 1935, in the Axis and in Italian participation in the Second World War. As a career diplomat would remember it after 1945, Corfu was a warning that the professionals might not be able to contain the Duce and treat him, as they had hoped, like the blood of Saint Januarius, that is to say, by exhibiting him only once a year.[32]

There can be little doubt that, in the circumstances of the summer of 1923, Mussolini's actions were crass and precipitate and did represent a peremptory prime ministerial intrusion into the making of foreign policy of a type which had become unfamiliar since the retirement of Crispi. However, it is hard to see Corfu as a drastic break with the Liberal past. The tactic of a sudden occupation was not new – Sonnino had used it in Asia Minor in 1919[33] – and one of the lingering issues of international diplomacy in 1923 was what to do about the Italian occupation of the Dodecanese Islands which had continued since 1912 and where possession was indeed turning out to be nine-tenths of the law.[34] Nor was Greece a country with which Italian friendship ran deep. Nitti had defined that nation as the spoiled child of the Entente.[35] Luigi Federzoni, the Nationalist leader and Mussolini's first Minister of Colonies, had long before expressed his contempt for 'the fragile screen of Greek pseudo-imperialism'.[36] In August 1923, Mussolini's action was endorsed by Giulio Cesare Montagna, the career diplomat who was ambassador in Athens, and, at least until a conflict with Britain threatened, by the Minister of the Navy, Admiral Paolo Thaon di Revel, and the rest of the naval leadership.[37]

Moreover, all commentators agree that the Fascist bombardment and occupation of Corfu were 'popular'. The elderly Salandra evinced his approval of it,[38] and the demonstrations of support which occurred in a number of Italian cities were largely spontaneous.[39] But the real issue raised by Corfu is another. What, at its most basic level, did the incident show about the making of Fascist foreign policy?

In his *Lectures on Fascism* first delivered to a Party school in Moscow in 1935, the leader-in-exile of the PCI, Palmiro Togliatti (called, appropriately, by Stalin '*il professore italiano*'),[40] laid down the dictum that Fascism was related to the Italian Nationalist Association (ANI) as was Rome to Greece. Though the ANI had been subsumed into the Fascist *stato totalitario*, Togliatti asserted, whenever there was a conflict between Fascists and ex-Nationalists, 'the substance of the solution to these problems has always come from the Nationalist Party'.[41]

Though some De Felicean historians have denied the accuracy of this analysis,[42] there can be little doubt that Nationalism gave a considerable imprint to Fascist foreign policy. It is quite clear, for example, that the ANI, which had been established in 1910, had many sympathisers among the younger generation of Italian diplomats, both before and after 1922.[43] Although they were very much the sons of Liberal fathers (and did not therefore really belong to that 'emerging middle class' which De Felice has discerned at the base of 'radical' Fascism), and although they were committed monarchists with many highly conservative domestic aims, the Nationalists lacked modesty and moderation in their international ambitions for Italy. Already in 1914–15, typical spokesmen had urged that the Mediterranean become neither a British nor a Slav lake but an Italian one, imagined that Constantinople was calling Italy 'back' and sensed that classical remains in Syria and Palestine 'palpitated' with *italianità*.[44] War, another patriot had then hoped, could deliver both Trieste and Tunis to Italy,[45] and it was under Nationalist impulse that the Ministry of Colonies, after 1915, drafted a wish-list in Africa and Asia Minor which, had it ever been granted, would indeed have constituted an Italian 'grab for world power'.[46]

Such Nationalist intemperance did not lessen in 1919 and can be found peeping out from the minds of many members of the ruling class throughout the Fascist regime. Despite, or because of, the elite background of many of the ANI membership, and their intellectuality, no Fascist foreign policy, however extreme or brutal, would ever exceed the imaginings of the Nationalists.

If the flurry over Corfu is set aside, it is surprising, nonetheless, how moderate Fascist foreign policy in the decade after 1922 was. Though, as refined and nourished by Nationalism, its ultimate ambitions may have been greater than the norm under the Liberal regime, the element of fear and the resultant opportunist common sense remained much the same. Until Nazism came to power in Berlin in 1933, Italy behaved in a predictable manner on the international stage.

Thus, in the first decade of Fascist power, some plots were laid, some advantage was sought in byways. The Italianisation of the Alto Adige did not improve relations with Germany and so subsidies and sympathy were from time to time sent to the enemies of the Weimar

Republic, including the infant Nazi movement,[47] though neither the ideological critique nor the subsidies greatly altered the basic situation in Germany where 'contempt for Italy was a national pastime'.[48] Somewhat half-heartedly, Italy meddled in the Balkans – Albania became an uneasy, unrewarding and wholly untrustworthy commercial satellite;[49] Croatian opponents of the new Yugoslavia were financed (as had already been envisaged in 1918–19);[50] Hungary and Bulgaria were enticed with the prospect of an Italian-led bloc which would oppose France's clients in the region (Yugoslavia, Czechoslovakia and Greece). There, as elsewhere, Italy pursued a policy of pinpricks directed at Paris,[51] which was scarcely surprising in the sense that, in the Balkans, the Mediterranean and East Africa, France remained 'public enemy number two', and, with the disappearance of Austria-Hungary, there was, at least in the short term, no longer a 'public enemy number one'. A more far-sighted diplomacy might have reckoned that Germany's return to commercial and political power in the Balkans and the rest of the continent could not be delayed for ever. Fascist Italy, however, with a certain panache and a certain gullibility, pursued its immediate European interests as though that time would never come.[52]

Dreams of empire survived, too, especially in Ethiopia, but Fascist Italy continued to postpone action there as Liberal Italy had so long done in Libya.[53] Mussolini enjoyed meeting or patronising dissident nationalists, from Chaim Weizmann to Mahatma Gandhi, and punted half-heartedly that revolution somewhere in the world and run by non-Marxists, who half-thought that Fascism was a revolutionary creed, might sometime and somehow bring Italy advantage.[54] In any case, there were publicity gains to be won from these endless mini-summits, and the consequent opportunity to be lionised was not to be passed up by a politician who allegedly read thirty-five newspapers each day.[55] The Italian diplomatic service, it was said, was 'fascistised', notably with a special intake of party faithfuls in 1928,[56] though the agent of fascistisation was Grandi rather than Mussolini and the new appointments were either rapidly duchessed by the already Nationalist officials, or were rusticated to centres beyond the ordinary diplomatic ken such as Detroit (Michigan) or Perth (Western Australia).[57]

For all that, and for all the rhetoric about the inevitability of war and its virtues in generating a virile Fascist manhood, about which Mussolini and the rest of the Fascist elite repeatedly wrote or speechified at home, no irreparable mistakes in foreign policy were made. Despite its claims to have defeated the communist menace within Italy, the Fascist regime pursued a more balanced and sensible policy towards the USSR than did most other states.[58] Italy, too, kept its squabbles with Britain to a minimum and, at Locarno or the Disarmament Conference, acted as something of a 'noble second' in British schemes of pacification. Italy duly signed the Kellogg–Briand pact (though Mussolini then mocked its 'transcendental nature' in a speech at home), and participated as keenly as any other in the secretariats of the League of Nations. Though Mussolini exaggerated when on one occasion he told the Senate, 'Italy today is a world power',[59] Fascist policy was not totally Eurocentric and, especially in the areas of finance and culture, official Italy began to acknowledge what the people of the Italies, unlike most European statesmen, had long understood – the ever-increasing power of the United States. An English wit thought it all amounted to 'pacifascism'.[60]

In general, then, as Fascist Italy, with noisy fanfare, celebrated in 1932 its *Decennale*, the tenth anniversary of the 'Fascist Revolution', the concert of the Great Powers regarded Mussolini, Grandi and the rest with some benevolence. They were as tolerable as most of their predecessors and less of a nuisance than some. It seemed perfectly true, as the regime said, that Fascism was not for export and, if Mussolini had his little ways at home, Italians, as springing in great part from the 'Mediterranean race', were deemed not naturally prone to discipline and order. Fascism was good for them, as it would not be for more advanced peoples,[61] and it had not yet caused those more advanced peoples major disquiet.

By the time Hitler took power, there were only two great apparent differences between Fascist and mainstream Liberal foreign policy. One was the marketing at home. In a curious Fascist version of the new diplomacy, the regime bombarded its citizens with rhetoric about Italian greatness and the necessity and inevitability of conflict. The second difference was a corollary of the first. Given the marriage of foreign policy and publicity and the need for open conflicts openly arrived at, in any crisis, even more than in the past, 'Italy must be there'. Crispi had had similar illusions and paid the penalty for them; Cavour, Visconti Venosta, Depretis and Giolitti had preferred rather to keep the option of inaction. Fascist foreign policy was by definition active, at least in appearance. Mussolini, reversing the sage advice of Teddy Roosevelt, trod the halls of power, speaking loudly and carrying a little stick.

In these circumstances, it was hardly surprising that, in 1933–4,

Fascist Italy was the first state to seek to do something about the Nazi rise to power; and, predictably, what Fascist Italy tried to do was highly traditional. The liberal internationalism of the 1920s had had its day; what was needed in the more dangerous world of the 1930s was an accommodation between the European Great Powers, the 'Four Power Pact' of Great Britain, France, Germany and Italy (no room now for such extra-European powers as the USSR, the USA or Japan). The 'congress system', constructed by Metternich and revived in one way or another after 1870 at Berlin or Algeciras, should be resuscitated. Between the Franco-British and German blocs, Italy, the *peso determinante*, could use its good offices (and hope to be paid for them). The Four Power Pact, or '*Il Patto Mussolini*' as a Nationalist writer called it, would see Italy 'resuming its primacy in the world'[62] (or at least in Europe narrowly defined).

Though such grandiose ambitions have now been set aside, the Pact continues to have a good press in Italian historiography. Rosaria Quartararo has used its failure as the starting-point for her thesis on the deplorable British renunciation of 'Anglo-Italian collaboration in Europe'. She claims that Mussolini had not forgotten the essence of the pact in 1940,[63] but her ideas are exaggerated and depend on that literal reading of evidence so typical of contemporary Italian neo-Rankeans. In fact, the Four Power Pact was more a moment of negotiation than a settled agreement regrettably not applied. In its rapid course to becoming a dead letter it carried two great disadvantages. One was its traditionality, its 'realism', its Eurocentrism; its exclusion, too, of a state like Poland, which would plainly carry huge significance in Nazi foreign policy. The other was Italy's international reputation; the smaller European states might have been willing to listen to Germany, Great Britain or France, but, both because Italy was Fascist and because Italy was Italy, it was hard to applaud a Mussolinian attempt to play at being Bismarck.[64]

If the pre-1914 style of diplomacy was not the answer, military power, or its threat, might be. In August 1934, Austrian Nazis murdered, with cold brutality, their clerical–fascist chancellor, Engelbert Dollfuss (whose wife was then holidaying with the Mussolini family on the Adriatic coast). Mussolini reacted swiftly to this affront both to his hospitality and to Italy's national interest. That interest plainly lay in averting an *Anschluss* which would return German power to Italy's borders, and ominously foreshadow German irredentist campaigns in the Alto Adige, Trieste and wherever the Habsburgs had once ruled. Italian troops were rushed to the Brenner

Pass and promised invasion were Hitler to condone the actions of his Austrian party comrades.[65] Mussolini even used the occasion to fulminate against Nazi racism: 'yesterday against Christian civilization, today against Latin civilization, tomorrow against the civilization of the whole world', who knew where the Nazi depredations would end? Those 'barbarians' could not comprehend the thirty centuries of Roman enlightenment and were the enemies, real or potential, of all humankind.[66]

But, once again, Mussolini's, Fascism's and Italy's reputation helped to undermine policy. For the moment, the Nazis did back off, but an *Anschluss* remained on the horizon and the Austrian populace, which, in March 1938, would welcome a Nazi invasion so warmly, was not allured by the prospect of becoming a client of Italy. Nor did Britain or France show any sign of wanting to stand up to Nazi Germany; rather, Britain was already commencing that policy of appeasement which, in 1935, would return the Saar to Hitler and sign the Anglo-German naval pact. If Britain and France were militarily unwilling, Italy alone could scarcely become the policeman of Europe.

The moment, it seemed, was one in which the international system had been jolted out of its usual course. The post-war settlement had collapsed; its replacement was hard to foresee. Probably this was one of those moments about which Italian philosophers, politicians and historians had so often talked, a moment at which an opportunity existed for the will to triumph against most odds. Fascism, Nationalism and the Italian understanding of the world since the Risorgimento suggested that something should be done. It would be – in Ethiopia.

The Ethiopian War of 1935–6 has spawned a literature more extensive than that on any other single aspect of Fascist foreign policy.[67] It is certainly impossible to narrate the whole crisis and, once again, summary becomes difficult. But a number of conclusions can be drawn. Whatever else it was, the Ethiopian War was not wholly 'new'. Italy had long-standing interests in Ethiopia. Crispi's intentions of immediate annexation had been thwarted at Adowa, but, in 1913–14, as the Ethiopian empire threatened to disintegrate internally after the death of Menelik, Italian officials again planned forward policies.[68] After 1922, these 'plans' were duly renewed. So moderate or normal an official as Raffaele Guariglia, who would become the first career head of the Italian Foreign Ministry after the fall of Fascism, can be found advising in 1931: 'to penetrate [Ethiopia] money is necessary – to take it probably war. But you get nothing in this world without force and effort. If we want an Empire it is necessary to win one'.[69]

Here, then, is another conundrum about Ethiopia. By 1935, both in the liberal capitalist world and in Nazi Germany, seizing an African empire seemed an old-fashioned ambition. 'Been there, done that', the leaders of Britain, France, Portugal, Belgium and the rest might have remarked, had they been so cynical; and indeed the upright, if realistic, British Chancellor of the Exchequer, Neville Chamberlain, jotted in his diary in July 1935, as international tension about Italy's foreign policy in Ethiopia grew: 'it was not her colonial aspirations but her proposal to achieve them by war that we objected to'.[70] The enigmatic attitudes of British conservatives towards Italian policy in Ethiopia were prompted by their sense that certainly there was nothing wrong with empire and, perhaps, even Italy could responsibly or reasonably bear some minor part of the white man's burden, but that such 'imperialist' sentiments should not be expressed too openly in polite circles any more, and should not be mentioned at all where mass opinion might be involved. In attacking Ethiopia, Fascist Italy had opted for a characteristic amalgam of what was really old but appeared new. Despite a military victory whose rapidity astonished most foreign observers and all Italians, Italy would eventually pay its cost.

In the short term, however, there were enormous domestic gains to be had and, in that sense, the war deserves De Felice's characterisation of it as 'Mussolini's masterpiece'.[71] When, on 9 May 1936, Italian troops stormed into an Addis Ababa from which the defending forces had already fled, and Mussolini proclaimed the foundation of a real Italian and Fascist empire, public delight was unrestrained.[72] Italy's historians from Croce to Chabod were among those who especially felt the tug of patriotism and were joyful at the prospect that Italy could at last exploit and experience the 'Glory, God and Gold' of empire.[73]

At the time, for many intellectuals outside Italy, their Italian colleagues' untrammelled imperialist fervour seemed either curiously dated or sadly corrupted by Fascism, although in the 1980s and 1990s the Falkland and Gulf Wars have shown how 'clean', 'cheap' campaigns in distant fields, fought against cultural or racial 'inferiors' and backed by a howlingly patriotic press, have by no means lost their intellectual or public appeal. Italy's war was quick; the major military advance began in January 1936 and five months later the fighting, at least of the official variety, was over. In the whole campaign only about 1,000 Italian soldiers died, though, as Denis Mack Smith has noted sardonically, leading Fascist boss Roberto Farinacci lost a hand while fishing with grenades on Lake Dessie.[74]

So far, so good, it seemed, as long as no hard questions were asked. When they are asked, however, it rapidly becomes apparent that 'Mussolini's masterpiece' possessed a multiplicity of flaws. The most immediate one was economic. To overwhelm an Ethiopian force which, in 1935, possessed only eleven slow, unarmed aircraft (three of which could not fly) and 371 bombs,[75] Mussolini had marshalled the best of Italian technology and more than 500,000 troops. The taking of the city of Addis Ababa, moreover, by no means entailed the pacification of the whole population and, in any case, Ethiopia was a desperately poor country. This empire had scarcely even fools' gold to offer. In October 1936, the lira was devalued by 40 per cent[76] and, despite Fascist trumpeting about the financial virtues of autarky, the Italian economy, required to pay for both aggression and empire, steadily deteriorated over the years that followed.[77]

Nor, after the excitement was over, was much glory won. In the long term, the Ethiopian War did nothing to repair Italy's reputation abroad and added brutality, 'the worst side of fascism', to those familiar ideas about military incompetence, cowardice, sly double-dealing and empty pride, none of which could be countermanded by a victory in Africa. Left and moderate right were appalled by the Fascist use of gas and the Fascist boasting, notably among members of Mussolini's own family, about the pleasure of watching from the air as Italian bombs blew apart Ethiopian villages and their inhabitants (the Futurist, Fortunato Depero, outrageously painted such events with a patriotic green, white and red motif).[78] While these stories figured in the news, Mussolini became the most morally detestable of the dictators and circumspect politicians placed the appeasing of Italy last on any list of priorities which might be influenced by morality or public opinion.[79]

The negative effects of the Ethiopian War did not end there. What, after all, had it been for? What were Italy's war aims? And by what process of decision-making had these aims been reached? To these questions, the simplest and most basic to be asked about any war, neither contemporaries nor later historians have been able to give clear answers. Perhaps, as De Felice has averred,[80] the die was cast by December 1934. But the die for what, precisely? For some, as yet undefined, gain in East Africa is the only response. Mussolini, like almost all members of the Italian elite, thought that an unstable Europe gave Italy some sort of opportunity. In the past, words had not always turned into deeds, but, now, if only because he was in a position to do so, Mussolini was willing to try this opportunity on, by transporting across the seas a massive armed force, maybe at first as a sort of travelling Fascist propaganda campaign. Although there were some difficulties – as late as May 1935 the chief Eritrean port of Massawa, after fifty years of colonial administration, had facilities to unload only one ship at a time[81] – Italy invaded Ethiopia because the propaganda campaign could not be sustained for ever, and because the campaign had elicited no other suggestions for deals or arrangements.

Thus far, apart from its Fascist dressage, the Ethiopian campaign had not been so different from that in Libya in 1911. Then, however, Giolitti, with much greater clarity of purpose and a keener control of the machinery of government than Mussolini possessed, swiftly decided that the only sensible policy was outright annexation, a clean cut in Africa, followed by a rapid return to the complexities and dangers of the European real world. Mussolini lacked such firmness and foresight. Instead, certainly before the Hoare–Laval Pact fiasco of November–December 1935[82] and probably until Italian troops were at the gates of Addis,[83] the Duce waited for someone else to start serious negotiations. When these did not commence, Fascist Italy occupied all of Ethiopia without really wanting it and without having the faintest idea of what to do with this huge accretion of territory and population.

Moreover, all the worst aspects of Mussolinian, Fascist and Italian foreign policy had been reinforced by this hollow African victory. It did not seem to matter that the Duce was bored by economics,[84] or given to changing his mind from one day to the next,[85] or tempestuously ready to proclaim that the phrases of a speech or a conversation amounted to 'plans'. All those lessons which Italian intellectuals had so often preached about faith being able to move mountains seemed, after all, to be true. Galeazzo Ciano, the young new Foreign Minister and son-in-law of Mussolini, joined the King, the military, big business, the intelligentsia, the Catholic Church and, not least, Mussolini himself, in walking behind the Duce's star and all of them cared less than ever before where they placed their feet.

The radical Anti-Fascist historian, Gaetano Salvemini, defined the Ethiopian campaign as the 'Prelude to World War II',[86] and certainly it was the prelude to Italy's version of that war. It had started a process which it did not seem possible to stop. In July 1936, before the euphoria of conquest wore off, Mussolini committed the cardinal sin of intervening in a foreign civil war, even though, in this case, the cardinals and bishops of the Vatican were delighted that Fascist Italy had joined Franco's 'crusade' against Iberian communists, anti-clericals and democrats. The Spanish Civil War was costly in finance, men and material. Neither Franco nor Spanish public opinion displayed much gratitude in either verbiage or practice.[87] Guadalajara (memorably defined by David Lloyd George as the 'Italian ske-daddle')[88] joined Caporetto on the long list of Italian military fiascos – the Fascist forces beaten there were apparently equipped only with a 1:400,000 Michelin road map of the contested terrain.[89]

Italian involvement in war now acquired a momentum of its own. As the spirit took him, Mussolini would boast 'when Spain is finished, I will think of something else. The character of the Italian people must be moulded by fighting',[90] and belatedly discovered that the whole purpose of Fascism was to make 'new men'. On Good Friday 1939, prompted both by the constant expansion of Germany and by the desire of the yuppy Ciano and his entourage to make a financial killing,[91] Italy occupied its erstwhile puppet, Albania, adding that poor and restless Balkan kingdom to the Fascist empire.

In all of this, Italy's real options were narrowing to a frightening degree. From 1935 to 1939, Europe, both commercially and politic-ally, was increasingly falling under the hegemony of a single state, Germany. The leader of this state viewed himself as a personal friend of Mussolini and as an artistic lover of Italian light, art and history, but was contemptuous of the great majority of the Italian people. Nazi Germany was also an expansionist state with irredentist claims on Italy itself, the old enemy of the Risorgimento, the state against which Italy had fought in the First World War, the state which since 1938 had sat so menacingly on Italy's borders. While Italy dispersed or augmented its foes to the south, west and east, the real problem lay to the north.[92] The Romanian diplomat, Grigore Gafencu, showed a fine insight into this dilemma at the base of Fascist foreign policy. Aided and abetted by Ciano, 'the more [Mussolini] felt compelled to proclaim his faith in the excellence of his policy', Gafencu noted, 'the more [the Duce] felt its disadvantages and risks'.[93]

This uneasy sense that the world was not sorting itself out aright dogged Fascist foreign policy even after the 'War for Danzig' com-menced. Though Italy was the ally of Nazi Germany, and though Mussolini had promised in the Pact of Steel that he would be 'ready' by '1943'[94] – what he actually meant, of course, was that 1943 was a long time off and that many things would happen between now and then – Italy, with no serious war aims and no economic, military or domestic preparations for combat, in September 1939 could merely adopt a policy of 'non-belligerency'. Although Mussolini hated the comparison with 1914–15,[95] Fascist Italy very much resumed the position of its Liberal predecessor. It all depended on what happened at the front. Ask the question 'who ruled in Rome?' in 1939–40 and there is no real answer. Contrary to all its rhetoric, the Fascist 'totalitarian state' was powerless in the face of international developments.[96]

Nor was there, despite legend, much sign of genuine division among the Fascist ruling elite, whether of 'Fascism regime' (King, Pope, army leadership, big business and bureaucracy) or 'Fascism movement' (Fascist Party, true believers). It was natural for Italians who mattered to eye the battlefront and, while Germany failed to launch another blitzkreig, contemplate past quarrels, present Nazi fanaticism and future threats. It was natural, too, for Mussolini to rage against his Fate, to recall his militant oratory, to tell himself that, with the coming to power of the Nazis, Fascism had become *the* ideology of the twentieth century and that Italians must eventually march shoulder to shoulder in war alongside their Nazi comrades.

The structural imperatives that lay behind these diverse thoughts and ensured that they would not turn into diverse acts, have not been acknowledged by a historiography which, for one reason or another, has been happy to endorse the eventual (and self-interested) claim of Winston Churchill that 'one man alone' had taken Italy into the war.[97] Actually, Mussolini waited almost exactly the same length of time that Salandra and Sonnino had in 1914–15. Fascist Italy's joining of the war on 10 June 1940 was a classic Italian case of entering a war after it was over, in order to get something at the peace-table, and with the hope in that gathering of confusing and weakening the swagger of the victor. Whereas other European states had entered the First World War with widespread popular backing, and the Second with a sullen, doubtful or resigned populace (this was true even of Nazi Germany), in Italy, in a way, the reverse occurred. In the special circumstances of the fortnight or so leading up to 10 June there is little evidence that anyone strongly disagreed with Mussolini's 'decision'.[98] Though almost always the butt of the historiography,[99] Ciano, who, in his meeting with Ribbentrop and Hitler at Salzburg, had seen 'the horror, the horror', and learned that Nazis said what they meant,[100] was the nearest to a tragic figure in the regime as he jotted into his diary (either then or later): 'May God help Italy.'[101] If those words expressed his real sentiments, then a silly young man[102] was showing some signs of maturing into sense.[103]

The entry into a Second World War, which was, after all, not over, in most ways ended Italy's aspirations as the least of the Great Powers. In his authoritative survey, Paul Kennedy has been particularly severe on the Italian record: 'fascist Italy', he notes, 'was, in power-political terms, spectacularly weak'. It failed in leadership, financial acuity and willingness to fight. 'Rarely in the history of human conflict has it been argued that the entry of an additional foe would hurt one's enemy more than oneself; but Mussolini's Italy was, in that way at least, unique.'[104]

Perhaps Kennedy exaggerates to a degree. But there can be no doubt that, as the conflict widened, Fascist Italy became, in power-political terms, the puppet of the Nazis as surely as Austria-Hungary had once been subordinated to Imperial Germany. Especially after the invasion of Greece in October 1940 turned into the most spectacular of Italian military humiliations, Italy no longer had space to pursue a foreign policy in any serious sense of the word.[105] As the Italophile Hitler would put it in September 1943: 'Italy never was a Power, is no Power today and will not be a Power in the future.'[106] Goebbels, who had been saddened at the news that Mussolini had been liberated to establish the Salò Republic, and wanted Germany to 'regain' all its 'lost territory' from Bologna to Trieste, was more peremptory: 'The Italian people', he confided to his diary in March 1945, at last expressing an opinion which he and most members of his party had always held, 'is not worth a row of beans.'[107] Friedrich Meinecke, from a rather different perspective, did not much disagree: 'The Italian people, rich in creative talents and imperishable contributions to civilisation, are not at all a soldier people. They were not adequate to the task put upon them by Mussolini of raising Italy to the rank of a world power.'[108]

What of Italy's international position at the war's end? What would be the basis of the foreign policy of that Italian Republic which was voted into existence in June 1946? And to what extent would this new regime change a course of Italian diplomacy which had been set by Cavour and which had, to a considerable degree, made its Second World War the 'fifth war for the Risorgimento'?[109]

The basic answers to these questions are simple. By 1945 Italy had, at last, and to its great benefit, been relegated; it was no longer a Great

Power in any sense of the word. At least in the area of foreign policy, the establishment of the Republic did mean a rupture in Italian history. It was true that not all members of the old elites were pleased by that breach. Some nostalgic (ex-Nationalist) Fascists like Luigi Villari[110] and Attilio Tamaro searched their dictionary of rhetoric to find words to deplore Italy's fall from grace. The 'Resistance', or rather 'collapse' and 'civil war', from 1943 to 1945, wrote Tamaro, had been 'a bloodbath unparalleled in our national history' and had resulted in a peace 'contrary to our dignity, our honour, and our interests as a great nation'. Fiume, Dalmatia and the lost colonies, he urged, should not be forgotten. Present defeat must one day be bloodily avenged.[111]

But the revelations about Auschwitz and genocide as well as the total military defeat in Italy left Fascism, for a generation at least, without nostalgic admirers in all but the most extreme circles. As preoccupying in retrospect were the objections of more responsible and more influential members of the Italian ruling elite who, by 1943, may have been glad to see Fascism go, but who also did not like the position to which Italy was reduced in the treatying at the end of the war. Alcide De Gasperi, Christian Democrat Prime Minister from 1946 to 1953, fought stubbornly (and successfully) to keep the Alto Adige[112] and Trieste,[113] and tried to use the sad state of the Italian economy and the rapid resumption of emigration as reasons why Italy should retain some sort of presence in Africa.[114] More surprisingly, as enlightened a figure as Croce could be heard defining the post-war settlement as a *Diktat*,[115] a word with menacing resonances, which he must, or ought to, have understood. Even the Communists were not then averse to bewailing what a conservative contemporary historian can still be found calling an 'unjust peace'.[116]

However, the better symbol of immediate post-war Italian diplomacy was the Foreign Minister (1947–51) Carlo Sforza, who, in his Giolittian phase, had already offered a genial[117] and even postmodern definition of Italy's ideal: 'in foreign policy, it is above all necessary to help the inevitable'.[118] For the Italy which existed in the world of atomic weapons brandished by others, for the Italy which had not yet begun to experience the 'economic miracle' of belated industrialisation, for this Italy it was time to abandon all those absurd and harmful ambitions to strut as masters in Mogadishu or to decree the law in Durazzo.[119]

Though, inevitably, Italy joined NATO in 1949,[120] Sforza and his Christian Democrat successors eagerly pushed ahead with schemes ranging from a Franco-Italian customs union[121] to that fully-fledged EEC which, for the foreseeable future, would end the sad history of Western European border conflicts.[122]

It was highly appropriate that Rome should be the place where, in 1957, the treaty inaugurating the Common Market was signed – De Gasperi, who never forgot his pre-1914 training in the Habsburg Empire, had said that the EEC stood for 'Christian [by which he meant Catholic] solidarity'.[123] For the first time since the Risorgimento, Rome, especially as the PCI after 1956 steadily sloughed off its Stalinism, had found a constructive continental mission.[124]

In the new, post-Second War world order, Italy nonetheless preserved some of its traditions of pursuing its own way. In 1943–4 it was already seeking the best possible relations with the USSR. The onset of the Cold War meant that the far wealthier and more powerful Americans became the more obvious and public patrons, especially as anti-communism or anti-Americanism automatically became part of a domestic political vocabulary. Pietro Nenni, for example, declared that NATO membership had made Italy into 'an aircraft carrier of imperialism',[125] though neither he, for the Socialists, nor Palmiro Togliatti, for the Communists, were too fervently committed to an urgent transfer of Italy from the Western to the Soviet bloc. And, while politicians orated from one camp or the other, Italy went on spending on defence the lowest proportion of GDP of any NATO ally.[126]

Italy became, especially in its internal politics, the border state of the capitalist world, in a sense the Yugoslavia of the West, and, from that somewhat ambiguous international position, nourished its idiosyncratic domestic system of *bipartitismo imperfetto*[127] – the imperfect bipartisanship in which the Christian Democrats were always in government and the Communists always in 'loyalish' opposition. Furthering the nation's low profile in foreign policy, each of these two major parties was as international and as parochial as it was national. Without having to put up with a De Gaulle, without having to decolonise in any serious and dislocating sense, without any real irredentist aims, without having to endure, as Britain did, too 'special' a relationship with the USA, Italians began to grow rich and, from 1946 to 1989, experienced, for all the frailties and continuing tyrannies, incompetencies and corruption of the Republic, the happiest years of their history.

It was perhaps just as well that few Italians saw matters as baldly as this. Indeed, Italians were assisted in their mental transference from imperial and Great Power ambitions to a world in which Europe, Italy and *paese* could happily coexist by two, rather contradictory, interpretations of history, two myths. The first, and more positive, was that of the Resistance, the idea that Fascism and all it stood for had been beaten to its lair by a spontaneous rising of a naturally humanist and Anti-Fascist Italian people.[128] Since Fascism had meant war, racism and aggression, Anti-Fascist Italy would seek peace, fraternity between peoples and international arbitration and concord. It is currently fashionable among conservative Italian historians and politicians to debunk the Resistance and to reduce it to a 'civil war' in which Fascists and partisans are scarcely morally distinguishable. But, whatever the historical 'reality' may have been, the myth of the Resistance was, for at least a generation, a most valuable aide to the Italian Republic's search for peace abroad, and at home.

The second myth, embodied in a suitably ambiguous way by Sforza and given expression by Croce, was that Fascism had only entailed a parenthesis in national history. Liberal Italy had been a democracy in the making; its foreign policy and entry into the First World War had been right and proper for a nation state. For many a moderate or conservative, it became all the easier to hide how radically Italy's situation had changed after 1945 by claiming an interrupted continuity with the Liberal past.

Thus most temptations were avoided. But, given the reality of Italian powerlessness, some dangers lurked in such a restored history. In 1956, the unreconstructed Fascist historian, Gioacchino Volpe, in his own old age regretted that Italy had given up making a great policy before it had ever been able to display its real national mettle.[129] The centenary of the Risorgimento in 1959–61 further stirred some currents of nationalism which still eddied at the bottom of Italian society and culture. As if to test the waters, and see if it was time for the aspirations of a Greater Italy to resurface, in the summer of 1960 there was political crisis. The Christian Democrat, Ferdinando Tambroni, proposed governing with the support of the neofascist and revanchist Movimento Sociale Italiano (MSI).[130] The result was a sort of spontaneous rising of those Anti-Fascist Italians who were determined that the Italian Republic would still incarnate the myth of the Resistance. Tambroni retired to obscurity and death. The MSI remained outside the system. Nationalism was held in check. Italians went back to their byzantine political and financial dealings and ignored foreign affairs. The contentment or prosperity of the greatest number of Italy's citizens continued to increase.

3

THE ITALIAN MILITARY IN WAR AND PEACE 1860–1960

In 1881, the English writer, Samuel Butler, published an account of a holiday tramp around alpine Italy. His mood had been euphoric: 'Who does not turn to Italy who has the chance of doing so? What, indeed, do we not owe to that most lovely and loveable country?' he asked himself as he began writing a journal of his trip.[1] And he duly had a fine time. But near Susa, in those pre-Fiat days not yet a resort town, he had an odd conversation which might even have been worrying to a less confident and less carefree spirit. While Butler was sketching mountain scenery, a local man approached him and asked if his engagement in this seemingly innocent activity meant that war was near. For, Butler explained not altogether convincingly, 'the people in this valley have bitter and comparatively recent experience of war, and are alarmed at anything which they fancy may indicate its recurrence'. Even though, as Butler added, there were no other British, French or German travellers in the neighbourhood, one *straniero* mapping out the environment conjured up for an inquisitive local the dread possibility of military conflict.[2]

But to which recent war was the *paesano* referring? His valley could not have seen direct action since unification, nor had it been directly affected by the battles of the Risorgimento itself. Armies may have marched to and fro but, if military combat was really being recalled, it could only have been before 1815, in the Napoleonic and revolutionary wars. At that time it seems unlikely that this *paesano* could have been born.

The conversation which Butler recorded in his diary and briskly explained away is of rather greater interest to the historian of peasant *mentalité* or of the grand questions of the relationship between *paese legale* and *paese reale* and between military and society in Italy. What Butler was hearing, it seems, was a small echo of these great schisms.

Though he did not understand its nuances, the *paesano* had made a telling remark. He bespoke a world in which one 'foreigner' was much the same as another, and, if each outsider should be approached with courtesy, none should be trusted. It was a rare intruder into the valley who bore no ill. And the worst of all the plagues, for all *paesani*, men and women alike, was war. In war, the agents of one state or another irrupted into the life of local men and women to tax, to conscript, to rape and to kill.

Ironically, Butler learned a rather different lesson from his stay in this locality. Firm in his Victorian (or Herderian) belief that the world was naturally divided into nations, Butler thought that he had happened upon a community of 'pure' Italians. 'Nothing struck me more than the easy terms on which every one, including the waiter [at the inn where he stayed], appeared to be with every one else.' Such happy and grave familiarity would have been impossible in England, the conservative writer added, 'because the general stand-ard of good breeding [in Italy] is distinctly higher than it is among ourselves'. There were fewer 'rude and unmannerly Italians' than Britons, and the reason was easy to see. Italians possessed an ancient civilisation which was engraven on even the humblest heart. Thus they had no sense of an aggressive and churlish 'frontier spirit'.[3]

For all their mutual misunderstanding, both peasant and tourist, 'Italian' or *paesano* and citizen of that British empire on which the sun never set, were thus in a sense agreed. Italians, whether by commission or omission, were not a people of war. Their world in its perfect or natural state was one of peace. Their definition of community excluded the philosophy and practice of arms.

A modern commentator reacts with suspicion to such general-isations and to such sentimentality. Can Italians really have avoided the rage of history in the twentieth century's 'age of violence'? What part did the military play in the history of the Italian state from 1860 to 1960? And how was that part received by Italian society? What especially did Fascism, with its stentorian claims to have equipped Italy with 'eight million bayonets', do to turn Italians into militarists? To what extent did it succeed in this ambition? How did the participation in two world wars, easily accepted as inevitable by Italian diplomatists and writers, condition Italian state and society? Arthur Marwick has suggested that these wars can well be viewed as a test case of the character of a modern state.[4] What happens when this test is applied to Italy?

United Italy had, of course, been born in war. Piedmont, that state which led the Risorgimento and then imparted its institutions to the new union, was renowned as the 'Prussia of the peninsula'. A member of the Savoy dynasty knew that he could trust the army to disperse, if necessary, all those liberal lawyers, townsmen and journalists who, in this piazza or that coffee shop, chatted so tiresomely about parliaments, modern business and liberty.[5] In Piedmontese history or legend, every ruler was meant to be a *re soldato*, though, if the historical record were scrutinised carefully, it seemed that the most adroit kings or dukes had exhibited the opportunist and Fabian skills of the diplomat (or bandit) as often as they had the dauntless but blind courage of the soldier. After 1860, each succeeding monarch of Italy nourished a special relationship with 'his' army. Even that most unlikely figure, Umberto, Prince of Piedmont, destined in 1946 to be the 'King of May', insisted during the Second World War on possessing a military command,[6] and thus emulating his father, grandfather and great-grandfather in 'active' service.

One reason why the King and his officer corps had not followed their naturally anti-liberal bent and dealt decisively with those scheming lawyers, journalists, businessmen and politicians of the Risorgimento was that such liberals were happy enough to employ the army. Cavour talked of setting 'fire to the four corners of the earth'[7] if that would assist the national cause, and many another liberal who, in 1848, had distrusted or despised the Piedmontese and their soldiers, was won over thereafter to accepting the utility in the real world of Savoyard monarchical and military power. Mazzini, far too principled or arrogant a revolutionary ever to compromise with Cavour or King Victor Emmanuel II, defined the nation as a world to win: 'Do not beguile yourselves with the hope of emancipation from unjust social conditions if you do not first conquer a Country for yourselves.'[8]

And yet, for all the half parallels, the Risorgimento was not a militarist event in the way that the unification of Germany was. Mazzini may have preached 'holy war' for the nation, 'let it, like the Nile, flood all the country that it is destined to make fertile', but he envisaged this 'insurrection, strenuous, ubiquitous' as a battle of and for the oppressed. Its chief targets should be the monarchy, the papacy and conventional military institutions.[9] Cavour as a young man had rejected the boredom and irrelevance of an officer's life and his public image, so superbly caught in the portrait by Francesco

Hayez,[10] was of a civilian 'new man', at once tough, businesslike and Pickwickian.

Still more fitting of the Risorgimento was the character of its quintessential and most lasting hero – Giuseppe Garibaldi. In another age this Hero of Two Worlds might have seemed just another pirate – he, whose sailing of the seven seas would eventually include landfall in (an uninhabited part of) Australia,[11] and who could order an execution or a military raid without taking the cigar from his lips.[12] In the special circumstances of the mid-nineteenth century, however, Garibaldi, bred of Napoleon, the Corsican everyman who conquered the world, and of Mazzini, the prophet of a post-national revolutionary utopia of the peoples, was an irresistible figure at home and abroad. When he reached England in 1864 not only did Garibaldi biscuits become everyone's taste but his shrewd or devoted followers even found a market for his locks and soapsuds.[13]

To Italian military history, Garibaldi left one obvious, if characteristically double-sided, bequest. Garibaldi the Hero embodied the triumph of the will. He was the soldier of the people rather than of the state (whose forces, indeed, would wound him so sacrilegiously in ankle and thigh at Aspromonte on 29 August 1862). He was the amateur, Cato-like in the sternness of his criticism of the Establishment and in his rejection of its ways. He was independent, recalcitrant of discipline, nobly ready to forgo political or financial advantage in order to be true to himself. His fate was to be invoked by Fascists and Communists, Socialists, Liberals and Republicans,[14] and indeed by almost everybody except the Vatican and the national army. Ideologies may have come and gone, but few municipal counsellors are yet willing to change the name of the Via Garibaldi which runs through every Italian *paese*. Even the devotees of the Lega Nord may find it damaging to renounce his 'heroic' legacy, and devotees of the Garibaldi myth will go on preferring the will and the dashing individual act to the formal discipline and order of a conventional army.

In his fine study on army, state and society in Liberal Italy, John Gooch has concluded that, in 1914, the army was 'distanced from society and state alike'.[15] In neither its social mores nor its political planning was Italy in any serious sense a militarist country. This distancing had already been apparent in the character of Garibaldi, but was reinforced by the events of Italian history after 1860. Though the Piedmontese officer corps had been by no means rigorously aristocratic, and though, as an Italian historian has declared, by the 1870s, the 'middle-class' element was predominant,[16] the military was almost by definition 'unpopular'. Its first task in United Italy was to provide an 'army of occupation' to defend the new Liberal system. The social war against Bourbonist, clerical or localist 'bandits' or peasants was duly won by the Italian army, a 'victory' which was all the greater because of the contrast with the humiliating failures of Italian soldiery at Custozza and the Italian navy at Lissa in the 1866 war against the Austrians. Confronted with the two great tasks of a modern state, the Italian military, it seemed, was better at preserving law and order (or keeping property in the hands of those who had it) than it was at defending the nation (or aggressively fighting for its cause).

Piedmont had introduced Napoleonic-style conscription in 1854 and further tightened its legislation three years later. Technically the period of service could last eight years, though the exemptions were many. Both the law, and its somewhat uneven practice, were duly passed on to United Italy, though the reformer, General Cesare Ricotti Magnani, cut compulsory service to three years and tried to ensure that it actually applied to most young men. For all his efforts, however, the army remained only partially 'modernised'; it still served a dynasty, and itself, as much as it did the nation.

Indeed, Italy's huge military expenditure – in 1889 it would consume 38 per cent of government revenue[17] – had a largely domestic purpose. It was typical that the royal and national police, the *carabinieri*, should be a militarised body and should, then and thereafter, be funded by the Ministry of War.[18] It was typical, too, that the new mass political movements, especially the Italian Socialist Party, should remain very suspicious of the army and its values.[19]

Nor were such suspicions unknown in other segments of society. Before 1860, Habsburg authorities had deemed the Milanese hopelessly unfitted for the military life and, after the Risorgimento, these attitudes survived. Soldiers were reported to prefer walking around the city in mufti rather than in their uniforms, since the latter exposed them to insult, even from the local police (the Pubblica Sicurezza, or PS). In Milan and elsewhere, officers carried poor value on the marriage market[20] (in any case, in 1894 only 3,833 officers were married as against 10,920 who were bachelors).[21] A Genoese merchant was reported to have remarked, on receiving one officer's proposal for his daughter's hand: 'What! You marry my daughter? When you don't have a proper job!!'[22] Giovanni Giolitti was similarly less than entranced by the military life and did not hide his view that only *deficienti* (dead-beats) went into the army. Sure in this knowledge or prejudice, he saw no reason to share with the officer corps such presumably useful information as the terms of the Triple Alliance or the likely timing of war in Libya.[23]

Nonetheless, there is some evidence of change in the situation of the Italian military during the decades before entry into the First World War. Professionally, a certain modernisation was occurring. In 1882 the position of Chief of Army General Staff was created and such incumbents as Enrico Cosenz (to 1893), Tancredi Saletta (1896–1908) and Alberto Pollio (1908–14) held office for lengthy periods and, especially in the case of Saletta, were of considerable competence. For a time under Giolitti, there was even brief (and unique) experiment with a civilian Minister of War, Severino Casana (1907–9). To some extent, the process of nationalising the armed forces had begun.

In 1860, one of the first problems confronting United Italy had been how to blend the officers and men, the practices and traditions, of the armies and navies of Piedmont, Naples–Sicily and the other old states of the peninsula. Though the military elite, conscious of its propinquity to the King, preserved much that was Piedmontese, a certain unification did gradually occur both in officer ranks and among the conscripts. By 1914 the army had at least some claim to being 'the first school of the nation', even though its mobilisation plans promised to deploy some 7,000 trains and thus nervously ensure that men from one region would always serve alongside men from another.[24]

Socially, a unification process had also proceeded to some extent, even though the comparative figures were not always encouraging. In 1913 Italy, as yet minimally a nation in arms, only called up about 25 per cent of the available annual cohort of conscripts as against 74 per cent in Germany and 87 per cent in France. At that time, Italy spent a higher proportion of its GDP on training than did France, but France trained about 70 per cent more of its youth.[25] Nonetheless, these figures were an improvement on the Italian situation in previous decades, even if the rich and the emigrant, as well as the physically feeble, frequently evaded the requirement to defend the nation and thus avoided the opportunity to be 'made' into Italians.

Ideologically, there were also some signs of a turn in the army's favour. In the 1890s the army was almost automatically deployed as an agent of domestic repression. As retired Chief of General Staff Cosenz would growl on New Year's Day 1894, 'softness' was no use against Sicilian discontent: 'Without *the actual use of its arms, the Army will grow demoralised*' [*sic*].[26] And in that decade the enemies of the army and the monarchical state seemed to lurk everywhere. They could be composed of peasant 'socialists' of the Sicilian *fasci* of 1893–4, or socialist workers and clerical sympathisers shot down in the '*fatti di Milano*' of May 1898.[27]

With the coming of the new century, and the 'Giolittian era', however, two changes became apparent. Though a rural strike[28] or the chaos created by an earthquake[29] could entail the suspension of civil rights with the army behaving like a force of occupation, Giolitti tried to rule on a lighter rein than had his predecessors and, during labour disputes, to do no more than 'hold the ring' between employers and landowners, on the one hand, and social protesters, on the other. To the extent that Italy was then a 'democracy in the making', the army became less openly needed to guarantee the survival of the state.

However, not all modern ideologies were automatically arrayed against the military. After the disturbances of 1898–9 were over, and Luigi Pelloux, the Piedmontese who was to be the last army officer to act as Prime Minister before Pietro Badoglio in 1943,[30] had retired, new alliances became possible. As it achieved rapprochement with the Liberal state, political Catholicism, however variegated a body, found that it shared some values with the military. During the First World War, Catholic chaplains would urge forward what they hoped were the Christian soldiers of the Italian army.[31] In Umbria, for example, the younger clergy were reported to be especially patriotic, while the defeat at Caporetto led one local Catholic paper to editorialise:

> Now it is no longer relevant to talk about interventionists or neutralists, supporters of peace or of action to the bitter end, socialists or catholics or nationalists. Neither the enemy nor the wider world make these distinctions. Rather we are Italians. And Italian are the cities and the land and the families which we must defend from the threatened enemy devastation. Italian is the name and Italian is the honour which we must avenge and save.

For such Catholic patriots eventual victory was sweet: 'the borders of Italy marked out by Divine Providence and for so long contested have now been reached'.[32]

The rise of the nationalist movement also promised new allies for the army, even if Luigi Federzoni, Nationalism's most successful politician, seemed to cleave to old hierarchies as, in 1911, he urged the army to be 'independent of the nature of the State which it is its duty to defend. The Army must be national and only that. The Army must know how to keep quiet, nothing other than how to keep quiet'.[33] Yet, if read closely, Federzoni's words did contain an exhortation to the military to behave in a more nationalist manner, to take ever more seriously their role as 'the school of the nation'. And, indeed, there was new evidence of the officers corps' determination to educate or obtain hegemony over its soldiery. Little military papers, like *Il giornale del soldato* published by a Captain Lo Monaco Aprile in Milan from 1899, began to appear. This publication was pronounced, not to say hysterical, in its patriotism. Adowa must be avenged, Italian greatness properly asserted. The Libyan War brought joy as it opened 'the *first* chapter of our *first* free and conscious appearance in a *world* policy'. The local Arabs, variously defined as 'vipers', 'dogs' or 'cowards and traitors like Judas', should be punished without mercy. Their land was rightly forfeit to the resurgent 'Third Italy'.[34]

In its rabid nationalism, *Il giornale del soldato* went too far even for contemporary tastes, and the paper sank into financial decline until rescued by government subsidies after 1915. Nonetheless, other less florid publications had expressed and continued to express military values. In 1908, the *Vita Militare* of Edmondo De Amicis, with its naive and traditional exhortations to a patriotism of service and Roman Republican *virtù*, reached its sixty-fifth edition after only forty years of publication and, along with the still more sentimental *Cuore* (at its 423rd edition by 1908 after being first published in 1886), was much used in elementary teaching. Read out reverentially in many a school lesson, the works of De Amicis, preaching class unity and the need for a natural bridge between army and people, were probably the most powerful cultural force assisting the nationalisation of the Italian masses before 1914.[35]

And to a certain degree this nationalisation was being achieved. For all the natural peasant distrust of the military and the fear of their intrusion into the rhythms of country life, it was accepted that the army could make a man of a lad. The soldiers of the Sardinian Brigata di Sassari might preserve an intense regionalism, go on using their own dialect in all familiar discourse and consider a posting to Bologna as the equivalent of foreign service. Yet the men could have a strong sense of loyalty to their unit, their comrades and even, on some occasions, their officers. The mores of the army and the peasant world of *padre, padrone* and *padreterno* were not by definition totally at odds.[36]

The role of the navy in Italian society, by contrast, has been almost entirely ignored. It is known that a Navy League (the Lega Navale) was established in 1897. Its membership remained small, however,[37] and its leadership seems often to have been more interested in navy contracts than in navalism.[38] Though the children of the bourgeoisie 'always wore sailor suits', as the fashion of the *belle époque* dictated, and some intellectuals would wax enthusiastic about the navy as the major force of racial vitality, navalism, except in such coastal cities as La Spezia or Venice, seems to have had little popular appeal.[39] Indeed, in June–July 1914, Ancona, a major Adriatic port, saw the temporary establishment of an anarchist republic as part of the disturbances of 'Red Week'.[40] The fiasco at Lissa in 1866 cast a long shadow and, as its historian has remarked, Liberal Italy's patriotic statuary notably excluded naval figures.[41] In the First World War, too, the navy would prefer inaction, a preference which changed little thereafter. As one English-language historian has acerbically remarked, the message that Italy would get, in 1940, from the sea was that 'for twenty-five years, the Italian navy had been preparing for the wrong war with the wrong enemy in the wrong way'.[42]

But there was one thing the navy officer corps had done before 1914. For once in agreement with the army leadership, with which it was typically in dispute over levels of government finance, the naval chiefs had taken the Triple Alliance at its word and in 1913–14 were developing detailed plans for association with the Austro-Hungarian fleet in time of war.[43] The army had gone at least as far, with Pollio, the Chief of General Staff, being sufficiently invigorated after attending German manoeuvres in April 1914, to urge on his bemused or compliant hosts the advantages of a preventive war against France and Russia.[44] Italy, whose planners had repeatedly contemplated violating Swiss neutrality,[45] would superbly link up with the left-wing of the German army, Pollio imagined, before Paris fell.

Such 'plans' remain a puzzle unless it is accepted that they were not plans at all, since the army and navy leadership had no serious role in the peacetime decision-making processes of Liberal Italy. In that regard it was perhaps appropriate that the post of Chief of General Staff of the Italian army was vacant for the first four weeks of the July crisis. Pollio had died a few days after Archduke Franz

Ferdinand and his replacement, Luigi Cadorna, from an old and pious Piedmontese military family and speaking Italian with a pronounced local accent, did not receive his appointment until 27 July (he had been convinced that Jews and Freemasons had previously blocked his promotion).[46]

It was Cadorna who, after the *intervento*, would lead Italian forces into the First World War. Italy's part in this war has a curious history or lack of history. English language and other non-Italian analytical works regularly exclude Italy. The image of the war, which, as Paul Fussell has so movingly shown,[47] has had such a profound and lasting impact, is almost always composed from scenes of the muddy trenches in Flanders or of unarmed and brutalised soldiers dying on the Eastern Front.[48] The Italian war in the rugged hills of the Carso, or on the precipitous slopes of Monte Grappa and the Valle del Pasubio, is all but unknown outside Italy. Only Caporetto, yet another Italian military disaster,[49] is remembered.

That ignorance and that recollection are the odder because, as has already been noted, the war continues to have a surprisingly good press in Italian historiography and is often claimed by Fascist and Anti-Fascist alike as a time of national grandeur and achievement.[50] As Piero Pieri, the doyen of war historians, has put it, the army in 1918 acted as 'the exponent of the living forces of the nation after fifty years of unity and liberty'.[51] Why? How did Italy fight the First World War and what did that mode of fighting do to Italy?

For a state like Liberal Italy the war effort was massive. Some 5.7 million Italian men would eventually pass through the war machine, a greater number than those who had exercised the right to vote in the 1913 elections.[52] Almost 600,000 died and some 500,000 were wounded and incapacitated (or 'mutilated', to use the more evocative Italian term). Financially, the Italian government spent more than twice its total expenditure from 1861 to 1913 on the war of 1915–18.[53]

Predictably enough, however, the war did not afflict all Italians equally. Peasant soldiers, who dominated the infantry where the casualty rate was 39.8 per cent (as against 4.1 per cent in the artillery and 3.5 per cent in the cavalry), were the most likely to die. In 1919, 63 per cent of war orphans belonged to peasant families.[54] Low pay (in 1914 an ordinary soldier earned 0.5 lire per day against a metalworker's then wage of 7.6 lire)[55] and brutal discipline (decimation, that is, the killing, in case of attempted mutiny, of every tenth man, was still practised)[56] made it a highly traditional army, as was appropriate in a state fighting merely for the dynastic advantages of *sacro egoismo*. Italian POWs, if they were Southerners, might write home to request a paternal blessing and offer in return a respectful kiss of the father's hand and right foot. Rumours from the worlds we have lost would be passed on, for example, about a hen which had laid an egg with '1917, 26 May, peace' in it. Correspondents would lapse into dialect when they expressed their views on love or sex, their health, or that of the Austrian or Italian political systems.[57] The 'Italies' could similarly display their resilience after Caporetto. Some 800,000 'Italians' were then left behind the lines, but they seem to have been little perturbed that Roman rule had ended. Priests responsibly accepted the leadership of their communities and peasants gladly took over the land of those liberal *signori* who had fled.[58]

Yet the story of Italy's First World War is not merely that of a 'peasant' war and of Italies enslaved to Italy. Rather, it is arguable that, on 4 November 1918, more Italians found their identity in the nation than ever had before and, perhaps, Fascist legend to the contrary, would again until the 1960s and 1970s.

The explanation of this surge in the processes of the nationalisation of the masses is a curious one. As has been related above (pp. 30–3), Italy, alone of the Great Powers, entered the war lacking a political or social *union sacrée*. Until Caporetto, the war continued to be waged by a traditional elite, with traditional means and for traditional ends. However, the nearness of total defeat (and thus of the collapse of the whole Liberal state) brought a degree of change. In the twelve months which followed Caporetto, Italy began to fight something like a modern national war.

This modernity was mainly exemplified in propaganda. Only on 1 November 1917 was an under-secretaryship for the press and foreign propaganda created, and entrusted to the nationalist, Romeo Gallenga Stuart.[59] In February 1918 the new ministry was accorded a budget of 9 million lire, not a huge sum, but a useful indication of the new governmental determination to forge an Italian 'idealism', to adapt its practices to that contemporary discourse, summed up so memorably by Arno Mayer under the title 'Wilson vs. Lenin'.[60] Other intellectuals with very different futures – Giovanni Amendola, Ugo Ojetti, G.A. Borgese, Federzoni, Volpe and, in his own way, Mussolini – became associated with Gallenga Stuart in these campaigns. At the front, officers now more urgently instructed their men on the justice of Italy's cause. Prime Minister Orlando even got around to promising land distribution to Italy's heroic peasant soldiers once the war was over, while later Anti-Fascist martyr Carlo

Rossell imagined at the war's end a '*union sacrée* of officers with soldiers, bourgeoisie with the people'.[61]

There was much that was brittle and superficial about this belated campaigning. Its very belatedness, nonetheless, meant that it was by definition short and was not therefore given the sort of searching examination which, for example, the hegemonising processes of the German government had received by 1918. On 4 November, the fact that there was what could be counted as a victory at Vittorio Veneto, and that Italy had 'redeemed' Trieste and Trento, undone its historic enemy and achieved its 'natural' frontiers did make it appear that the war had been the greatest triumph in 'national history'. It was an appearance, however, which would be of very short duration.

From the real Vittorio Veneto of an economy uneasily modernised (but dependent on state subsidy and a rigorous policing of the workforce) and a population only partially nationalised (where peasants and workers, patriots, bourgeoisie and *paesani* had, however, had such a diverse experience of the war) sprang Fascism. Here, at last, it seemed in 1922, was a regime which would take as one of its first purposes the task of integrating the military into Italian society. Whatever had been the nation's past failings, under Fascism the legions would march afresh as proudly fascistised 'new men' and, in the wider world, forcibly assure all Italians a 'real' respect.

From the very beginning Fascism made great play of its commitment to educating Italians into a more militant view of the world. In 1923 Mussolini spoke of the plans of Giovanni Gentile, right-wing philosopher turned Minister of Education, as 'the most fascist of reforms'.[62] Especially in the next decade, the Fascist regime hailed its paramilitary youth organisations as the best example of totalitarian achievement. In launching the School Charter in 1939, ex-Nationalist, Roman Fascist and aspirant ideologue Giuseppe Bottai[63] proclaimed that the new schooling system would 'serve neither bourgeois truth nor proletarian truth but rather a human and national truth' based on 'the culture of the people inspired by the eternal values of the Italian race and its civilization'. Education would 'create the new man, educating him in a living and modern concept of culture and life', which would not be at all rhetorical but would produce 'a precise moral renewal'. One precious aid to this process would be new textbooks, written by historians, generals and admirals and full of 'military culture'.[64]

Though a critical reader might catch just a hint of rhetoric in Bottai's phrases and wonder anyway why they were necessary after almost two decades of Fascist rule, it was true that in 1937 more than 6 million Italians were enrolled in the various Party youth organisations: 2,478,768 in the Balilla, 2,130,530 in the Piccole Italiane, 960,118 in the Avanguardisti, 483,145 in the Giovane Italiane (assisted by a bureaucratic staff of 129,277 then under radical Fascist *ras*, Renato Ricci).[65] Back in 1930, Ricci had already requested that each Balilla gym be equipped with arms, since the first purpose of Fascist scouting was preparation for war.[66] And ten years later, a Fascist propagandist was still boasting: 'The Nation had become . . . a big school; a school in which Italy has found a Teacher.'[67]

By that time, however, voices more critical of the Fascist boast through its iron will to have tempered a nation in arms were being heard. In 1942, the journal, *Libro e moschetto* (whose title echoed the Mussolinian slogan *'Libro e moschetto/Fascista perfetto'* – Book and rifle/perfect Fascist), complained bitterly that 'the great part of youth is apathetic, detached from the gravity of the moment'.[68] There were limits, it seemed, to the Fascist penetration of the popular mind.

There were limits, also, to the Fascist penetration of the army. The story of General, then Marshal (and having won the empire to be created Duke of Addis Ababa), Pietro Badoglio, is typical. Badoglio, a Piedmontese monarchist, rose to be Chief of General Staff in 1919–21, despite claims that his military incompetence had been responsible to some extent for the Caporetto collapse. Following the March on Rome, his future seemed doubtful – because of his ideology, because of his military record[69] and because those members of the Fascist Party most interested in military affairs had proclaimed that Fascism stood for *'una nazione armata'* and that they would bring their 'revolution' to the military hierarchy and systems as surely as they would to Italian society.[70]

For the next two or three years a battle was fought over the army's future. The result, however, was a victory not for revolution or militancy but for tradition, continuity[71] and, naturally enough, for Mussolini himself. In 1925 Badoglio was reinstated as Chief of General Staff, though any personal threat which he might have offered to the Duce was checked by the appointment of General Francesco Saverio Grazioli, a fervent Fascist and a personal enemy of Badoglio, as his deputy. The rank of Marshal was created so the elite of the army would not be too embarrassed socially when they had to attend international military gatherings. Officers' pay was increased. And, in case there were any further problems, Mussolini himself assumed the post of Minister of War. Giorgio Rochat, the historian of these events, has concluded his superb study with the remark that Italy was left possessing 'an army with too many officers, too few soldiers, half empty stores, an antiquated structure, financially costly and wasteful, and with too great ambitions'.[72] Little would be done thereafter to change this situation and Badoglio would remain at his post to organise the fiasco in Greece. He was only dismissed on 29 November 1940, well after the extent of that Balkan defeat had become clear.

Despite the passage of the years, the state of Italian military preparedness had not improved. Though much money was spent,[73] the new arms and equipment which were purchased were rapidly exhausted in imperial campaigns, in the Spanish Civil War or, as ever, in police and propaganda duties at home. Notoriously, the Italian army would enter the Second World War utilising artillery left over from the First war, some of it being Austrian.[74] When, in June 1941, Italy joined Operation Barbarossa, it would dispatch 20,000 mules to Russia but no sleds and few winter uniforms.[75] Its steel production figures before and during the war were so low that they have been defined by a leading historian as 'risible'.[76]

Coordination between army, navy and air force officer corps had broken down as early as 1927,[77] and a level of inter-service conflict, worse than that which had been common in Liberal Italy, developed. The new air force became a particularly good example of the strengths and weaknesses of Fascist military policy. A pilot's life seemed ideal for the new Fascist man – it combined modern technology, speed and daring. Alone in an open cockpit, a man engaged with nature in a specially 'modern' way. He confronted Destiny, while still a knightly crusader for the nation. One Fascist painter expressed it all a little crudely by portraying a woman (who may also have represented 'Italy') being inseminated or raped by a propeller-driven plane as it swooped low over her naked and yielding body.[78]

In 1925 an Air Ministry had duly been created and the following year given to the leading Fascist, Italo Balbo, as its under-secretary (in September 1929 he became minister).[79] Balbo was an indefatigable propagandist of this *arma fascistissima* and led a series of international 'raids', in which numbers of Italian planes flew to the USA or Brazil, to the delight of the press (and of Italian emigrant communities). Mussolini, too, enjoyed the publicity thereby generated (though his mistrust of Balbo's popularity mounted and Balbo's phone was regularly tapped). As the Duce told his minister in a public letter: 'Your long-distance flight was undertaken in a black shirt because it was the flight which consecrated the fascist revolution in the skies of two continents.'[80]

Balbo also acted as a sponsor of Giulio Douhet, a theoretician of attack as the supreme virtue, 'a novelist and comic writer of a minor sort, a painter, and a cinematic scenographer'.[81] It was Douhet who, in the 1920s, urged that 'the air force . . . represents the ideal means to ensure victory, independently of any other circumstance whatever'.[82] A historiographical debate continues about Douhet's virtues as a strategic thinker,[83] but all commentators agree that much of his contemporary success was due to the drastic nature of his ideas and the fluency with which he expressed them.

What neither Balbo nor Douhet did anything to amend was the gap between the theory and the practice of Italian air power. The Fascist air force turned out to be less than ready for a winged blitzkreig which might effortlessly carry Italian power to the wider world. In 1939 the claim that Italy possessed 8,528 war planes was suddenly revised downward to 840.[84] In fact, aircraft production was one of those areas where Fascist Italy most drastically failed the 'test of war'. By 1942, the United States, now so absurdly added to the list of Fascism's enemies, was turning out from its factories in a week more planes than Italy could manufacture in a year.[85] Even in the haven of its Mediterranean sideshow, Italy could not draw comfort from such a comparison.

Contrary to all its assertions about the creation of a totalitarian state and the engendering of new men, Fascist Italy in general performed far worse as a state, a society and a military force in the Second World War than had Liberal Italy in the First. When the Australians took Bardia in Libya in January 1941, Anthony Eden, the British Foreign Secretary, commented sardonically that 'never had so much been surrendered by so many to so few'.[86] In its performance at the front, Fascist Italy, in its weakness and confusion, regularly confirmed both allies and enemies in their long-standing beliefs about the unsuitability of Italians for military life.

What were the reasons for this military failure? To a considerable degree they were economic. As Alan Milward, the most authoritative economic historian of the war, has remarked briefly:

> The immense investment and productive effort which characterized the war effort of the other combatants did not take place in Italy. . . . Stagnating production and raging inflation soon made . . . [the] situation hopeless. The fascist experiment,

whose economic foundations had been shaky at the best of times, collapsed into occupation and penury. None of the economic benefits of war . . . [was] reaped in Italy; its disasters were reaped in full.[87]

And even James Sadkovich, a persistent if unconvincing advocate of the significance of the Italian war effort, has acknowledged that Italy could deploy but 'slender resources'.[88]

If the economy was unprepared for major war, Fascism had similarly done little to modernise Italian society. For all the talk about a united Italian 'race', class differences were as evident as ever; for all the emphasis on cultural fascistisation, Italians still nourished in their hearts their Catholicism, their liberalism, their socialism and their other pre-1922 beliefs. The bourgeoisie successfully sought to save its sons from war service. The proletariat rediscovered its sense of self in a series of spontaneous strikes in 1943. Even intellectuals began to doubt Mussolini's charisma; and the peasantry, still the most likely to be doing the real fighting, continued to dream of family, *paese* and 'America', rather than of Mussolini, Fascism and Italy. In the First World War it had been reported by one perceptive officer that peasants viewed soldiering as another form of emigration, 'hard, serious, grinding labour among unknown folk whom they do not love, under unknown regulations into which they don't inquire'.[89] Nothing had changed in the second conflict when, as one survivor would remember, officers and men still literally spoke dissonant languages.[90]

It was thus appropriate in very many ways that the fall of Fascism in July 1943 and Italy's withdrawal from the war forty-five days later would be triggered by an Allied bombing raid on Rome. In Britain, Germany and Russia (as later in North Vietnam), bombing usually stiffened resistance. In Rome, it exposed the hollowness of the Fascist revolution. Romans, no longer especially desirous of being Italian and unmoved by all the propaganda about the new Roman Empire, sought succour from the Pope, just as they had in times of troubles before 1860. Fighting for Italy was still not their business.

Despite this attitude, the elites of pre-Fascist national or Liberal Italy, as they tried to slough off twenty years of fellow-travelling with Mussolini, turned back to the army as a last resort. As once Umberto I had called on Pelloux, and Victor Emmanuel II on a number of military chiefs, so Victor Emmanuel III summoned Badoglio to be Prime Minister (1943–4), in what Claudio Pavone has defined as a *'mancato incontro'* (a meeting which never happened) between the Italian army and people.[91] It was true, too, that the Salò Republic, the puppet radical–fascist regime headed by the rescued Mussolini after September 1943, re-emphasised its militant commitment to the 'new man' and attracted the support of so eminent a military figure as Marshal Rodolfo Graziani, Badoglio's old rival, who now became Minister of Defence. (Predictably Graziani was especially anxious that a national army assert itself over party militias. Salò, in its short and vicious life, spawned a variety of competing armed groups.)[92] But, in practice, Italy had lost its military independence. The 'Kingdom of the South' was in the hands of the Anglo-American occupiers and, as Goebbels put it in March 1945, Mussolini's restored *repubblichino* regime was 'so impotent' that it was 'fairly immaterial' who held its offices. Field Marshal Keitel of the *Wehrmacht* did not repine: 'the only Italian army which cannot betray us is one which does not exist'.[93]

In most senses, an Italian military relationship with the wider world ends here, though Republican Italy would duly be granted membership of NATO.[94] A new Italian army would be constructed and in August 1953 sent to the Trieste border at a low point in negotiating the fate of that city. Italian soldiers, retired or in service, would occasionally attract the attention of Republican Italian politicians, especially those who belonged to the neo-fascist MSI.[95] But the Italian military had lost their last pretensions to strut on a wider stage.

One final matter deserves mention, all the more because it has been discussed in a finely textured book, Roger Absalom's *A Strange Alliance: Aspects of Escape and Survival in Italy 1943–5*. Absalom relates the story of the Allied POWs cast adrift in Northern Italy by the botched attempt of the Badoglio government to get Italy out of the war and the resultant 'immediate, spontaneous response to . . . [the POWs'] plight of tens of thousands of Italian civilians'.[96] Nuances abound. The peasants were traditionally suspicious of outsiders, but war and conscription meant that they were presently short of labour and the protracted functioning of a black market sometimes gave them an unusual surplus of food. Women, especially inured to the casual sexism of peasant life, were flattered to be able to help men who might well be the sons of foreign *signori*, and it was even better to be respected and liked by them for giving charity: 'the grateful dependence of the escaper was a sure sign that the reign of justice had at last begun'.[97] Echoes of those Italies which had not been confined by the borders of the Fascist empire or the Italian state could also frequently be heard:

> a constant among helpers everywhere in Italy was a vision of an America, whether personally experienced by them as emigrants or simply transmitted through the informal culture, as a promised land of abundance, generosity and loyal friend-ship, in some sense even a representation of the millenialistic 'world turned upside down' which remained a deep collective fantasy.[98]

For those like the family near Marano Lagunare which con-temporaneously fed New Zealand escapers, Italian partisans and German troops, politics or ideology were only a trifling part of the human condition, even though, naturally enough, a *furbo* would always try to be on both sides of an even money bet. As Absalom has explained it:

> few peasants were strongly influenced by the official ideo-logies of either Fascism or antifascism, but their 'common-sense' provided models of interpretation and response which reflected a long history of exploitation and more or less successful passive resistance to it, while they possessed a traditional technique of survival through concealment and displacement, and a framework of values tending to legitimate such behaviour.[99]

Among Italy's own POWs, the equivalent of these wise and guileful helpers were some soldiers who were penned in a camp in rural New South Wales when in 1943 their Japanese colleagues broke out *en masse* to kill or 'to die like the carp'. Though the Japanese opened the gates of the Italian compound, the Italians remained inside. However alien much of Australian country life must have been, they were sensible enough to know that in wartime (and even in peace, since Australia was then a rich country, and ample meat filled the POWs' diet) they had never had it so good.[100]

The helpers in the mountains or on the Po Valley plain, the POWs in Australia, all kept to some version of Christ's second command-ment even while they broke the ten of the Old Testament. In so doing they, like the *paesano* of Susa who had met Samuel Butler sixty years earlier, incarnated the 'banality of good' more surely than did many other combatants in this or other wars. In however partial and self-interested a manner, these Italians had delivered themselves from the fury of the militarisers and the nationalisers. Their understanding why the peacemakers are blessed and why individuals need 'society' helps to explain how those who study modern Italian history often feel reason with Gramsci to retain an optimism of the will, even while it is necessarily accompanied by a pessimism of the intellect.

4

ITALIAN COMMERCE AND THE WIDER WORLD 1860–1960

In the late 1980s, commentators suddenly decided that Italy was much wealthier than had previously been reckoned. For some years, statistics had underestimated the national GDP by 30 per cent or more.[1] Now it was agreed that 15 per cent should be added to official totals in order to make allowance for the 'black economy', that is, for those sections of business and industry which operated outside government ken. The result of this new tallying was that Italy suddenly overtook Great Britain in domestic product and drew close to France. A bookkeeping change made Italy the fifth or even the fourth greatest economic power in the world.[2] In a short-lived interruption to the normal national discourse about permanent crisis, experts declared that Italy was a success. Its growth rate, averaging 5 per cent since 1945, was the highest in Europe. 'Democracy Italian style' had brought positive results which could only be compared with those of that other highly idiosyncratic society and economy, Japan.[3]

At the moment of writing, this euphoria has evaporated and commentators have resumed their accustomed vocabulary of corruption, incompetence, permanent crisis and imminent disaster. If the words of economists and other savants are to be believed, Italy is experiencing yet another commercial and monetary 'Caporetto' and who knows where the rescue will come from this time?[4] Indeed, a historian surveying the literature of the last century might conclude that, with some exceptions during the Fascist period, the major constant of Italy's economic place in the world has been its perceived precariousness. This perception may also explain why Italy, even in the first decades of its existence,[5] always stimulated in onlookers and participants brief bouts of high optimism which were rapidly succeeded by repentance and fear (and by some sort of economic shake-out).

Precariousness is certainly a factor to be acknowledged in any survey of Italian economic history. But so, too, and especially since 1945, is growth. Whether fourth, fifth, sixth or seventh in GDP, Italy undoubtedly now possesses one of the world's largest economies. Fiat, Olivetti, Pirelli, Varese, Valentino, Benetton, Barilla and Cinzano are familiar names in many a household in many a country. ENI, the state-owned holding company, until privatisation was a huge enterprise, controlling Alitalia, AGIP and many other concerns. The Banca Nazionale del Lavoro, the Banca Commerciale Italiana, the Credito Italiano and the Banco di Roma are among the most important financial institutions in Europe (and the Mafia is undoubtedly the world's best-known criminal 'multinational'). Still more important are innumerable small businesses, from the restaurants and hotels of the tourist industry to the vast number of shops, which have such a characteristic place in every Italian town, and the small manufacturers, notably of furniture, furnishings, textiles and other quality products based on Italy's frequently acknowledged world leadership in design. In some circles, 'Italian' is now thought to be synonymous with 'style', and recollections of Rome and the Renaissance render this thought seemingly permanent. Whatever past or present fashionability, it is plain that, since the Risorgimento, Italy has experienced a rise in wealth and expectation quite unparalleled in any other century of the history of the peninsula. The nation state has been quickened by the successive industrial and technological revolutions of the recent past. It is today, and has been for some time, a full participant in the order of world capitalism.

Yet, as was true of Italian foreign and military history, so Italian economic history has many individual features. Italy moved through the gigantic economic changes unleashed by the first Industrial Revolution at its own speed and in its own fashion, and lived in its own special way a story of growth and uncertainty, innovation and imitation, 'backwardness' and super-modernity, continuity and violent change.

As has already been noted, if rhetoric about coming liberty and national grandeur is set aside, then the basic purpose of the Risorgimento was economic. Italy was united not so much by as for the railway, for that heavy (foreign)[6] industry which would manufacture the locomotives and the tracks and for the enhanced communications and increased commerce which the railway would provide. Rosario Romeo,[7] in his polemic with the dead Antonio Gramsci[8] and the live Alexander Gerschenkron,[9] would be wrong in many things but he would be right in his understanding that a United Italy could only make sense if it succeeded economically. Such success remains the fundamental justification for the retention of an Italian nation state.

Perhaps his Sicilian background helped Romeo understand just how far the kingdoms, republics and theocracy of the period before unification had fallen behind Britain, Belgium, the Germanies and France. As Gino Luzzatto has noted, until 1860, and even beyond, the Industrial Revolution had stimulated but 'weak and sporadic reflexes'[10] in the economies of what would become Italy. In 1859, the peninsula possessed only 1,476 miles of railway (649 in Piedmont, 503 in Lombardy–Venetia, 195 in Tuscany, 70.75 in Naples–Sicily, 58.25 in Rome).[11] Some of the lights and shadows of this uneasy 'modernisation' were reflected in the formal opening ceremony in February 1854 of the Turin–Genoa line. Built through very difficult terrain, the railway was something of an engineering triumph and was duly saluted by King Victor Emmanuel II. To his royal benediction was added God's – the Archbishop of Genoa took the opportunity both to bless the endeavour and to baptise three locomotives,[12] a modern gesture by a prelate of a church whose former Pope, Gregory XVI, had labelled railways an invention of the devil.[13] Nor was this Pope alone in his abomination of the greatest invention of the Industrial Revolution. In normally enlightened Tuscany, for example, it was reported that the inhabitants disliked the spread of railway tracks since they were sure that locomotives caused vine blight.[14]

Still more ambiguous for the future economic history of United Italy was its inheritance from the Kingdom of Naples–Sicily. This realm was the largest of the Italian states; its capital, Naples, a genuine metropolis of a kind, was, in 1800, Europe's third most populous city after London and Paris.[15] In the eighteenth century, the Enlightenment had flourished more palmily in Naples than in Rome or Turin. Nor, after the French Revolution, did the kingdom sink entirely into reactionary lassitude. Rather, Naples–Sicily saw the launching of Italy's first steamship (1818), the initiation of its first Mediterranean shipping line (1823), the construction of its first iron bridge (1832), the opening of its first railway (1839) and the provision of the first gas lighting to an Italian city (1840), even as the Habsburg Emperor, in his capacity as ruler of Lombardy, was banning the publication of 'socially disruptive' stock market reports (1839).[16] King Ferdinand II (1830–59), who would earn the soubriquet 'Bomba' for his suppression of the 1848 revolution in Messina, took a professional and somewhat modernising interest in his army and, for a time, his state was regarded by contemporaries as a relatively serious military power (though it was not so clear that they were affrighted by his promotion in 1834 of Saint Ignatius Loyola to be, at least in spirit, a Field Marshal in the royal force).[17]

Indeed, for all the glimpses of modernity which can be detected there, Naples–Sicily was an almost entirely traditional society and one in which there had been regression rather than economic development since 1800. The population of Naples was numerous, as were those of Palermo, Catania and Messina; even in 1880, the old Kingdom of Naples–Sicily still boasted four of the eleven Italian cities with more than 100,000 inhabitants.[18] But, at the same time, Naples lacked anything that might be defined as industry or an industrial class. In 1840, a handful of the population was involved in other than the most local commerce,[19] and, sixty years later, the 'industrial' workforce amounted to a mere 10,000 men.[20] In every way the Bourbon capital was a city of the court. The urban masses (*lazzaroni*) lived by their wits, by begging, charity, prostitution and 'dealing'. The city was parasitic on its agrarian hinterland, that swathe of fertile land at the foot of Mount Vesuvius. Since further inland the terrain became very rugged, administration there was likely to be contested by bandits, and roads were tracks for goats, donkeys and human pedestrians. As the population of Naples continued to grow, the Bourbon monarchs regarded the first task of their governance as the shipping of grain from Puglia (it could not be carried to the capital by any other means). But even such shipping was a fragile business. Ports in Puglia were little more than open roadsteads and memories of piratical raids remained vivid. In both the ports and other centres in this region, diseases such as malaria and pellagra were endemic and, well into the twentieth century, the standard of living of ordinary peasants was abysmal. Marasmus, or simple starvation, took a daily toll.[21] In Naples, the bread riots of 1844 and 1847 were one face of urban life;[22] the cholera epidemics of 1836–7 and 1884 another.[23] As late as 1863, it was thought, 100,000 Neapolitans lived without access to a toilet of any kind except the street.[24]

In a series of studies, the English historian John Davis has completed a detailed analysis of the economy of Naples–Sicily. His conclusion is that the kingdom was a place where 'investment in poverty was both remunerative and self-perpetuating'.[25] The beneficiaries were the King and the court, and, rather more, external investors – the English, for example, in the marsala industry of western Sicily[26] and the sulphur 'mines'[27] in the eastern part of that island; the French and other foreign entrepreneurs in Naples itself.[28]

Ironically, then, given popular parlance, Naples–Sicily actually was part of 'Africa' in the sense that it was a prey to the classic mechanisms of imperialist exploitation. The 'state' (such as it was) and its foreign backers and contacts were the only permitted vehicles of economic activity. Even a good harvest was feared by the authorities for providing work too readily, and for cutting prices. After 1860, Naples–Sicily would be absorbed tardily and arduously into the national economy not because it was 'backward' in the sense of lacking contacts with the wider world, but because it was backward in consequence of them.

In their enthusiasm as new men operating the new systems of the moment, few of the leaders of the Risorgimento much remarked on this difficult inheritance. Rather they were confident that, by making Italy, they could readily spread economic benefits across the peninsula. Had not Cavour, with happy circularity, defined political economy as 'the science of the love of country'?[29] Actually running the national finances, however, soon proved a rather more complicated matter than adepts of Cavour and believers in his maxim had assumed. In a way which still needs further clarification, Italy was born, and in the 1860s preserved, with the sympathetic approval of foreign financiers and investors more generous with 'risk' capital than those who had effortlessly drawn their profits from Naples–Sicily. English railway entrepreneurs, French bankers, Swiss or Belgian financiers and many other European businessmen had decided that a United Italy would be a better market for their exports and would give a better return on their investments than had the small states. In the mid-1860s it was a cliché that the new nation had been 'made by foreign capital'; foreigners had taken up at least a third of the national debt.[30] Moreover, the prompt construction of railways in the first decades after the Risorgimento was the work of foreign bankers and engineers (and Italian, generally 'Northern' Italian,[31] labourers). By 1878, the Società delle Strade Ferrate dell'Alta Italia had purchased 247 locomotives manufactured in Alsace, 25 in Britain, 125 in France, 110 in Belgium, 90 in Austria, 3 in Bavaria and 39 in Italy (2 from Verona and 37 from the Ansaldo factory – originally established in the 1840s by an English engineer named Taylor – near Genoa).[32] The diffusion of the railway thus only minimally industrialised Italy, but, instead, reflected (and enhanced) the industrialisation of other parts of Europe.

At the basis of the ideology of the Risorgimento had lain three great concepts – liberty, the nation and free trade. The ambiguities of the first two are commonplace and have been noted in the preceding chapters. The commitment to free trade proved similarly protean when politicians tried to move from theory to practice. It was true that Liberal Italy swiftly and rather innocently began to seek commercial arrangements with its trading partners which would peg tariffs at as low a level as possible. Treaties in that regard were signed with France (1863), Switzerland (1867) and Austria (1868),[33] and the negotiation of bilateral agreements became one of the set ideas of Italian international commercial practice until the First World War and beyond.

However, the business of national and international finance soon showed itself neither painless nor straightforward. In 1866 the Liberal government experienced a major economic crisis in which both its banking system and its foreign credit tottered, a financial tremor which helped to explain the poor military performance against Austria that year. The fiscal solution decided on was a policy of rigid deflation in pursuit of a balanced budget, a goal achieved technically in 1875–6.[34] The greatest beneficiary of these policies was probably Italy's then major trading partner and financier, France; the major casualty, Italy's own industrialisation (and its government's ability to increase public welfare and foster 'liberty'). Nonetheless, by the time the new state achieved that always difficult task, the first passing of government from one ideological group to another, with the replacement of the *Destra* by the *Sinistra* in 1876, Italy had earned a respectable position on international markets.

At that time the unified state was still something of a client of France, but, by 1881, its imports from France were only minimally greater than those from Britain (364.8 million lire from France, 361.5 million from Britain and 218.7 million from Austria).[35] A decade later, however, Italy was obtaining 23.3 per cent of its imports from Britain as against 12.8 per cent from France, 11.9 per cent from Germany and 10.8 per cent from Austria.[36] These trade figures would continue to fluctuate in what, given long-term and worldwide economic trends, was a largely predictable way. Thus, by 1900, France and Britain had been ousted by Germany as Italy's largest trading partner, and Germany's leadership in turn was being threatened by the rise of the USA as a world economic power.[37] Italy's foreign policy of an alliance with the Central Powers and friendship with the Triple Entente (and emigration to the USA) was accurately enough matched by the national trading figures: for example, in 1910 Italy received 25.1 per cent of its imports from the Central Powers and sent its allies 22 per cent of its exports; 33.2 per cent of its imports came from Britain, France and Russia who purchased 23 per cent of Italian exports.

These raw figures, however, hide a number of more specific matters which deserve emphasis. The nation's high level of imports from Britain – Italy always ran a considerable balance of payments deficit with that country – were most notably composed of coal, a product which was needed in ever greater amounts because of Italy's own economic growth and lack of mineral resources.[38] With time, hydroelectricity began offering something of a domestic energy source, but, in 1914, Italy's dependence on British coal was perhaps the most powerful of all the unspoken assumptions in Italian pre-war diplomacy. Even in 1939–40 the most unresolved question of Mussolini's period of non-belligerency was where reliable energy supplies would come from if not from Britain.[39] Ironically, it was only in the 1950s, when Italy had ceased to aspire to Great Power status, that the discovery and exploitation of natural gas meant that domestic energy resources could meet a not inconsiderable part of the national demand.[40]

With France, by contrast, relations had not run smooth. The deference and clientelism of the 1860s were replaced in the 1880s by suspicion and hostility, and eventually by a 'full-scale trade war'[41] which, to a commentator like Bonaldo Stringher, the director of the Bank of Italy, writing in 1912, seemed to have been the one great caesura in Liberal commercial policy.[42] Certainly Crispi had pursued the commercial conflict with a flamboyance and a neglect of domestic ramifications[43] which were all his own. In the financial world, one unplanned result of the dispute was a long-running banking crisis which culminated in 1892–3 in the 'Banca Romana scandal'[44] – at this time the celebrated criminologist, Cesare Lombroso, searched without success to distinguish a particular 'criminal type' in the world of high finance.[45] The severity of the crisis was only abated when the ramshackle national banking system (until then four banks still had the right to print currency) was modernised and switched from 'French' to 'German' fiscal practice.[46]

Despite all the high words of this period and other alarums, France and Belgium continued to be the chief sources of foreign investment in Italy.[47] Nonetheless, in the last few years before the outbreak of the First World War, it was Germany's 'penetration' of the Italian economy which provoked most debate. The new Banca Commerciale Italiana had become the financial institution nearest to Giovanni Giolitti and therefore to that variety of modernisation and industrialisation which occurred in the 'Giolittian decade' 1903–14.[48] The BCI was led by men like Otto Joel or Giuseppe Toeplitz who, during the First World War, would be pilloried for their policies, names or ancestries by xenophobic nationalists.[49] In recent times, American historian Richard Webster has engaged in a scholarly analysis of Imperial German trading policies in Liberal Italy and, without justifying the paranoia of the nationalists, has found examples of German dumping and other exploitative commercial actions.[50] Such sharp practice, he says, steeled Italian resentment and opposition and helped to forge an Italian military–industrial complex anxious eventually to break out of the Triple Alliance and, in the interim, determined on more aggressive imperial policies.[51]

In the light of available evidence, however, Webster seems to exaggerate both the abnormality of German–Italian trade relations and the idea of an economic drive as the crucial propellant of Italian new imperialism. If any bank pushed Italy into imperialism, it was, ironically enough, the Vatican-owned Banco di Roma which, from 1907, threatened to have its fingers burned in Tripoli unless rescued by the arrival of Italian armed forces.[52]

In retrospect, at least, the most successful entrepreneur in Giolittian Italy was Giovanni Agnelli. Born in 1866, Agnelli was a Piedmontese landowner and, for a time, cavalry officer, who, in an aristocratic and upper middle-class *circolo* in Turin, heard the gospel being preached in Paris and elsewhere of the modern automobile. From dreaming of fast cars, Agnelli took to manufacturing them, establishing the Fabbrica Italiana Automobili Torino, or Fiat, in July 1899.[53] At first Fiat was only one company among many, and, in the financial downturn of 1907, it went close to failure. But Agnelli proved himself energetic and tough, and, perhaps more importantly, willing and able to utilise Swiss capital and American factory techniques. Fiat became a company which moved with the times and which also tried to avoid too overt a political exposure. Thus, in 1914, although some key figures in the management were flirting with new nationalism, Agnelli himself had eagerly signed contracts with the Russian army and with both the German and British navies. As for the chairman's views on whether or not, or when, Italy should enter the war, they remained, his biographer has said, 'an enigma'. Indeed, so far as all politics were concerned, Agnelli was already following his later dictum: 'we businessmen are supporters of the present government by definition'.[54]

So far as Fiat at least is concerned, its pre-1914 history provides little evidence for the thesis that modern industrialists and financiers had taken over the Liberal Italian state. As Adrian Lyttelton has remarked, Italy was more precocious in its production of doctors, lawyers and humanist university professors[55] than of engineers and modern industrialists. It was true to an extent that men of technology criticised the political and cultural hegemony of men of the arts, but there is little evidence during the Liberal regime that they supplanted them at the levers of power. Any sociological analysis of the membership of the Giolittian parliament, for example, reveals the continued dominance of lawyers and other clerical professions and only a minuscule representation of industrialists (or peasants).[56] Some of these 'humanist intellectuals' were undoubtedly the agents of bankers and businessmen, but others reflected more traditional values and a more antique power structure.

Outside the parliament, the truth was, of course, that Italy remained very much an agrarian country. One historian has estimated that, in 1901, only 8.5 per cent of national wealth sprang from industry and commerce,[57] and, despite genuine progress in industrialisation during the Giolittian decade, the level would rise only slowly. It was not that 'agriculture' was a single or simple matter, however. An aspiration to modernise agricultural production had provided one of the great economic thrusts to the Risorgimento.[58] Fifty years later, the agriculture of the Po Valley was notably characterised by capitalist practices – the flat terrain, rare elsewhere in Italy, was easily accessible to farm machinery – and much land, for example, in the sugar beet industry,[59] was in the hands not of individual landowners but of 'anonymous' companies.

Elsewhere on the peninsula, however, the land was worked, owned and leased in many different ways. There were small private estates in Piedmont, sharecropping arrangements in Tuscany and *latifondi* (big estates with absentee landowners) in some parts of Sicily and Calabria. But even here variation[60] was always the rule, and both 'peasant' and 'landowner' are terms which require a scrupulously accurate setting in place and time. Nor was agriculture a solely domestic business. The export of citrus juice to Britain in the 1860s and its conversion there to cordials or citric acid, wine sales to France in the 1880s, the fruit trade with Austria in the 1900s were all basic factors in Italian commercial policy. Indeed, in so far as unspoken assumptions are concerned, agricultural trade may well have influenced such great landowners as Francesco Guicciardini and Antonino Di San Giuliano during their terms of office rather more directly than did the needs of modern industry. Until 1914 Giulio Prinetti, a bicycle manufacturer, was the only industrialist to hold the office of Italian Foreign Minister.

Stuart Woolf has remarked accurately that the 'remoteness' of the state has been the most obvious feature of the national history of Italy since the Risorgimento.[61] And yet his remark deserves some qualification so far as economic policy is concerned. From a naive reliance on the 'market', by its very nature never a source of free competition except in the self-interested illusions of some contemporary monetarist economists, those managing the Italian economy rapidly realised that personal profit and potential national power could be brought into association and then nourished in a myriad of ways by the modern state. Especially in the Giolittian decade before 1914, as industrialisation rates increased it became simple common sense that the state must indeed manage the economy (the railways were finally nationalised in 1905),[62] and that the basic field of action and accounting for business was the nation. The years before 1914 saw the creation of a whole series of commercial pressure groups (usually on French or German models) – Confindustria, established in 1910, was the most powerful – which, often in alliance with the nationalists, urged the establishment of a newly authoritative and authoritarian state, more receptive to their purposes and needs.[63]

These processes were duly accelerated by the experience of running a war economy between 1915 and 1918.[64] Though industrialists were not especially influential[65] in the *intervento*, with the advent of war they could be heard preaching order and discipline and demanding a state which would be committed to production and 'productive forces' (and profits).[66] During the conflict, Fiat's workforce grew from 4,000 to 40,000, Ansaldo's capital from 30 million lire (1916) to 500 million (1918),[67] and many small industries and modernised agricultural holdings similarly leaped forward. State employees also advanced in number – from 280,000 in 1907 to 500,000 in 1919.[68] By the war's end, Liberal economist Riccardo Bachi observed, the state had become the basic motor of Italian industrial growth. If a military–industrial complex was hard to find in 1915, traces of it now existed and, at least according to some of its partisans, it would be all the more necessary in the future.[69]

In fact, during the rise of Fascism a certain confusion spread about the proper bases of Italian commercial and economic policy, the place of the state and the possible meaning of industrial democratisation. The most graphic example occurred in 1919, when, during the social troubles which would culminate the next year in the 'occupation of the factories',[70] Giovanni Agnelli, the boss of Fiat, seems in the short run genuinely to have contemplated his factory being converted into a cooperative. He believed, in a curious example of business utopianism which appropriately reflected the spirit of the times, that Fiat's products would thus acquire 'a brand name known to the whole world'.[71] Nor, once in power, did the Fascists altogether overcome past ambiguities. On the one hand, the regime was ostentatiously generous in bringing the state to the aid of the rich or 'productive' – a large loan was granted to bail out the Banco di Roma;[72] the telephone system was privatised; punitive taxes, imposed by Giolitti on rapacious war 'profiteers', were repealed.[73] And, as if to show purity of heart, Mussolini appointed Alberto De Stefani, a professional paladin of the virtues of free trade, as his first Minister of Finance.[74]

During its first decade of power, then, the Fascist regime in its economic policies seemed scarcely revolutionary but, instead, only a somewhat idiosyncratic engine of what Charles Maier has felicitously labelled the 'recasting of bourgeois Europe'.[75] In its international trading policies, Fascism was still more orthodox. It eschewed ideology in becoming a realistic and rewarded trading partner of the USSR,[76] and, much more importantly, it deferentially accepted that the leading power of world capitalism was now unquestionably the USA. Already before 1914, Vilfredo Pareto had reported that Italian business was alert to stock market rises and falls in New York,[77] perhaps because emigration had made America a place with which all Italians reckoned. Fascism was even more attuned to financial tidings in the New World and, whether because of Italian attention to detail or Fascist Italian ideological acceptability, loans flowed in from J.P. Morgan and other American financiers.[78] After 1922, the Italian economy experienced some growth,[79] though the adoption of a high valuation of the lira in 1927 (90 to the US dollar),[80] a decision still being debated by economic historians,[81] slowed development thereafter (and to an extent saved Italy both from the pre-1929 boom and the subsequent bust).[82] For all the Fascist rhetoric about radical change, Italy, as one recent commentator has noted, continued to possess an economic establishment, and continued to pursue, internally and externally, commercial policies, 'clearly rooted in ... the pre-First World War business structure'.[83]

Yet there was something particular about Fascist economics, apart, that is, from its repression of non-Fascist[84] labour organisations, rigid control of wages, rhetorical flirtation with the supreme virtues of rural life and acquiesence in Italy's drift into becoming a commercial client of Nazi Germany.[85] Perhaps the best way briefly to unveil that particularity is through two vignettes of figures who did good business both at home and abroad during the Fascist years.

The first is Giuseppe Volpi, 'Count of Misurata' or 'the last doge'. Volpi was a man of many parts. After his admired elder brother had died 'for the nation' at Adowa,[86] Volpi rose in the Giolittian era through deals certainly with the Banca Commerciale and probably with the royal family. He made a name for himself as a man with good contacts in the Balkans and Asia Minor and, in 1912, was therefore selected by Giolitti to ease the negotiating processes of the Treaty of Ouchy which ended the Libyan War.[87] The Nationalist *L'Idea Nazionale* was particularly disgusted by this appointment – what, its somewhat idealist ideological purity suggested, did Italian power want with 'a [mere] businessman, a man who lives in the environment of international finance'?[88]

Thereafter Volpi had a 'good' First World War, making friends, as his most recent biographer puts it, with all political parties and economic groups. Particularly he favoured the growth of Porto Marghera, that 'planned' industrial development, which, in some eyes, promised to save Venice from a terminal decline or a tourist fate worse than death, and, in others, would lead to its irredeemable pollution. Volpi's great skill, however, lay in snaring government contracts, 'not so much an industrialist as a financier and a supplier of services'.[89] By 1922 he was listed as a shareholder in fifty-five companies and sat on the boards of forty-six. He was also Governor of Tripolitania, a post to which he had been appointed by the liberal democrat Giovanni Amendola.

Despite his liberal or democratic friendships, Volpi made the switch to Fascism without apparent pain. He joined the party in July 1923 (its secretariat graciously agreed to backdate his membership to January 1922).[90] After some irritation from both radical Fascists and personal enemies, Volpi cemented his position as boss of Venice, acquiring control over the local newspaper, *Il Gazzettino*, and happily patronising the international art and cinema exhibitions which helped preserve the tourist fame of that city.[91] He did not restrict himself merely to local deals, however. In the 1920s he was a prominent negotiator of both governmental and private loans in the USA, which, a historian has observed, tended to favour sectors of the economy in which Volpi himself was active.[92] From 1934 to 1943, he also held the post of President of Confindustria in Rome, appropriately installed just across the Piazza Venezia from the Duce.[93] He disliked the noises of war from 1938 to May 1940, however, and, after June 1940, swiftly adopted, in good company, a pessimistic stance about the Fascist war effort,[94] though some events at the front could briefly cheer him. The fall of Singapore, for example, led him to doubt an American comeback in the Pacific – 'wars are not only made with wealth and material goods', he remarked sagely in words which appear so frequently in Italian discourse, 'but also with the spirit'.[95] Volpi lived long enough to be condemned as a Fascist and then granted amnesty, and died a very wealthy man in November 1947.[96]

As typical a figure, if less adventurous in character, was Arturo Osio, from 1925 to 1942 director of the Banca Nazionale del Lavoro e della Cooperazione,[97] now more simply called the Banca Nazionale del Lavoro (BNL). Though this institution was by the Second World War a Fascist bank, it had sprung from a moderate democratic and socialist past and Osio himself had belonged to the Catholic Partito Popolare. He was also an enemy of Volpi who, for a time in the 1920s, probably under the influence of the Banca Commerciale, favoured the BNL's dissolution. In attaching himself to Roberto Farinacci, the extremist *ras* of Cremona,[98] however, Osio found a reliable patron and, from 1926, he had the extra security of regular meetings with Mussolini.

Thus safeguarded, Osio's BNL found the times fruitful. It backed the successful (and protected) Fascist cinema industry.[99] It opened branches in Asmara and Massawa in 1935, in Burgos, Seville and Salamanca in 1937, and later in occupied Valona, Paris and Athens.[100] It became a sort of Fascist state bank, with Osio being careful always to widen his circle of friends and acquaintances. As the BNL's official historian has put it: 'Judging from his correspondence, in practice Osio established contact with every single political figure in the regime and with every bureaucrat great or small.'[101] Though, in 1942, Osio fell victim to one of those familiar Mussolinian 'changings of the guard' (perhaps stimulated by the Petacci family) and the bank had a disturbed history in the last months of the war, the BNL was rapidly able to forget its cohabitation with Fascism, and by the 1950s was flourishing again, swelled by American loans and emigrant remittances (it had become especially involved in the emigration arena during the late Fascist years).[102]

The stories of Volpi and Osio are indicative of the opportunities which businessmen could exploit in Fascist Italy and of their operating methods in a world in which political and personal skills were at least as important as financial ones, and productivity some-times of only marginal account. Perhaps life was easier in the 1920s, but there is also every sign that the commercial and industrial class coped readily enough with the apparently more intrusive and Fascist policies of the regime after the Depression and the Nazi rise to power. Business did not lose by the creation of the Istituto per la ricostruzione industriale (IRI) in 1933, with its promise or threat of state interference or largesse, from the policy of autarky – well defined as one in which the state would control everything except profits[103] – from imperialism, from the Axis and even from anti-Semitism. All could be endured, manipulated or enjoyed with greater or lesser enthusiasm and advantage. At Munich and between August 1939 and May 1940, Italian business leaders, even while they looked for gain from the fact that, by 1939, Nazi Germany was Italy's leading trading partner, undoubtedly favoured peace and feared the unprofitable fanaticism of their German ally.[104] The stock market rose noticeably at the initial news in September 1939 of Italian 'non-belligerency'.[105] A successful short war, businessmen probably viewed in a different light, though, once it was plain that the Second World War would be long and harsh, the wealthy of all kinds rapidly detached themselves from Fascism and from any responsibility which others may have thought they possessed for Mussolini's regime and its policies.[106]

Whether due to opportunism or realism, or because of personal and ideological ties never fully sundered, in 1943–4 industrial and commercial Italy hastened to renew its relationship with the United States.[107] In so doing, it refurbished those processes and contracts which had already been evident in the 1920s, and again recast itself for a world in which the United States would be both the undisputed superpower and the generator of world commercial activity. In considerable part, Italy's history, from 1943 to the Christian Demo-crat (DC), American-funded,[108] Cold War, electoral triumph of

1948, was that of a business community anxious to follow American practices (anti-communism, deflation, free trade) and in search of a reasonably reliable and reasonably conservative party which would approve of this new world in which the business of Italy was business. If De Gasperi understood commercial practice through the eyes of a Social Christian from *fin de siècle* Vienna,[109] and party members as diverse as Luigi Gedda, Amintore Fanfani and Giulio Andreotti[110] treasured in their hearts some sort of corporatist 'third way' between socialism and liberal capitalism, the Catholicism or piety of the DC could be readily enough controlled. Indeed, the public connection between the DC and the Pope was a highly saleable product, both to the influential (and rich) Italo-American community and more generally. The link with such a revered and age-old institution as the Vatican made the DC (and Italy) look reliable, even if the party was actually 'diverse', to use that characteristic and redolent Italian term. In the jargon of modern advertising the Christianity or Catholicism of the DC promised Republican Italy favourable 'product recognition'.

At the same time, the DC's diversity also had its uses. Italy had ended the war with what is now estimated to have been a loss of some 18 per cent of its economic patrimony (not as high a figure as was originally assumed). Using the 1938 figures as an index of 100, industrial production in the dismal winter of 1945–6 stood at 29, agriculture at 63.3. Up to 20 per cent of the workforce was then unemployed and real wages were half the level they had been before the war.[111] For the next two or three years rumours spread that Italy would go bankrupt and Italian diplomatists were not averse to beating up this possibility, if they thought that the fear of a communist take-over which it evoked could improve peace terms, open paths of emigration or bring benefit in loan negotiations.[112]

Gradually, the period of weakness was forgotten. By the mid-1950s, the Italian economy began to boom and, in the 'economic miracle', Italy industrialised as never before. For some time this growth occurred in a *laissez-faire* way – unions were weak and political opponents the object of police repression, first-generation ex-peasant workers preserved a culture of 'deferred gratification' and much of the Italian left continued to regale its followers with easy rhetoric about the 'crisis of capitalism'. Meanwhile, real wages in 1957 were still blocked at the level of 1948,[113] and, despite the establishment of the Cassa per il Mezzogiorno in 1950, the regional gap between South and North continued to worsen.[114] It was really only after the *autunni caldi* (hot autumns – that is, periods of major union and other social conflicts) of the late 1960s and early 1970s that ordinary Italians began to find in their pay-packets and lifestyles some of the profits of industrialisation.

In its international commercial policies, Republican Italy, as has already been noted in Chapter 2 (pp. 54–6), had generally accepted that it was now a 'country of limited sovereignty'. And yet, within or because of those limits, Italy could find its own position. If the USA, the master of NATO, was one patron, others might exist in Europe. Doubtless Italy had joined the EEC because there was no other possible course to follow and yet that body did, in its very essence, recall a sort of social Catholicism and a corporatism which made appropriate De Gasperi's fame as one of its ideological 'fathers'. But the most graphic exemplification of this latest age of Italian capitalism and of what rendered it still a little *sui generis* was Enrico Mattei, as emblematic a figure of Italian industry and commerce in the 1950s as were Volpi and Osio of the inter-war period.

After a later much debated career as an Anti-Fascist Christian Democrat partisan,[115] Mattei in 1945 became manager of the northern section of AGIP, itself a part of the large state holding company ENI, and, at the time, in purist eyes, a Fascist autarkic left-over destined for urgent privatisation. But the discovery of natural gas and, even more, the propaganda exploitation of the hydrocarbons brought to the surface at Cortemaggiore in 1949 allowed Mattei and his friends in high places to claim that Italy had 'won the battle for oil' and to market AGIP's '*Supercortemaggiore*' as 'the powerful Italian petrol'.[116]

Considerable gas resources were indeed available, both in the North, especially around Ravenna, and in south-eastern Sicily. National petroleum production, by contrast, remained slight, but, secure in his position as the highly independent manager of a great state enterprise and bolstered by the publicity advantages of his purchase of the Milan daily, *Il Giorno*, Mattei swiftly secured oil deals for AGIP with Iraq, Egypt and the USSR,[117] this last a country with which Italy would continue to develop major and rewarding trade ties. In so far as Italy had, by the early 1960s, an independent international commercial policy, it was directed by Mattei. This policy was, in a sense, that of the greatest of the middling powers. It was a policy which saw trade and profit (and possible domestic advantage) as far outweighing ideology and a loyal or passive commitment to (American-style) international morality. Mattei's successes also enhanced support for the ideal of state capitalism and, at the same time, left Italy with an increasingly peculiar economy in which more than half of industrial production lay in state rather than private hands. Even if not all commentators were convinced, to the optimists Italy seemed to offer a model to the world of how to achieve a uniquely happy and prosperous relationship between capitalism and socialism.[118]

Mattei himself had not lived triumphantly to continue his independent or adventurous policies. On 27 October 1962 he perished when his jet, flying from Sicily to Milan, crashed. As was becoming normal in Republican Italy, no one was quite sure whether the crash was an accident or not, and the fact that Mattei had flown out of Palermo led to dark rumours about a possible Mafia plot. These rumours are a reminder that no survey of the Italian economy after 1860, nor of Italy's international commercial dealings, would be complete without some mention of 'organised' crime, be it the Sicilian Mafia, the Calabrian *'ndrangheta*[119] or the Neapolitan *camorra*.[120] In turn, however, an analyst confronts the problem of a topic beset by hearsay and innuendo, and by the possibility, maintained in at least some scholarly circles, that a body such as the Mafia is, to a considerable extent, 'all in the mind', the invention of that foreign, 'Northern', 'Italian' state which has so uneasily and so inadequately policed the South since 1860.[121] To rephrase Massimo D'Azeglio, *'fatta la Mafia, dobbiamo fare i mafiosi'* ('having made the Mafia, we must make the *mafiosi*').[122]

Any analysis of the international dealings of the Mafia and its fraternal criminal associations is further vitiated by the racist response of host societies to the arrival of Italian, and especially 'Southern' Italian, immigrants. Common in this regard were the ready and frequently unjustified allegations that such racial inferiors rallied and plotted, murdered and thieved, in secret conclaves known as the 'Black Hand', the 'Honoured Society' or the Mafia. Scandals, thus, are many; proof is often weak. In particular, there is no serious evidence before 1945 of a multinational Mafia 'empire'. Where Mafia-style *cosche* existed in inter-war New York or Chicago, they did so as part of the anarcho-feudal culture which the immigrants had imported from western Sicily and which proved adaptable to the existing cultures of American business, crime and politics. Even if, in 1943, 'Mafia contacts' opened some paths in Sicily to invading Allied troops, the Mafias of the new world and the Mafias of the old seem mostly to have run in parallel rather than in harness. Generally locked in brutal internecine conflict as much as they were at war with state and society, these Mafias only indirectly reflected the international commercial policies of the Italies.

After the fall of Fascism, however, and especially in the most recent decades, there is evidence of a change in direction and character. As Pino Arlacchi has convincingly argued, Italian organised crime has now become 'entrepreneurial'[123] or monetarist and opted for a criminal version of the efficient and ruthless internal and external policies of legal business concerns. Even so local and localist a group as the *'ndrangheta* has, to an extent, gone 'multinational' and can as readily be found trading drugs, laundering money and condoning or organising murder in Canada or Australia as in profitably defending honour and shame in Platì or Nicastro[124] (though the characteristic local 'industry' or 'art' of kidnapping only rarely has been exported). Much graver, however, has been the expansion of these criminal organisations of the Italies into Italy. By the 1960s, the Mafia, for example, was no longer confined to western Sicily but had spread throughout the island and to those Northern cities to which Sicilians were emigrating. Today, support for the federalist or separatist *leghe* owes quite a lot to a Northern sense, notably among small businessmen, that more than a century of Italian government has failed to 'legalise' the South, that is, has failed to construct either law or justice in that part of the country, and that this practice of and belief in injustice and illegality is spreading in the North. In the eyes of the *leghisti*, the Italian state, in five generations of existence, has been better at fostering *mafiosi* than at making Italians.

It would be wrong, however, to end an account of the economy of United Italy on such a pessimistic note. Issues undoubtedly remain to be resolved and an ordinary sense of historical realism or scepticism teaches that the huge acceleration in prosperity since the establishment of a Republic cannot proceed for ever at the same pace. Nonetheless, Italy since 1860, and especially since 1945, has by most estimates made do spectacularly well. Despite, or because of, an uneven education system, a humanist intelligentsia, a weak polity and an often bureaucratised management, Italians have been fertile in ideas and adept at selling their products in many commercial spheres – engineering, design, fashion, food, film and vast areas of the leisure and entertainment business. Italians worked hard and, when not distracted by military or imperial ambition, had, by 1960, already given Italy an economy which the world has had to gauge.

5

THE RISE AND FALL OF
THE ITALIAN EMPIRE
1860–1960

In 1949, a writer for the conservative and patriotic Rome newspaper, *Il Tempo*, grew nostalgic about the loss of empire. After all, he wrote, Italian imperialism had been of a special kind. Italy had only managed to win

> poor lands for the cursed work of poor men, lands for unemployed day labourers, lands for peasants lacking their own fertile fields who broke their backs to make flinty soil productive. They were lands of that last resource of poverty which says: 'Better than nothing'; which says: 'Better than to die of hunger'.[1]

Though his phrasing is different and his nostalgia less, Ronald Robinson, a major English historian of empire, does not altogether disagree. Italy, he says, especially Fascist Italy, was 'unique' in creating an empire for its unemployed proletariat. Italy's imperialism was thus pursued for internal benefits regardless of cost, and, in fact, required 'heroic over-investment' by an economy harnessed to its cause.[2]

Both Robinson and *Il Tempo* thus see imperialism as an important part of Italian history. Other perceptions are possible. In 1937, shortly after Ethiopia had fallen to Italian arms, the Fascist journalist, Giorgio Pini, was sardonic: '*Fatta l'impero*', he wrote in somewhat untotalitarian echo of Massimo D'Azeglio's aphorism about the making of Italy, '*dobbiamo fare gli imperialisti*' ('Having made the Empire, we must make the imperialists').[3]

Which of these views best comprehends Italian imperialism? As has already been established, Italy did for a time govern Eritrea, Somalia, Libya, the Dodecanese Islands, Ethiopia and Albania and looked for further advantage in Tunis or Yemen, Asia Minor or the

Caucasus. Was imperialism integral to the relationship between United Italy and the wider world and, if so, why and to what end? What did Italy do to its empire and what did that empire do to Italy?

The first point to emphasise, one fondly made by Fascist and nationalist commentators, was that, in many a mind, the words 'Italy' and 'empire' were indissolubly bound. Had not the empire of the 'First Rome' at one time stretched from the Irish Sea to the Persian Gulf[4] and provided a military, administrative and legal achievement unequalled in the annals of Europe? The idea of a reconstituted *mare nostrum*, even as early as the 1870s and 1880s, could set off patriotic rhetoricians. Italian classicists[5] and archaeologists,[6] then and thereafter, were particularly likely to be gladdened by the redolence and luminosity which they detected in the ruins of Carthage, Leptis Magna, the cities of the Asia Minor coast or the roads of the Balkans, and to urge that the sword should follow the pen or the spade.

Nor was the Roman Empire the only one to have sprung from the Italian peninsula. In the Middle Ages, Genoese colonies had spread across the eastern Mediterranean from the Morea to Syria to Constantinople and even to the Crimea. Their 'history' was sometimes recalled by Italians who, before and after 1914, aspired to create a 'zone of influence' in some part of the dying Ottoman Empire.[7] Venice was an even more lustrous site. Under the leadership of 120 doges from 687 to 1797, Venice had dominated the eastern Mediterranean and Adriatic. The *Serenissima's* most famous son was Marco Polo (*c.* 1254–1324), who travelled to China and beyond and opened routes of commercial and cultural exchange, matched only by those of the Genoese-born Cristoforo Colombo (1447–1506).

In Venice, memories lingered. Gabriele D'Annunzio, that *fin de siècle* world expert in self-dramatisation, found Venice the natural base from which to launch, during the First World War, his dashing or theatrical raids on Austro-Hungarian forces. In March 1919, he deemed the Loggetta a suitable stage from which to 'affirm solemnly Italic rights to all the lands of Saint Mark'.[8] Irredentist intellectuals, who applauded the poet's heroism, had already tended to settle in Venice before 1914.[9] One characteristic figure was Piero Foscari, proud of descent from one of the dogal families. Long a zealot of 'the Greater Italy', Foscari was an early Nationalist deputy who remained a generous patron and financier of D'Annunzio[10] and a friend and business partner of Giuseppe Volpi.[11]

Though neither the Venetian nor Genoese Republics had been able to survive the French revolutionary wars, the greatest 'Italian' 'empire' had. That empire was, of course, the Roman Catholic Church, which governed a religious, cultural and financial domain on which the sun never set. The role of the church in structuring Italians' relationship with the wider world will be discussed further in Chapter 7 (pp. 148–52); suffice it to say here that this body, with its Italian Popes and essentially Italian administration, became vulnerable to some extent after 1860 to the process of 'the nationalisation of the masses'. Though Latin remained its language of formal usage, Italian was the ordinary speech of many a clerical meeting, and non-Italian Catholic prelates and clergy often acquired a knowledge of the Italian language and an interest in Italian cuisine, politics, intellectual debate and finance through time spent in Rome.[12] In many a clerical mind, it was easy to fuse the economic and imperial interests of the church with those of the Italian state.

Outside the church, as the Italian national state rose and, through compulsory education, imposed its fabricated national language and invented history on 'Italians', the Italian language had lost ground. In the eighteenth century, it was still one of the 'historic languages', in much the same sense that Italians were recognised as one of the 'historic peoples' of the Habsburg Empire. Dr Johnson, aspiring in his youth to be a man of culture, automatically acquired it.[13] Italian was the language of music (Mozart's operas were usually sung in it) and sometimes, especially in the Mediterranean basin, of medicine and cooking, engineering and love.[14] Decades later it was still natural for an urbane and erudite politician like W.E. Gladstone to be a fluent Italian speaker,[15] a skill which few foreigners in the twentieth century would share. In time remembered, the peoples of the Italies had also been busily taking Italian, or, more accurately, their own dialects, abroad. Oblivious of the borders and certainties of the modern nation state, the fishermen of Molfetta, mentioned in the Introduction as finding sanctuary in Western Australia (p. 5), had also established their own 'colonies' in Alexandria and other eastern Mediterranean ports.[16] There they would winter or seek refuge from pirates or a storm; there they conserved their culture; there they were citizens of what still was a 'Mediterranean world'.[17] This 'citizenship', this 'Latinity', would soon no longer make sense in a world of nation states; ironically, given much of the rhetoric to come, unification ended any Italian pretensions of centrality in a *mare nostrum*.

These shadows of imperialisms past, whether official or unofficial, would do little directly to assist the construction of the empire of United Italy after 1860. Just as, for all the talk about a Ri-sorgimento, modern Italy had new borders not old ones, so, too, the Italian empire would, in large part, govern territories never before in subjection to the peoples of the Italian peninsula. Though nationalist historians did not like to admit it, Italy caught its *'mal d'Africa'*[18] not so much from its 'own' past as from the present escapades of those Greater Powers whose company it now sought. The only thing really old about its empire was that Italy was laggard in doing what other modern European states had already done.

It was true that the settlement at the Congress of Vienna, by handing over Liguria to the Kingdom of Sardinia, had armed Piedmont and 'turned its prow towards the sea'. Already in 1825, the Savoys could be found mounting a naval demonstration against Tripoli.[19] As the decades passed, other Italians dreamed of empire in New Guinea or Taiwan[20] and spread a network of consular agents which, in Piedmont's case, by the 1850s had already extended as far as Australia.[21]

The most obvious and major imperial interest for Liberal Italy, however, lay in North or East Africa or, just possibly, in Albania and some other parts of the Ottoman Empire, especially after the opening of the Suez Canal brought 'modernity' and instability to the region. Foreign diplomatists were not behindhand in suggesting that Italy could find a toe-hold in the scramble for imperial power. Appetite came with offering. When in September 1877, the inexperienced Crispi tried to get Bismarck's backing for the transfer to Italy of Trieste and the Trentino in return for an Austrian governance of Bosnia and Herzegovina, the German Chancellor cheerfully indicated Albania instead, and Lord Derby, the British Foreign Secretary, seconded the idea.[22] The Austrian Foreign Minister, Count Gyula Andrassy, less impressed by this suggestion since Austria itself might have eventual ambitions on Albania, thought Italy might like to pick up 'an island, a port, Tunis or Tripoli'.[23]

If ever Italy had a logical imperial interest it was indeed in Tunis. Even as late as 1936, official statisticians declared that 94,000 Italians lived there (as against 108,000 French), and Fascist propagandists implied that the real figure was much higher.[24] Tommaso Tittoni, Foreign Minister (1903–5, 1906–9), had been equally certain that Italy possessed 'permanent rights' in Tunis. 'The Africa which the Romans occupied', he added to clinch his case, 'was not very different from that of today', and the Silver Age poet, Statius, he averred, could still be read to justify an Italian drive to express their language and culture in the shadow of Carthage.[25]

But, however much conviction or self-satisfaction Tittoni and his colleagues gained from this parade of classical knowledge, by the inter-war period such claims were mere wishful thinking. The French occupation of Tunis had, according to one recent authority, provoked 'effectively ... the first popular participation in a foreign policy crisis' in Liberal Italy.[26] The applicability of the word 'popular' may be questioned – 1880s Italy was in no sense a democracy – but there can be no doubt that the loss of Tunis quickly threw Italian imperial policy askew. Without Tunis, the Italian flag would only be carried to places where virtually no 'Italians' lived and Italian expansionism in the Mediterranean world would never find a genuine popular base.

Nonetheless, such expansionism was soon underway. Its first site was 'Eritrea', that is, those lands now given an appropriately classical name which lay along the Red Sea and were under the highly nominal control of the Ottoman Empire. In 1882, the officially-sponsored Rubattino shipping line acquired the tiny harbour of Assab, near the Horn of Africa, as a coaling station to service its vessels plying to India. The Rubattino company then rapidly handed over the responsibility for administering this port to the national government. As imperial propagandists had always predicted, a first step soon led to others. In February 1885, Prime Minister Depretis and his Foreign Minister Pasquale Stanislao Mancini, each a somewhat reluctant colonialist, agreed to send an expedition to another Eritrean port, Massawa. They were prompted by domestic pressure from Sonnino and his friends, who enjoyed orating about Italy's imminent 'grandiose colonial future', and by some self-interested enticement from Great Britain, then on the lookout for associates who might help to realise its own Egyptian and Sudanese policies.[27] With both Massawa and Assab occupied, Italy became the owner of its first overseas colony.

The possession of Eritrea would continue to need justification, all the more because it brought so little obvious reward. In 1913, sixty-one colonists were established there, and by 1932 this number had risen to only 161. In 1934 the entire local armed force consisted of 125 officers, 136 NCOs, 90 men and 4,300 *ascari*. Nor was development swift or profound. It was said of the Asmara–Massawa trunk road that 'like all Eritrean roads it was constructed more for an animal caravan than for motor traffic'.[28] Even when Fascist attention was directed elsewhere, the colony regularly ran at a deficit. Nonetheless, 'Africanists' could always find reasons to be proud that Italy had acquired Eritrea. The simplest and most persuasive argument in defence of the colony was a variety of social Darwinism. In going to Eritrea Italy had joined the great struggle of the internationally fittest, a failure to compete in which would mean 'national death'. As a young army officer would muse in the 1890s, ruling Eritrea

> was a historic necessity created for our country by the same natural and special causes which also drove other nations to expand. It was impossible to exempt Italy from those fatal laws which govern nature, and force it to be inert when in fact it had and has within itself so much youthful strength.[29]

Others expressed themselves more subtly. Ferdinando Martini, Governor of Eritrea 1897–1907, would amuse himself building Tuscanate colonnades in his inland capital, Asmara, and assert that he was thus constructing a concrete base for Italy's 'civilising mission' (even if he, from time to time, intemperately argued that Italian rule would be best assisted by a genocide of the local peoples).[30] Nationalists contemplated cunning deals for further expansion to Djibouti, the Jubaland[31] or British Somaliland, and hailed the Yemen, across the Red Sea, as the 'necessary complement of Eritrea'.[32] A Fascist historian would argue that influence acquired at San'a through the dispatch there of two Italian doctors and five planes, and the participation of Italian engineers in an electrification scheme, would in turn open the gates to Jeddah,[33] and who could forsee what power and delight lay beyond that holy city?

The idea of a Muslim Roman empire might seem an incongruous one, but Italy had indeed gradually moved beyond Massawa. In the 1870s and 1880s its explorers, traders, missionaries and even some members of the royal family had already penetrated the territory to the south of the Horn of Africa, especially that part of it known to contemporaries as the 'Benadir coasts', which was believed by Europeans to be under the nominal suzerainty of the Sultan of Zanzibar.[34] Though the region was poor and its trade in such products as hides and cotton small – caravans to the interior 'rarely numbered more than fifteen or twenty camels'[35] – Italy, by the 1890s, had developed appreciable commercial interests there, mostly through private companies, and established an uneasy protectorate over the port of Mogadishu (Muqdisho) and its surrounding territory. In 1905, this control was formalised by the creation of the colony of 'Somalia italiana'.

It was a difficult time to assume an imperium because the forces of Muhammad Abdullah Hassan, then called by Europeans the 'Mad Mullah' but later proclaimed the national hero of the Somali Republic, were doing their best to drive British, French and Italian intruders into the sea and, that year, armies owing allegiance to the Ethiopian Emperor Menelik also penetrated to within a day's march of Mogadishu. Even after European forces achieved a paramountcy, Somalia italiana remained a barren place. Formal administration was one thing, genuine 'pacification' another. The Fascist, monarchist, historian and war hero, Cesare De Vecchi di Val Cismon, appointed to the colony's governorship in December 1923, would write his memoirs in the third person in imitation of Caesar's *Gallic Wars*, and pride himself on being a militant successor to the greatest Roman of them all. He did erect a large new Catholic cathedral in Mogadishu but, despite this victory for Christian soldiers, he had to admit that his generalship had still not ended the resistance of his local foes – the stubbornly independent Somalis were 'Africa's Irish', he somewhat lamely explained.[36] Less sanguine visitors remarked that so enervating was the climate that, in Mogadishu, even Buitoni spaghetti, that most resilient of products, grew worms on the pantry shelf.[37] Of all postings in the Italian realm, Somalia was the one best avoided. In 1935 about 250 Italian civilians lived in the colony's capital city and only ten of them were women.[38]

Such figures make it plain that Italy's excess population problems were not resolved in Somalia. The colony's trade was equally discouraging. On official figures, its exports in 1905–6 totalled only 2.23 million lire, whereas its imports were then 2.94 million. By 1934–5 this commerce still only amounted to 30.39 million for exports and 59.19 million for imports.[39]

The most recent analysis of Italian rule in Somalia has indicated again how extraordinarily superficial it was. Italian administrators failed to keep satisfactory records of local droughts and, especially inland, even under Fascism, their writ scarcely ran. 'Both practically and philosophically, Italian officialdom before World War II was inclined to leave the nomads [with their traditional pastoral ecology] alone.'[40] Still more ironically for a country whose leaders frequently claimed that it needed colonies because of its huge emigration, 'Italian colonists and officials would find the shortage of manual labor to be the major obstacle to the development of a profitable agricultural colony in Somalia.'[41]

Culturally, the results of Italian administration in East Africa were equally meagre. Despite regular missions, in 1928 only 8,473

Eritreans admitted to being Catholic, as against 239,000 who declared themselves to be Coptic Orthodox.[42] For Somalis, being Muslim was at the very centre of their identity, though a local proverb has an individualist rigour which might make even a *mafioso* feel soft and malleable: 'I and my clan against the world. I and my brother against the clan. I against my brother.'[43] But, if the religions of neither nation nor Pope deeply penetrated East African souls, some locals, *ascari* as they were called, enrolled in the Italian army and proved themselves brave, disciplined and brutal troops.[44] Both Liberal and Fascist governments were a little uncertain of their deployment. However useful was the *ascari's* service outside their own village or region, Italy ignored the models of Spain and France and created neither a foreign legion nor a fully-fledged imperial army.

In any case, all these matters, financial, demographic and cultural, were in the final analysis irrelevant. The Italian flag waved over Massawa and Mogadishu for one reason, and one reason alone. The ports only made sense as the launching point for the penetration or acquisition of Ethiopia, by the 1890s the only major part of Africa not yet under direct or indirect white rule. Ethiopia itself was a genuine empire, if in most senses a new and highly unstable one, possessed of shifting borders and riven by religious, tribal and political schism.[45] Its poverty and inaccessibility had preserved it from the other Great Powers.

In the classic manner of Italy's imperialism, the first drive on Addis Ababa was speeded more by words than by any cool and rational assessment of advantage. Commentators claimed that a commercial initiative by Cavour in the region had given United Italy a leitmotif from which it should not stray.[46] As that sometimes sober Milan newspaper, *Corriere della Sera*, would herald action against Massawa, Italy must act in the region lest it 'cease to have any pretence to assume the role of a Great Power and . . . [thus] have to content itself with being a big Switzerland'.[47] With every little victory or defeat on the Eritrean frontier, nationalist passion flared, and newspapers sold. When hundreds of troops were ambushed at Dogali in January 1887 – 430 died, eighty-two were wounded – patriotic demagogues cried for vengeance[48] (and, rounding off the number, the town planners of Rome constructed a Piazza del Cinquecento at the top of the new Via Nazionale). When Italian arms were briefly victorious, as at Agordat in January 1894, King Umberto I was persuaded that the victory had 'greatly raised the name and reputation of Italy' among the populace of all Africa and had even made the English jealous.[49]

But, soon, East Africa was another place where nothing failed like success. In 1896, the commercial deals, the missionary hopes, the plans of possible settlement, the strategic plotting, were all aborted when General Oreste Baratieri, whipped into action by desperate and sarcastic cables from Crispi, lost the battle of Adowa to Emperor Menelik II. The furies, it seemed, had fallen on Italian imperialism for a second time. Banned from the Tunisian Garden of the Hesperides by the power and ruthlessness of the French 'step-sister', Italy had now failed when 'only' Africans were the enemy. Solomon, in his legendary marriage to the Queen of Sheba, of which Menelik's dynasty was so proud,[50] may once have connected the Mediterranean with the Ethiopian plateau. Liberal Italy lacked the wisdom, determination or power to follow in his footsteps.

For Italian imperialists, the months after Adowa were a time of sackcloth and ashes. One official bewailed, 'in our colony it is no longer possible to live. We have lost any prestige with the natives'. Diarist Farini fulminated against the Ethiopians: 'they are people to treat as you would apes – fire and sword – if you can and if you have the stomach for it; or you can bury yourself in a tomb of impotence'.[51] Large sections of the Italian populace, by contrast, made manifest their opposition to African adventures, sometimes uneasily sensing that it was unjust to try to take away land that belonged to others. Among those anxious to withdraw from the race for empire were the businessmen of Turin and Milan, the socialists (who, in an emphatically anti-clerical gesture would, on Christmas Day 1896, inaugurate their national daily newspaper *Avanti!* in Rome) and many Catholics (Farini was troubled lest the Pope steal a march on liberalism by swiftly negotiating the release of Italian POWs).[52] Rather than papering over his domestic weakness through imperial triumph, Adowa ended Crispi's career and seriously undermined such near-supporters as the King, the army leadership and many conservative politicians.

It is often assumed that Adowa meant the end of Italian ambition in the Horn of Africa until that ambition was revived under Fascism. But such an assumption is quite wrong. What happened instead was that Italian policy in the area retreated from the high ground of military action into the more familiar back alleys of diplomacy. For a time, fear, especially fear of domestic contestation, counselled extreme caution, but, among large sections of the Italian ruling and intellectual elite, the ambition to penetrate Ethiopia had not disappeared (and, despite occasional rumours about Russia, France,

Germany, Britain or even Japan, no other Great Power proved itself seriously anxious to take over the Italian role there).

Rather, Italian Africanists, diplomats, journalists, politicians, Catholic missionaries and the occasional trader waited. And, gradually, an Italian influence in the region revived. Eritrea and Somalia had not been surrendered. In December 1906 an Anglo-Franco-Italian agreement on Ethiopia was signed; it included secret clauses envisaging a division of spheres of interests between the European powers. A new Italian war plan for action against Ethiopia from an Eritrean base was drafted in 1908. As Menelik drifted to dotage and death, his empire eroded and, by 1913–14, Italy contemplated again the possibility or threat of some sort of armed intervention in Ethiopia. Foreign Minister Di San Giuliano, who greatly enjoyed driving a hard bargain, said that his minimum eventual price was a territorial connection between Eritrea and Somalia which would necessarily run through the Tigray and the Galla (Oromo) parts of the Ethiopian empire.[53]

Di San Giuliano, however, saw no reason to be precipitate. By that time, Italy had already won new provinces for its empire of a rather greater size and significance than Eritrea and Somalia. In 1911–12 Italy conquered what its propagandists, with their accustomed *romanità*, denominated Libya. This new acquisition would eventually comprise the ex-Turkish vilayets of Tripolitania and Cyrenaica and the inland territory of Fezzan. Italy had entered what Salvemini would unkindly call its 'African sand-box'[54] through a military and diplomatic campaign which *The Economist* of London would characteristically define as a 'detestable outbreak of chauvinism and brigandage'.[55] Liberal Italy had located its 'fourth shore'.

There is a very considerable literature on the Italian acquisition of Libya[56] and space does not permit its reiteration here. Suffice it to say that perhaps the victory and certainly the acquisition were more nominal than real. Like the East African colonies, Libya did little to resolve Italy's strategic, economic, demographic and status problems.

It has already been noted how ruthlessly Giolitti played the diplomatic game during the Libyan War (p. 50). Even though he would eventually urge, piously, that the local population should not 'be treated like enemies but as our equals since I do not admit that there is a great difference between one man and the next', he had not been squeamish in his treatment of Libyan prisoners of war.[57] The army, too, however proud of its 'crusading' achievement in pioneering the usage of air planes and dirigibles in battle, would not act with kid gloves in its imperial actions. Wherever it could, both during the Libyan War and in its administration thereafter, Liberal Italy sought to deploy that overwhelming superiority of technology and fire-power which underpinned every European empire. Between 1911 and 1921, two-thirds of the livestock of Cyrenaica was killed and nationalist intellectuals talked carelessly of the advantages of genocide. Italians, wrote Maffeo Pantaleoni, should consider Libyans in the same way that General Sherman regarded red-skins, 'that is, that the only good ones were dead ones'.[58]

But Italy's superiority was typically fragile. For most of 1911–12, Italian generals, conscious of the humiliation once suffered by Baratieri, stayed cautiously inside the walls of the coastal forts. Once the initial landing had been made, the real action of the Libyan War occurred in European chancelleries, or in Levantine meeting-places where Giolittian agents sought to persuade Turkish politicians to abandon a territory which had brought their empire no profit. After an Italo-Turkish peace treaty was signed at Lausanne in October 1912, Giolitti rapidly lost interest in the new colony and, by 1914, those Italian soldiers who remained there cowered anew in their fortresses. With Italy and Turkey again opposed in the First World War from October 1915, the interior remained in the hands of its local inhabitants, who may not have obeyed the summons from Constantinople to launch a jihad against the Italian infidels, but who wanted to live in their own way for their own purposes.

Thus, by the time the First World War ended, Italy's possession of its Libyan colony had been reduced to a precarious hold on a scattering of coastal towns, though an archaeological museum was opened in Tripoli, with some fanfare, in 1919.[59] Whatever the echoes of the past, active colonisation was confined to eighty-nine meagre allotments; the families which worked them were 'the equivalent of the smallest rural settlement in Italy'.[60] But, once again, weakness had not entailed a will to surrender or withdraw. Instead, as the systems of ordinary government strove to assert themselves within Italy, so, too, an active colonial policy resumed. It was the Liberal democrat and soon to be martyr to Fascism, Giovanni Amendola, who, while Minister of Colonies from February 1922, demanded a more forward policy and harshly set about the genuine 'pacification' of the colony.[61] Fascist policies, especially as implemented by Giuseppe Volpi and by the monarchist and unpurged Italian army, thus displayed a very considerable continuity with what had gone before, though, as the years passed, Fascists did become more 'thorough' in their approach. By the early 1930s, Libya was at last securely in Italian hands. The cost was paid directly by some 100,000 Cyrenaicans, deported to coastal concentration camps after June 1930 in what two critical historians have called one of the most rapid examples of genocide in history.[62] Since the Fascist forces also killed livestock and poisoned wells, the population continued to decline by 'natural' wastage until the arrival of Italo Balbo as governor.

For all this ruthlessness – as one ex-Liberal turned Mussolinian notable put it, Fascism's implacable realism could have no truck with 'those who exalted the sterile anarchy of primitive regimes'[63] – it was not at all clear what Fascist Italy wanted to do with Libya. Its propagandists could regularly wax lyrical about its cities' 'non-African' climate,[64] the opportunities which Fascist law and order offered to archaeologists[65] and the economic benefits which would accrue from an improvement in salt production.[66] Or, as one Fascist propagandist put it briefly: 'today, the real America for all Italians is Libya'.[67] But, in 1930, an authoritative survey admitted that the colony spent 215 million lire on imports while its exports were only valued at 36 million. The same report concluded that mineral resources were limited to traces of manganese and zinc. Moreover, throughout their colonial rule, Italy's administrators stubbornly ignored what, at least in retrospect, seems clear evidence of the area's oil reserves.[68] But, as nationalist writer, Roberto Cantalupo, explained, in the Fascist world dominated by the will, tawdry economic matters were of trifling concern, and, in any case, the classics offered the incontestable lesson that agriculture had once been the key to Libyan development, and would be again.[69]

Not until the very end of the Fascist period was there some alteration in these attitudes. In 1934 the colony produced only about 25 per cent of what it cost to administer and in 1937 had still received only 1,299 Italian peasant families as immigrants.[70] By the late 1930s, however, things were beginning to change to a degree in the colony because of the activities of Balbo, the new Governor. A sort of Fascist 'leader of the opposition', Balbo had been rewarded with rustication to Libya precisely because the Duce disliked and feared his urbanity, self-confidence and popularity.[71] The new Governor, who had won agreement from Mussolini that the two territories of Tripolitania and Cyrenaica should be united into a single unit under his command, arrived in the colony on 1 January 1934. He soon launched a major immigration scheme in a blaze of publicity – though whether

Mussolini was pleased to learn that three babies born on the first convoy of 20,000 immigrants were named, in order, Italo, Vittorio and Benito might be another question.[72]

Balbo also seems to have got on reasonably well with the local Arabs, especially the chiefs,[73] and his ostentatious objection to the anti-Semitic campaign launched from 1938 onwards in Rome nourished his popularity among Libya's ancient Jewish community.[74] Nonetheless, it is hard to believe that Balbo's settlement policies would have won local favour for long or that he was destined to be much appreciated by thrifty officials in Rome. In the five years after 1937, Italy spent more on Libya than it had in the previous two and a half decades of possession. As Angelo Del Boca, the leading contemporary historian of Italian colonialism, has noted, the land colonised was acquired through 'a colossal theft, one of the most blatant and hateful ever committed in Africa'. Fascist empire-building, he says, was merely for show, 'every one of these great projects of demographic colonisation soon demonstrated itself a total economic and financial failure. But the Fascist state could not care less if its budgets did not balance'.[75] Perhaps it was lucky for Balbo's historical reputation, both in Libya and in Italy, that he was one of the early casualties of Italy's Second World War, shot down on 28 June 1940 by his own nervous anti-aircraft gunners as he dauntlessly and fascistically tried to land his plane at Tobruk airport. By that time the number of Italians who had settled in Libya had reached 140,000.

For a country which by then had sent 20 million emigrants abroad since the Risorgimento that was still a tiny figure, but Libya was the only colony which could boast even this small achievement. In 1934, there seemed no reason not to accept King Victor Emmanuel III's complaint that 'in the carving up of Africa, Italy had been given the bone of the joint'.[76] Apart from Libya, other possessions similarly exploited the funds of the Roman treasury but gave even less promise of reward. The Dodecanese Islands, for example, had been seized in 1912 but remained an object of international treatying until they were secured for Italy in 1923. Fascist rule gradually became more intrusive there as administration of the islands passed from ex-Liberal diplomat Alessandro De Bosdari to Nationalist Mario Lago (1922–36) to Fascist Cesare De Vecchi di Val Cismon (1936–40). Lago, who got on well with the local Jewish traders, seems to have left a reasonable reputation behind, even though in 1926 he instituted compulsory Italian courses for the islands' Greek population.[77]

Perhaps Lago's fame has been enhanced by his being succeeded by De Vecchi, a boastful incompetent who, in a lengthy and variegated career, turned anything he touched to dross.[78] It was De Vecchi who seriously applied 'fascistisation' to the islands, instituting in 1937 a school programme identical with that of Italy, pursuing anti-Semitic legislation in 1938 and, in 1939, committing the ultimate sin of closing the Greek Orthodox schools.[79] In 1912 owning the islands may have made some sense had Italy engaged in major commercial or colonial expansion in Asia Minor. By 1939 the Fascist Dodecanese brought no profit, could not be defended and, naturally, had never offered the chance to settle any Italian emigrants.

But the heart of Italian imperialism did not beat in Rhodes or Leptis Magna. Rather, the real Fascist empire lay in Ethiopia. There, in 1935–6, Crispi would be avenged and the Fascists would do what the Liberals had so notoriously failed to do. The new fascist man would shoulder the white man's burden and loyal supporters of the regime throughout the world would exult in 'Mussolini's master-piece' and hymn the final creation of a real Italian empire.

In fact, as has already been noted in Chapter 2 (pp. 50–1), there were remarkable parallels between the Fascist Ethiopian and the Liberal Libyan Wars. If the former was the 'prelude to World War II', the latter was the prelude to the First World War and it seems almost necessary to proclaim two historical laws for the first half of the twentieth century: European conflict threatens when Italy finally seizes territory in Africa for which planning in Rome had begun many years before; Italy acts in Africa when and because the situation in Europe is spiralling out of control. But the parallels do not end there. Italian troops reached Addis Ababa on 5 May 1936, shortly after Emperor Haile Selassie fled his capital. This much-vaunted 'Roman victory', however, scarcely meant that Italy had secured its possession of the new colony. In the months after 1936, the Fascist regime confronted the problem of making its writ run throughout those vast territories which even the most centralising previous emperors had perforce ruled with a light hand.

The story grows predictable. Fascist Italy began with brutality, though also with plenty of infighting between army regulars, Fascist ideologues and ill-trained career officials.[80] When, on 19 February 1937, there was an attempt on the life of the Fascist Governor, General Rodolfo Graziani, troops of both the Italian army and of Fascist paramilitary forces were encouraged to rage through the huts of Addis Ababa, killing, raping and burning. The massacres spread to the monastery at Debra Lebanos, where an attempt was also made to wipe out the sacred texts of Ethiopian history and thus symbolically to close the chapter of Ethiopia's native past. Some estimates say 30,000 Ethiopians died.[81]

Mussolini for a time light-heartedly encouraged such brutality, but these events amounted more to revenge killing than planned genocide. In the long run, Italy hoped to manage an empire with the style and methods of the British and the French rather than the deadly and technologised fanaticism which the Nazis would soon employ in their European *Lebensraum*. In November 1937, the young, handsome and tubercular Duke of Aosta, from the Nationalist branch of the royal family, a prince who looked wonderfully elegant in his white uniform and pith helmet, almost a pukka sahib, replaced Graziani as Governor. Though Aosta's administration was milder and less blatantly corrupt than Graziani's, he was completely unable to resolve the typical dilemmas of Italian imperial rule. Administering Ethiopia, instead of bringing wealth, proved costly. The annual estimates for 1936–7 promised to double the total national expenditure for that year, and Aosta's governorship continued to be plagued by financial troubles.[82] If, whatever its cost, the empire was meant to resolve Italy's 'demographic problem', it proved unable to do so. By 1941, only some 3,200 Italian colonists were farming in the Ethiopian highlands. By then, if any Italians were benefiting from the expansion of empire, they were unheroic middlemen and traders, those with good contacts when government contracts were disbursed.[83]

Moreover, although Ethiopia now joined Somalia and Eritrea in what was called 'Africa Orientale Italiana' (AOI – Italian East Africa), and although roads were built and other public works initiated, the territory remained absolutely indefensible against British colonial power. In a brief campaign in 1941 only some 1,500 Italians died in defence of this longest coveted part of the Italian empire and by 5 May Haile Selassie was back in his capital. The superficiality of Italian rule over Ethiopia is most clearly revealed in the memoirs of Lino Calabrò, an official who had reached the colony certainly full of a romantic *mal d'Africa* and perhaps because his father, a colonialist professor of history at Palermo University, had taught the Duke of Aosta. Sent up country, Calabrò claims to have been popular among the locals, especially the Coptic clergy, but, he says, with unconscious frankness, the locals could predict where he was going before he went.[84] If Sicilians, since 1860, had known a thing or two about how to resist or temper Roman centralism and kept their own track of official visitations, the peoples of Ethiopia comprehended at least as much.

As so far related, the story of Italian empire is a bathetic one. It is a tale of rather absurd ambition, with an essentially European intention, pursued in a less than wholehearted manner, and at a certain cost, which bore most heavily on the peoples of the empire rather than on Italians themselves. But there was one sphere in which 'Africa' did seriously afflict Italy – the sphere of race. It has often been argued that the domestic effect of the Libyan War was to destroy the political system of its artificer, Giolitti. In a curious sense, the Ethiopian War would also leave a heritage, one which would bring Fascism down. Mussolini's masterpiece would prove brittle indeed. Rather than resulting in deification, his Roman triumph would lead to death and dishonour, not only for Mussolini himself but also for his historical reputation.

Nostalgic writers, like the journalist of *Il Tempo* cited at the beginning of this chapter, have frequently claimed that Italians were better colonisers than other Europeans because they lacked a rigid racial sense and happily accepted the humanity of the people among whom they lived.[85] Italian soldiers in Ethiopia made the song *'Faccetta nera'* ('Little Black Face') top of the pops in 1936[86] in a way scarcely emulated by their German comrades when they invaded Poland or Russia. Italian settlers had commercial and sexual dealings with local men and women in a more open way than did the British in India, for example.

This alleged blindness to racial differences may, however, be doubted. The lyrics of *'Faccetta nera'* scarcely bespeak a romantic love between equals and, where Italians and locals did muck in together, the better explanation is based on class rather than on ethnicity. The poor have no choice but to live together, though in their hearts, and with 'education', they may well nurture the prejudices and biases held by those further up the social scale.[87] Certainly the Italian elite seems to have possessed as strong a sense of colour as did any other. That pillar of responsible or academic liberalism, F.S. Nitti, for example, can be found in 1922 writing scabrous stories about the black French troops who occupied the Rhineland. How deplorable it was, he said, to drive German women 'to prostitute themselves' and 'gratify the lust of negroes'. The Rhine had seen many bitter conflicts but 'never, until now, did the river sacred to battles and glory reflect from its green shores the black faces of African cannibals, brought thither to enforce the rights of the victor on the most cultured people in the world'.[88]

Such commonplace prejudices were sometimes half hidden by a recurrent parochialism among Italian intellectuals and policy-makers. Italians talked little about race because their empire was small and the nation's ruling elite (as distinct from the peoples of the Italies) rarely travelled abroad. Only in wartime or during the last years of Fascism did Italy in any major sense flirt with a *Weltpolitik*. In March 1937, during an official visit to Libya, which, unfortunately for Fascist propagandists, coincided with the Guadalajara rout in Spain, Mussolini drew the 'sword of Islam' from its scabbard, and thereafter his agents did something to foment national independence movements in Egypt, Palestine, Iraq and even India. In at least the eastern Mediterranean, Fascist historians could readily aver, Musso-lini's 'people's regime' would aim at a 'new reign of justice and prosperity'. Fascism would do all it could to help Egypt, it was said, though this stated modesty of ambition did not accord well with reminders that Augustus had once transported there both 'the eternal light of Roman virtue' and Roman legions.[89] Renzo De Felice, who has done the most research on the subject, is inclined to take very seriously Fascist policy in the Near and Far East,[90] but perhaps he should accept a caution from Luigi Goglia, a younger historian of Italian imperialism. Fascism, Goglia has said, did not really possess a policy on the Arab world (let alone, it might be added, on the Indian or Chinese ones). Its intrusions into these regions were merely 'an instrument used or brandished by the Duce to strike against, to irritate and to create diversions for and put pressure on Great Britain'.[91] In no way did Mussolini, except in regard to that stubborn Italian belief that anything was possible, really hope to ride in triumph through Persepolis.

Fascist Italy's most notorious descent into racist prejudice was, of course, the anti-Semitic legislation which began to be drafted after the publication of the 'Race Manifesto' and its endorsement by Mussolini in July 1938. The most widespread interpretation of this racial legislation, and the one which was automatically accepted by the Italian populace at large,[92] is that it was a price which Italy paid for its alliance with Nazi Germany. As a recent historian has averred: 'Italian anti-Semitism had no ideological base, but was the product of mindless and cynical opportunism.'[93] Certainly efforts to detect an anti-Semitic tradition either in Italy or in Italian Fascism have not got very far. Perhaps Liberal Italy was not entirely free from anti-

Semitic prejudice. Nationalist commentators could be troubled by Zionists who allegedly wanted to have 'two fatherlands', or could declare that the battle between Rome and Carthage had been fought between the Mediterranean and Semitic 'races'.[94] An austerely conservative prefect could complain that Jewish financiers owned too much of Venice and fostered its physical and moral degredation,[95] and other men in high places could mutter in a gentlemanly way that there were too many Jews in the Senate (there were twenty-four in 1922), or in the Academy.[96] Roman Catholicism was not always untainted by anti-Semitic ideas (*Civiltà Cattolica* can be found sighing about the absence of an Italian Drumont),[97] though their public expression occurred more often in France or Poland than in Italy. According to Gramsci, peasants did usually believe that 'the Jews' had killed Christ, but they also remembered that there were 'good ones' like Nicodemus, and actually had only the remotest understanding anyway of what a Jew might be.[98] All in all, the great majority of commentators agree, Liberal Italy, which had possessed a Jewish Minister of War, a Jewish Secretary-General of the Foreign Ministry, a Jewish Mayor of Rome and where, in 1910, one Jewish Prime Minister succeeded another of Jewish extraction, was the least anti-Semitic country in Europe.[99]

Nor did the situation alter much after 1922. So notorious a racist as the journalist Giovanni Preziosi did belong to the Fascist Party, but any influence he might have had was curtailed by a host of Jewish Fascists and *fiancheggiatori*. Among these were Emanuele Pugliese, the General who sagely advised King Victor Emmanuel during the March on Rome that he could rely on the army but that its loyalty was better not put to the test, Aldo Finzi, the Under-Secretary of the Interior most nearly involved in the Matteotti murder, Oscar Sinigaglia, a leading financier of extreme nationalist causes, and Guido Jung, who was still Minister of Finance in 1935. If a number of distinguished Anti-Fascists were Jewish, five Jews had attended the foundation of the Fascist Party at the Piazza San Sepolcro, three were 'martyrs' to the cause between 1919 and 1922 and 230 were officially recognised as having joined the March on Rome.[100]

Similarly, Jews had figured largely in the Risorgimento, in the Nationalist movement and at the front in the First World War. In October 1920 Mussolini himself pronounced that Italy 'did not know anti-Semitism and we believe that it will never be known here'.[101] Later he would meet Zionist leader, Chaim Weizmann, on a number of occasions with every sign of cordiality, and even act as a father of the Israeli navy by sponsoring from 1934 to 1938 a Revisionist Zionist naval school at Civitavecchia.[102] His sarcastic words about early Nazi ventures into anti-Semitic practice are too familiar to need repeating here.

Why, then, the anti-Semitic legislation? And, indeed, why the Italian participation in the Holocaust which, at least under the Salò Republic after September 1943, brought death to thousands of Italian and other Jews, who had taken refuge in Italian territory? It was then that the 'banality of good'[103] proved no longer sufficient.[104] There can be no doubt that part of the answer to these questions is indeed 'conformism and mimicry', a Fascist desire to ingratiate themselves with the Germans, a Fascist nervousness that their movement was not 'real' or 'fascist' unless it did what the Germans were doing, an angry realisation that, even after a generation in power, the 'new Fascist man' who could match an ordinary German soldier was not yet born. But there was also one other explanation – Fascist racism was the worst *mal d'Africa*. As a 1938 decree would maintain: 'The Jewish problem is only the metropolitan face of a problem with a more general character.'[105]

During the conflict in Ethiopia, xenophobia had mounted. The hostility of the world press and the campaigns of the League of Nations provided some evidence to the paranoid mind that Fascism was being persecuted by international Jewry.[106] But the greater pressure was imperial in a more direct sense. If the Italians really were to rule an empire, the Fascist leadership decided, they must act like those imperialists whom Pini, in 1937, had wanted 'made'. Fraternisation with the natives must be legislated against, and once this legislation began to be promulgated, it seemed sensible and necessary for it also to cover Libya and the Italian peninsula, and to extend to the Jews. In this way, recent historians maintain, the absence of any specific evidence of a German request in 1938 for Italy to adopt anti-Semitic measures is explained. Thus is revealed how Fascist racism, they claim, came, at least partially, from 'below'. Those intellectuals who signed the 'Race Manifesto' made their decisions on their own accounts as much as they acted at the behest of Mussolini. In this sense, this variety of revisionism concludes, it is appropriate that both Fascism and the Italian empire ended at 'Auschwitz'.

In practice, well before the fall of Fascism in July 1943, the Italian empire had collapsed. Eventually, not everyone in the Republic would be glad about this failure and, as has been noted above, some post-Fascist politicians, intellectuals and diplomats made feeble attempts to retain Libya (especially Tripolitania), Eritrea and Somalia, the so-called 'Liberal colonies' (they modestly forbore to remember that the Dodecanese had been Liberal colonies, too). At least in the case of Somalia, Italy did not lose a formal role as a mandatory power until 1 July 1960. Libya was granted its independence in 1952, and expelled its last 30,000 Italian settlers after Colonel Gadhafi's coup in September 1969. Eritrea was, until 1993, uneasily absorbed into the renewed Ethiopian empire. In all cases, Italy retained cultural, commercial and even political influence, though whether that greatly benefited either Italy or the locals is another question.[107]

The informal empire which did matter to 1950s Italy was, rather, one of influence in the oil-rich Arab world, as narrated in the foregoing chapter. The successes of Enrico Mattei and of Christian Democratic policy in the region owed much to the fact that Italy was not by then usually perceived as an imperial power. At the same time, and also to its good fortune, Italy missed out on the domestic travails of decolonisation which so dogged the post-Second World War histories of France and Britain, and which so afflict 1990s Russia. To the advantage of Italians, Albanians, Dodecanese Greeks and North and East Africans, the brief history of the Italian empire now seems little more than a mirage, and its historical imprint on Italy's relationship with the wider world to have been insubstantial indeed. Italy may have briefly possessed an empire, but the Italian nation state had 'made' imperialists in only the most superficial of senses. Or have I been writing about the wrong empire? In the next decades, if the *leghe* get their way, will it be Piedmont (or Sicily) which will have to decolonise? That would seem a rather more traumatic prospect for the inhabitants of the Italian peninsula, and for those who abandoned that peninsula some time in the century after 1860 and constructed by their emigration the empire of the Italies.

6

THE RISE AND RISE OF THE EMPIRE OF THE ITALIES

Emigration 1860–1960

Propagandists of the Italian empire habitually talked blithely about the Third Rome, even as they sent Italian legions to places where the Roman eagle had never been and constructed an imperium not of marble nor yet of tufa, but more of papier mâché or grains of sand. However, while politicians plotted and intellectuals penned their clever lines, the people of the Italies pursued an external policy of their own. Political Italy boasted about national grandeur and fearfully or covertly sought to imitate the really powerful, all the time living in the little worlds of Europe or East Africa or the Mediterranean. The peoples of the Italies, driven by an amalgam of compulsions, hopes, delusions and ambitions, went out onto the paths of the wider world and admixed their cultures to those of Patagonia and Pittsburg, Scotland and South Africa, Marseilles and Manjimup. If students wish to locate an Italian *Weltpolitik*, they are more likely to find it in 'real' than in 'legal' Italy.

Before the First World War, for example, semi-official commentators noted that only a handful of Italians had settled in Eritrea or in Somalia whereas 135,000 resided in Switzerland, 35,000 in Egypt, 20,000 in England and Wales, 450,000 in France and millions in the non-European world.[1] In 1911, Francesco Saverio Nitti, with that love of pedantic accuracy which so typified the man, declared that 5,547,746 Italians lived abroad, not counting those who had abandoned their nationality.[2] Though the world after 1918 was more hostile towards emigrants, Italians continued to leave (or to return, or to leave again, or to return again). It has been estimated that, by the outbreak of the Second World War, about 20 million Italians had been through the emigration process since 1860, of whom some 14 million remained 'permanently' domiciled outside Italy (see Tables 6.1 and 6.2).[3]

Table 6.1 Emigration from Italy 1876–1975

Year	Number (millions)
1876–85	1.31
1886–95	2.39
1896–1905	4.32
1906–15	6.00
1916–25	2.60
1926–35	1.49
1936–45	0.26
1946–55	2.47
1956–65	3.17
1966–75	1.71

Source: Adapted from G. Rosoli (ed.), *Un secolo di emigrazione italiana 1876–1976*, Rome, 1978, pp. 350–5

Table 6.2 Repatriation to Italy 1905–74

Year	Number (millions)
1905–14	1.80
1915–24	0.92
1925–34	1.15
1935–44	0.36
1945–54	0.78
1955–64	1.78
1965–74	1.53

Source: Adapted from G. Rosoli (ed.), *Un secolo di emigrazione italiana 1876–1976*, Rome, 1978, pp. 348–9

After 1945 this 'flux', as Italian scholarship graphically describes it, began again. In the next two and a half decades a further 7 million left. Those who departed were gradually outnumbered by Italians moving within the peninsula – generally from still agrarian regions to the industrial cities and manufacturing centres of the North. In the 1950s, the first decade of the 'economic miracle', 10 million Italians, one-fifth of the total population, uprooted themselves and departed to new places of work or habitation within Italy, within Europe or across the seas.[4] Then, suddenly, from the 1970s, the process halted. The birthrate declined precipitously, wealth, however unevenly, increased as never before, and Italy, to its surprise and in some confusion, was transmogrified into a country of immigration. Some of these immigrants were 'Italians', the children, grandchildren or great-grandchildren of emigrants, returning from places where neither wealth nor happiness seemed as easy to win as in present-day Italy; but others were Iranians, Filipinos and Singhalese or, in an ironical reversal of the imperialism of the previous generation, Ethiopians, Libyans, Tunisians and Somalis.

It may be that the history of Italian emigration and its habitual discourse impose a special requirement on contemporary Italy to be flexible and humane in dealing with immigrant 'problems', but such issues lie outside the ambit of this book. Rather our questions must be who were these 'Italians' who emigrated? Where did they go? Why? When? With what effect on their host society, on Italy and on themselves? If they went back to Italy, why did they do so and, again, with what effect? What were the changing lineaments of the 'empire of the Italies' from 1860 to 1960?

In approaching these topics, a historian must start by acknowledging how crucial a part emigration played in Italy's relationship with the wider world and how deeply the issues of emigration, and the 'knowledge' which such issues inspired about that wider world, penetrated into Italian political and popular minds. One example must suffice. In November 1942, Mussolini received proof of the genocidal policies being pursued by his German ally in Eastern Europe. 'They're making [the Jews] emigrate . . . to another world',[5] he remarked, in a sentence which simultaneously bespoke his brutal cynicism and his abject helplessness before his terrible allies who said what they meant and did what they said. But Mussolini's words, however distasteful and unjust, had a further significance. To narrate an ultimate event, Mussolini selected what for him and many Italians was a visceral metaphor. The fate of the Jews, the Duce implied, bore some relation to the experience of Italian emigrant *poveri cristi*, himself included,[6] over the past century. In their way, Italians, too, had been rendered homeless, dispersed and deprived of family, village and nation. Before Fascist military and moral defeat, emigration was the most obvious failure of the Italian nation state. For decade after decade, emigration had made it manifest that the pretensions of the Italian state to feed and defend its peoples, to possess and deserve popular sovereignty, to carry out the most basic activities of any state, were limited or false.

Basilar the significance of emigration may have been in Italian history, yet its themes have scarcely resounded through the pages of Italian historiography.[7] Rather, the study of emigration has been mostly confined to the hands of demographers, economists and other social scientists. Their scholarship has unearthed a huge array of statistics and other 'facts', but their professional duty to engage in 'problem-solving' for the governments of host or emigrant societies has made some of their questions and many of their answers naive or crassly present-centred. Historians, so often fixated by the history of the nation state, have been ill-equipped or timidly reluctant to pursue the tortuous and transnational paths of emigration. Only in the last twenty years, and especially in North America through the fine work of Robert Harney, Donna Gabaccia, Rudi Vecoli, Dino Cinel and others, has migration history come into its own, and then usually through monographic studies rather than more wide-ranging accounts.[8] One of the better general studies available in any language remains that written by R.F. Foerster[9] in 1919. Italian scholarship, with some honourable exceptions,[10] is particularly disappointing in this area and far too frequently remains deferentially linked to the requirements of contemporary politics and the contemporary state. Perhaps more than in any other field, migration history, so easily overwhelmed by the detail made available through social science, is vulnerable to neo-Rankean objectivity (or patriotism) and 'documentary fetishism'. Narrating 'what actually happened', without a fresh and rigorous examination of the questions to be asked, hardly helps construct a credible history of the migrant experience.

The subject, then, is massive, the information vast (but often narrow or slanted), the historiography weak. Nonetheless, certain issues do rapidly become apparent from a brief examination of Italy's emigrant history. Some Italians, like so many other citizens of this world, had always migrated, either seasonally, or for a period of years, or permanently. Yet the great wave of emigration ran its course from *c.* 1865 to *c.* 1965 and thus coincided almost exactly with the history of the Italian state. How did that state, in its successive Liberal, Fascist and Republican regimes, confront the issue of emigration? As ideologies rose and fell did policies greatly change? How did the aims and actions of the national state affect the emigrants (or returnees) themselves?

For Liberals, emigration was, by definition, a problem. Their ideology was posited on the principle of *laissez-faire* and thus on the notion that a government should not intrude too far into the lives of its people. As Sonnino mused in 1880, liberal Britain had never blocked emigration and this commitment to liberty was the mainspring of its greatness.[11] Such devotion to an ideal was all very well, but, as the years passed, the numbers of those departing continued to increase and still national greatness did not come. In 1876 100,000 left, in 1895 293,000, in 1913 the total exceeded 872,000, or more than one in forty of the entire national population. Simultaneously, more emigrants began to seek distant transoceanic destinations rather than ones within Europe. During the period before the outbreak of the First World War, the focus of emigration also shifted from North to South, though always with significant regional and local variations. In a thoroughly 'pre-modern' pastoral economy like Sardinia, emigration counted little; it lost significance, too, whenever industrialisation, full-scale agrarian modernisation and socialism were strong. Emigration was less likely to be, or to be imagined to be, possible for landless labourers on great estates (*latifondi*), and far more probable among peasants into whose lives a market economy was intruding and in whose region land sales were occurring. Men always left in larger numbers than did women (see Tables 6.3 and 6.4).

Table 6.3 Emigration by gender 1876–1975

| Year | Number (millions) | |
	Male	Female
1876–85	1.12	0.20
1886–95	1.86	0.53
1896–1905	3.53	0.80
1906–15	4.86	1.14
1916–25	1.80	0.81
1926–35	0.99	0.50
1936–45	0.15	0.11
1946–55	1.62	0.85
1956–65	2.39	0.77
1966–75	1.17	0.54

Source: Adapted from G. Rosoli (ed.), *Un secolo di emigrazione italiana 1876–1976*, Rome, 1978, pp. 375–7

Politicians did not have to grasp the full complexity of these problems in order to ask three questions. Should the many blatant forms of exploitation inflicted on emigrants (before departure, on the journey – notably on the always foetid and sometimes unseaworthy ships which plied the Atlantic – and after arrival) be curbed or policed by a government responsibly concerned with its subjects' welfare? Second, how could Rome best benefit economically from its emigrants? Already, in 1907, emigrants through accountable channels repatriated 550 million lire (465 million from overseas, 85 million from Europe),[12] and by 1914 these remittances, with the matching

Table 6.4 Emigration by region 1876–1975

Year	Number (millions)
a North-West (i.e., Piedmont, Lombardy and Liguria)	
1876–85	0.56
1886–95	0.57
1896–1905	0.73
1906–15	1.26
1916–25	0.72
1926–35	0.41
1936–45	0.04
1946–55	0.30
1956–65	0.23
1966–75	0.18
b North-East (i.e., Trentino (after 1918), Veneto, Friuli, Venezia–Giulia)	
1876–85	0.37
1886–95	0.88
1896–1905	1.04
1906–15	0.94
1916–25	0.46
1926–35	0.34
1936–45	0.09
1946–55	0.63
1956–65	0.47
1966–75	0.24
c Centre (i.e., Emilia, Tuscany, Umbria, Marches, Lazio, Abruzzo)	
1876–85	0.16
1886–95	0.28
1896–1905	0.93
1906–15	1.44
1916–25	0.51
1926–35	0.29
1936–45	0.04
1946–55	0.58
1956–65	0.61
1966–75	0.24
d South (i.e., Molise, Campania, Puglia, Basilicata, Calabria, Sicily, Sardinia)	
1876–85	0.24
1886–95	0.66
1896–1905	1.62
1906–15	2.36
1916–25	0.92
1926–35	0.45
1936–45	0.09
1946–55	0.96
1956–65	2.86
1966–75	1.05

Source: Adapted from G. Rosoli (ed.), *Un secolo di emigrazione italiana 1876–1976*, Rome, 1978, pp. 356–65

sum expended by foreign tourists within Italy, together permitted a balancing of the national budget.[13] Could any government afford to ignore such vast sums? And finally, what did emigration mean for Italian reputation and power and for the well-being of the Italian 'race'? Were emigrants lost souls and lost bodies whose blood haemorrhaged out of the nation[14] to be absorbed to the benefit of others, as one commentator put it, 'like drops of rain in the sand'?[15] Did, as Catholic radical Romolo Murri wondered, Italians in emigration sometimes become more conscious of their nationality?[16] Or, as Luigi Villari, the nationalist son of the distinguished conservative historian and 'Southernist' Pasquale Villari, suspected, were they poor illiterates, 'an army without generals', deprived of an intellectual leadership[17] and needing to be instructed in *italianità* by well-primed consuls, generously funded Italian schools and elegant or popular national cultural societies?[18]

These issues of welfare, finance and national grandeur became those around which a long-running debate about emigration arose. Giovanni Giolitti and many other liberals went on believing either that emigration was some sort of socio-political 'safety-valve', or, as Luigi Luzzatti would declare in 1901, a plain necessity about whose goodness or evil too much oratory was pointless.[19] But, gradually, the Italian government did pass legislation about emigration. There had been discussion of some measures as early as 1868, and from 1873 prefects were obliged to keep accurate statistics of departures from their region. Crispian imperialism was thereafter particularly inclined to emphasise that only an Italian empire could properly resolve the emigration problem. Such views were enhanced by the spreading of Italophobia in host societies, as was evidenced in the lynching of eleven immigrants in New Orleans in 1891 who were thought to be members of the 'Black Hand',[20] in the murder of at least nine Italians and the assault on hundreds more at Aigues Mortes in southern France in 1893,[21] and in public contempt displayed by the Swiss at the end of the decade towards those Italians, who, despite appalling working conditions, dug the Simplon tunnel through the Alps.[22]

After 1896, the collapse of imperial ambition, at least for the time being, further exacerbated the debate about emigration and, in 1901, the government passed its most thoroughgoing legislation so far, requiring its agents at home and abroad to supervise and assist emigrants and establishing a Commissariato dell'Emigrazione in Rome to centralise their efforts.[23] Further than that the Liberal state would not and did not go, but the political leadership continued to have to fend off criticism of its inaction or moderation.

Nationalists recalled Crispi with nostalgia. One leading ideologue, Enrico Corradini, foresaw a great future for Japan which conserved its people, in contrast to Italy which allowed its lifeblood to drain away.[24] 'Political' Catholics, like the Bishop of Piacenza, G.B. Scalabrini, and the Bishop of Cremona, Geremia Bonomelli, bewailed the fate of emigrants pitilessly exposed to those perils of the deep, and of that soul-destroying Protestantism or godless materialism and socialism which waited upon them in the New World. Pope Leo XIII had produced a critical encyclical, *Quam aerumnosa*, as early as 1888 and both the Scalabrinian fathers and the Opera Bonomelli sought to institutionalise Catholic welfare and Catholic piety in emigrant communities. In so doing, they often drifted into a coalition with local consuls or nationalist intellectuals, which did not yet seem proper within an Italy where the issue of Temporal Power remained unresolved. Above their redoubts, the Scalabrinians flew an Italian tricolour with *'religione e patria'* emblazoned on it, and Bishop Scalabrini told emigrants to revere Italy as 'their common mother'.[25] Bishop Bonomelli remarked that God had instructed the 'strong peoples' to go out and multiply, and in 1911 he publicly endorsed the Libyan War.[26] In France, the *ralliement* of the 1890s had been prefigured by collaboration between church and state in the French empire the decade before. In Italy, by 1914, the same process of accommodation was occurring, but through the empire of the Italies as much as through that of Italy.

One reason why, by then, anti-clericalism no longer seemed so relevant or rewarding a doctrine for European liberal elites or for the Vatican was the rise of socialism. Italy's socialists, however, were relatively slow to refine a policy on migration. Already, in 1893, the welfare organisation, L'Umanitaria, had been established in Milan[27] and henceforth it collected information about emigrant travail for deployment against the complacency of advocates of the 'safety-valve'. Nonetheless, as late as 1900, *Critica Sociale*, the Socialist Party's chief ideological organ, had not mentioned the issue of emigration,[28] and socialist chiefs, loyal to the principles of inter-nationalism, were still advising Italian workers abroad to join local unions and to forget 'nationalist particularism'.[29] In the decades which followed, such wide-ranging intellectuals as Gramsci and Togliatti were usually silent about the issue and, for many socialists, the real message about emigration was 'Don't'. Workers and peasants should stay home and unite to fight the bosses. This rejection of emigration, accompanied by a certain feeling that emigrants were deserters from the class front, helps to explain why regions in which socialism or, later, communism were strong, tended to have low emigration rates,[30] and, at the same time, why the left-wing political movements frequently had only a limited appeal among Italian communities abroad.

Fascism would eventually be even more peremptory in its rejection of emigration. In 1927, Dino Grandi, with Fascist fanfare, announced the abolition of the very word 'emigrant' at much the same time that the regime committed itself to winning 'the Battle of the Births' and thus rapidly augmenting the national population.[31] Grandi maintained that permanent emigration would no longer be permitted, and from 1928 formal legal restrictions on it were introduced. In the 1930s Fascism became still more strident in its demand that such emigration as there was must be channelled into an Italian empire. As Under-Secretary for Colonies, Alessandro Lessona, explained at the time of the Ethiopian War, the regime had stemmed the 'immense haemorrhage' of the past. It had understood that, properly regulated, emigration could sustain and nourish imperialism: 'Fascism [had] closed the emigration era audaciously to open the colonial one.'[32]

Another Fascist preoccupation was to attach to the regime the 9 million or more Italians who lived outside Italy.[33] By 1923 it had begun to set up a formal network of Fasci all'estero. In 1927 the Commissariato Generale dell'Emigrazione was merged into the Direzione Generale degli Italiani all'estero, and its director, the career bureaucrat Giuseppe De Michaelis, was succeeded by the Fascist official Piero Parini, even though Fasci all'estero were responsibly, or timidly, instructed not to disturb diplomatic relations or to involve themselves in the internal affairs of the host countries and, in the emigration and labour fields, Fascist Italy was long an active member of the League of Nations.[34] In 1924 the socialists' Umanitaria was closed down, and four year later the Opera Bonomelli suffered a similar fate. The regime tried to harness the financial side of emigration through the Istituto di Credito per il lavoro italiano all'estero and, eventually, in 1939, established a Commissione permanente per il rimpatrio. Government funds underwrote Italian language papers in Argentina or Belgium; vice-consuls paraded their Fascism to factory workers in Detroit or fishermen in Fremantle;[35] visiting Fascist airmen, victorious sportsmen and patriotic priests cheered and were cheered by emigrant communities; and, above all, the name of Mussolini was broadcast wherever one emigrant met another. With the spirit of Mussolini to sustain them, emigrants could walk tall as never before. Such at least was the theory of the Fascist totalitarian state which, as Grandi explained, would mean that every Italian action abroad fell under the ultimate authority of Rome and of the Duce.[36]

As with so many other aspects of Fascism, practice was not quite the same as theory. For one thing, the much trumpeted Fascist rejection of continuing emigration was as much justificatory and reactive as ideological. Mussolini himself, in April 1923, had been heard intoning: 'For whatever good or ill, emigration is a physiological necessity for the Italian people', and in May 1924 he had acted as the genial and statesmanlike host to the International Migration Conference which assembled in Rome.[37]

This international meeting, and an earlier one which had been held in 1921, had been summoned because the post-war atmosphere had turned so hostile towards emigration. In 1917 the United States had introduced a Literacy Act to curtail its immigration flow, and Canada had enacted similar legislation two years later. In 1921, United States policies became overtly racist with a quota system which limited the total of Italian immigrants in any one year to 41,721 (calculated as 3 per cent of the number of Italians in the United States population in 1910). In 1924 the figure was cut to almost zero (2 per cent of the component in 1890). During the next decade, Canada, Brazil and Australia also restricted their intake of Italians,[38] making little attempt to hide the racial motivation of their policies. Perhaps Fascism would in any case have wanted to utilise emigrants for its own benefit and certainly it was always likely to become a colonialist and imperialist regime. But the actual chronology shows that Mussolini turned his face against emigration only after the traditional host societies had shut their doors against Italians.

If there is something post hoc in Fascist attitudes to emigration, the regime's policies are not always easy to distinguish from Nationalist ones. Just as Lessona's haemorrhage metaphor of 1935 was unoriginal, so the Fasci all'estero imitated those Istituti Coloniali Italiani which had been established by Nationalists and Liberals before 1914. In the 1920s, too, it was often ex-Nationalists who most fervently publicised their concern about the 'migration problem' – historian Gioacchino Volpe was one who early indicated that the only way by which the 'open wound' of emigration could be salved was through a clear-sighted and tough-minded linking of foreign and migration policies; in other words, by creating a real Italian empire.[39] At the very least there was much continuity between Nationalist words before 1922 and Fascist deeds after 1927.

Nor was 'Fascist totalitarianism' entirely reliable in its practice in emigrant 'communities'. The cohesion of such bodies is always doubtful. Battles between local true believers ('fascism movement') and *fiancheggiatori* (fellow travellers), who were as automatically the allies of a Fascist regime as once they had been of a Liberal one and as eventually they would be of the Christian Democratic Republic, were common and were usually won by the *fiancheggiatori*.[40] The institutions of Fascism abroad promiscuously mingled monarchism, Catholicism, capitalism and Fascism, though a generic nationalism associated with a naive 'Mussolinism' was the most pervasive ideology. Perhaps petit bourgeois migrants, some local version of the 'emerging middle classes', now were more prominent in the 'rites of community' than in the past.[41] Consuls did keep dossiers on the politics of their flock and pressure could be exerted against small-time Anti-Fascists. Most important of all, Fascism's proclamation of its faith in itself and in the 'myth of Mussolini'[42] helped some Italians defend their *italianità* or sense of self in pubs, clubs and on street corners in many diverse places just as, after 1945, it would leave many such emigrants as nostalgic admirers of the Duce. But totalitarian 'control' did not always go much further than that.

The typical emigrant 'Fascist' is well-embodied in the Melbourne businessman, Gualtiero Vaccari. This sometime agent for Fiat, Snia Viscosa and other Italian companies in Australia was, for a long time, *persona gratissima* at the local consulate and seems to have provided Fascist officials with useful information. Simultaneously, however, he was not averse to contacts with the Australian secret service, itself anxious to know something about a migrant community perversely inclined to conduct its dealings in a foreign tongue. Thus doubly useful and doubly protected, in 1943 Vaccari could emerge from the war as the special spokesman of Italian Catholicism and be recognised by the Australian Labor government, influenced by its own Irish Catholic Minister of Immigration, as the 'leader' of the 'Italian community'. Here was one *furbo* who was a Fascist with the Fascists, a capitalist with the capitalists, a Catholic with the Catholics and a democrat with the democrats. Vaccari, who would briefly style himself a convinced Anti-Fascist, drew the line only against communists and their comrades (though he also had his doubts about Jews).[43]

Replete with figures like Vaccari, the emigrant world was not normally an especially suitable place for the flourishing of organised Anti-Fascism. It was true that the steady imposition of the *stato totalitario* had, in the 1920s, driven a number of dissident politicians and intellectuals abroad. These were the *fuorusciti* ('those who had left the fold') and included Carlo and Nello Rosselli (based in Paris), Gaetano Salvemini, Carlo Sforza and Luigi Sturzo (in the UK or the USA) and Palmiro Togliatti and other party cadres who took refuge, not always with Togliatti's happy fate, in Stalin's USSR.[44] In their several ways, such figures kept flying the banners of liberalism, socialism, communism and Christian Democracy. They launched political movements, most notably Giustizia e Libertà, established in Paris in 1929, newspapers and journals. They negotiated among themselves (in August 1934 setting up a reasonably united Anti-Fascist popular front after the Communists, in obedience to another change of plan in Moscow, ended their denunciation of socialists and liberals as 'social fascists'). They indefatigably orated or wrote against Mussolini's regime – Gaetano Salvemini, for one, engaged in a polemic of scores of letters and articles against Luigi Villari, the regime's most committed and prolix propagandist in the Anglo-Saxon world.[45] Except for the Communists, whose discipline and experience helped them always to keep some contact with supporters in Italy, these Anti-Fascists' 'genuine popular base' was slight indeed.

A humble but emblematic figure was Omero Schiassi, ex-volunteer, moderate socialist, lover of Dante, intellectual leader of Anti-Fascism in the Italian community in Melbourne and, until the anti-Semitic legislation brought new immigrants to Australia, Vaccari's great enemy. Reduced to living in a garret and surviving on a pittance earned by teaching his native language, Schiassi refused to compromise either in his Anti-Fascist writing and orating or in that style of dressing and mode of speech which expressed the fact that he was a gentleman and an intellectual.[46]

A critical historian has written unkindly that Schiassi had only a 'one-person organisation'[47] and, though this gibe may be an ex-aggeration, it is true that, at least until Italy's entry into the Second World War, the *fuorusciti*, whether dwelling in Australia, North America or non-fascist Europe, were often lonely and isolated, oppressed by a sense of irrelevance or failure, prey to ideological and personal bickering or to a sense of lost nationality[48] and, of course, to persecution by the local representatives of Fascism. Paris, because of that city's intellectual prestige, its nearness to Italy and the long-standing and relatively organised nature of France's Italian immigrant community, provoked the most notorious example of Fascist violence. In 1937 the Rosselli brothers were murdered by Cagoulards, French fascists working in the pay and at the behest of the Rome government.[49]

An Anti-Fascist brought up in Mussolini's regime confided honestly to his diary: 'without the war I would have remained an intellectual with predominantly literary interests'.[50] What he had to say may be applied to the *fuorusciti*. It was only the war which gave them the chance to end their irrelevance and to leave their exile. At least by 1942, the Italia Libera movement, with branches throughout the emigrant world, had been recognised as a serious body by the Anglo-American leadership, and, in 1945, the government of Ferruccio Parri would try to implement its ideals and introduce democracy, *Giustizia e Libertà* (or Anglo-American) style, into Italy.

Notoriously Parri would fail. His short-lived Partito d'Azione aroused enthusiasm only among intellectuals of goodwill. In this failure to find a mass base, the Partito d'Azione made manifest in Italy what had always been true of the Anti-Fascists in emigrant communities. Despite some recent myth-making to the contrary, the emigrants from the Italies had been little affected by intellectual Anti-Fascism. If anyone was to translate the 'spirit of the Resistance' abroad, it would have to be those Italians who, after 1945, resumed their departures from the peninsula with an alacrity, knowledge and sense of inevitability which seemed to imply, in regard to emigration at least, that Fascism had indeed been a parenthesis in Italian history.

Nor was political discourse within Italy much amended after 1945. Beset by economic crisis and fearing the politics of the unemployed, the Christian Democrat Prime Minister, Alcide De Gasperi, whose personal Resistance had been assisted by a job in the Vatican Library (there, perhaps appropriately, he introduced the Dewey system), and who had not joined the *fuorusciti*, suggested in 1948, after an electoral tour of the South, that the best solution for poor Italians was 'to learn a language and go abroad'.[51] His younger colleague and future Prime Minister, Mariano Rumor, praised emigration in a more clinical metaphor as that process which might 'safeguard the domestic balance against the pressure of the masses'.[52] Other moderate politicians did not demur, and even the Partito d'Azione had to admit that emigration was a necessary tonic for Italy's social problems.[53] In March 1949, the Director-General of Emigration, whose job had been restored with the fall of Fascism, thought, for the sake of good order and the country, 4 million Italians urgently had to go.[54]

Only from the extremes of the new Republican political system were there objections. Communists, including Antonio Giolitti, who was denying at least some family traditions, condemned the re-utilisation of the safety-valve either as a metaphor or as a practice and demanded protection for all emigrants against capitalist exploitation.[55] Nationalists and Fascists recalled how Italy was 'a lighthouse of civilisation and a Great Power of work' and demanded that it not accept being treated as a museum or a cemetery. It was unfair, they said, that Italy had lost all its colonies. A change of regime had not meant an alteration in vital national interests.[56]

Neither De Gasperi nor Pope Pius XII was completely averse to this sort of language but, as has been seen in the previous chapter (pp. 112–13), the Christian Democrat Republic realistically accepted that 'Africa' was lost forever. Instead, the best policy, as enunciated, for example, in the Papal Allocution, *Exsul Familia*, in 1952, was for government agents and priests to do all that they could to smooth the paths of emigration and to expedite the 'assimilation' of immigrants into the systems of at least the Catholic parts of their host societies. Only in the late 1960s, 1970s and 1980s, as emigration dwindled and finally ceased, would Italian state and church reassert their right or duty to preserve, foster or reinvent *italianità* abroad.[57]

With the partial exception of the Fascist era, the story of official Italian policy towards emigrants from the Italies between 1860 and 1960 is, thus, largely a negative one. As far as the Italian state was concerned, in the final analysis the emigrants were on their own. What, then, of the policies of the states in which they settled, in which emigrants turned into immigrants?

Here the issues dealt with in this book become even more vast and any summary can only be superficial. Nevertheless, some observations can be made. The first is, of course, that of variety. Situations changed over time and altered from place to place. The history of Italian immigration is the history of a host of processes in many diverse countries.

Take the issues of image, of social position and of status, for example. It is a commonplace that Italian emigrants were poor (though modern research has indicated that they were not the poorest of the poor) and rural (though that general term cries out for precise definition). It is also usually thought that peasants had a tough time, at least in the early years of their immigration, and could only

Table 6.5 Emigration by destination 1876–1975

Year	Number (millions)	
a Within Europe		
1876–85	0.85	
1886–95	0.97	
1896–05	1.89	
1906–1915	2.43	
1916–25	1.29	
1926–35	0.81	
1936–45	0.15	
1946–55	1.30	
1956–65	2.43	
1966–75	1.30	
b US and Canada	*US*	*Canada*
1876–85	0.09	0.001
1886–95	0.38	0.007
1896–1905	1.30	0.02
1906–15	2.38	0.12
1916–25	0.74	0.03
1926–35	0.26	0.01
1936–45	0.05	0.001
1946–55	0.15	0.12
1956–65	0.17	0.20
1966–75	0.16	0.11
c South America	*Argentina*	*South America in total*
1876–85	0.18	0.33
1886–95	0.41	1.00
1896–1905	0.49	1.01
1906–15	0.72	0.97
1916–25	0.38	0.47
1926–35	0.26	0.32
1936–45	0.03	0.04
1946–55	0.44	0.72
1956–65	0.05	0.18
1966–75	0.01	0.03
d Oceania		
1876–85	0.0001	
1886–95	0.002	
1896–1905	0.006	
1906–15	0.009	
1916–25	0.02	
1926–35	0.02	
1936–45	0.009	
1946–55	0.12	
1956–65	0.15	
1966–75	0.08	

Source: Adapted from G. Rosoli (ed.), *Un secolo di emigrazione italiana 1876–1976*, Rome, 1978, pp. 345–7

with difficulty find a place in the financial, intellectual and power structures of their host countries.

But do these generalisations hold wherever Italians went? Over recent decades S.L. Baily[58] and others have shown that there were great differences in the experiences of Italians who emigrated to South rather than to North America. In Argentina, Italians had an especially massive presence. They composed 57 per cent of foreign immigrants in the decade from 1881 to 1890, 62 per cent in 1891–1900, 45 per cent in 1901–10, and again 57 per cent from 1947 to 1951.[59] At least in the short term, Italians did well there. In a country in which it was estimated in 1895 that 81 per cent of the industrial workforce was Italian, as was a third to a half of the urban population of Buenos Aires,[60] an Italian contribution has been celebrated in music, architecture, literature, science, educational theory and practice, engineering and psychology,[61] and might also be admitted in Peronism and some Argentinian military thought and action. But it was as workers that Italians were especially sought after and admired. In 1911, it has recently been recalled with pride, a commentator could state that Argentina had been 'made' by the combination of English capital and Italian labour.[62] Italians pioneered the trade unions both in Argentina and Brazil. As Baily had noted, in South American societies, Italians were not piece-workers or black-legs but the aristocrats of labour.

This idea of an Italian triumph should not be pushed too far, however. Romolo Murri, in his journey through South America, had also noted how rapidly many Italians merged into the existing Spanish and Portuguese communities (he claimed, not altogether convincingly, that women immigrants were the first to slough off their nationality).[63] The hopes of liberal economist, Luigi Einaudi, in 1898 that Argentina contained a rising and greater Italy, which could give the same cultural and financial stimulation to the homeland that the USA had brought to the UK, were soon dashed,[64] even though, at least until 1914, patriotic Argentinian politicians would anxiously urge that the *argentinizzazione* of Italian immigrants be accelerated. A network of Italian patriotic and religious (and religio-patriotic) institutions did spread in Argentina, as it had in Brazil, both before and after 1914, but, even so, it was reported in the latter country that Fascism was no more than a vague and generic concept, even among the leadership of the Italian community.[65] *Italianità* in South America would remain a nebulous matter, except where subsidy or public occasion encouraged its disclosure. For immigrants, there as elsewhere, their Italian ethnicity, defined as the 'core values' of the Italian nation state, was only a part, and generally a small part, of their identity and to be cherished only in particular circumstances. 'Latins', such emigrants might frequently remain; Italians, they usually were not.

It is normally assumed that Italians fared worse in Anglo-Saxon countries than in the Latin world, that they were more unpopular and, if tolerated at all, were the objects of more strenuous official assimilationism. Acceptance could come only after Italians had abandoned their history and culture; otherwise they represented the 'olive peril'. In Britain, for example, *The Times* was already, in 1820, inveighing against Italian boy organ-grinders. In the face of continuing immigration to Britain there followed, throughout the nineteenth century, a general decline in Italy's image, perhaps best expressed by the medical journal the *Lancet*, which, in 1879, warned knowingly that 'the Italian colony would soon become a standing menace to the public health of London'.[66] Nonetheless, 'Italians', the most numerous group being from the Upper Valtaro in the hinterland of Parma, did establish themselves in London (especially near Holborn), Glasgow, Bristol, Bedford and other places. They found employment in restaurants and fish and chip shops – in South Wales, somewhat oddly, they dominated the temperance café market[67] – as ice-cream vendors, barbers, entertainers of some description, models (a French paper remarked with Gallic lightness: '*l'Italie qui était jadis un modèle de pays est devenu le pays des modèles*')[68] or mosaic and other construction workers. As a young historian in Scotland has accurately but somewhat insouciantly remarked: 'fortunately none of these categories threatened the existing native workforce'.[69]

If work was best done quietly, 'community' organisation was also most effective when its real character was left covert and private. Such ambassadors as Antonino Di San Giuliano, before the First World War, and Dino Grandi, in the 1930s, were unusually active as nationalist or Fascist propagandists, but such formal politics trickled slowly and reluctantly into immigrant minds. Politics from below could also have an innocent or uncertain side as was the case with the patriotic Cafaro brothers in Glasgow. In 1908 they took to publishing the four-page *La Scozia*. Filippo Cafaro pressed its sales from an 'office of legal information', which retailed 'information of all kinds' and 'white and brown bread' daily.[70] As historian Lucio Sponza has remarked in a comment which holds true in many Italian 'communities', at best 'the Italian papers published in London (and

... Glasgow) ... were important vehicles of conservatism and conformism, and never ceased to persevere in this role which they wrapped in a vague emotional appeal to national values and nationalistic pride'.[71]

The significance of the Cricket Club Italiano, opened in 1897,[72] may be questioned and a Mutual Aid (Mutuo Soccorso) society failed in Glasgow amid recrimination. But there can be little doubt that the clubs and societies and the financial currents and hierarchies of status and power which lay behind them constituted the most significant glue of any community. Typical was the Società italiana di mutuo soccorso e collocamento fra impiegati d'Albergo e Ristorante of London. This body promised that it would protect its members' economic interests and help to place the more humble or most newly arrived in employment. It probably did so, but, Sponza has indicated, it also policed the many gradations in the life of hotel clerks, cooks and waiters and ensured that the pecking order, established by the first arrivals and maintained thereafter by the most wealthy and powerful, would survive.[73]

In Britain, it seems, the Italian 'community', for all its small size, for all its eventual prosperity and for all the prejudice and ignorance of its British hosts, was a complex place of political and economic struggle. But the major meeting ground of Italians and Anglo-Saxons was the United States. The very word 'America' evoked the promise of wealth and freedom inscribed in many a peasant heart and the phrase *'fare l'America'* entered speech as the equivalent of 'to make a fortune'. To a considerable extent, the story of Italo-Americans has been sketched above. It is a tale of a massive and always increasing migration, especially, by the twentieth century, of 'Southerners'. Many would try to be *furbi* and some would succeed. In the oral history archive *Voices from Ellis Island* there is a lovely account of a poor Abruzzese getting a dozen bottles of 'Centerbain' (*sic* – really Cent'erbe) past United States customs officials on the grounds that this 90 per cent proof *liquore* was medicinal. His family, the migrant swore, believed that the magical elixir would cure any known sickness.[74]

For most immigrants, however, manipulating the system was a more onerous or unrewarding task. All Italians were likely to confront the profound sense of racial superiority held by Anglo-Saxon, German, Irish and even sometimes black[75] Americans towards the new arrivals. Perhaps this racial prejudice had its most damaging effects when it was simply part of ordinary Americans' 'unspoken assumptions' as, for example, when in the 1930s a commentator opined that Italians were instinctively good at fishing in the same ways that gulls were.[76]

Such views were nourished by the partially justified suspicion that many immigrants were 'sojourners' – sometimes the phrase '*fare l'America*' ran on '*e cumprare lu campu*'[77] ('to make your fortune in America is to buy land back home'). But the more normal, and wholly unjustified, stimulus to Italophobia was simple racial theoretics, the fear that Italians, with their 'Mediterranean' stock, would pollute Aryan America's racial purity. It was this racism which was the essential trigger for the anti-Italian legislation of 1917, 1921 and 1924. It would still be powerful after the war against Fascism and Nazi racism had been won, and was expressed anew in the McCarran–Walter Act of 1952.[78] This last piece of legislation, which reaffirmed the earlier restriction on Italians, would not be repealed until 1965.

Obfuscating to some extent the racist bases of United States immigration policies was the ideology of 'the melting pot'. In that crucible of Americanness, all immigrants were meant willingly to deposit their histories and languages, cultures and identities, so that they could emerge as new men and women, tempered by truth, justice and the American way.

American policies towards immigrants may have had their racist features but they were scarcely unique in that regard. Even after 1945, both Germany and Switzerland assessed their Italian immigrants as no more than 'guest workers', who should be denied both any permanent place in local culture and any serious political rights. Still in the 1960s, signs saying 'no dogs or Italians allowed' could appear in parts of the Germanic world without much sanction or rebuke.[79] In Australia, which, in the early 1950s, Italian planners briefly deemed a 'new America' in terms of prosperity, potential (and racial prejudice), liberal social scientists could define Italians as 'black' and endorse official objections to the use of 'the foreign language' (*sic*) in public places. A good Australian, such experts advised, would acknowledge the supremacy of the 'Anglo-Saxon race' throughout time and space.[80]

However, already by then, some intellectuals, notably in the United States, began to see how unjust were the recipes of the melting pot and how uneven were its results. In the 1960s and 1970s it became possible for Italo-Americans to admit to having 'roots' and a historiography began to develop explaining just what those roots might be.

It is time to turn aside from the more or less illiberal 'planning' or fumbling of governments, either Italian or of the host countries, and examine the emigrants themselves, as they sought to avoid or manipulate official attention and manage their own lives. Who were the migrants? Why did they leave? Why did some of them go back? How did the experience of the wider world impinge on them?

Given, certainly, the present state of scholarship and, perhaps, the historical reality, any attempt to depict those ordinary immigrants must be impressionistic. Dots of individual detail may merge to suggest a general outline, at least if the advice of nineteenth-century sociologist Stefano Jacini that every *paese* was not 'a closed world but participated in the life of all the rest of the social world',[81] or of modern historian Charles Tilly that 'the history of European migration is the history of European social life', is to be believed.[82]

Take the village of Sambuca in western Sicily, for example. In the best monograph so far published on Italian emigration, Donna Gabaccia has vividly depicted the complexity of that *paese*'s relations with the United States (and with Italy). Though the people of Sambuca were unusual in their political militancy (in the twentieth century the *paese* would acquire the reputation of being Sicily's 'little Moscow'), they were not, says Gabaccia, anomalous. Rather, she urges, emigration should everywhere be pondered as an aspect of international 'class formation'.[83] Moreover, the original *paese* and any 'community' of *Sambuchesi* established abroad should necessarily be reviewed in E.P. Thompsonian terms, as a happening and not a thing: 'at best, communities resembled quarrelsome families: a communal orientation structured conflict, it did not eliminate it'.[84]

Those who emigrated were thus not merely *Sambuchesi* (let alone 'Southern' 'amoral familists'[85] or puppets of the other ridiculously all-embracing categories once favoured by social science). Instead, with graphic detail, Gabaccia has estimated that, between 1881 and 1935, 11 per cent of the village elite migrated, 13 per cent of shepherds, 37 per cent of artisans, 42 per cent of the poorest peasants and 23 per cent of middle peasants. Men were more likely to go than women. Family positioning was also significant. Since the youngest child often inherited the land, oldest children were wont to leave. Some 75 per cent of illegitimates departed. A family death, too, could precipitate emigration (Gabaccia detects a 'fear of stepmother' syndrome). Those about to be called up frequently emigrated, and so did an unusually high number of dentists. As Gabaccia concludes convincingly: in Sambuca 'much more than economics influenced any individual's decision' to emigrate.[86]

Nor did the diversity end there. In the United States *paesani* might go to the Louisiana sugar fields. If they did, many would become 'birds of passage' (despite the arrival of women immigrants from the 1890s) and eventually return to Sicily. In Louisiana they were not likely to be militant (though some mutual aid societies flourished in New Orleans), but rather comprised a sort of 'classless ethnic community'. In Illinois, by contrast, middlemen played a key role and dominated community welfare societies, sometimes criminalising them. Labour militancy was again weak, except in some mining towns in the south of the state. Fascism, on the other hand, had a relatively high appeal in Italo-American Chicago. Florida and New York were different again. In the Tampa tobacco factories, unionism, Anti-Fascism and anti-clericalism were strong, as was inter-ethnic collaboration with Hispanic and even black Cuban fellow workers. In Brooklyn, the unity was similar but weaker, especially because artisan emigrants often viewed themselves as superior and tried to obtain local hegemony, for example through a *Sambuchese festa*, organised from 1889. As Gabaccia concludes challengingly: 'Sambucesi [*sic*] appeared in various locations as peasant leftists, migrant harvesters, padrone slaves, immigrant familists, militant factory workers and factionalized small businessmen. Who would guess that all were also fellow villagers',[87] let alone fellow Sicilians and fellow Italians?

Nor does the buffeting of too simple an image of the 'Italian community' and what it means to be an 'Italo-American', an 'Italian ethnic' or even 'an Italian' which results from such a conclusion end there. A detailed study of Tampa, for example, gives more insight into the 'Latin alliance' (and its radical anarchist or socialist political purpose) which flourished in local factories until the Depression.[88] A similar bloc has been located among *Molisano* and Basque sugar workers in inter-war north Queensland;[89] and between Sicilians and Maltese in post-1945 western England.[90] A *più grande Italia*, it seems, may exist in the hearts of the denizens of many a 'little Italy'; it just cannot be relied on to have the same borders lusted after by the leaders of the Italian nation state. Frontiers in the immigrant world are always likely to escape the science of the map-makers. As a pre-1914 woman immigrant to Melbourne has put it: 'I migrated to America. It did not occur to me that Australia was not in fact America.'[91]

Nonetheless, even where Latin alliances bloomed, more con-ventional *italianità* could also be constructed. In Tampa, L'Unione Italiana was set up in 1894 with a Sicilian imprint – one of its earliest preoccupations was how to ensure the retention of Sicilian funeral customs. By 1900 L'Unione had triumphantly purchased its own 'Italian cemetery'; Sicilianness was merging into Italianness. This process continued. When the club erected its own clubhouse it would be 'built in the Italian Renaissance style, decorated with classic columns, terra-cotta relief, and a profusion of marble'. It would also boast a theatre (where visiting opera companies could be accom-modated), a cinema, a dance-floor, a library (notably of leftist tracts), a *cantina*, a bowling alley and other recreation areas.[92] There, members could eat, drink, gamble, negotiate business deals, find information, organise family marriages and expand or contract their identities. All sorts of Italies and quite a number of Americas thronged its rooms, as they did in the myriad of 'Italian' clubs which sprang up in every immigrant centre.

Amid this eclecticism can any generalisations still be made? One who thinks so is Dino Cinel. In a fine local study of Italians in San Francisco[93] and a less convincing one of return migration, Cinel has reiterated a familiar theme in recent social history by emphasising the extent to which emigrants controlled their own destinies. His Italo-Americans are instigators of 'conservative change'. They emig-rate in order to achieve certain ends in Italy (the purchase of land, higher social status), and, whether they return or not, they never forget their ties with the old country (even though the Second World War taught them to be American). They are thus 'traditional modernisers': 'traditions may even have been the strongest resources immigrants had for effecting change'.[94] Simultaneously they may well be possessed by a traumatic sense of exile[95] and failure. Com-posing a kind of 'emerging middle class'[96] (Cinel replicates without comment De Felice's term for the mass basis of Fascism) which has never won full recognition, emigrants, despite their many regional variations, do have much in common.

In a study of Italians in Toronto, John Zucchi has similarly located some unity in all the diversity. His 'Italo-Torontans' successfully balance multiple identities – they can be Italians or *paesani*, Italo-Torontans or Canadians, depending on need or situation.[97] Zucchi also follows Robert Harney[98] in indicating that *padroni* or bosses had duties as well as rights, and he demonstrates that both local commercial networks and the local church usually operated on the assumption that all 'Italian' immigrants were Italian. So, too, did the Canadian internment authorities, and their British and Australian[99] counterparts in 1940 (the USA, after 1941, would be more liberal: as President F.D. Roosevelt remarked, not altogether benignly, the 'wops' were 'a lot of opera singers' and did not frighten him as a potential fifth column[100]). In many an aspect of life, whatever the reality, the processes of Italian nationalisation pressed in upon the immigrant.

And yet Gabaccia's emphasis on the textured nature of emigrant societies is highly persuasive. No student of Italian emigration should forget that being an Italian and being an emigrant are matters that are subject to change, and that any emigrant 'community' will be a cover for rival factions and forces. Italians in emigration varied by region, by gender, by age, by skill or employment, by class, by politics, by venue, by time of departure, by whether the group was composed of family, *paesani*, people from the same region or other 'Italians', and doubtless by a myriad of further things. Harney remarked wisely on one occasion that class analysis should not be diverted by an ethnic one, *ubi panis, ibi patria*,[101] and the same generalisation can be made about all the other ways in which people are distinguished. Similarly, American historian Larry Levine has explained:

> Contemporary scholars have demonstrated again and again that, in penetrating the culture of a neglected group, historians often find more than they bargained for. What looked like a group becomes an amalgam of groups; what looked like a culture becomes a series of cultures.[102]

Nonetheless, despite this endless fluidity and variegation, some patterns can be seen or imagined. With all the qualifications and movement, with all the change over time and space, with all the subjectivity or situationality of Italianness, the emigrants, as they pursued the highways and byways of the world, did carry with them cultural baggage, even as they often, willingly or unwillingly, consciously or unconsciously, added to it on the way. Some of that baggage was transported from that other great and ambiguous 'Italian' organisation, the Universal or Roman Catholic Church, some from the Italies and rather less from the official culture of 'United' 'Italy'.

7

CULTURES AND IDEOLOGY FOR EXPORT
Italy and the Italies 1860–1960

In 1931, Giuseppe Prezzolini, an intellectual who in his arrogance and cynicism had been as responsible as any for the rise of Fascism but by then had a certain aura of dissidence, was managing the Casa Italiana, the 'house' of Italian culture, in New York. It was, he confided to his diary, something of a labour of Sisyphus, especially so far as his emigrant co-nationals were concerned: 'They are not Italians', he noted,

> because they have never been Italians. Here they have taken on certain American habits, but at base they have remained southern peasants without a culture, without learning, without a language, people for whom the moment of '*italianità*' has never arrived. They leave Italy before being Italians. They have settled here but have not become real Americans.[1]

It is a wonderfully, if largely unconsciously, evocative passage, full of the bafflement, the uneasy contempt, the fear, the disappointment, which, after 1860, so often divided an intellectual 'maker of Italy' from the people of the Italies. Prezzolini's diary entry is a sort of 'order of the day' in the continuing battle between legal Italy and real Italy, between the homogenising processes of the 'nationalisation of the masses', as commanded by the 'lesser examination-passing classes',[2] and the heterogeneity of real life. It is also an order of the day which, like many proclaimed by the Italian army, needs to be read between the lines. Male, bourgeois, intellectual and a nationalist, Prezzolini was bound to write certain things, even in the privacy of his diary. His words and phrases were little more than clichés which could be repeated by a wealthy Neapolitan liberal like Croce, by an 'educated' northern Scalabrinian missionary priest and by many another real or aspirant member of the Italian elite. But even while they enthusiastically embraced 'modernity', such Italians knew that it was an ersatz product and that their own most heartfelt identities owed at least as much to the culture of the Italies.

But what were these cultures? One place to start answering such a question is with the women of the Italies and especially with those who, in one form or another, experienced emigration and in some fashion participated in the *Weltpolitiken* of the *paesi*.

On the surface, Italy has seemed until very recently a highly sexist country. Amid the euphoria of the Risorgimento, Cristina Belgiojoso, in the very first issue of *Nuova Antologia*, may have announced 'that woman is neither morally nor intellectually inferior to man ... is a matter now generally recognised and admitted', and predicted that the new Italy, which did not 'fear to separate itself from things of the past', would swiftly accept and duly benefit from a reasoned equality between the genders,[3] but this happy future was slow to arrive. Criminologist Cesare Lombroso, one of the few Italian intellectuals of his era with a genuine international reputation, was as convinced of the physiological and thus permanent inferiority of women (those 'weak' and 'susceptible' beings) as he was, more scandalously at the time, of the phrenological differences between 'Northerners' and 'Southerners'.[4] If Liberal Italy in any sense constituted a 'democracy in the making', it was not one which included women.

Fascism hardly improved matters. Though initially there were a few futuro-fascist women in the radical urban sections of the movement (and the first all-woman *fascio* was set up in Monza in March 1920), once in power Mussolini's regime determinedly restricted a woman, certainly in discourse and perhaps in reality, to her 'traditional' role of *sposa e madre esemplare* (exemplary wife and mother)[5] – a phrase still to be found engraven on many an Italian woman's tombstone.[6] Mussolini's own myth was blatantly masculist – his sexual prowess was flaunted; he was pre-eminently a man 'with balls' (though his ulcer problems from the mid-1920s might prompt some doubt about the actual sexual appetite and performance of the mature Duce). More oppressive perhaps for Italian women was the entente cordiale between Fascism and the Catholic Church. It was the church which was the more prurient and which meddled most obtrusively in Italian bedrooms. If Luisa Passerini's moving account of the 'passive dissent' of Turin housewives is to be believed,[7] questions like abortion and birth control, in which the church led and Fascism followed, ensured most directly that many women remained alienated from the processes of nationalisation and fascist-isation. Though Fascism, in its ambiguous commitment to 'modern-ity', offered, in its parades, clubs and other areas of dressage, some opportunities of freedom or independence to some young women, Mussolini's regime scarcely brought women to the forefront of political and cultural life.[8]

Women were finally granted the vote in Republican Italy, due to both the active female participation in the armed Resistance after 1943 and international fashion. Nonetheless, the Christian Democrat Italy incarnated in a figure like Pope Pius XII had scarcely moderated its reactionary views on gender and indeed zealously propagandised the sanctity of a figure such as the new saint, Maria Goretti, who, aged twelve, had defended her virginity and honour at the expense of her life.[9] Only after 1968, and especially as reflected in the referenda on divorce (1974) and abortion (1981), did Italian women at last gain some of the political acceptance which Belgiojoso had foreshadowed in 1866.

If progress was slow in 'legal' Italy, it seemed no more rapid in the *paesi*. Gender relations were one of the issues which made Italy a suitable object of study for modern anthropologists and thus, by definition, a place of 'otherness'.[10] Anthropologists alleged that concepts of 'honour' and 'shame' lay at the heart of 'Southern' society. The myth of the 'ram' and the 'billy-goat' was deemed pervasive in Sicily, and a man's greatest preoccupation was to avoid being '*incornuto*' ('wearing horns', being made a cuckold).[11] The maxim '*Moglie e buoi dai paesi tuoi*' ('Wife and oxen from your own village') was said to echo through every *paesano*'s mind.

Recent historiography, though still limited in its extent, has begun to amend the static and unilateral nature of this image. In this amendment the fundamental reason being adduced as to why gender relations in the *paesi* were not as simple as some anthropologists had maintained is emigration.

As already noted in the previous chapter, it is a commonplace that men tended to emigrate first. In particular, those numerous emig-rants who saw themselves as 'birds of passage' and who had gone confident that eventually they would return, usually left their women (and children) at home. In the flux of an emigrant's life, they might sometimes return home, conceive another child and then depart again; they might also sometimes take with them an elder son, or gradually summon their sons and eventually their wife and daughters to join them. The women, left on their own in the *paese* for a year, a decade or more, were called *vedove bianche*, 'white widows'.[12]

Already, before 1914, commentators began noticing that, in the absence of their men, these *vedove bianche* managed. They worked; they ran the household finances, selling and owning property on their own account; they brought up and educated their children, and arranged and defined their own family life. Perhaps they nurtured that mother–son relationship which has led contemporary Italians to joke that Christ must have been a fellow national 'because he lived at home until he was thirty, presumed his mother was a virgin, and she certainly believed he was God'.[13] These were women, who, whether by force of circumstance or not, whether breaking from tradition or not, empowered themselves. Their special version of family and society was brilliantly described by a visiting English-woman, Anne Macdonell, in 1908. Journeying into the Abruzzi, that ruggedly mountainous region which ran from the east of Rome to the Adriatic coast, Macdonell found that emigration was an ancient part of life, amended recently by large-scale departure to the USA: 'the commonest decoration of an Abruzzo village [nowadays] is the emigration advertisement of the Transatlantic liners'.[14] This emigration, however, had different effects on male and female:

> As yet very rarely do the women go; and when they begin to go in great numbers it is all over with the Abruzzo, for they are the sap of its life. You have always to take the woman into account. One gathers from old tales and old records of the country that she has ever been prominent as chief organizer and counsellor. Today, however, a great deal more of the bread-winning falls to her share. You may say, indeed, that all the careers are open to her – especially the hard ones. As a rule, she is better developed physically than her men-folk and handsomer, too.

Indeed, Macdonell ran on, there were

> places where one is hardly aware of the men. Woman fills the picture. Household work and child-bearing form only part of her life. She gathers the winter fuel – a formidable task that lasts the summer through; she bakes the bread; she spins the wool and the flax; she dyes the cloth; she makes the clothes; she keeps the home-flock; she builds the houses even – or does the most arduous part of the masonry; she is an astonishing porter, and,

with majestic gait, will carry anything you like on her head, from your heaviest luggage to a plough or an iron bedstead. As yet I have seen no woman blacksmith, but should not be surprised to hear that there were many.[15]

Macdonell's story of women empowered was not confined to the physical sphere. Women bought and sold land. Women were said sometimes to be warriors or brigands. Women defined a family very different from that which cliché teaches us to expect:

> To hear the children talk of their homes, you might believe that a matriarchy existed. Their introduction of themselves to you is never complete till they have given full information as to the Christian name and cognomen of their mother, sometimes even of their grandmother. The father may be quite creditable and even useful; he may even have paid for the boots on the little feet; more often he is the man who sends strange postage stamps from across the sea. But the mother is to be obeyed. She rules across the hearth, and shapes the young lives. She is the guardian of the faith, and of the old lore that will long compete with the newer science of the schoolmaster,[16]

the 'science', of course, of the 'nationalisation of the masses'.

Nor did this power necessarily leach away if the women emigrated, for often in emigration, as in Italy, a Sicilian saying applied: 'The husband is like the government at Rome, all pomp; the wife is like the Mafia, all power.'[17]

Let one emblematic story suffice. It is that of Emma Ciccotosto,[18] an emigrant who came from that same region of the Abruzzi described by Macdonell, but journeyed to Western Australia rather than to the United States. Emma Ciccotosto was born at Casalbordino, on the hills above Vasto, in 1926. She was brought up by her mother and grandmother and these women instructed her in natural lore and appropriate behaviour, in cooking and in Casalbordino's and their family's own special history.

In due time, the father came back from America, having lost what fortune he had made on an earlier trip. But, indefatigable, he sold what little land he had, handed over his wife and three children to the mercy of a landlord and departed again, this time for Western Australia. There, despite the Depression and the primitive conditions of bush life, he began to prosper. Remittances reached Casalbordino. Finally in 1937, a ticket arrived for his son and, two years later, opportunely before Italy's entry into the Second World War, Emma and her mother also boarded ship for Australia (an elder sister, who was already married, stayed at Casalbordino). On landfall, Emma would recall,

> the first person we recognised was my brother, who was waving at us, and then my mother said, 'There is your father'. I looked at him, he had a moustache, and I felt very strange. I said to myself, 'I can't call him papa'.[19]

In Australia, eventually, Emma made good, first on a farm in the bush and then at Fremantle, the port of Perth. She married young and brought up three sons and a daughter. She worked on the farm and then in a biscuit factory. She cherished and controlled a husband who lacked her canny monetary sense and who sometimes had a roving eye. Before he died, she and her husband made a return trip to Italy, going back to Casalbordino and, like any foreigners, also tramping the tourist beat through Venice, Florence and Rome. Emma Ciccotosto endured and throve and loved her neighbours and herself (while remaining a little sceptical of priests, politicians and intellectuals). Today she still radiates a certain sort of 'Italian' 'culture'. It mingles materialism, generosity and hospitality, good or abundant cooking, a willingness to touch and to sing, to argue and to talk, a fierce determination, a truthfulness, a narrowness, a literalness, a loyalty, a power, a love and, above all, a sense of her own human value.

It is tempting to conclude that, in this amalgam of qualities, Emma Ciccotosto embodies the Italian family, and that it is this family which is the most characteristic export of emigration. But, if such is their conclusion, historians at once confront a complication. As historical anthropologist R.M. Bell has noted, the family, like everything else, is a process and not a thing and is subject to change over time and space.[20] This change, it seems, may accelerate with emigration, either because of the effect on the family of the long-term and repeated absence of its male 'head' or because of the changes induced by translocation.

It is Donna Gabaccia who has written most pertinently on this subject. In her first book, a study of Sicilian migration to New York, Gabaccia argued that '*la famiglia*' was, to a very considerable degree, a product of the new urban environment of emigration.[21] The 'Italian family' was not a timeless affair but a necessary product of the crowded tenements of the late nineteenth- and early twentieth-century North American city. It was new, a response by emigrants to new conditions and, if it eventually became 'Italian', that was because it was reimported to Italy with returning migrants, or with ideas borrowed from the much admired New World.

The Sicilian family in the nineteenth century, Gabaccia warns sensibly, should not be assumed to replicate that of the twentieth. Rather, she argues, a sense of kin and of the materialist purpose of that family and its strategy in managing its members' fortunes was greatly enhanced by emigration. At the same time, the intricate hierarchies of artisan and peasant life in the *paese*, and their accompanying ceremonies, were simplified by emigration and by the practical realities of tenement living. Even parent–child relations were drastically altered in America as parents, saving for their own house in a world where renting was more common and costly than at home, themselves infringed family solidarity and altered traditional parent–child relations. All these revolutionary domestic events, concludes Gabaccia, had their frightening starkness and radicalism cloaked, in migrant minds, by the claim that basic ideals in the New World remained identical with those in the old, by the myth of the all-embracing 'Italian family'.[22]

Other recent historians tell a somewhat similar story. Fortunata Piselli, in a fine study of Calabria, has concentrated less on what the family did in emigration than on what emigration did to the family. She sees the Second World War as a sort of watershed. Before then emigration tended to reinforce family ties. After 1950, when Calabria was exposed directly to the attractions and perils of the market economy, emigration became more likely to destroy the family in a general atmosphere of each person for himself and the devil take the hindmost. Traditionally emigration acted, she says, as a sort of safety-valve, not so much for Italian politics as for the rigid and complex structures of the extended family. In particular, emigration could condition the more extreme requirements of the *comparaggio* (or godparent) relationship, and offer a partial outlet from the sometimes hereditary and always crucial patron–client networks which criss-crossed the *paese* and dominated so many of its dealings with the world (and even, she says, with the priesthood).[23] As a hortatory and monitory local saying went: 'Your godfather is your godfather until death, even if you don't come back for fifty years.'[24] But, in fact, if neither *comparaggio* nor the rest of the family was working well, emigration could be a way of escape from such elemental troubles. By contrast, post-Fascist emigration, which was still more massive than before, imposed on Calabria and *compaesani* emigrants a sort of free market in kinship and marriage, which was manipulated for materialist and power ends more ruthlessly and aggressively than in the past. So, too, was *comparaggio*. Every part of life was adjusted to the national politics of clientelism[25] and to a 'criminalised' *mentalité* and reality in which, at least according to one English commentator, the *'ndrangheta*, the local version of the Mafia, acted as an all-powerful cultural system.[26]

However they may differ as to detail, Piselli and Gabaccia, in their sensitivity to local, national and multinational contexts, act as a useful corrective to a too nostalgic reading of the history of the Italian family. From 1860 to 1960, the 'Italian family' was not a single nor a sempiternal entity and was as subject to international influences as any other. And yet it would be equally mistaken to conclude that the family had little meaning for Italians. If only because the national state was ineffectual or unrealistic in its policies and ambitions, and emigrants were by their very nature people who sought to prevent too much intrusion into their lives and fortunes by nationalising and homogenising officials or intellectuals, Italians at home and abroad did frequently find a special part of their identity in their family, however much the definition and lived reality of that family was changing over time.

But what happened when family spread out into a 'community' and into a so-called *ambiente* – that certain architecture and design, that aroma of garlic and coffee and olive oil and tomato, that special atmosphere which Italians are thought to create in every 'little Italy' and, of course, in every lively piazza and every luminous *centro storico* on the peninsula itself? To what extent did Italians carry this *ambiente* with them along the paths of emigration?

Here the literature is divided in its answers. According to some analysts Italians in emigration do indeed try to re-create the character of that *paese* which they left behind.[27] The distribution of houses around a bay, or on the emigrants' 'mental map' of their city,[28] the ornamentation of architecture, the plants grown (sometimes illegally) in a back garden, the products retailed in local 'Italian' shops, the way in which these shops are laid out, the ceremonies of sale and purchase, not to mention those of birth, death and marriage, the food consumed at many a table – all will be coloured by a nostalgia for Italy (or the Italies). They may also be curiously frozen in time, replicating the situation which existed at the moment of departure from the *paese*, the 'Italy' that was, rather than the ever-changing

Italy that is. This fractured sense of time[29] is thought, in turn, sometimes to prompt disapproval, dislike, dismay or alienation, when emigrants make a return trip 'back home' (and even more strongly if that 'back home' means not so much the *paese* as Venice, Florence and Rome).

Undoubtedly there is something in this concept of an *ambiente*. It is, after all, natural for those stranded among the unfamiliar to search out and treasure the familiar and, where possible, to savour a 'little taste of home'. On the other hand, it is also important not to be too naive about the construction of an *ambiente* or about any other part of 'heritage'.[30] In restaging the past, Italians in emigration are at least as fond of 'fakes'[31] as are most people. 'Genuine' gondolas in Las Vegas, or a 'genuine' replica of the Tower of Pisa projected at one stage for Sydney, lie at one extreme of faking, but much 'genuine' Italian food and quite a lot of 'genuine' Italian culture are not so different. According to one recent, provocative, commentator, 'Calabrian regional food', as understood today, was invented in the United States, and *spaghetti pomodoro*, that most basic of 'Italian dishes', became an everyday food only after the commencement of the canning industry.[32] Manufacturing authenticity, it seems, is probably more common than its 'genuine' generation in the distant past. An advertisement may read 'Buy an Italian suit and feel yourself Italian',[33] but the meaning of such feeling may be in the words and in the moment of their expression as much as in the art, the cloth or the tailoring.

Much more important is the fact that any *ambiente*, no matter how small or large the 'little Italy' which houses it, is itself in movement, and intricately embroidered with threads of political and economic interest. Such threads usually connect with the original *paese*, with Italy (especially when the national government can disburse contracts and favours) and with the host country. As Robert Harney perceptively remarked of the Italian community in Toronto, even the most flourishing *ambiente* 'has no typical people, no valid stereotypes and no ethnicity, except as functional politics'.[34]

A fine place to view these struggles of identity, marketing, religion and power is the *festa*. Many an Italian immigrant community, once it reaches a certain size, status and level of prosperity, will seek to restage a local version of the annual festival of the saint from the home *paese* (or one of the saints from the *paese*, since even quite small Italian villages often have their own 'suburban' or parish divisions). San Ubaldo of Gubbio has his *ceri* replicated in

Pittsburgh,[35] and Molfetta's Madonna dei Martiri is celebrated in Fremantle, Port Pirie (South Australia) and Hoboken (New Jersey).[36] In 1920s Marseilles, 'Italian' fishermen revered Saints Cosma and Damiano if they had originated in Gaeta, Saint Silverio if they came from Ponza, and Saint Andrew if from Amalfi,[37] and many other saints or emanations of the Madonna were and are carried in procession through the innumerable towns and cities of the Italian diaspora.

What is the meaning of these *feste*? The most detailed study of a *festa* in emigration is that by the American sociologist, R.A. Orsi, of the Madonna of Mt Carmel in New York, the Madonna of 115th Street.[38] This Madonna started her career in 1881, when emigrants from Polla in Salerno province organised a Madonna Mutual Aid society. Endorsed, somewhat unusually, by a local Irish-American priest, the Madonna gradually advanced from a *paesano* to a national identification (and thus beat off a number of rival saints and manifestations of the Virgin). New York *mafiosi*, Fascists, post-1945 American loyalists and anti-communists recognised, in their turn, the Mt Carmel Madonna as the special vehicle of 'the history of the people of Italian Harlem'. At least according to Orsi, the Madonna's festival also became a magic moment of a 'theology of the streets', in which ordinary men and women, the 'working class' (though, he says, 'everyone was a child again during the festa'), 'redeemed time'.[39] In the *festa*, the Italians of New York, no matter how humble, could publicly lay claim to a 'real' history and to a continuity from a past in which they could be proud and in which they could anchor their identity.

The sceptical historian needs to be a little careful before accepting the more grandiose of Orsi's claims. Even by his own account, the Madonna of 115th Street does not sound an entirely innocent being, and her special version of history did not automatically free all the Italian men, let alone all the Italian women, of New York from the structures which oppressed and channelled them. Rather, as usual, it may be presumed that, in her *festa*, some history was being gained and some lost. The Madonna acted as an agent of commercialisation, 'disciplinisation' (especially within the church) and Americanisation, as well as of a rather folkloric, 'little Italies'-style Italianisation. As they worshipped her, communed with each other and nourished their identities, her devotees were manufacturing (the classic myths of) 'the Italian family'.

The equivocations and complexities evident on 115th Street can readily be found in other *feste*. Take those of Italo-Australia, for example. In suburban Adelaide, the festival of San Pellegrino (of Altavilla Irpina, Avellino province) was moved, with a hint of political rather than religious purpose, from 25 August to coincide with Australia Day (26 January). Its historian claims, nonetheless, that it is always a roaring success:

> To turn to the social side of the celebration. It has to be experienced. There were hurdy gurdies, moon walks, trampolines, merry-go-rounds, shooting galleries, coconut shies, the lot. There were spaghetti eating competitions, games of bowls, races on a wet sheet of plastic, tugs of war . . . a brass band . . . . There were food stalls, water melons [always so patriotically red, white and green], pizzas . . . BBQ chops, icecream, fairy floss . . . coca cola.[40]

For a different set of South Australian Campanians there was another, graver problem. When in 1955 they desired a statue of their own *Madonna bruna*, they sought 'authenticity' by ordering it 'from home', though in this case, as often, not from their *paese* but from a well-known firm in Florence. Great was their dismay when, on unwrapping a package from Italy, they discovered that they had been sent 'someone else's Madonna' (though honour was satisfied for the inaugural *festa* of 1956 when 'one of the more artistic [Capuchin] Fathers' did a skilled job of retouching).[41]

There were other ambiguities. In Western Australia, the Madonna dei Martiri of the Molfettese segment of Fremantle seems to be following the path of the Madonna of 115th Street and becoming the Queen of Italo-Western Australia. As she transmutes into a local 'star' who can grant identity, other saints lose status, following and credibility. In a world of change, the boast by one Abruzzese as he rejoiced in the establishment of a *festa* for Pollutri's San Nicola, that 'One fact is certain. Pollutri has existed for more than two thousand years. And in those two thousand years the Commune [in Chieti province] and its inhabitants have preserved intact their own special characteristics', could only be false.[42]

And yet, for a historian of Italian cultures abroad, the fact of this boast is more interesting and more enlightening than is its 'falsity'. What the *paesano* from Pollutri was expressing was the view that his own culture and his own identity possessed a past which stretched far back in time. A *paesano* of Pollutri had roots superior to 'new' Australia (Italian commentators over the years have frequently been inclined to argue that Australia is too new to have a 'real history').[43] At the same time, Pollutri has a history more antique than that of the nation state, Italy, which is, by one reckoning, even newer than Australia. This frequently evinced sense that the old is better than the new makes it all the more appropriate that the demonstration of a *paese*'s longevity should come most commonly during a religious ceremony under the official auspices of that other 'age-old' 'Italian' institution, the Roman Catholic Church.

This church, in practice, was another body with its own rhythms and diversities. That special victim of the Risorgimento, Pope Pius IX, in the Syllabus of Errors (1864) and the Declaration of Infall-ibility (1870),[44] had ostentatiously placed the church at odds with Italy, with any idea of democracy and, indeed, with most of the modern world. In 1871, *Civiltà Cattolica* paralleled that Liberal Italy which, in 'sacrilegious wars', had dispossessed the papacy of the Temporal Power, to the regimes of Nero, Domitian, Caracalla and Napoleon. The Jesuit journal pledged its unbroken loyalty to the 'old cause'[45] and thus, if opportunity came, to the demolition of newly united Italy. In 1896 it deemed Adowa a 'providential lesson for Italians' and wondered at the sublime geographical and historical wisdom of a Deity who had once chastised the Pharaoh, and was now, in adjacent lands, plaguing Liberal Italy.[46]

But, as has already been noted, there were by then plenty of signs of a rapprochement between Catholic Church and Liberal state, a coming together prompted on the one hand by a mutual realisation that socialism was a greater enemy,[47] and, on the other, by a joint collaboration in the practice of welfare and the preaching of patriot-ism to Italian emigrants. Indeed, as the years passed, it was possible to see the Vatican and, even more so, the Italian priesthood, at home and abroad, as an object of that nationalisation of the aristocracies, bourgeoisies and intelligentsias which is familiar elsewhere in the late nineteenth and the twentieth centuries. A church which increasingly spoke Italian, invested in Italy and multiplied its Italian organ-isations[48] – from cooperative banks, to 'white' unions, to newspapers – could not but gradually itself become more Italian.

Thus it is no surprise to find some sections of the church loudly proclaiming that Liberal Italy was sending Christian soldiers onward to Libya in 1911, the purity of their mission seemingly enhanced by the likelihood that they would, once there, restore the fortunes of the troubled and Vatican-owned Banco di Roma. In the First World War, Pope Benedict XV, dismayed to find his co-religionists on both sides of the battle front, clung piously to papal neutrality and half-heartedly sought to foster a compromise peace. But even as the Pope imitated the Prince of Peace, military chaplains urged on Italian forces to their victory of justice or national power.[49]

By 1919, the Risorgimento split between church and state in Italy was largely repaired. Making manifest a Catholic return to Italian politics was the Partito Popolare (Popular Party or PPI). That characteristically heterogeneous institution of 'political Catholicism' briefly promised to become a major actor on the national stage until it fell victim to Fascist 'totalitarianism' in what some commentators have regarded as a less than honourable deal between Mussolini's regime and the Vatican.[50]

The high point of an identification of church and state in Italy, however, would be reached during the pontificates of Pius XI (1922–39) and Pius XII (1939–58), notably with the signature of the Lateran Pacts in 1929.[51] Only the introduction of anti-Semitic legislation from 1938 onwards caused any drastic reconsideration by the church of its cohabitation with Fascism, and the Vatican more or less openly blessed Fascist foreign policies in Ethiopia, Spain and Albania, while, in Malta, the church was rather more Italian nation-alist than were the Fascists. Even the Second World War did not diminish the church's commitment to what most in the ruling elite agreed were Italian national interests, and the great majority of the church hierarchy, including the future Pope John XXIII (1958–63),[52] regarded the Axis invasion of the USSR as a 'crusade' for Christianity (or Catholicism).

The fall of Fascism meant that Italy and Roman Catholicism became even more closely identified. Pius XII, with his studied policy of 'triumphalism', and John XXIII, with his more natural charisma, seemed to the wider world legitimate and august Kings of Rome in a way that no Victor Emmanuel or Umberto had ever been. As the post-war years passed, however, the reality was, ironically, that the Vatican was being reinternationalised, or at least Ameri-canised, and was thus converting itself into another ordinary 'cor-porate multinational' part of the capitalist West. Behind Bernini's great square, English had become as useful a language as Italian and the Bahamas as crucial a centre of Vatican finances as was Brescia. The church was being prepared for the pathetic figure of Pope John Paul I (1978), struggling with taped English lessons as he made his lonely beginning to another weary and baffling day,[53] and for the more powerful and confident John Paul II (1978–), the '*Papa polacco*' as Italians denominate him, not always with enthusiasm. This second John Paul would be a warrior of the West, a major artificer of the fall of communism and the rise of the monetarist (and utopian) new world order. For his church, the rights or wrongs of Italian influence at Massawa and what should be the ideal Vatican policies towards them had faded into a distant memory indeed. Perhaps it would also be appropriate that Italian-style Christian Democracy would collapse in his reign.

But even while Popes, notably between the wars, had emphasised the Vatican's hierarchical character and the tight discipline which bound both priesthood and laity to their religious superiors, in fact the church remained anything but a monolithic organisation. One ideal place from which to view this disunity was the Italian emigrant world. There it was all very well for the Scalabrinians to preach the gospel of their nationalising and disciplinising welfare policies, but a favourable reception among emigrants from the Italies for this medley was by no means guaranteed. Such Italians, by tradition and especially if they were male, were neither regular attenders at Mass nor automatic respecters of the clergy. They might well be generous donors to the church, but they preferred to give in their own way, at the *festa* or as a special *ex voto* donation.[54] They objected to the newly organised policies of the church, which aimed to extract a regular and pledged tithe every week. Why should a priest replicate the methods of the hated state or a feared bank? Similarly, should not priests bring material benefits to their laity in a way that neither the state nor banks could be relied upon to do? Why, too, should a priest, committed to the new piety or austerity of the twentieth-century church, set himself above the people? A suspicion of priestly hypocrisy, greed and lubricity had always been widespread among Italians, whose folklore and gossip frequently repeated stories which more lettered readers enjoyed in the prose of Boccaccio or Aretino. A priest, by definition, was thought to have a cushy job; a popular, pre-1914 song suggested brightly that the easiest means through which a peasant's son could avoid emigration was by accepting vocation as a fat priest.[55] However, even while singing along with gusto or retailing the latest scandal about those 'half men' in skirts, Italians would readily overlook venial sins if a priest was, in his *rapporti umani* (that characteristic Italian term inadequately translated as 'human relations'), at one with his flock. Pride, intellectual or racial, was ignored or forgiven with greater difficulty.

Between church and the Italies there were thus many grounds for misunderstanding. In Chicopee, Kansas, on one occasion, a member of the clergy was pelted with rocks and vegetables by his disgruntled parishioners, and, on reaching a mainly Sicilian-American parish, a priest of Tuscan origin mumbled in bewilderment and lament, 'is it possible that these are Italians?'[56] Even in post-Second World War Australia, a learned Scalabrinian could maintain that the peculiarity of 'Southerners' was a product of ancient 'Moslem influences'.[57] Their ostentatious shrines were no more than 'gaudy aberrations',[58] leftovers from a peasant world which would and must fade away. They served no purpose in the austere or 'disciplinised' religion of this 'missionary' to the migrants.

If Italian did not necessarily comprehend Italian, how much worse was it when Italians had to deal with those parts of the church dominated by other ethnic groups? In the United States, as in Australia, the most dramatic conflict in *mentalités* occurred with the Irish, whose earlier presence in these new worlds had allowed them to dominate the local episcopates.

Throughout the world Irish bishops were almost universally hostile to what they deemed the 'pagan' practices of the *feste*, and could also be highly suspicious of 'Italian' apostolic delegates who arrived in their dioceses from the Vatican on some supervisory mission or other.[59] However, perhaps the most profound moment of mutual bafflement occurred in Australia in 1949 when the tall, loud and very Irish-Catholic Minister for Immigration, Arthur Calwell, met the elegant, diminutive, anti-clerical, *noblesse de robe*, Neapolitan, Giulio del Balzo, the first Italian diplomatic representative to post-war Australia. 'You have one job, here', bellowed Calwell in his domineering way to his blanching new acquaintance: 'Get the Italians to go to mass.'[60] It would take another two decades before Irish, Italian and other Catholics moved very far towards an understanding of their different pieties and religiosities. In 1969 Pope Paul VI, in an encyclical entitled *Pastoralis Migratorum*, finally set the church on a course towards what is today called multiculturalism.[61]

However tardy were the agencies of the church in recognising its richly human diversity, the proclaimed universality of the church's mission was a factor woven into the identity of many Italians. Their origin in a nation which harboured so naturally 'multinational' an institution as the Vatican became another reason why Italians' place in the world was not merely crafted from their Italianness. 'Belonging' in some way to both the church and the *paese*, Italians almost inevitably embodied a localist internationalism and an international localism as much as, or more than, they did the national mission of United Italy.

After 1945, a third great stream, in which currents of localism and internationalism similarly mingled, reinforced this drift. The special Italian variety of Marxism, as expressed, however ambiguously on occasion, by the Italian Communist Party (PCI), by its various intellectual fellow-travellers and by all those who believed in the 'myth of the Resistance',[62] ensured yet again that the national community would not be the only one which Italians could imagine. Though PCI members were always, to some extent, the faithful children of Moscow – in 1924 Gramsci had opined: 'he who is independent of the Soviet Union is "independent" of the working class and thus "dependent" on the bourgeois class'[63] – such fidelity did not entail an inability to criticise, or to see and pursue national and local interests.

Indeed, the PCI's special history, as an object of persecution by a Fascist dictatorship and, then, as the political leader of armed Resistance from 1943 to 1945, naturally enhanced its independence. Under the Republic, the rules of the game of *bipartitismo imperfetto* (the imperfect two-party system) increasingly made the PCI the main party of opposition. At the same time, it was a party which could never enter the national government in Rome and was obliged to restrict itself to local and regional administration. In these circumstances it was inevitable that matters national would only be part of the PCI's image and reality. Had not Gramsci, whose myth was so carefully marketed to potential believers at home and abroad,[64] already advised: 'The Italian people are the people with the greatest "national" interest in a modern form of cosmopolitanism'?[65] If, actually, there were plenty of 'national populist' ambiguities about Gramsci and his myth as a modern and Marxist St Francis of Assisi, Communist practice in such showcases as Bologna[66] also emphasised the party's local face. In its essence the PCI was a movement which could not afford to distinguish too clearly between localism, regionalism, nationalism and internationalism. The cadres who united under its banners were ideally men and women who deemed themselves simultaneously Bolognese, Romagnole, Italian and workers of the world.

Before such huge forces and such a wealth of history and reference, how petty would seem the culture of the Italian nation state, how limited its possession of time, how feeble its penetration of the masses and its associated nationalising of the foreign understanding of

'Italy'. And yet could a United Italy exist without a cultural mission? As has already been noted, the memories which eddied through the streets of 'eternal' Rome seemed, in an age when 'history' was the natural legitimiser of a state, to require that they be harnessed for some grandiose purpose. As Mussolini, echoing many others, muttered on one occasion: of all cities Rome could not be reduced to being 'merely the capital of a little people of antiquarians'.[67]

This desire to find a mission, to locate for the 'Third Italy' an ideology for export, had been present at the very birth of the Italian nation state. Had not the Risorgimento been the fruitful product of action *and* thought?[68] If Italy had been made by the devious diplomacy of Cavour and the military prowess of Garibaldi, had not Mazzini, Cesare Balbo, Gioberti, Rosmini, Cattaneo, Verdi, Manzoni and all who attended the 'scientific' congresses of the 1830s and 1840s[69] also contributed to national unification? Was not Italy, as Croce would maintain,[70] a triumph of the will and the idea, the handiwork of 'active minorities' and the creation of what was coming to be called an intelligentsia? But what ideas did this intelligentsia have and how successful was it in exporting them from Liberal, Fascist and Republican Italy?

Immediately after unification, a search for great ideas began. As the editor of *Nuova Antologia*, that most characteristic purveyor of Establishment views from 1866 to the present, put it in his first issue: 'A judicious man foresees little good for a political risorgimento when an intellectual surge ['*moto*'] does not accompany it or follow it near behind.'[71] What did contributors to *Nuova Antologia* discuss in its pages? In that first issue there was that very liberal and surprisingly feminist article by Princess Belgiojoso cited earlier in this chapter (p. 138). There was a long article about Rome in which readers were reminded that Cavour had prophesied that the Eternal City must 'be by the law of nature and necessity the venerated head of Italy'. There was a review of the role of Virgil in literary tradition before Dante.[72]

Classical reference, then, was dominant and would remain highly significant thereafter in nationalist and Fascist politico-archaeological discourse about both Italy and the whole *mare nostrum*. A pronouncement of Cesare De Vecchi di Val Cismon, the editor of the *Rassegna Storica del Risorgimento*, in 1936, was typical. The 'facts', he said, showed that Italians were 'not the "sons of Europe" but rather of ourselves, and of the teeming womb of Rome which has from one period to the next known how to produce its own history'.[73]

Also likely to ignite patriotic fervour was the figure of Dante Alighieri. As a youth Mazzini wrote about the sustenance which he drew from the '*amor patria di Dante*'.[74] When, in 1889, nationalists in-the-making wanted to launch a patriotic cultural association which bore some local resemblance to the Pan German League, they called it the Dante Alighieri Society.[75] When they wished to make a superb gesture against the 'Germanisation' of the South Tyrol, they opened a monument to Dante in Habsburg Trento in 1896 – fifteen years later, irredentist patriots would organise an automobile 'caravan' in the tracks of Dante and trust thus that they would be stirred 'by the genius and commitment of their great and inspiring Duce'.[76] Other nationalists found from their reading that Dante, a social Darwinist before his time, had said that one nation grew strong only when another grew weak.[77] A Minister of Education sonorously reiterated Dante's demand that emigrants preserve their language which was their soul.[78] Liberal Italy called one of its first Dreadnought battleships the *Dante Alighieri*. The Fascist anthem, *Giovinezza*, in its chorus, cited the poet as the one who had marked out in a sacred manner Italy's borders on the Quarnaro River, and thus required that Istria join the *madrepatria*,[79] while, for the Fascist *Decennale*, a Somali village, Hafun, was solemnly renamed Dante.[80] According to at least one sentimental account, Dante himself had portrayed his Beatrice as dressed in the green, white and red of the Italian tricolour (the emblem of the three Christian graces).[81] For all these reasons, it is scarcely surprising that, in the lexicon of Italian street names, a via Dante still is second in frequency only to a via Garibaldi. In Italian schools and universities and, even more, in Italian courses taught in tertiary institutions in the wider world, Dante, similarly, almost always holds pride of place. In prestige, at least, Dante remains the pre-eminent export of the Italian culture industry.

Why? What is it about a Tuscan religious poet of the fourteenth century that has made him such a living reference for United Italy? A full-scale study of the nature of the Dante myth has not been written, but it is clear that Dante has been read as a patriot before his time, as a man of liberty who would not kow-tow to papal pressure, as an anti-clerical (though simultaneously a man of piety, a true Catholic) and even as a Fascist. But the essence of Dante's fame and vitality is something simpler. What he embodied, every commentator agreed, was there in his pages. It was the Italian language; Dante incarnated Italian even more than Shakespeare did English.

Yet, matters were not really so simple. Indeed, an unkind commentator might remark, Dante was needed to express the Italian language because there was no Italian language. Just as, geographically, the new Italy had borders which no state had possessed before, so, after 1860, new words, new grammar and a new pronunciation, the new language we call 'Italian', needed to be taught to the 'Italian' people. Until the impact on Italy of mass TV in the 1960s and 1970s, and even after that in many emigrant communities, Italians quite literally spoke with many tongues. When, as cited at the beginning of this chapter (p. 137), Prezzolini bewailed the fact that the people of the Italies had no 'language' and no 'culture', all that he was actually saying was that the emigrants did not possess his bourgeois intellectual culture and language. They were not as manufactured an Italian as he was. Their flesh had not yet been made word.

Throughout this century, one of the most redolent ironies in the expression of Italian culture abroad has been present in those Italian classes held by the Dante Alighieri Society, in this centre or that, wherein emigrant Italians sought instruction in 'their' national language. The results have been fitful and, as Tullio De Mauro has remarked, most evidence indicates that emigration has enhanced and preserved the use of dialects (while sometimes prompting further linguistic inventions – 'what a shame! I have *smasciato* my *carro*', as some Italo-Australians are wont to say).[82]

Language, thus, was a crucial sphere in which ambiguity and frustration clung to the post-Risorgimento intelligentsia. How footling it was to seek out a universal national mission while the very words which one Italian used to another were not understood. And, as if reflecting its weakness at home, 'Italian' culture, after 1860, lost ground in its 'foreign policy'. For Italian painters and writers to be recognised in Paris (or even in Vienna) was more important than their critical reception in Rome. In the *belle époque*, only the studied exoticism of D'Annunzio could really make the French sit up, listen (and pay). The Futurists launched their manifesto in French in *Le Figaro* but, when nobody in Paris seemed much impressed, had to make do with Italian fame. In historiography, philosophy and music, by contrast, finding a place in the Germanic world was what mattered more. In the last regard, Verdi and Puccini, each such a fine emblem of his age, triumphantly preserved an audience for 'Italian' music but lost ground critically, first to Wagnerian intellectualising and, after

1900, to the new assumptions and techniques of Stravinsky and Schönberg. Already in 1884 an American critic had dismissed Italian opera as 'the sweetmeats of the hurdy-gurdy repertory', corrupted by and corrupting in its 'African' origins.[83] Nor would Verdi and Puccini have successors, except in the sense that Frank Sinatra, Dean Martin and other musicians of Italo-America were their heirs. The reader might like to contemplate the reaction of the ghost of Puccini to the suggestion that Madonna, too, should be numbered among his progeny.

On the still wider stage, the Italian language, even as it was being fabricated, lessened in influence. The coming of a mass age meant that far more people spoke the great imperial languages – English, Spanish, Chinese, French, Russian, Arabic, Hindi, German and Portuguese – than they did Italian. Though Italy's participation in the First World War was rewarded in England by the belated funding of chairs in Italian at the Universities of Oxford, Cambridge and Birmingham,[84] Italian as the language and culture of a modern state was increasingly viewed as of only provincial significance. If diplomatically Italy, until 1943, aspired uneasily to the title of least of the Great Powers, national Italian culture was even less able seriously to sustain its claims to be in the first rank.

One of the great boasts of Fascism, of course, was that it would check and overcome this inferiority. Mussolini's regime certainly paid a great deal of attention to public relations and the targets of such superb or showy displays as the *Decennale* of 1932 or the *Esposizione Universale* planned for 1942 were not only Italian. Mussolini was indefatigable in meeting foreign dignitaries and, with his charm and bower-bird mind, was able, momentarily at least, to impress many of his guests. His reception list could embrace so humble a figure as a visiting Australian doctor, albeit one who was convinced that Rome was refulgent with the 'immanence of creation' and that the Duce was the greatest man of his age.[85]

Buoyed by such admirers, the Mussolinian regime, following a tradition established in Liberal Italy, generously disbursed funds to its real or presumed friends, be they Italians or foreigners, intellectuals, journalists or politicians. In that last regard the Fascist financial support of dissident nationalists in the Weimar Republic and of Croatian separatists is notorious, and Fascism also rewarded its sympathisers in the Anglo-Saxon world[86] – in emigrant communities politically deferential Italian-language newspapers could rely on at least some government largesse (as they would similarly be able to do after 1945).[87]

Such expenditure was not always well targeted, however. In 1930s Switzerland, for example, the authorities believed that they were sustaining Ticinese autonomism, but their crafty 'client' actually used the bribes from Rome for his own purposes and was actively hostile to Fascist interference in his country.[88] In this as on other occasions, Italian cultural policy and Italian plotting had to confront the realities of force. Germany, the USSR, Britain, the USA, France and Japan, all had more loyal and more dutiful foreign admirers because they had more power. It was all very well for Mussolini to talk about Fascism as *the* doctrine of the twentieth century and to patronise a Fascist International,[89] but few were seriously impressed until Nazism, that rather different version of fascism, ruled in Berlin.

In its cultural policy, the Italian Republic preferred a quieter life to that of its Liberal or Fascist predecessors. At last, it seemed, the Italian nation state had given up its delusions about a universal mission and opted instead for its own path to the future. Foreign commentators wondered just what sort of curious beast Christian Democracy might be, but argued that it and the PCI, which, after 1956, increasingly possessed a similar amorphousness or ideological eclecticism, constituted the '*via italiana*' or 'democracy, Italian style'.[90] In the 1950s, the most common image of Italy was that of a Catholic, Americanised, capitalist or *paesano* place, in which Don Camillo and Peppone jockeyed for a hollow power, watched by such elegant, cynical, worldly-wise and wary observers as Luigi Barzini.[91] Italian writers, painters, film directors and composers, philosophers, economists, scientists and historians might make a splash at this or that conference, concert or exhibition, but they did so as individuals more than as representatives of the culture of the Italian nation state.

Nonetheless, it would be a mistake to conclude too abruptly that there has never been much to this culture. Just as over the years Italian was becoming the language which Italians spoke and even dreamed in, so, too, foreigners had increasingly accepted the permanence of the Italian nation state and given some cognisance to the existence of an Italian national culture. In 1960 Italy was rewarded for its 'progress' since 1945, for its economic 'miracle', for its legitimacy as a member of the capitalist West, for the solidity of its institutions and for the attractions of its culture, by being accorded the right to stage the Olympic Games. Inevitably, they were held in Rome, city of the Caesars, where the architecture of the main stadium still flaunted the Fascist version of classicism; city of the church, where Pope John XXIII, that universal and *strapaese* 'peasant' figure, now reigned; city of *La Dolce Vita*, of the sweet life, of 'three coins in the fountain', of artichokes *alla romana*, of *vino*, of Latin lovers; Rome, the city of those ever more massive battalions of tourists, who, since 1860, had regularly brought a glimpse of the wider world to Italy, and carried away a new memory or a previously existing prejudice, a suntan, a postcard and a gladness that Italian culture did exist (one Italian culture or another, that is).

8

VISITING ITALY
Tourism and Leisure 1860–1960

In August 1923 Italy announced its newly Fascist presence in the Mediterranean by bombarding the Greek island of Corfu. A French cartoonist revealed what he thought of this show of force by depicting the attacking ships as a flotilla of armoured gondolas milling around at sea. One gondola bore the less than frightening name *O Sole Mio*.[1] For this cartoonist, it seems, 'Italy' bespoke tourism and leisure, carnival in Venice, fun and sun and a yawling tenor in Naples, rather more than it did naval conquest.

Perhaps because it is such a leisurely matter, tourism has been hard for commentators to take seriously. Even as late as 1971, when American novelist Mary McCarthy had one of her characters (a sociologist standing in the crowded Sistine Chapel) preach 'tourism is all around us, a central fact of our mobile civilisation, so much taken for granted that nobody has stopped to ponder on it',[2] her intention was satirical. Her sociologist was searching for a way to go on a permanent and all-expenses-paid holiday.

Yet, especially when placed in his context of Rome and Italy, the sociologist was right. In the century from 1860 to 1960, Italy's biggest and most lucrative industry, the one certainly with the largest number of employees and perhaps with the most satisfied customers, was tourism. For all its importance as an earner of foreign currency, and for all the obvious fact that it was through visiting the country, in anticipation and retrospect as well as realisation, that most foreigners experienced Italy, tourism has achieved a remarkably small place in the historiography. A literature, often rather sentimental and descriptive, does exist about foreign 'images' of Italy, but there is no serious economic or administrative history of the tourist industry and no social history of hoteliers, waiters, cooks or other employees. Only scattered studies can be located of the modern 'invention' or conceptualisation of mountains, lakes, spas, bathing resorts, religious sites, art works, classical remains, 'history', museums and other components of the tourist business. Thousands of pages recount Italy's costly, damaging and unsuccessful policies in Albania or Eritrea; very few direct attention to that most basic, pleasurable or profitable way in which Italy and the wider world have interrelated.

This small book again is scarcely an appropriate place in which to remedy such a glaring omission. But some questions at least can be asked. Did the rhythms of tourism fit those of politics and formal power? What happened to the leisure industries in war, or when Italy was controlled by an ostensibly xenophobic ideology like Fascism? Who, anyway, were the tourists? Where did they come from? Where did they go? What sites did they visit and fail to visit? How spontaneous were their choices or how much were they directed by Italian tourist operators and the Italian state? What prejudices and knowledge did the tourists arrive with? Did they leave in the same condition? What knowledge and prejudices did Italians acquire in return, as they managed one of the great mass tourist industries of the modern world? What, in sum, did tourism do to Italy and what did Italy do to the tourists?

Like emigration, with which it would be repeatedly linked or compared, tourism existed before Italian unification. From at least the seventeenth century, tourists, or *stranieri* (foreigners) as they were long generically called,[3] played an obvious and important part in the life and finances of most Italian states. Already by the 1840s, Charles Dickens was having difficulty squeezing himself into that Sistine Chapel[4] which would later inspire philosophical lucubrations in Mary McCarthy's imaginary sociologist. Three generations earlier, Dr Samuel Johnson, whose own plans to visit the peninsula were always thwarted, homilised about a journey there in words which would echo down the decades:

A man who has not been in Italy is always conscious of an inferiority, from his having not seen what it is expected a man should see. The grand object of travelling is to see the shores of the Mediterranean. On those shores were the four great empires of the world: the Assyrian, the Persian, the Grecian and the Roman – all our religion, almost all our law, almost all our arts, almost all that sets us above savages, has come to us from the shores of the Mediterranean.[5]

Whether spurred by these or other attractions, the Grand Tour had become the entertainment of the age for French, English, German and Russian visitors, and soon Americans were arriving, too. In the nineteenth century, as the middle classes rose in their 'age of improvement', they sought out Italy for the fruits of its soil, its climate, its art and its history, discovering also its present decadence and thus the comforting final wisdom that, after all, home was best. Dickens characteristically moralised about dirt in Genoa, beggars in Pisa[6] and a public execution in Rome (which did not run on time).[7] 'Old Italian towns', like Piacenza, Parma or Ferrara, taught him what it meant to be lazy. There, he remarked, 'any attempt to think would be accompanied with a creaking noise'; in those places 'there is nothing . . . to be done, or needing to be done . . . there is no more human progress, motion, effort, or advancement of any kind'; there, 'the whole scheme stopped . . . centuries ago, and laid down to rest until the Day of Judgment'.[8] The only hope of amendment sprang from the railway. That little engine of modernity which ran between Pisa and Livorno had, concluded Dickens, 'already begun to astonish Italy with a precedent of punctuality, order, plain dealing, and improvement – the most dangerous and heretical astonisher of all'.[9]

For all their ready recourse to such effortless superiority, visitors continued to flock into Italy. It has been estimated that, by the 1840s, 11,000 Britons were in residence in Florence alone, and four English-language travel guides were being published each year. In Venice, where the first bathing establishment on the Lido opened in 1833, Britons were outnumbered by Germans, but sufficient numbers tramped that city's bridges and alleyways for Robert Browning to bewail its 'Liverpoolising'.[10] As throngs turned into hordes (more than 110,000 foreigners visited Venice in 1843), the great institutions of mass tourism were being founded – the initial Baedeker Guide was released in 1828, American Express opened for business in 1841, Thomas Cook organised his first 'tour' in 1845 (to Liverpool! – he would not penetrate Italy until 1864).[11]

An ambiguous tourist 'love' of Italy thus acted as an important accompaniment to many of the events of the Risorgimento. Even Dickens confessed that, despite the dirt, he grew fond of Genoa and hoped for the national 'resurrection' of Italy.[12] For both Italians and foreigners such rebirth would be a recurrent metaphor and a semiotician might wonder how much this recurrence owed to the viewing of early Renaissance, Pre-Raphaelite, religious paintings. Half-remembered tourist days undoubtedly augmented, for many,

Garibaldi's charisma and, more generally, may have stimulated foreign politicians and businessmen to be interested in and sympathetic to the new Italy. It was thus natural that Baedeker should publish its first guide to Italy in 1863, urging that unification had simplified and cheapened the business of travel to the great sites of the peninsula. For many a foreigner, the greatest freedom made available by the Risorgimento was the freedom to travel.

At that time, one growing centre, just over the border from the Riviera, was San Remo, which, by the 1870s, had become an Italian extension of it. As Massimo Scattarreggia, a local historian, has related, San Remo tripled in population between 1871 and 1915 and, at the same time, was more generally modernised. The flourishing of the tourist industry resulted in the introduction of drains, street-lighting, rubbish collection and leisure outlets (from sports fields to brothels), even though these 'improvements' always reached the tourist part of the town before those places in which the locals lived. The tourists themselves, still in the *fin de siècle* way likely to 'winter' in San Remo, conducted themselves rather like immigrants, however more wealthy they were than the Italians contemporaneously reaching the Americas. As Scattarreggia explains:

> In the first phase of their 'colonisation' of the San Remo area, the Nordic guests tended to form closed societies and to ignore the more backward local population. They set up their own exclusive clubs, opened Protestant or Orthodox churches, joined special sporting associations, built hotels and shops, founded banks and printed newspapers in their own languages.[13]

If San Remo grew as a bathing resort, Salsomaggiore flourished as a spa. This village in the hills south of Parma had acquired a curative reputation in the 1840s, and thereafter gradually expanded on the model of spas like Vichy and Baden Baden in France and Germany. In the 1890s a businessman, Giuseppe Magnaghi, who had happened to take the waters, launched a building boom. Despite Magnaghi's death in 1898, a new Grand Hôtel des Thermes – the French name, it was hoped, guaranteed cachet – was opened in 1900. Salsomaggiore developed a highly *belle époque* image, and became celebrated for the design work of Galileo Chini, an artist who lived in Bangkok from 1911 to 1914 and practised a style which might be defined as *thai-oiserie*. Profits were not automatic, however. In 1911 local hotels counted 13,813 paying guests as against Vichy's 103,742 and Baden's

77,743. The solution was a characteristic one; the Italian state took over the enterprise. It would remain in control, except during an attempt at Fascist privatisation from 1923 to 1933. What really happened was that Salsomaggiore became an essentially Italian resort, in its way part of the Italian medical and welfare system. Foreigners went elsewhere.[14]

Of course, they had plenty of resorts from which to choose. There were great artistic and historical centres like Venice, Florence and Rome. There was the 'Italian Riviera' which spread south-east from San Remo and had as its jewels Rapallo and Lerici. There were the hill towns of Tuscany and Umbria, still sometimes difficult of access before 1914, but, in Siena, San Gimignano, Gubbio, Assisi and the rest, of limitless potential in art, history, religion, cuisine and 'ambience'. Further south lay Pompei, Agrigento, Capri and Taormina, places from which more daringly to view or to practise beauty and decadence.[15]

Faced with such developments, it was not long before the leaders of that new Italy began, in the spirit of the times, to argue that what they still awkwardly called 'the influx of foreigners' should be subjected to 'scientific review'. In 1898, Guido Paravicini, troubled by the social and economic crisis of that time, noted that what he called '*Touristes*' gave crucial benefit to the national exchequer. Tourism, he declared, had massive ramifications, for example in floriculture, and Italians must urgently commence 'a vast intellectual preparation', on the model of what Switzerland already did, in order best and most productively to welcome the visitors.[16] The following year Luigi Bodio, an economist and Senator, made a more precise attempt exactly to tally the monetary value of tourism. By counting the quantity of railway tickets sold to those crossing the national frontiers and reckoning on a daily level of expenditure, he estimated that, in 1897, Italy had gained 300 million lire from its tourists. In 1912, immediately after the grandiose patriotic celebration of the *Cinquantennio* which may have helped to boost tourist numbers, Bonaldo Stringher, the director of the Banca d'Italia, applying Bodio's methods, reckoned that the income had now risen to 450 million, earned from some 900,000 visitors. This total, Stringher noted, using an equation which was tirelessly reiterated by later commentators, equalled that provided by emigrant remittances. Together, he maintained, these two great 'invisible assets' permitted the national economy to flourish despite its persistent balance of payments deficit.[17]

At the time when Stringher was making this assessment, tourism, again in parallel with emigration, was becoming one of the more significant debating points of Italian political and commercial life. In the tourist field, 'science' and 'organisation' were urgently needed, it seemed; otherwise Italy would lose out to more resourceful and more ruthlessly self-interested competitors. One who made public his thoughts in this regard was the Piedmontese businessman, Maggiorino Ferraris. Very much a member of the ruling elite of Liberal Italy, Ferraris had a seat in the Chamber of Deputies and was the owner–editor of *Nuova Antologia*. Politically he was close to Sidney Sonnino and, in his banking practices and enthusiasm for the new nationalism, Ferraris belonged to that circle of conservative critics of the Giolittian system who would help pave the way for Fascism.

Between 1899 and 1913 Ferraris, following up the work begun by Paravicini and Bodio, wrote a series of articles about tourism and published them in his own journal. His first point was that tourism underpinned Italy's present economic performance and its future expectations. If visitors presently brought in 450 million lire to the national economy, there was no reason why, with proper planning, they should not soon deliver 1 billion. The traces of tourism could be seen almost everywhere. They extended 'from the railways to the coachmen in any city square'.[18] (Ferraris was an enthusiast for taxi-meters and for the replacement of horse-drawn cabs, still ubiquitous in 1913, by motor cars.[19]) Profits would also be garnered 'by big fashion shops and theatres, by artists and by the rather too many ambulatory sellers of guides and post-cards. And, most of all', he added, 'land-owners should be interested because of the huge sale of quality goods – wines, meat, chickens, eggs, fruit, flowers etc.' All these products were 'consumed by this mass of visitors who, if they were put together in a single centre, would constitute one of the most populous, rich and lively cities in the world'.[20] Tourism, Ferraris declared in repeated refrain, was the most profitable and least studied industry in Italy. Viewed properly, it was Italy's premier 'export'.[21]

As a tourist venue, Italy's attractions were infinite. They ran 'from the Alps to Sicily' (and, by 1913, on to Libya).[22]

It is only necessary to have lived for a short time in a family even of modest means in Britain or Germany to feel the allure which Venice by moonlight, or Naples with Vesuvius erupting, or the ruins of Rome, or the temples and gardens of Sicily, exert on whole generations and especially on the young. . . . A journey to Italy becomes the dream of their life.[23]

In England, even workers now travelled for pleasure.[24] With Ferraris' every thought, the potential customers for an Italian holiday grew and grew again.

But perils also lurked in this tantalising world. Foreigners – Swiss, French, Greek, Egyptian – were actively engaged in diverting the flood of visitors to their own resorts. Italy, amid its beauties, also contained some irritations – tipping, dirt, unreliable trains[25] and interfering customs officials. A tradition of toadying to eccentric foreign millionaires resulted in Italians ignoring opportunities for more lucrative mass tourism. Abroad, malign rumours circulated that Italy was a place of thieves and vagabonds. Worse, some foreigners flaunted their technological lead over Italy. Germans and Swedes had taxi-meters. The French and the Belgians placed seductive photographs of their own beach resorts in the compartments and corridors of their trains. German spa owners more readily co-operated with each other than did Italians, who, as a nation, were, unfortunately, slow to understand that, 'whether a matter of pleasure or not, ours is the era of unions [*sindacati*] and *trusts*'.[26] Italy, concluded Ferraris, must accept that it lived in a Darwinian economic and political world. 'Those people and individuals conquer who know first how to adopt the most efficient and modern means.'[27] 'The real need which Italy must feel at this moment is to enrich itself .... Whoever works for wealth is working for national grandeur.'[28]

To attain this dearly sought and well-rewarded modernity, planning was necessary. Private associations were good; state encouragement, supervision and subsidies were better. In this regard, some positive events had occurred and a network of organisations, designed to channel and charm the incoming tourists, was spreading. Ferraris himself was a leading advocate of the Associazione nazionale italiana per il movimento dei forestieri (ANMF or the National Tourist Association), which had been constituted in Rome in 1900. This body saw itself as centralising the efforts of such local groups as the Pro Napoli society and the Associazione pel bene economico of Palermo (this last was backed by such Sicilian magnates as Ignazio Florio and the prominent Lanza and Whittaker families, and was especially proud of having induced a certain Dr Lindsay to publish in the *Lancet* an article promoting 'Sicily as a Health Resort').[29] Closely linked to the ANMF was the Società italiana degli albergatori (SIA or Italian Hoteliers' Association), founded at Como in 1899, thereafter based in Genoa and by 1904 already claiming a membership list of 400 hotels.[30] In June 1900, the Hoteliers' Association had held their first national congress in Rome and debated such issues as better hygiene in hotel rooms and restaurants, a more structured training system for staff, a pension scheme, the possibility of more cooperative purchasing (eating foreign food in Italian hotels was deemed costly and unpatriotic) and ways of controlling tipping ('which had now become a real moral torture for a traveller').[31] As usual, Ferraris' mind raced ahead as he urged that the SIA and the ANMF should launch an

> Italian society . . . in each of the main cities of the world from Australia to America. These societies would bring together friends of our country – those who have visited it and those who dream of visiting it. Thus Italy could be made better known and appreciated abroad and attract a stream of guests and visitors.[32]

Nor was Ferraris alone in preaching planning and organisation. Rather, and very typically of Italy in the years before 1915, there flourished a whole host of associations more or less directly linked to tourism and to other leisure activities. In Venice, which for some years would remain Italy's most frequented tourist attraction, Michelangelo Jesurum, a lace manufacturer and hotelier, had been an early advocate of collective action, though his inspiration remained more local than national.[33]

In Milan, the Touring Club Italiano, which in the end would prove the most powerful and durable of all the tourist organisations, commenced activity in 1894. It had arisen on the private initiative of local gymnasts and cyclists and, until 1900, was called the Touring Club Ciclistico Italiano.[34] Its first president was Federigo Johnson, a businessman of English descent, who simultaneously presided over Milan's Veloce Club. Despite enduring occasional patriotic attacks on his English ancestry, Johnson remained in office until 1919, although the most active spokesman for the TCI quickly became the self-made businessman, Luigi Vittorio Bertarelli (founding member, vice-president from 1906, director-general from 1919 until his death in 1926).[35] Bertarelli gave special impetus to what soon became the flourishing publications wing of the TCI. From a humble beginning in 1895 with a *Guida delle grandi communicazioni stradali*, which aimed to be of assistance to lost cyclists (Bertarelli would remain an active propagandist of the need to improve the nation's roads),[36] the TCI, two years later, started distributing a monthly information sheet to its members. Sometimes almost entirely written by Bertarelli, this monthly acquired a decidedly lavish format and, in 1921, was renamed *Le Vie d'Italia* (*Italy's Highways and Byways*). Membership in the TCI spiralled upwards from 21,000 in 1900, to 84,000 in 1910, to 401,000 in 1930. Eight years earlier, in 1922, the Club had claimed assets of some 20 million lire, with an annual budget of 5 million.[37] Further enhancing the Club's profits and reputation were Bertarelli's celebrated multi-volume *Guide d'Italia*, which still remain the most authoritative introductions to many Italian tourist sites.[38]

Senior to the TCI was the Club Alpino Italiano, which had been established in Turin in 1863 by Quintino Sella,[39] a leading Liberal politician, whom, later, radical Fascists would hail as a precursor.[40] The Club Alpino enmeshed 'sport' and travel even more directly than would the TCI, and had sprung from the very heart of the Piedmontese Establishment, with its partisans boasting that the young Carlo Emanuele, in climbing Rocciamelone in 1658, had engaged on 'the first ascent by a sovereign in the Alps'. In the decades after its foundation, the Club and its members would expound the moral and physical benefits of the 'good air' of the mountains, pioneer alpine photography and cement its appeal to (gilded) youth by opening a university branch in 1905. The Club Alpino remained more elite in social composition than the Touring Club, possessing, by the 1920s, some 40,000 members.[41]

To these bodies, which directly favoured the growth of tourism, can be added a number of others. It was predictable, for example, that Italy's first sports newspaper should be published in tourist Venice,[42] and that the first Congresso Ginnastico Italiano should also be held in that city, in 1869.[43] Genoa, by contrast, would be the port through which modern football reached Italy, and that city's team, the first national champions, would be steeled by such English players as Dapples, Spensley and Baird.[44]

A pattern can thus be seen emerging. Liberal Italy was increasingly a place of clubs and associations. Their membership, which frequently overlapped, came from the higher rather than the lower social classes and often had the closest ties with the political establishment. Generations of Sellas figured prominently in the Club Alpino; the TCI, when it opened a branch in Venice, took over members of the Veloce Club Veneziano, which inevitably included scions of the Jesurum, Danieli and Foscari families prominent in the politics and hotel industry of their city. Prince Pietro Lanza di Scalea, who would be Under-Secretary of State for Foreign Affairs between

1911 and 1914, Fascist Minister of Colonies between 1924 and 1926 and a long time 'Mafia deputy' in western Sicily, went on cycling trips and was an important member of the TCI and the ANMF;[45] Francesco Guicciardini, from one of the oldest Tuscan landowning families (which would eventually sponsor the peculiarly vicious brand of Fascism in Tuscany)[46] and Sonnino's Minister of Foreign Affairs in 1905 and between 1909 and 1910, similarly proselytised tourist and athletic causes.

The Clubs were mostly northern in their origins and a reluctance was sometimes evinced when suggestions were made that a particular association would be best centred in Rome, where a national purpose might outweigh a local one. The sporting or tourist organisations, in turn, were the natural running mates of such overtly political organisations as the Dante Alighieri Society, the Istituti Coloniali Italiani and the Lega Navale. All accepted that Italy was engaged in a (Darwinian) international competition. The Italian 'race' must look to itself; as Angelo Mosso, a keen *alpinista*[47] and great advocate of the introduction of compulsory physical education into Italian schools and universities, put it in a book entitled *Mens sana in corpore sano*, unless Italians undertook more rigorous courses in hygiene and physical development, they could never hope to catch up with 'more civilised countries'.[48] (Mosso also thought it unlucky that Italians had the shortest legs in Europe, but believed that the adoption of the goose-step during military training might remedy that sad situation.)[49]

The basic message of those grouped in the tourist, sporting and political clubs was thus ameliorist; Italians must act now, improve their physiques and accelerate their economic growth in order to cope with the modern world. It was also emulative: the models which Italy needed to adopt were almost always foreign – the Club Alpino followed the British Alpine Club (1857) and the Austrian one (1862);[50] the Club Automobile d'Italia opened in Turin in 1905 and patterned itself on the Royal Automobile Club in Britain (1897). Italy may have pioneered international cycling races, but its first national association, the Unione Velocipedistica Italiana, set up in 1885 under the aegis of Count Agostino Bigliare di Viarigi, lagged behind the English and the French. The TCI had a British antecendent, while the French Touring Club boasted almost 50,000 members by 1897.[51] Gymnastics came from Germany, and Swiss schools had made physical education compulsory as early as 1828.[52] The Americans were pioneering sport for women.[53] Pressure groups designed to enhance tourism flourished earlier and were better organised in France and Switzerland.

In their dedication to 'power and the pursuit of peace', the membership of these 'clubs of the ruling class' reflected a *mentalité* which, earlier in the century, had led to the promotion of such international institutions as the Postal Union and the Red Cross, and was presently giving a solid base to the International Court of Justice in the Hague.[54] Club members thought of themselves as advocating an 'improvement' which well fitted the economic growth and rising national optimism of the Giolittian era.

But there were limits to the innocence of this zest for international competition and this openness to the possibility of learning from more 'advanced' foreigners. As Liberals surveyed the world and sought wider contacts through sport, tourism or the sponsoring of international congresses and exhibitions, they did so as men (and, indeed, women, since early Italian feminist organisations were proud of their wide-ranging contacts)[55] of their time, with a positive belief in human progress and in continuing peace. Contemporaneously, the Liberal elite understood their nation to be confronted by ever fiercer competition from abroad. Power was indeed at play as well as peace, and in this competition eventually there would be casualties. As Ferraris had argued in one of his publications aimed at promoting tourist organisation, there, as elsewhere, Italy 'had a great national treasure to develop and defend. In the present context of bitter international struggle, the weak and the isolated go under'.[56] The more many Liberals experienced the wider world and the more they learned from it, the more they felt impelled to defend their nation and to assert its grandeur. Above all else, the clubs and pressure groups, as they perceived or constructed this pervasive international competition, were nationalising their membership. As Bertarelli had stated as early as 1901 in a phrase which would be much invoked by his institution under Fascism: the knowledge gained in travelling around the peninsula would mean that 'Italy – and here the Touring will be of assistance – Italy will make Italians'.[57] Within Liberal Italy would be achieved a nationalisation of the bourgeoisie and intelligentsia, if not the masses. Men and women of good will or good sense, and even more, their sons and daughters, must temper Italy for the war of tomorrow.

When that war came, it had one obvious and immediate effect, though one of some puzzlement to contemporaries.[58] War was bad for tourism, just as it was bad for emigration and bad for the national budget and estate – in January 1915, the TCI leadership was still asserting naively that their work in proselytising tourism was 'essentially pacific'.[59] One inevitable victim of the war was Venice, Italy's premier tourist site with particular links to the Germanic world, though cheerful or insouciant nationalists saw the collapse of the Venetian tourist industry as the chance to restore to that city its proper mission. Maybe tourism was not an automatically pacific activity, after all. Some Italians, it now turned out, felt suffocated by foreigners' love of Venice and repaid such feelings with resentment or hate – the Futurist Marinetti would contemplate with pleasure the prospect of the city razed to the ground under aerial bombardment.

For the tourists who crowded into Piazza San Marco, by contrast, Venice had many charms. It was a fabulous place – Dickens comprehended it in a 'dream';[60] Ruskin proclaimed the Doge's Palace 'the central building of the world';[61] years after, Théophile Gautier could still see in his mind's eye the colour of the peaches which he had bought on the Frezzaria.[62] But to the Victorian and *fin de siècle* mind, such sensual beauty and pleasure carried a strong hint of sin. In the writings of figures as diverse as 'Baron Corvo', Maurice Barrès or Thomas Mann, Venice became the special symbol of decadence,[63] lust, adultery and homosexuality, this last still at the time that unnamed sexual perversion which thrilled so many northern Europeans with its possibilities. In its genteel, *belle époque* way, Italy, especially on Capri,[64] in Calabria[65] or at Taormina, where Baron Wilhelm von Gloeden won something of a European monopoly in artistic photographs of naked boys,[66] was the natural venue for what is now called a 'sex tour'. While more predatory visitors sought release further south, Venice, to innocent minds, was instead a cliché; as Henry James had remarked, 'of all the cities in the world ... it [was] the easiest to visit without going there'. 'The Venice of today', he went on,

> is a vast museum where the little wicket that admits you is perpetually turning and creaking, and you march through the institution with a herd of fellow-gazers. There is nothing left to discover or describe, and originality of attitude is completely impossible.[67]

Given this admixture of foreigners' salaciousness and contempt, it is not surprising to find some Italians searching out a different role for Venice. Before 1914, the intellectual who had most publicly made himself into a Venetian was Gabriele D'Annunzio. This self-defined 'world's greatest lover' pledged, for the 'Queen of the Adriatic', a naval and imperial mission which might once again hold the gorgeous east in fee and convert 'all the oceans into ... [Italy's] own sea'.[68] D'Annunzio's carefully constructed and marketed persona and prose style were nothing if not ambiguous, arch and artful, and did little to redeem Venice's image of luxury and transgression; the diminutive 'Archangel Gabriele' seemed to be one who indulged in each of the seven deadly sins before breakfast (at 2 p.m.), and such ostentatious shamelessness assisted his fame and his sales in Paris, that other epicentre of sin, culture and tourism. In his vortex of self-advertisement, D'Annunzio often seemed to convert patriotism into little more than another rhetorical device, designed in the final analysis merely to sell his wares.

With war, however, such doubts and inconsistencies could be set aside. Venice lay near the front, subject to enemy aerial bombardment and, after Caporetto, became a place from which a majority of the civilian populace had been evacuated. While D'Annunzio plotted another dauntless and well-publicised mission against the *tedeschi*,[69] other nationalist intellectuals made Venice into a symbol of that new Italy in which they placed their post-war hopes. Ezio Maria Gray was typical of this group. In 1915, Gray had published a paranoid account of spying in Italy (he is perhaps the only person in world history to have cited William Le Queux as an authoritative source), and eagerly helped organise the Comitato italiano contro le insidie straniere (Italian Committee Against Foreign Plots).[70] His proof of German perfidy had included tourist shops throughout the peninsula which, he declared, never seemed to sell anything, the German and 'Swiss' (they were all really Germans, he warned) clientele and ownership of too many Italian hotels and the regularity of the Kaiser's visits to Venice (or Taormina).[71]

In 1917, when he, like a number of other nationalist intellectuals, was doing regular service from the roofs of the city as an anti-aircraft gunner, Gray amplified his attack on tourism in a study of Venice in war. Before 1914, Gray wrote, the Giolittian elite had consigned Venice 'into the hands of foreigners who do not understand it, do not respect it and do not honour it'. The merchandising of such tourist specialities as 'alabaster gondolas, cheap post-cards and ... [with a disgraceful if predictable ignorance of place] Florentine hand-made paper' had reduced the city to a 'Tunisian souk'. High cultural activities did not rehabilitate Venice. The *Esposizione Internazionale d'Arte* in the summer of 1914 had, in his opinion, transmogrified the

Lido into 'a suburb of Budapest'. Everywhere, and on all occasions, the city breathed falsity. At the Excelsior Hotel, Gray recalled,

> I was invested by overpowering perfume which did not remind me of any real flowers; I heard snippets of conversation in French, English, Russian, Hungarian and each of these languages was spoken in a foreign way. At the same time the phrases had a strictly limited vocabulary: love affairs, little scandals, eccentricities, paradoxes. The voices were as fake as were the ideas.[72]

For Gray, there was one insistent answer – Venice must stop prostituting itself. Luzzatti should be condemned for hoping that the tourist industry would revive after the war; Salandra should be praised for urging 'fewer hotels and more factories'. The city had never looked more beautiful than in wartime, with the tourists gone and a blackout in force. It must never again become a place in which Italian could not be heard. Venice's new destiny must be national and only that.[73]

Gray's ideas were, of course, completely unrealistic, more rhetorical and 'false' than the most petty *oggetto d'arte* foisted by a brazen cicerone on some guileless tourist. (In his earlier book Gray had listed as another of the succubi of Germandom Giuseppe Volpi, that entrepreneur who in the inter-war period would lead the industrialisation of Venice at Porto Marghera and Mestre.)[74] But, in rejecting tourism as servile and corrupting, Gray had also expressed sentiments which would become an important aspect of Fascism and which, in Italy and elsewhere, remain an inescapable debating point in any consideration of the long-term value of a tourist industry.[75]

The war over, Italy's political and commercial worlds, which had paid little attention to Gray's intellectual posturing, sought rapidly to revive tourism. In 1919 Prime Minister Nitti[76] and his Minister for Commerce and Industry, Meuccio Ruini, finally did what Maggiorino Ferraris had long advocated and established a national tourist board. The Ente Nazionale per le Industrie Turistiche (ENIT) was soon busily at work, having hired such distinguished statisticians as Angelo Mariotti[77] and Marco Avancini[78] who, in the 1920s, would give Italy the international reputation[79] of having the most accurate and detailed tourist statistics in the world. Government 'planning', or at least bureaucratic supervision of tourism, had at last been achieved.

After 1918, tourists had quickly remembered Italy's attractions, though, doubtless, they were dismayed by waiters' strikes which, on at least two occasions in 1919–20, made life difficult for visitors to Venice.[80] In 1922, despite the continuing political instability, more than half a million foreigners crossed the national borders – 131,000 reached Venice, 67,000 Naples, 66,000 Rome, 30,000 Florence, thirty-five Potenza and fourteen Sassari. July was the most popular month of entry, January the least. Germans were the most numerous visitors to Venice, and Americans to Florence. The French composed 75 per cent of Lucca's tourists.[81] Most of those arriving still travelled by train, though 3,005 cars entered Italy that year, 199 over the Brenner Pass, seventy over the Little St Bernard and ten intrepid chauffeurs drove their employers over the Colle della Maddalena.[82] To Italy's familiar allure were now added the battle-fields,[83] so freshly reeking of blood and so redolent of heroism. According to Mariotti,[84] Italy had special advantages there, since the Carso and Monte Grappa[85] possessed natural scenic beauty of their own, and the former lay close by the newly acquired Abbazia, one of pre-war Europe's premier bathing resorts.

As well as sponsoring the collection of fuller and ever more accurate statistics, the Liberal regime was undertaking tighter state supervision of the hotel trade; new legislation had been passed even before the war ended.[86] ENIT, meanwhile, pressed for better training of hotel staff. The Touring Club had somewhat inauspiciously opened the first proper Italian 'leisure industry' school only in September 1914, whereas Switzerland had started tourist instruction in 1893 and thirty years later would possess at least 100 such centres.[87] Now, with the war over, a state-approved Italian school could commence its training programmes at Montecatini. Its seventy-three alumni, Mariotti rather naively noted, were 'all the sons of hoteliers or of the owners of restaurants, *pensioni* or bars'.[88]

Fascism at first appears to have had very little impact on this reviving activity. Mussolini and *Popolo d'Italia* both regularly underlined the economic importance of tourist promotion, even if they could not help boasting that Italy had a natural 'tourist primacy in the world'.[89] The Duce was an early visitor to the Touring Club, now plainly the most successful and popular of the tourist associations, and in 1926 took out a well-publicised membership ticket.[90] The Hoteliers' Association turned into the Federazione Nazionale Fascista Alberghi e Turismo and went about its business.[91] The state promised further assistance or control, in 1927 setting up the Compagnia Italiana Turismo (CIT), which operated mainly as a travel agency (E.M. Gray was its somewhat inappropriate first president), and, in 1934, the Direzione Generale per il Turismo (DGT), which, characteristically of later Fascism, was designed to supervise the supervisors. In the next year, a decree established yet another body, the Ente Provinciale per il Turismo.[92]

The DGT fell under the authority of the Ministry of Press and Propaganda and the Fascist regime was active in continuing to bruit abroad Italy's attractions as a tourist venue. During the Ethiopian crisis, for example, much care was taken to proclaim that tourist conditions in Italy were 'quite normal'.[93] In 1936, despite sanctions, the regime went out of its way to give foreign tourists access to petrol supplies and retained their usual discount. Similarly, a satisfied British customer was featured in the media as saying that sanctions had actually improved hotel food, rendering it more tasty and 'national'.[94] The empire was also to be opened to tourists. As Governor of Libya, Italo Balbo took special delight in patronising the fine local archaeological museum.[95] His efforts must have convinced the holidaying Durack sisters, daughters of one of Western Australia's leading pastoral, political and literary families, who, in 1937, came home remarking that what had been done in Libya could be done in Ethiopia: 'We are absolutely won round to [the Fascist] conquest of Abyssinia and feel sure that they will make a wonderful job of it and be extremely good rulers to the Abyssinian people.'[96] Even in 1942, Venice welcomed a convention of Axis journalists[97] and, two years later, that city was still holding art exhibitions[98] 'under one bombardment or another'.[99]

In 1931 Mussolini had declared grandly that tourism was one of Italy's four ways to the future.[100] He needed to be positive because by then the industry had been afflicted by something of a crisis. After the Fascist accession to power, progress had at first been easy. Tourist numbers increased exponentially year by year. In 1925 the total of arrivals numbered 1,350,000 (up by more than 100 per cent since 1922). They were estimated to have spent some 3,600 million lire and thus that year to have wiped out 61 per cent of Italy's budget deficit.[101] This triumphant expansion had been greatly assisted by the fact that 1925 was *L'Anno Santo* (Holy Year), an event which was scheduled to occur only once every twenty-five years, and which was marked by many special religious celebrations that automatically brought many faithful Catholics to Rome. Thereafter, times became more difficult. The high valuation of the lira in 1927 acted as a special disincentive,[102] and in 1929 only some 900,000 tourists came, spending 2,418 million, covering an estimated 35 per cent of the balance of payments deficit.[103] Germans visitors were now more numerous than Americans, although official planners reckoned that Americans per capita spent twice as much as did Europeans, and solemnly wondered how best they might be wooed – by trains that ran on time? By freely available bottle openers? By an increase in the number of golf courses? By the elimination of tips or the *coperta* fee in restaurants? By the invitation to put a 'Do Not Disturb' sign on their hotel room doors?[104]

But while such weighty matters were pondered by the bureaucrats of the tourist industry, an economic crisis had enveloped both Germany and the United States, and the value of tourism continued to decline. It reached its nadir in 1932, when the advantage to the national budget was reckoned to be only 1,004 million lire, though propagandists of the industry trumpeted that this sum nonetheless amounted to 58 per cent of the budget deficit. (What they did not say was that in a contracting national economy budgetary figures were smaller than before.)[105]

During the following years, the world slowly emerged from the Depression and tourist numbers and spending increased again. The automobile had replaced the train as the major vehicle of tourist travel and, in 1934, the Fascist government counted 2,138,950 foreigners who reached Italy by road, a new record.[106] Italy, they were proud to say, had confirmed its standing as the third tourist venue of the world, behind France and Canada.[107] In 1937, more than 5 million foreign visitors crossed its national borders (see Table 8.1).

For all the brave words about Italy's tourist performance, however, a certain contradiction hung over the industry in the 1930s, as international crises multiplied, and as the Fascist regime highlighted its nationalism and xenophobia and its commitment to economic autarky. In September 1935 Rotary International displayed a modicum of unease about holding its regional conference in Venice at the very moment that Fascism was preparing so ostentatiously to invade Ethiopia.[108] A decade before, Mussolini had expressed the hope that, rather than always emphasising international contacts, the government would concentrate on drawing to Italy 'foreigners of our own blood', that is, the children of emigrants, and on giving them 'an immersion in Italianness', *'un bagno d'italianità'*.[109] In the aftermath of this declaration, ENIT, CIT, TCI and the rest had loyally or deferentially opened branches in New York and Buenos Aires and had presumably done good business there.

Table 8.1 Tourists visiting Italy and their means of access 1931–56

Year	By rail	By road	By ship	By air	Total
1931	919,484	1,156,943	108,273	1,605	2,186,305
1932	705,725	1,102,177	94,705	1,963	1,904,570
1933	922,042	1,494,675	109,202	2,389	2,528,308
1934	881,617	2,138,950	119,111	2,694	3,142,372
1935	882,468	2,042,764	110,547	5,041	3,040,820
1936	941,805	2,326,684	116,883	7,390	3,392,762
1937	1,468,356	3,375,753	163,321	11,276	5,018,706
1938	1,362,500	2,449,929	158,346	12,220	3,982,995
1939	938,531	1,429,122	101,911	12,430	2,481,994
1940	245,024	144,548	24,769	4,798	419,139
1948	842,849	627,883	50,869	68,432	1,590,033
1949	1,202,236	1,980,461	91,948	127,017	3,401,662
1950	1,934,484	2,588,726	137,127	178,939	4,839,276
1951	2,076,240	3,028,242	113,225	188,156	5,405,863
1952	2,116,571	3,572,523	155,433	214,770	6,059,297
1953	2,319,999	4,926,770	176,297	258,804	7,681,870
1954	2,492,921	6,305,742	225,354	303,495	9,327,512
1955	2,800,114	7,384,704	258,107	343,093	10,786,018
1956	3,218,463	8,772,944	264,096	409,457	12,664,960

Source: G. Carone, *Il turismo nell'economia internazionale*, Milan, 1959, p. 292

But the regime had also emphasised its commitment to making holidays available for its own people. Quite a lot was done, especially for children and especially in Northern Italy, as the Balilla or *dopolavoro* organised summer camps or weekend treks.[110] An official policy of organised tourism and other forms of leisure for Italians within Italy was accompanied by a determination that Italy succeed in international sporting competition – Fascist propagandists exulted over cycling champions, over Primo Carnera, who, in 1936, challenged for the world heavyweight boxing title but lost,[111] and over the national football team's victorious participation in the 1934 and 1938 World Cups. Similarly, the regime boasted that 'everyone recognised' that Italy had been 'third' in the 1928 Olympic Games and 'second' in those of 1932.[112]

Under Fascism, much more directly than in the past, all forms of leisure were to have a nationalising and eugenic purpose. Whatever effete foreigners were doing, Italians could only play and holiday for their own and their regime's good. The 1934 *Manuale* of the Touring Club was emblematic in this regard. It predictably endorsed tourism, and happily contrasted the many achievements of the Fascist regime with the situation which the *Manuale* claimed had existed before 1922, in which period 'the flood of subversion' had discouraged so many from travelling around the nation. But, for Italians, the *Manuale* emphasised stoically, the best way to see their country was on foot, 'the oldest, the healthiest and the cheapest form of tourism'. In words which may not have appealed to peasants and women, and which hinted that the nationalisation of the masses was not yet complete, the *Manuale* continued:

> Modern man, condemned for so long to the segregated, sedentary and noisy life of the city . . . in the open air needs to tone up his body and to calm his spirit by serenely viewing the countryside and by direct contact with nature.

Great poets, great artists and great thinkers had always been at their best on a tramp – Dante, Petrarch, Shelley, D'Annunzio, Pascoli, Virgil, Beethoven, Nietzsche, Carducci, Pope Pius XI (the '*Pontefice alpinista*') and, of course, Benito Mussolini were the proof of that.[113]

In practice, however, Italy was marching to war and to another period of tourist ruin, even if, in 1942, comforting official noises would be made about the substantial place which would eventually be granted to tourism in the 'New Order'.[114] The dilemmas of the era were well summed up in the story of the Hotel Anglo-Americano in Florence. In 1940 its owners, engaged on a sisyphean search to be politically correct, amended the name to Albergo America; in 1941 to the Regina; in 1943 to the Mercurio. In 1944, however, they took out the old Hotel Anglo-Americano signs once more.[115] But war did not assault only the façade of the tourist industry. In the campaigns of 1943–5 which slowly traversed all of Italy, the infrastructure of tourism was damaged far more gravely than it had been between 1915 and 1918. By its end, the war had destroyed 40 per cent of hotels and damaged another 20 per cent, leaving only 176,000 beds available in the whole country in 1946.[116]

Nonetheless, once again the 'structure' of tourism soon shrugged off the mere 'event' of a war. In 1950 Pius XII presided over the most triumphalist of Holy Years and pious customers arrived daily, almost equalling the previous record figures of 1937, and more than trebling the tourist total of 1948. Within six years the number of tourists had trebled again, and then, in August–September 1960, the Olympic Games drew some 100,000 visitors to Rome each day. Of all the economic miracles, tourism was the greatest (see Tables 8.2 and 8.3). Between 1955 and 1959, the number of beds in Italian hotels increased by almost 50 per cent and the number of bathrooms doubled. More than 188,000 Italians were by then employed in the hotel industry alone.[117] In 1964, 10 million foreigners took their holidays in Italy, and a further 12 million visited the country for a couple of days. The number of tourists spiralled upwards by more than 10 per cent each year.[118]

Table 8.2 Number of tourists to certain countries 1953 and 1956

Country	1953	1956
Italy	4,812,000	7,000,000
France	3,190,000	4,305,000
Germany	2,751,000	4,289,000
Switzerland	3,218,000	3,831,000
Austria	1,601,000	2,836,000
Great Britain	819,000	1,107,000
Greece	76,000	206,000

Source: Figures adapted from G. Carone, *Il turismo nell'economia internazionale*, Milan, 1959, p. 39

Table 8.3 Hotel and other accommodation in certain regions, 30 June 1957

Region	Hotels and pensioni	Locande	Rooms	Beds	Bathrooms
Piedmont	1,004	2,448	31,329	52,617	5,090
Lombardy	1,423	3,277	41,832	71,492	8,396
Veneto	1,196	1,493	39,188	66,799	8,319
Emilia–Romagna	2,389	1,394	52,939	93,077	13,882
Tuscany	1,590	740	37,111	63,291	10,296
Lazio	795	373	21,849	36,499	7,866
Campania	517	551	15,129	27,061	5,863
Basilicata	28	245	1,262	2,257	155
Sicily	331	688	11,476	20,215	3,034
Sardinia	87	157	2,518	4,203	680

Source: Figures adapted from G. Carone, *Il turismo nell'economia internazionale*, Milan, 1959, p. 304

Nothing daunted, the statisticians of ENIT, one of many state institutions which had easily forgotten its Fascist past, provided yet more information. A survey compiled in 1965 indicated that, of all visitors, Belgians, Germans and Dutch were most attracted by Italian weather. 'History' and 'art' interested Spaniards and Americans. Local food and wine impressed the Swedes and the British most (and the French the least). Catholicism enticed the Lebanese and the Irish. The 'national character' of Italians had won over the French and the Swedes.[119] A gender breakdown was also available. Women, who had been an important part of the tourist armies for generations,[120] now made up the majority of Finnish and French visitors and 48.1 per cent of American ones (as against only 38.5 per cent of British and 35.5 per cent of Spanish tourists).[121]

Thus, the democratisation of tourism, which Maggiorino Ferraris had foreseen at the turn of the century, was still gathering pace. By the end of the 1980s the world was spending an estimated US $2 trillion annually on tourism, equal to 12 per cent of the global economy.[122] Italy, whose officials liked to boast that the country held in its innumerable museums and galleries more than 50 per cent of the world's artistic patrimony and that Tuscany alone possessed more classified sites and artistic treasures than any single European country,[123] claimed 10 per cent of the trade and had indeed finally won a civil and financial primacy in tourism.[124]

Tourism and emigration had continued to shadow each other through Italian history. In the 1950s and 1960s, for example, young Australians, leaving in unparalleled numbers to see the world, took over the berths vacated by arriving Italian immigrants on Flotta Lauro or Lloyd Triestino ships. By the 1970s and 1980s, as emigration ceased, and Italy began its still equivocal history as an immigrant country, Italians, for the first time in vast numbers, began democratically to holiday for pleasure at home and abroad. In now importing immigrants and exporting tourists, Italy threatened again to do unto others as had been done unto its own citizens.

It was true, of course, that Italy had experienced tourism, sport and all leisure activities in an uneven way. As the figures cited above have already demonstrated, Venice, Florence and Rome attracted hundreds of thousands of tourists while only an intrepid handful reached such poor or distant outposts as Potenza, Nuoro or a *paese* in the Calabrian hills. According to Norman Douglas, ordinary Italians, at least before 1914, saw northern European visitors as belonging to 'a vast perambulatory lunatic asylum'.[125] Then and thereafter, tourism, sport and leisure flourished best in urban areas, or in such resort towns as San Remo and Viareggio,[126] in the great spas of Salsomaggiore and Montecatini[127] and in alpine retreats like Cortina d'Ampezzo and Susa. While peasants still formed a signific-ant proportion of the population, tourism rarely affected them in any direct sense, and they were also the last social class to think of taking holidays of their own. In a region like the Salento, or in rural Sardinia, the very concept of a hotel remained alien until at least the 1960s.[128]

Such regional and class variation and exclusiveness, along with the many blatant types of exploitation perennially involved, make it easy to score points off tourism both as an industry and as an activity. Intellectuals from E.M. Gray onwards have been especially ready to bewail the ignorance, corruption and pollution which accompanies the growth of tourism, and to deplore the latest equivalent of 'Florentine' paper retailed in Venice or of an alabaster gondola clutched in the sweaty hand of an ill-dressed, ill-kempt, ill-fed and ill-informed foreign tourist.[129] Such elitist arrogance should be kept under tight rein, however. For all the degradation of the coastline caused by the mass discovery of the sea-as-holiday from the 1950s onwards,[130] for all the tawdriness of the trinkets of 'genuine' art, history or religion retailed at Florence, Rome, Assisi and a thousand other centres, for all the environmental and spiritual pollution, it seems reasonable to conclude that the rise and rise of tourism has brought more benefit than loss, and occasioned more pleasure than harm.

No matter how dimly, on many occasions it has taught the world something about Italy. It has brought vast sums of money into the peninsula. In harness with emigration, it has helped, despite products of such dubious attraction as tinned spaghetti and the frozen pizza, to give hundreds of millions a taste for Italian cuisine: a social history of garlic 1860 to 1960 might start with John Ruskin being offended by its 'close smell' at a dirty inn in Mestre,[131] and end with recent medical advice on the advantages of the 'Mediterranean diet'.[132] Perhaps one day an *equipe* of *Annales* historians will develop a 'garlic index' and draw a graph of the relationship between the appreciation of this herb and Italy's place in the world. Similarly tourism has assisted the triumphs of Italian design – once it is accepted that the Doge's Palace, or a Ravenna mosaic, or a Duccio painting, or a temple at Paestum are the epitome of style and beauty, it becomes hard to overlook the skill of an Italian couturier. The drivers of cars which traversed Italian *autostrade* have learned about Italian engineering skill and carried the news back home. Tourism has sold Italian cinema, and perhaps helps to explain why so often the 'best' Italian films win their most appreciative audiences outside Italy.[133]

Perhaps, too, tourism has prompted that 'banality of good' which may sometimes characterise Italy or the Italies. Bertarelli of the TCI was right to deem it a pacific act. Tourism is another of those areas of human life which, in its very essence, is both universal and local, social and individual. For all its ambitions to do so, the Italian national state has never wholly organised and controlled tourism (and its statistics, for all their plenitude, are inevitably unreliable); the industry has been another sphere in which state weakness has been as evident as state strength – according to a recent estimate, governmental figures may underestimate the number employed in tourism in Italy by 100 or 150 per cent.[134] Yet, somehow, the industry has survived and flourished, the holidays have been taken and enjoyed, the outsiders received and, at least to some extent, accepted. In the final analysis, Italy's visitors have come, seen and, often enough, been conquered, of course by Italy's past, but also by its present and future, and Italians have learned to treasure such peaceful, happy and lucrative contacts with the wider world.

CONCLUSION

This book was written at a time of trauma in Italy. *The Economist*, the most authoritative organ of monetarist dogma, has been welcoming the prospect of 'tumbrils' rolling metaphorically through the streets of Milan and Rome,[1] and has regularly enthused about a 'revolution' which, it believes, will sweep away the corruption, inefficiency (and welfare state) of the 'First' Republic: 'in the heart of Western Europe, an entire political order is collapsing. It's about time'.[2] Whatever else Silvio Berlusconi and Forza Italia, Gianfranco Fini and his re-legitimated or post-Fascist Alleanza Nazionale and Umberto Bossi and the Lega Nord represent, at least, we are told, they will constitute a break with the past, an overcoming of Italian history.

This book was also written in a special place, that Australia which, after 1945, welcomed Italian immigrants in unexpected numbers, but in which, now, the 'second generation' of Italo-Australians is drifting into the third and in which direct contact with Italy steadily diminishes. The most clear-eyed of Italo-Australian writers has recently remarked that, already in her girlhood, 'Italy' could be deployed in some very particular ways: 'Nostalgia', she says, 'was becoming the older generation's strongest defence' against the new:

> Our parents needed intercession, holy favours. The figure of Saint Italy began to appear and intervene in bitter family arguments. Saint Italy was Person, Place and Spirit. Whenever we teenagers wanted to do anything – go on a school camp, buy white leather knee-high boots, play guitar, go swimming with friends – Saint Italy the Perfect, Saint Italy the Good, Saint Italy the Merciful and Bountiful and Beautiful would come up .... *The doctors are smarter in Italy*, said my mother of her

182

aches and pains that never responded to treatment. . . . *The young people are more modest in Italy. . . . There are no rapes and murders in Italy. . . . There is more respect for parents in Italy. . . . There are no drugs, mini-skirts or The Beatles in Italy. . . . Girls do not have boyfriends in Italy. . . . Italians do not say 'piss off' or 'stuff you' in Italy. . . . There is no premarital sex in Italy . . . therefore unmarried women do not have babies in Italy. . . . There is no violent crime in Italy.*[3]

Italy, the corrupt; Italy, in permanent need of schooling and amendment; Italy, the magical; Italy, the giver of solace; Italy, the deployable; Italy, like many another nation, the manipulative creation of the 'lesser examination-passing classes';[4] Saint Italy, in which the people believe – the many meanings of Italy, it is plain, are still located in the eyes of the beholders. Or is it just that, in the endless human process of remembering, inventing and forgetting, some Italies are always dying out, even as *The Economist* gives counsel, emigrants reforge their identities, and I write?

Certainly it seems reasonable to argue in conclusion to this book that much of Italy's relationship with the wider world in the century after unification is best defined negatively. Italy and its people did not suffer from imperial delusions and responsibilities to the same extent that the British, the French and the Americans have done. Italians never attempted or endured a revolution as all-embracing as the Soviet one. Fascist Italy could not compete with Nazi Germany in fanaticism of thought and deed. The Italian Army could not emulate the feats of the *Wehrmacht* on the field of battle nor those of the Spanish or French armies at home. Italians were never as certain that they 'possessed' 2,000 years of history as many Japanese were. Apart from some nationalist rhodomontades, Italians with difficulty conceived themselves as coming from the 'Middle Kingdom', even if 'Italian' emigrants could and can be found in every part of the globe. For all Gioberti's hopes and delusions in the Risorgimento, the civil and moral primacy of Italians in this or that field was never unreservedly achieved.

Certainly a primacy was not won diplomatically. In the halls and corridors of international power, Liberal, Fascist and (First) Republican Italians aspired in the final analysis to recognition more than anything else. Italy should behave like a Great Power, join the race for empire, participate in world wars, practise capitalism, uphold a national culture, instruct and entertain those foreigners who crossed its frontiers, but never too wholeheartedly, never too credulously, never (or, rather, seldom) too rashly. Italy was the border country of many a mind – its Catholics were more sceptical than were Poles, Irish or Croats (and were less persuaded that their God had been nationalised); its Communists looked for an Italian path to socialism or indeed any path that would not be Muscovite; its Fascists were aghast at the German ally which meant what it said; its Liberals knew as much about patron–client networks as about the 'free' market; its emigrants, sometimes *paesani*, sometimes 'Latins' and sometimes assimilated, were rarely content with the single identity of being Italian.

By one understanding Italy from 1860 to 1960 thus resembled that Venice depicted by a contemporary post-modernist novelist. It was

> the city of mazes. You may set off from the same place every day and never go by the same route. If you do so it will be by mistake. . . . This is the city of uncertainty where routes and faces look alike and are not. . . . In this enchanted city all things seem possible. Time stops. . . . They say this city can absorb anyone. It does seem that every nationality is here in some part. . . . They are all looking for something, travelling the seven seas but looking for a reason to stay.[5]

Italy is the place where there is always another play within a play, and each Pagliacci is destined to discover that the *commedia* is not quite *finita*. Italy is the society always grappling with 'an awful mess on the Via Merulana', in which the honest detective, however, is destined never to reveal his solution on the last page.[6] Italy is the country whose most renowned contemporary intellectual is a semio-tician named Eco, good at finding and celebrating fakes, in a world he comprehends as one of *cogito interruptus*.[7]

As if to legitimise further the claim that understanding best comes through a series of flickering images, Italy has possessed, and to some extent still possesses, one of the great national film industries. By 1909 500 films had already been produced in that country. Italians became adept in making documentaries that were not documentaries – both the Messina earthquake and the war in Libya were constructed on the screen, but by art not 'reality'.[8] Liberal Italy, that culture so uncertain about its own history, also pioneered 'historical' block-busters which, by means of the camera, cheerfully illustrated an identity between the first and the third Romes.[9] Nor did the mixed messages cease during the Fascist regime. For all his aspiration to serve a totalitarian culture, Giuseppe Bottai advised in 1931:

> Too openly propagandist films or those too overtly moralising perhaps will not meet with public favour. Even a production which is backing up religious or political ideas must concentrate on its artistic and commercial sides and not lose sight of what leads to 'success', the real reason for the cinema's existence.[10]

Such realism did not necessarily bring rewards, however. In 1938 almost three-quarters of ticket sales in Fascist Italy went to films made in the USA – Mussolini himself was known to be a devoted fan of '*Stanley e Olio*' (Laurel and Hardy).[11] Though, for the next years, autarky and war stemmed the United States invasion, the popular cultural ground was left well tilled for a Hollywood revival after 1945.

Film in the Italian Republic retained some anomalies. In the immediate post-war period, 'neo-realism' restored Italy's cultural fame with a cinema which seemed beautifully to express both the 'spirit of the Resistance' and a timeless humanism.[12] Cesare Zavattini, the movement's most sophisticated theorist, explained that these films sprang from a post-Fascist 'sense of obligation' on the part of the film-makers, 'as Italians, to break free from false absolutes and to enter into the essence of things'.[13] Christ with a camera, he maintained against the criticism of such Christian Democrat moralists as Giulio Andreotti, would have been a neo-realist.[14]

No doubt many films of the genre reflected a moral purpose just as they marked a departure from a Fascist past, but the change in character was rendered ambiguous by the fact that such celebrated neo-realists as Vittorio De Sica, Roberto Rossellini and Zavattini himself had been well launched in their careers by 1939. The 'first' neo-realist classic, Luchino Visconti's *Ossessione* (1942), was, arguably, a piece of Fascist populism, with a certain (paradoxical) admixture from contemporary United States and French cinema. Similarly undermining of any simple assumption that neo-realism embodied the new Italian Republic's civic culture were ticket sales. Outside Italy, the films were critically acclaimed and sold well to sophisticated audiences, but they were generally far less successful with local cinema-goers. Italians preferred the products of Hollywood.[15] Stanley and Olio still worked their spell.

For all the constancy of American competition, many marvellous films would be produced in Republican Italy. But perhaps the outstanding director of the post-Fascist period, until his death in 1993, was Federico Fellini. In his way Fellini agreed with the comment of Italo Svevo cited in the introduction to this book that humanity lived and lives in a world of mixed tenses. Fellini's greatest films, *La Strada*, *8½* and *Amarcord*, brought to the screen images of complexity and ambiguity – as often as not Fellini was another unveiling the play within the play, the mask beneath the mask, the image within the image; he was the film-maker playing with the problem of making films. As for meaning, Fellini eschewed final solutions:

> I don't like people who pretend to save humanity with a picture. . . . I have never thought of making a film moved by considerations of political morality or by any social sense. I have only wanted to tell a story, almost in a narcissistic way, something that concerns myself, deeply, and, since I don't think that I am a kind of inhuman monster, when I speak for myself I feel that I have spoken for everyone.[16]

His audiences, both in Italy and in the wider world, were viewing images manufactured by an individual, even as they then forged their own personal comprehensions of Fellini's 'Italian' cinema. (Half-understood) messages continued to redound.

Fellini's words, with their ambiguous promise of humanity, are as good a place as any to end this excursion through the highways and byways of Italy's place in the world. Many Anglo-Saxon historians have over the years come to the highly romantic conclusion that the Italian people are good, even as Italian politicians are bad. The Italies, they have tended to argue, have reflected an enduring sense of love and charity, even while a Mussolini strutted, or an Andreotti set up another morally dubious deal. Though the powerless are always in a sense blessed, it is an unsatisfactory antithesis. Generally speaking, Italians, like most people, were ruled by something like the governments which they deserved, and, even if large sections of the populace were, until at least 1960, scarcely active participants in a functioning democracy, the excluded social groups were no more certainly bearers of virtue than were those in power.

And yet, somehow, Italians and their nation state, the regions of Italy, the various *paesi*, the Italian family in all its change and contradiction, endured, and there will be many grounds for regret if, by some fell chance, there is no place in the newest new world order for Italy and the Italies. A certain charm, a certain elegance, a certain beauty, a certain humility, a certain perseverance, a certain resilience, a certain energy, a certain sense of work and of play, of love and of charity, a certain openness, a certain willingness to engage in *rapporti umani*, will, among other, not always so positive, matters, be lost. But, whatever the future, the history, from 1860 to 1960, of Italy and Italians, and of their place in the wider world, should be remembered as a time of good and evil, in which the banality of the evil was, on balance, outweighed by the banality of the good. After all, as an Australian novelist sometime resident in Tuscany has noted, there 'Italy' is only a 'misty, metaphysical concept' and when an old *paesana* remarked to him 'we're all Italians' she was intending thus to celebrate and to treasure the commonality of humankind.[17]

NOTES

PREFACE

1 A.B. Facey, *A Fortunate Life*, Ringwood, Victoria, 1981.
2 E. Ciccotosto and M. Bosworth, *Emma: A Translated Life*, Fremantle, 1990.

INTRODUCTION: THE PROBLEM OF ITALY AND THE WIDER WORLD 1860–1960

1 L. Baldassar, 'Italo-Australian youth in Perth (Space speaks and clothes communicate)', in R. Bosworth and R. Ugolini (eds), *War, Internment and Mass Migration: The Italo-Australian Experience 1940–1990*, Rome, 1992, pp. 207–24.
2 D. Lowenthal, 'The timeless past: some Anglo-American historical perceptions', *Journal of American History*, 75, 1989, p. 1267.
3 M.D. Steinberg, 'Culture and class in a Russian industry: the printers of St. Petersburg, 1860–1905', *Journal of Social History*, 23, 1990, p. 520; D.P. Koenker and W.G. Rosenberg, *Strikes and Revolution in Russia, 1917*, Princeton, 1989, p. 110.
4 A. Hitler, *Table Talk 1941–4* (ed. H.R. Trevor-Roper), London, 1953, p. 10.
5 Antonio Gramsci (1891–1937) was the greatest humanist Marxist philosopher of this century. For some introduction, see J. Joll, *Gramsci*, London, 1977.
6 S. Colarizi, *L'opinione degli italiani sotto il regime 1929–1943*, Bari, 1991, p. 337 on the sudden ambitions of Roman crowds, as unleashed by the events of May 1940.
7 For a very fine general history of the Italian language in the period under study, see T. De Mauro, *Storia linguistica dell'Italia unita*, Bari, 1963.
8 See, e.g., E. Serra, *La diplomazia in Italia*, Milan, 1984, pp. 60–2.
9 The best English-language introduction to this world can be found in J.A. Davis, *Conflict and Control: Law and Order in Nineteenth Century Italy*, London, 1988.

10 For the best factual introduction, see G. Rosoli (ed.), *Un secolo di emigrazione italiana: 1876–1976*, Rome, 1978.

11 For one case-study of these *paesi* of the mind, see W.A. Douglass, *Emigration in a South Italian Town: An Anthropological History*, New Brunswick, NJ, 1984.

12 R. and M. Bosworth, *Fremantle's Italy*, Rome, 1993, pp. 48–9.

13 For some introduction, see D. Gabaccia, *From Sicily to Elizabeth St.: Housing and Social Change Among Italian Immigrants, 1880–1930*, Albany, NY, 1984; and, more generally, P. Melograni (ed.), *La famiglia italiana*, Bari, 1988; D.I. Kertzer and R.P. Saller, *The Family in Italy from Antiquity to the Present*, New Haven, Conn., 1991.

14 The most dramatic example is J. Le Goff, 'Is politics the backbone of history?', *Daedalus*, 100, 1971, pp. 1–19.

15 The three classic studies of this process are G. Mosse, *The Nationalisation of the Masses*, New York, 1975; E. Hobsbawm and T. Ranger (eds), *The Invention of Tradition*, Cambridge, 1983; B. Anderson, *Imagined Communities*, London, 1983.

16 G. Volpe, *Scritti su Casa Savoia*, Rome, 1983, pp. 274–5; cf. his *Storia della Corsica Italiana*, Milan, 1939. Italian geographers were also accustomed automatically to list Corsica as geographically part of Italy.

17 For some introduction to historiographical crises at the time, see R.J.B. Bosworth, *Explaining Auschwitz and Hiroshima: History Writing and the Second World War 1945–1990*, London, 1993, p. 131; and for similar changes in US diplomatic historiography, see P. Novick, *That Noble Dream: The 'Objectivity' Question and the American Historical Profession*, Cambridge, 1988, pp. 445–7.

18 J. Joll, '1914: the unspoken assumptions', in H.W. Koch (ed.), *The Origins of the First World War: Great Power Rivalry and German War Aims*, London, 1972, pp. 307–28.

19 N. Rodolico in *Nuova Antologia*, f. 1789, January 1950, p. 96.

20 S. Romano, 'Gli storici e la politica', in G. Arnaldi *et al.*, *Incontro con gli storici*, Bari, 1986, p. 191.

21 S. Romano, *Crispi*, Milan, 1986, p. 18.

22 For further comments on this subject, see R. Bosworth, 'Italy's historians and the myth of fascism', in R. Langhorne (ed.), *Diplomacy and Intelligence During the Second World War*, Cambridge, 1985; and my *Explaining Auschwitz and Hiroshima*, pp. 118–41. For a defence of De Felice, if one very poorly translated from Italian to English, see N. Zapponi, 'Fascism in Italian historiography, 1986–1993: a fading national identity', *Journal of Contemporary History*, 29, 1994, pp. 547–68.

23 R. De Felice, *Mussolini l'alleato 1940–5: 1. L'Italia in guerra 1940–1943*, Turin, 1990, p. 163.

24 *Ibid.*, pp. 770–1, 828, 959.

25 *Ibid.*, p. 671.

26 In English, cf. the sometimes wrong-headed 'revisionist' work of Sadkovich, often also cited with approval by De Felice. J.J. Sadkovich, 'Understanding defeat: reappraising Italy's role in World War II', *Journal of Contemporary History*, 24, 1989, pp. 27–61, 'Of myths and

men: Rommel and the Italians in North Africa, 1940–1942', *International History Review*, XIII, 1991, pp. 284–313, 'The Italo-Greek war in context: Italian priorities and Axis diplomacy', *Journal of Contemporary History*, 28, 1993, pp. 439–64, 'Italian morale during the Italo-Greek war of 1940–1941', *War and Society*, 12, 1994, pp. 97–123, *The Italian Navy in World War II*, Westport, Conn., 1994; his *Italian Support for Croatian Separatism 1927–1937*, New York, 1987, is more credible.

27 F. Chabod, *Storia della politica estera italiana dal 1870 al 1896*, Bari, 1951, p. 10.

28 *Ibid.*, pp. 290, 292–3.

29 *Ibid.*, pp. 296–302.

30 S. Soave, *Federico Chabod politico*, Turin, 1989, p. 16. Appropriately, if a little ambiguously, Chabod would eventually take the partisan name of Lazarus (*ibid.*, p. 10).

31 For an introduction, see K.D. Erdmann, 'A history of the International Historical Congress. Work in progress', *Storia della Storiografia*, 8, 1985, p. 3.

32 F. Valsecchi, 'La storiografia mondiale a congresso', *Nuova Antologia*, f. 1858, October 1955, p. 147.

33 *Ibid.*, p. 149.

34 B. Vigezzi (ed.), *Federico Chabod e la 'nuova storiografia' italiana dal primo al secondo dopoguerra (1919–1950)*, Milan, 1983, p. 554.

35 *Ibid.*, pp. 692–3.

36 Note, for example, the claims of Roberto Vivarelli that, in any case, the rhythms of intellectual life did not match those of political history. See *ibid.*, p. 489.

37 See, especially, B. Vigezzi, *Politica estera e opinione pubblica in Italia dall'Unità ai giorni nostri: orientamenti degli studi e prospettive della ricerca*, Milan, 1991; E. Di Nolfo, *Le paure e le speranze degli italiani (1943–1953)*, Milan, 1986; L. Tosi, 'Romeo A. Gallenga Stuart e la propaganda di guerra all'estero (1917–1918)', *Storia contemporanea*, 2, 1971, pp. 519–43.

38 C.M. Santoro, *La politica estera di una media potenza: L'Italia dall'Unità ad oggi*, Bologna, 1991, p. 10.

39 *Ibid.*, pp. 38, 75.

40 *Ibid.*, pp. 159, 163.

41 The nearest to a general history is C. Lowe and F. Marzari, *Italian Foreign Policy 1870–1940*, London, 1975.

42 For a review, see R. Bosworth, 'Denis Mack Smith and the Third Italy', *International History Review*, XI, 1990, pp. 782–92. 'Radicalism' is always a loose term. At least if press reports are to be believed, by 1995 Mack Smith was saying that, had he been an Italian, he would have voted for Berlusconi at the elections of the previous year, though his great hope for Italy remained that it should acquire a 'genuine' conservative party like the English Tories. See *L'Espresso*, XLI, 20 January 1995.

43 D. Mack Smith, *Italy: A Modern History*, Ann Arbor, 1959.

44 R. Romeo, *Dal Piemonte sabaudo all'Italia liberale*, Bari, 1974, p. 320.

45 F. Fischer, *Germany's Aims in the First World War*, London, 1967; A.J.P. Taylor, *The Origins of the Second World War*, Harmondsworth, 1964.

46 D. Mack Smith, *Mussolini's Roman Empire*, London, 1976, p. v.

47 For his first statement of this thesis, see D. Mack Smith, 'Mussolini, artist in propaganda', *History Today*, IX, 1959, pp. 223–32.
48 J. Steinberg, *All or Nothing, the Axis and the Holocaust 1941–1943*, London, 1990, p. 6.
49 P.N. Furbank, *Italo Svevo: The Man and the Writer*, London, 1966, pp. 3, 204; the most readily available English-language edition of the novel is I. Svevo, *Confessions of Zeno*, Harmondsworth, 1976.

1 ITALIAN DIPLOMACY AND EUROPEAN POWER POLITICS 1860–1922

1 H. Nicolson, *Diplomacy*, rev. edn, London, 1963, pp. 151–3. Cf. his earlier comment (p. 29) 'It may have been regrettable that [Renaissance] Italy should have become the mother of organised or professional diplomacy; but it was also inevitable.'
2 See, e.g., C. Thayer, *Diplomat*, London, 1960; or, for similar French assumptions, P. Milza, 'L'Italie dans les manuels français de l'après guerre', in J.B. Duroselle and E. Serra (eds), *Italia e Francia (1946–1954)*, Milan, 1988, pp. 218–20.
3 R.J.B. Bosworth, 'Mito e linguaggio nella politica estera italiana', in R.J.B. Bosworth and S. Romano (eds), *La politica estera italiana, 1860–1985*, Bologna, 1991, pp. 35–67.
4 G. Ciano, *Diario 1937–1943* (ed. R. De Felice), Milan, 1980, p. 414; R. De Felice, *Mussolini il duce: II. Lo stato totalitario, 1936–1940*, Turin, 1981, p. 679; G. Bottai, *Diario 1935–1944* (ed. G.B. Guerri), Milan, 1982, p. 175.
5 For a modern variant, see the claim of liberal historian, Roberto Vivarelli, that Italian history has not been taken as seriously as it should be owing to a sort of 'Anglo-Saxon' conspiracy: 'due to sheer ignorance and subsequent misrepresentation Italy has been practically expelled from the historical map of modern Europe' (R. Vivarelli, 'Interpretations of the origins of Fascism', *Journal of Modern History*, 63, 1991, pp. 29–30). Vivarelli is wrong to single out Anglo-Saxons but is right to see lingering anti-Italian prejudice in the literature. For a recent example from a professor of German at Lyon, see E. Demm, 'Propaganda and caricature in the First World War', *Journal of Contemporary History*, 28, 1993, p. 181.
6 For a brief English-language summary, see D. Mack Smith (ed.), *The Making of Italy 1796–1870*, New York, 1968, pp. 73–84. Cf. also the views of Giovanni Spadolini that the Risorgimento leaders 'in their moral elevation and their Italian passion compose the greatest real moral patrimony of the nation. . . . This patrimony it is our task to transmit intact to the new generations' (A.A. Mola (ed.), *Garibaldi: generale della libertà*, Rome, 1984, p. 14).
7 For a brilliant account of an epidemic and its (mis)treatment as late as the twentieth century, see F. Snowden, 'Cholera: Barletta 1910', *Past and Present*, 132, 1991, pp. 67–103.

8 A. Forti Messina, *Società ed epidemia: il colera a Napoli nel 1836*, Naples, 1979, p. 43.
9 For the background, see C. Vidal, *Charles-Albert et le Risorgimento italien (1831–1848)*, Paris, 1927.
10 Cavour had proclaimed in regard to his own peasants, 'a severe subordination is the first requisite of good administration'. See R. Romeo, *Cavour e il suo tempo, 1842–1854*, vol. 1, Bari, 1977, p. 133.
11 A. Helps, *Life and Labours of Mr. Brassey*, London, 1969, p. 175.
12 The best evocation of such mockery is Verga's short story 'Liberty'. See G. Verga, *Little Novels of Sicily*, Harmondsworth, 1973, pp. 133–40.
13 G. Volpe, *L'Italia in cammino: l'ultimo cinquantennio*, Milan, 1928. The book was part of the Library of Political Culture of the Istituto Nazionale Fascista di Cultura.
14 The English liberal G.M. Trevelyan's biography of Garibaldi is the most accessible example of the genre. Though very much a period piece, it continues to sell and may retain some influence, notably among those who compile historical introductions for opera programmes. See G.M. Trevelyan, *Garibaldi's Defence of the Roman Republic 1848–9, Garibaldi and the Thousand, Garibaldi and the Making of Italy*, London, 1907–11; and cf. his *Manin and the Venetian Revolution of 1848*, London, 1923. Most recently, F.J. Coppa, *The Origins of the Italian Wars of Independence*, London, 1992, has tended to restate the *rivoluzione nazionale* thesis.
15 P. Farneti, *Sistema politico e società civile*, Turin, 1971, pp. 117–20; cf. in English, P. Farneti, *The Italian Party System (1945–1980)*, London, 1985.
16 D. Beales, *The Risorgimento and the Unification of Italy*, London, 1971, p. 13.
17 See D. Varè, *Laughing Diplomat*, London, 1938 and *The Two Imposters*, London, 1949.
18 For a more developed introduction to these matters, see R. Bosworth, *Italy and the Approach of the First World War*, London, 1983, pp. 7–27.
19 A. Herzen, *My Past and Thoughts*, London, 1968, vol. 3, p. 1029. (Cf. vol. 2, p. 697 on Mazzini's inflexibility or madness and p. 694 on his dislike of contradiction and his 'habit of ruling'.) By contrast, Denis Mack Smith, in a new biography, has portrayed Mazzini as an apostle of European Union. See D. Mack Smith, *Mazzini*, New Haven, Conn., 1994.
20 J. Mazzini, *The Duties of Man and Other Essays*, London, 1907, pp. 53, 245.
21 D. Mack Smith, *Cavour*, London, 1985, p. 256.
22 S.J. Woolf, *A History of Italy 1700–1860*, London, 1979, p. 175.
23 A. Heriot, *The French in Italy 1796–1799*, London, 1957, pp. 52–5.
24 G. Abba, *The Diary of One of Garibaldi's Thousand* (ed. E.R. Vincent), London, 1962, p. 44.
25 See, e.g., R.M. Bell, *Fate and Honor, Family and Village: Demographic and Cultural Change in Rural Italy since 1800*, Chicago, 1979, pp. 1–4.
26 E. Lussu, *Il cinghiale del diavolo e altri scritti sulla Sardegna*, Turin, 1976, pp. 90–1. Among peasants unusually dispersed into the Apulian country-side and living in cone-shaped houses called *trulli*, a recent anthropo-

logist has noted, 'trullo doors traditionally had holes bored in them for a shotgun muzzle and large iron hooks and eyes which braced them securely shut from inside' (A.H. Galt, *Far from the Church Bells: Settlement and Society in an Apulian Town*, Cambridge, 1991, p. 160).

27 F. Molfese, *Storia del brigantaggio dopo l'Unità*, Milan, 1964, p. 132.

28 *Ibid.*, p. 89.

29 As Gramsci duly noted, arguing that the usage went back at least to the time of Victor Amadeus II (1675–1730), A. Gramsci, *Il Risorgimento*, Turin, 1975, p. 207.

30 For this and similar metaphors see R. Bosworth, *Italy and the Approach of the First World War*, pp. 3–4.

31 F. Crispi, *Memoirs* (ed. T. Palamenghi-Crispi), London, 1912, vol. 2, p. 1.

32 For a review of his career, see S. Romano, *Crispi*, Milan, 1986.

33 There is an old but still readable English language account of the battle, G.F-H. Berkeley, *The Campaign of Adowa and the Rise of Menelik*, London, n.d., p. xxxiii (pp. 168–73 describe the battle). The Italians took casualties of 70 per cent if their prisoners are included; for a very competent biography of Menelik, see H.G. Marcus, *The Life and Times of Menelik II: Ethiopia 1844–1913*, Oxford, 1975.

34 D. Farini, *Diario di fine secolo* (ed. E. Morelli), Rome, 1961, p. 594.

35 See, e.g., R. Truffi (ed.), *Precursori dell'Impero Africano: lettere inedite*, Rome, 1936 (with an enthusiastic preface from G. Volpe) (emphasis in original).

36 See, e.g., D. Farini, *Diario*, p. 1294; and cf. G. Fortunato, *Carteggio 1912–1922* (ed. E. Gentile), Bari, 1979, pp. 276–7 (letter to Croce) for a wonderful evocation of the sense of a highly honourable and caring intellectual and landowner that he was besieged in his own study. Outside its walls lay a wholly unpredictable darkness.

37 J. Pemble, *The Mediterranean Passion: Victorians and Edwardians in the South*, Oxford, 1987, p. 128, citing Harriet Taylor who ran on characteristically 'as they are the curse of England' (emphasis in original).

38 For some account of ministerial attempts to invent a nationalist public opinion, see R.J.B. Bosworth, *Italy, the Least of the Great Powers: Italian Foreign Policy before the First World War*, Cambridge, 1979, pp. 39–67. There is very little evidence in Italy of the sort of popular humus of nationalism found by Geoff Eley in Germany. See G. Eley, *Reshaping the German Right: Radical Nationalism and Political Change after Bismarck*, London, 1980, and, for some of his voluminous essays, *From Unification to Nazism: Reinterpreting the German Past*, Boston, 1986.

39 D. Farini, *Diario*, pp. 559, 628.

40 For more detail, see R. Bosworth, *Italy and the Approach of the First World War*, pp. 21–2.

41 J. Redlich, *Emperor Francis Joseph of Austria: A Biography*, Hamden, Conn., 1965, p. 273.

42 For a detailed anthropological account of ethnic variation, see J.W. Cole and E.R. Wolf, *The Hidden Frontier: Ecology and Ethnicity in an Alpine Valley*, New York, 1974.

43 See R.J.B. Bosworth, 'Mito e linguaggio', p. 50; and M. De Marco, *Il*

Gazzettino: storia di un quotidiano, Venice, 1976, p. 30. This paper, originally 'democratic' but turning conservative and to become Fascist, characteristically bore the headline on 15 May 1915, 'The hour is tragic, but great and Roman. It is the hour of destiny. The venture is before us. Let us defend ourselves as our fathers did when the *patria* was in danger' (*ibid.*, p. 38).

44 For one microcosmic story, see R. Bosworth, 'The Albanian forests of Signor Giacomo Vismara: a case study of Italian economic imperialism during the foreign ministry of Antonino Di San Giuliano', *Historical Journal*, XVIII, 1975, pp. 571–86.

45 For a typical evocation of *romanità* by a later Foreign Minister, see A. Di San Giuliano, *Lettere sull'Albania*, Rome, 1903, p. 37.

46 For a highly patriotic account of their difficulties, see P. Pastorelli, *L'Albania nella politica estera italiana 1914–1920*, Naples, 1970.

47 For basic information, see A. Pribram, *The Secret Treaties of Austria-Hungary, 1879–1914*, 2 vols, Cambridge, Mass., 1920–1; and for a recent and very useful study, see R. Petrignani, *Neutralità e alleanza: le scelte di politica estera dell'Italia dopo l'Unità*, Bologna, 1987.

48 D. Farini, *Diario*, p. 5.

49 For one case, see R. Bosworth, 'The Messina earthquake of 28 December 1908', *European Studies Review*, 11, 1981, pp. 201–2.

50 D. Farini, *Diario*, p. 38.

51 C.A. Avenati, 'Italianità della Savoia (attraverso documenti inediti del 1848)', *Rassegna Storica del Risorgimento*, XXVII, 1940, pp. 158, 168.

52 J. Gooch, *Army, State and Society in Italy, 1870–1915*, London, 1989, p. 97.

53 R. Petrignani, *Neutralità e alleanza*, p. 223. For further detail, see also R. Rainero, *L'anticolonialismo italiano da Assab ad Adua (1869–1896)*, Milan, 1971.

54 For a droll account, see F.E. Manuel, 'The Palestine question in Italian diplomacy, 1917–1920', *Journal of Modern History*, 27, 1955; and see generally R. Bosworth, 'Italy and the end of the Ottoman Empire', in M. Kent (ed.), *The Great Powers and the End of the Ottoman Empire*, London, 1984, pp. 52–75.

55 King Umberto was also typically captivated by the apparent efficiency and power of the German system. For a typical example, see D. Farini, *Diario*, pp. 116–18.

56 Cf. the young Mario Missiroli who, on joining *Resto del Carlino* in 1908, proclaimed his enthusiasm for '*Germania . . . giovane e proletaria*' (G. Afeltra, *Mario Missiroli e i suoi tempi*, Milan, 1985, p. 16).

57 See R. Webster, *Industrial Imperialism in Italy 1908–1915*, Berkeley, 1975, p. 16, for an analysis of the loves and hatreds of this relationship.

58 H. von Treitschke, *Politics* (ed. H. Kohn), New York, 1963, pp. 61, 292–3. In his biography of Cavour, Rosario Romeo endorsed Treitschke's view of history and morality as a way of countering the nefarious influence of Mack Smith. See R. Romeo, *Cavour e il suo tempo*, vol. 3, p. 928.

59 R. Romeo, *Italia moderna fra storia e storiografia*, Florence, 1977, p. 94.

60 Little King Victor Emmanuel III, in the 1890s before his succession,

NOTES

especially resented imperial twitting about his delayed marriage. D. Farini, *Diario*, p. 728, and Farini himself (p. 840) noted his mistrust of the '*Imperatore chiaccherone*' (Mr Emperor Big Talk).

61 The fullest, if now very dated, account in English of this period is A.W. Salomone, *Italy in the Giolittian Era: Italian Democracy in the Making, 1900–14*, rev. edn, Philadelphia, 1960.

62 For more detail, see R. Bosworth, *Italy and the Approach of the First World War*, pp. 17–19, and *Italy, the Least of the Great Powers, passim.*

63 S. Romano, *Giolitti: lo stile del potere*, Milan, 1989, pp. 113, 193, 198–9.

64 See R.J.B. Bosworth, *Italy, the Least of the Great Powers*, p. 2.

65 For the latest English-language narrative of the diplomacy of this war, see T.W. Childs, *Italo-Turkish Diplomacy and the War over Libya 1911–1912*, Leiden, 1990.

66 A.J.P. Taylor, *The Struggle for Mastery in Europe 1848–1918*, Oxford, 1954, p. xxiii, n. 4.

67 R. Grew, *A Sterner Plan for Italian Unity: The Italian National Society in the Risorgimento*, Princeton, 1963, p. 29.

68 *Ibid.*, p. 11.

69 D. Mack Smith, *Cavour*, p. 197.

70 D. Mack Smith, *Cavour and Garibaldi 1860*, rev. edn, Cambridge, 1989, p. 91.

71 Cf. R. Bosworth, *Italy and the Approach of the First World War*, pp. 35–6.

72 Cf. D. Farini, *Diario*, p. 1476 on the able, unscrupulous and very ambitious young politician of the 1890s.

73 Many of Sonnino's writings and papers are available, see S. Sonnino, *Discorsi parlamentari*, 3 vols, Rome, 1925, *Diario* (ed. B.F. Brown and P. Pastorelli) 3 vols, Bari, 1972, *Scritti e discorsi extraparlamentari, 1870–1922* (ed. B.F. Brown), 2 vols, Bari, 1972.

74 For his own account, see A. Salandra, *Italy and the Great War, From Neutrality to Intervention*, London, 1932.

75 For some comments, and for similar views of such major intellectuals as conservative philosopher Giovanni Gentile, see R.J.B. Bosworth, 'Mito e linguaggio', pp. 51–2.

76 Richard Webster, with his attempt to transfer to Italy the 'social imperialist', 'military–industrial complex' model, made familiar in Germany by the Bielefeld school, is the major critic of my own views; cf. his *Industrial Imperialism in Italy, 1908–1915*.

77 Denis Mack Smith has published a useful if rather superficial history of the Italian monarchy: D. Mack Smith, *Italy and Its Monarchy*, New Haven, Conn., 1989.

78 For a detailed English-language study of Visconti Venosta's methods, at least during one crisis, see S.W. Halperin, *Diplomat under Stress: Visconti Venosta and the Crisis of July 1870*, Chicago, 1963.

79 There is one, rather curiously phrased, organised and argued, English-language account of such forces before 1900: R. Drake, *Byzantium into Rome*, Chapel Hill, NC, 1980.

80 The only serious account of this highly significant institution is A.A.

Mola, *Storia della massoneria italiana dall'Unità alla repubblica*, Milan, 1976.

81 S. Romano, *Giolitti: lo stile del potere*, p. 230.

82 There is now a detailed, if descriptive, English-language narrative: W.A. Renzi, *In the Shadow of the Sword: Italy's Neutrality and Entrance into the Great War 1914–1915*, New York, 1987.

83 B. Vigezzi, *Da Giolitti a Salandra*, Florence, 1969, p. 59.

84 For a massive and unfinished introduction to this public opinion, see B. Vigezzi, *L'Italia di fronte alla prima guerra mondiale*, Milan, 1966, vol. 1.

85 For Turati, see, in English, S. Di Scala, *Dilemmas of Italian Socialism: The Politics of Filippo Turati*, Amherst, Mass., 1980.

86 For Agnelli, see V. Castronovo, *G. Agnelli: Fiat dal 1899–1945*, Turin, 1977; and cf. the highly characteristic diary, E. Conti, *Dal taccuino di un borghese*, Cremona, 1946.

87 For a useful English-language introduction to the intelligentsia and the coming of the war, see W.L. Adamson, *Avant-Garde Florence: From Modernism to Fascism*, Cambridge, Mass., 1993, especially pp. 153–203.

88 S. Kern, *The Culture of Time and Space 1880–1918*, London, 1983.

89 A.J.P. Taylor, *The Origins of the Second World War*, rev. edn, Harmondsworth, 1964, p. 42.

90 R. Romeo, *L'Italia unita e la prima guerra mondiale*, Bari, 1978, p. 157.

91 L. Villari, *Le avventure di un capitano d'industria*, Turin, 1991, p. 32. Patriotic Australians have, of course, often told me that it was Australia which expended the most . . . .

92 For his own account, see V.E. Orlando, *Memorie, 1915–19* (ed. R. Mosca), Milan, 1960.

93 For a crucial interpretation, which, typical of so much literature both of the war and the peacemaking, pays little attention to Italy, see A.J. Mayer, *Wilson vs. Lenin: Political Origins of the New Diplomacy 1917–1918*, New Haven, Conn., 1959, and *Politics and Diplomacy of Peacemaking: Containment and Counter-Revolution at Versailles, 1918–1919*, London, 1968.

94 The basic and fair-minded, 'realist' account remains, R. Albrecht-Carrié, *Italy at the Paris Peace Conference*, Hamden, Conn., 1966; and cf. H.J. Burgwyn, *The Legend of the Mutilated Victory: Italy, the Great War, and the Paris Peace Conference, 1915–1919*, Westport, Conn., 1993.

95 In English, see M. Ledeen, *The First Duce: D'Annunzio at Fiume*, Baltimore, 1977, for a 'De Felicean' account.

96 For some of Nitti's writing in English, see his *Peaceless Europe*, London, 1922, and *The Decadence of Europe*, London, 1923.

97 Sforza also wrote a good deal after 1922. See C. Sforza, *Diplomatic Europe since the Treaty of Versailles*, New Haven, Conn., 1928, *Europe and the Europeans*, London, 1936, *Italy and the Italians*, London, 1948.

98 For a useful study of Sforza, see G. Giordano, *Carlo Sforza: la diplomazia 1896–1921*, Milan, 1987.

99 The basic English-language account of the rise of Fascism is A. Lyttelton, *The Seizure of Power: Fascism in Italy 1919–1929*, London, 1973. The most important in the genre of local studies are P. Corner, *Fascism in*

Ferrara 1915–1925, Oxford, 1975; F.M. Snowden, *Violence and Great Estates in the South of Italy: Apulia, 1900–1922*, Cambridge, 1986, and his *The Fascist Revolution in Tuscany 1919–1922*, Cambridge, 1989. The most recent Italian attempt exhaustively to study the subject is R. Vivarelli, *Storia delle origini del fascismo*, 2 vols, Bologna, 1991.

100 C. Seton-Watson, *Italy from Liberalism to Fascism 1870–1925*, London, 1967, p. 630.

2 ITALIAN DIPLOMACY AND EUROPEAN POWER POLITICS 1922–60

1 B. Mussolini, *Opera omnia* (ed. G. Pini and E. Susmel), Florence, 1951–80, vol. XXIX, pp. 364–7.
2 For the original, brilliantly provocative, usage, see A.J.P. Taylor, *The Origins of the Second World War*, rev. edn, Harmondsworth, 1964, p. 27.
3 For a succinct English-language statement of this case, see E. Gentile, 'Fascism in Italian historiography: in search of an individual historical identity?', *Journal of Contemporary History*, 21, 1986, pp. 179–203.
4 E. Gentile, *Storia del Partito Fascista 1919–1922: movimento e milizia*, Bari, 1989, p. viii. The italics are Gentile's. Cf. also, and still more stridently, his *Il culto del littorio: la sacralizzazione della politica nell'Italia fascista*, Bari, 1993.
5 S. Colarizi, *L'opinione degli italiani sotto il regime 1929–1943*, Bari, 1991, p. 3. It is typical of the nastier side of contemporary Italian academic life that Colarizi, nowhere in her text or footnotes, refers to the work of Luisa Passerini, whose own *Fascism in Popular Memory: The Cultural Experience of the Turin Working Class*, Cambridge, 1987, is the best known earlier study of 'consensus'. Passerini is not a follower of De Felice; Colarizi is.
6 D.L. Germino, *The Fascist Party in Power: A Study in Totalitarian Rule*, rev. edn, New York, 1971, p. 144. For some introduction to the 'totalitarianists' in the context of the 1950s, see R.J.B. Bosworth, *Explaining Auschwitz and Hiroshima: History Writing and the Second World War 1945–1990*, London, 1993, pp. 21–6.
7 C.J. Friedrich and Z.K. Brzezinski, *Totalitarian Dictatorship and Autocracy*, Cambridge, Mass., 1956.
8 R. De Felice, *Mussolini il duce: I. Gli anni del consenso 1929–1936*, Turin, 1974, p. 337.
9 G. Rumi, *Alle origini della politica estera fascista (1918–1923)*, Bari, 1968, pp. ix, 246–7.
10 R. De Felice (ed.), *Italia fra tedeschi e alleati: la politica estera fascista e la seconda guerra mondiale*, Bologna, 1973, pp. 58–9.
11 G. Carocci, 'Appunti sull' imperialismo fascista negli anni '20', *Studi Storici*, VIII, 1967, pp. 113–37, *La politica estera dell'Italia fascista (1925–1928)*, Bari, 1969, and in English, his *Italian Fascism*, Harmondsworth, 1974.
12 R. Quartararo, *Roma tra Londra e Berlino: la politica estera fascista dal 1931 al 1940*, Rome, 1980, pp. 32–5 (emphasis in original); cf., in a rather

different key, D. Bolech Cecchi, *Non bruciare i ponti con Roma*, Milan, 1986, a largely narrative book from the school of Ennio Di Nolfo, which is nonetheless severe on France for failing to take up the opportunities to appease Fascist Italy.

13 For a useful early study, see F.W. Deakin, *The Brutal Friendship: Mussolini, Hitler and the Fall of Italian Fascism*, Harmondsworth, 1966.

14 R. Quartararo, *Roma tra Londra e Berlino*, p. 536.

15 For a De Felicean biography, see P. Nello, *Dino Grandi: la formazione di un leader fascista*, Bologna, 1987, and *Un fedele disubbidiente: Dino Grandi*, Bologna, 1993; cf. also M. Knox, 'I testi "aggiustati" dei discorsi segreti di Grandi', *Passato e Presente*, 13, 1987, pp. 97–117 for evidence of some dubious adjustments of Grandi's record.

16 R. De Felice, *Mussolini il duce: II. Lo stato totalitario 1936–1940*, Turin, 1981, pp. 843–4; *Mussolini l'alleato 1940–1945: 1. L'Italia in guerra 1940–1943*, Turin, 1990, pp. 3–4.

17 R. De Felice, *L'Italia in guerra 1940–1943*, pp. 103–10.

18 M. Knox, *Mussolini Unleashed 1939–41: Politics and Strategy in Fascist Italy's Last War*, Cambridge, 1982, pp. 1–2, 5. Although Knox claimed his intention was merely to explain 'what actually happened' (p. ix), his immersion into the world of Italian historiography led to his book being translated by Riuniti, scholarly publishing house of the PCI.

19 M. Knox, 'Fascist Italy assesses its enemies, 1935–1940', in E.R. May (ed.), *Knowing One's Enemies: Intelligence Assessment before the Two World Wars*, Princeton, 1984, p. 348.

20 M. Knox, 'Conquest, foreign and domestic, in Fascist Italy and Nazi Germany', *Journal of Modern History*, 56, 1984, p. 10.

21 R. De Felice, *L'Italia in guerra 1940–1943*, pp. x, 594–5.

22 E. Di Nolfo, *Mussolini e la politica estera italiana (1919–1933)*, Padua, 1960, p. 1.

23 *Ibid.*, p. 10.

24 B. Mussolini, *Opera omnia*, vol. XV, pp. 28–9 (11 June 1920), vol. XVI, pp. 104–6 (7–8 January 1921), 150–60 (8 February 1921), vol. XVII, pp. 117–19 (1 September 1921), vol. XVIII, pp. 119–24 (25 March 1922), 179–80 (5 May 1922).

25 *Ibid.*, vol. XVIII, pp. 465–6 (29 October 1922), vol. XIX, pp. 3–4 (3 November 1922), pp. 128–33 (10 February 1923).

26 Notably the Secretary General of the Ministry of Foreign Affairs, Salvatore Contarini, who had retreated to Ischia. E. Di Nolfo, *Mussolini e la politica estera italiana*, p. 90.

27 For a detailed English-language narrative, see J. Barros, *The Corfu Incident of 1923: Mussolini and the League of Nations*, Princeton, 1965.

28 *The Times*, 31 August, 1 September 1923; and cf. R.J.B. Bosworth, 'The British press, the conservatives, and Mussolini, 1920–34', *Journal of Contemporary History*, 5, 1970, pp. 169–70.

29 J. Barros, *Corfu Incident*, pp. 313–14; cf. also P.J. Yearwood, '"Consistently, with honour"; Great Britain, the League of Nations and the Corfu crisis of 1923', *Journal of Contemporary History*, 21, 1986, pp. 559–79.

30 D. Mack Smith, *Mussolini's Roman Empire*, London, 1976, p. 7.

31 A. Cassels, *Mussolini's Early Diplomacy*, Princeton, 1970, p. 126.

32 M. Luciolli, *Palazzo Chigi: anni roventi. Ricordi di una vita diplomatica italiana dal 1933 al 1948*, Milan, 1976, p. 53.

33 G. Giordano, *Carlo Sforza: la diplomazia 1896–1921*, Milan, 1987, pp. 97–8. Sonnino decreed that in the region Italy should behave as with peasants: 'It is at the market and at the last minute that I agree on the price.'

34 See R.J.B. Bosworth, *Italy, the Least of the Great Powers: Italian Foreign Policy before the First World War*, Cambridge, 1979, pp. 299–336; A. Cassels, *Mussolini's Early Diplomacy*, pp. 216–25. The islands were, of course, ethnically Greek.

35 F.S. Nitti, *Peaceless Europe*, London, 1922, p. 168.

36 L. Federzoni, *Presagi alla nazione: discorsi politici*, Milan, 1924, p. 340.

37 J. Barros, 'Mussolini's first aggression: the Corfu ultimatum', *Balkan Studies*, 2, 1961, pp. 250–1, 283.

38 R. De Felice, *Mussolini il fascista I. La conquista del potere 1921–1925*, Turin, 1966, pp. 562–3.

39 J. Barros, 'Mussolini's first aggression', p. 273.

40 G. Cerreti, *Con Togliatti e Thorez: quarant'anni di lotte politiche*, Milan, 1973, p. 11.

41 P. Togliatti, *Lectures on Fascism*, London, 1976, p. 36.

42 Cf., e.g., F. Perfetti, *Il nazionalismo italiano dalle origini alla fusione col fascismo*, Bologna, 1977, pp. 5–7.

43 R.J.B. Bosworth, *Italy, the Least of the Great Powers*, pp. 95–126; in 1922 only one career diplomat resigned over the Fascist seizure of power. Even Carlo Sforza, who would soon go into exile, advised his younger ex-colleagues at the ministry to stay, pointing out that they could serve Fascism with dignity. G. Cora, 'Un diplomatico durante l'era fascista', *Storia e Politica*, V, 1966, p. 88.

44 L. Medici del Vascello, *Per l'Italia!*, Bari, 1916, pp. 180, 183, 185. Medici also favoured war because it would end tourism and lead to the industrialisation of Rome.

45 G. Curàtolo, *Francia e Italia: pagine di storia, 1849–1914*, Turin, 1915, p. viii.

46 For an English-language account, see R.L. Hess, 'Italy and Africa: colonial ambitions in the First World War', *Journal of African History*, 4, 1963, pp. 105–26.

47 See, e.g., A. Cassels, 'Mussolini and German nationalism, 1922–5', *Journal of Modern History*, 35, 1963, pp. 137–57.

48 H.J. Burgwyn, 'Conclusion' to debate on 'Italy in the aftermath of the First World War', *International History Review*, 8, 1986, p. 84.

49 See, e.g., A. Cassels, *Mussolini's Early Diplomacy*, pp. 315–34.

50 J.J. Sadkovich, *Italian Support for Croatian Separatism 1927–1937*, New York, 1987, pp. 3–4, 45–6. In reviewing this whole story, Sadkovich concluded (p. 303) that 'the cold war that Italy and Yugoslavia fought during the inter-war period was the result of a number of factors, perhaps the least of which was the installation of a Fascist regime in Italy'.

51 For a detailed review in English, see W.I. Shorrock, *From Ally to Enemy:*

The Enigma of Fascist Italy in French Diplomacy, 1920–1940, Kent, OH, 1988.

52 See Shula Marks' sensible comments in this regard: S. Marks, 'Mussolini and the Ruhr crisis', *International History Review*, 8, 1986, pp. 68–9, and cf. her 'Mussolini and Locarno: Fascist foreign policy in microcosm', *Journal of Contemporary History*, 14, 1979, pp. 423–39.

53 For an example, see S. Minardi, 'La missione diplomatica del marchese Paternò ad Addis Abeba (settembre 1930–novembre 1931)', in A. Migliazza and E. Decleva (eds), *Diplomazia e storia delle relazioni internazionali: studi in onore di Enrico Serra*, Milan, 1991, pp. 365–90.

54 The best review of Italian foreign policy in this regard, though often too literal in its reading of the evidence, is R. De Felice, *Il Fascismo e l'Oriente: Arabi, ebrei e indiani nella politica di Mussolini*, Bologna, 1988.

55 G. Giuriati, *La parabola di Mussolini nei ricordi di un gerarca* (ed. E. Gentile), Bari, 1981, p. 43.

56 See, in English, the rather exaggerated account in H.S. Hughes, 'The early diplomacy of Italian Fascism, 1922–1932', in G.A. Craig and F. Gilbert (eds), *The Diplomats 1919–1939*, rev. edn, New York, 1963, pp. 210–33.

57 For Detroit see P.V. Cannistraro, 'Fascism and Italian-Americans in Detroit', *International Migration Review*, 9, 1975, pp. 29–40; for Perth, R. Bosworth, 'Luigi Mistrorigo and *La Stampa Italiana*: the strange story of a Fascist journalist in Perth', in R. Bosworth and M. Melia (eds), *Aspects of Ethnicity: Studies in Western Australian History*, XII, Nedlands, WA, 1991, pp. 61–70; R.J.B. Bosworth, 'Renato Citarelli, Fascist Vice Consul in Perth: a documentary note', *Papers in Labour History*, 14, 1994, pp. 91–6.

58 For a narration, see G. Petracchi, 'Ideology and realpolitik: Italo-Soviet relations 1917–1932', *Journal of Italian History*, 2, 1979, pp. 473–519. In English, there is a naive account: J. Calvitt Clarke III, *Russia and Italy Against Hitler: The Bolshevik–Fascist Rapprochement of the 1930s*, Westport, Conn., 1991.

59 B. Mussolini, *Opera omnia*, vol. XXIII, pp. 158–92 (5 June 1928), pp. 265–73 (8 December 1928).

60 The papers of Lord Vansittart of Denham (Churchill College, Cambridge), memorandum of 1 January 1932. For a narration of US–Italian relations, see G.G. Migone, *Gli Stati Uniti e il fascismo: alle origini dell'egemonia americana in Italia*, Milan, 1980; C. Damiani, *Mussolini e gli Stati Uniti 1922–1935*, Bologna, 1980.

61 For this sort of belief, see R.J.B. Bosworth, 'The British press, the conservatives and Mussolini', pp. 163–82 and contrast it with the exaggerated views of the De Feliceans that Mussolini was greatly admired abroad (S. Colarizi, *L'opinione degli italiani*, pp. 105–7; R. Quartararo, *Roma tra Londra e Berlino*, p. 16.) Fascists, outside Italy, usually had to explain how native was their version of the ideology and how little it borrowed from Rome.

62 F. Salata, *Il Patto Mussolini*, Milan, 1933, p. 41.

63 R. Quartararo, *Roma tra Londra e Berlino*, pp. 25, 38; cf. F. Suvich, *Memorie 1932–1936* (ed. G. Bianchi), Milan, 1984, p. 143.

64 See, e.g., J. Lipski, *Diplomat in Berlin 1933–1939: Papers and Memoirs* (ed. W. Jedrzejewicz), New York, 1968, pp. 64–5.

65 For the most detailed account of Italo-German relations at this time, see G.L. Weinberg, *The Foreign Policy of Hitler's Germany: Diplomatic Revolution in Europe 1933–1936*, Chicago, 1970.

66 B. Mussolini, *Opera omnia*, vol. XXVI, pp. 232–3 (26 May 1934), pp. 318–20 (6 September 1934).

67 In English, the basic narrative is found in G.W. Baer, *The Coming of the Italo-Ethiopian War*, Cambridge, Mass., 1967, and *Test Case: Italy, Ethiopia and the League of Nations*, Stanford, 1976.

68 R.J.B. Bosworth, *Italy, the Least of the Great Powers*, pp. 329–36.

69 R. De Felice, *Gli anni del consenso 1929–1936*, p. 399.

70 Cited by G.W. Baer, *Test Case*, p. 4.

71 R. De Felice, *Gli anni del consenso 1929–1936*, pp. 758–808 provides a summary of what he believes was Mussolini's triumphant position after the conquest of Ethiopia; R. Quartararo, by contrast, defined the conflict as a '*guerra bianca*' for Anglo-Italian control of the Mediterranean (R. Quartararo, *Roma tra Londra e Berlino*, p. 148). For an account of the controversy occasioned by De Felice's views, see P. Meldini (ed.), *Un monumento al duce?*, Florence, 1976.

72 B. Mussolini, *Opera omnia*, vol. XXVII, pp. 265–6 (5 May 1936), 268–9 (9 May 1936).

73 Of old Liberals, V.E. Orlando and Luigi Albertini rallied to the war and King Victor Emmanuel III can be found remarking in November 1935 that 'we have lost forty years' (G. Bottai, *Diario 1935–1944* (ed. G.B. Guerri), Milan, 1982, p. 54).

74 D. Mack Smith, *Mussolini's Roman Empire*, p. 74.

75 G. W. Baer, *Test Case*, p. 79.

76 R. De Felice, *Gli anni del consenso 1929–1936*, p. 784.

77 See, e.g., S. La Francesca, *La politica economica del fascismo*, Bari, 1972, pp. 79–118.

78 For a gentler introduction, see M. Scudiero (ed.), *Depero per Campari*, Milan, 1989.

79 Haile Selassie was *Time* magazine's man of the year for 1935.

80 R. De Felice, *Gli anni del consenso 1929–1936*, pp. 605–8.

81 A. Pavolini, *Disperata*, Florence, 1937, p. 16.

82 For a narration, see A.J.P. Taylor, *The Origins of the Second World War*, pp. 126–30.

83 For example, see A. Lessona, *Verso l'impero*, Florence, 1939, p. 215.

84 F. Suvich, *Memorie*, p. 6 (though the young economist, and post-war Christian Democrat leader, Amintore Fanfani, argued in 1936 that empire was a necessity and not a luxury for Italy). O. Del Buono, *Eia, Eia, Eia, Alalà! la stampa italiana sotto il fascismo 1919–43*, Milan, 1971, p. 301.

85 F. Suvich, *Memorie*, pp. 283–4.

86 G. Salvemini, *Prelude to World War II*, London, 1953.

87 For the basic analysis in English, see J.F. Coverdale, *Italian Intervention in the Spanish Civil War*, Princeton, 1975. Italy's main pre-war contacts and clients had been Spanish monarchists.

88 Quoted by M. Knox, *Mussolini Unleashed*, p. 6.
89 *Ibid.*, p. 28.
90 Cited by J. F. Coverdale, *Italian Intervention*, p. 11. The war cost Italy 3,819 dead, 759 planes, 1,801 cannon, 157 tanks, 3,436 machine guns and 8.5 billion lire. See R. De Felice, *Lo stato totalitario 1936–1940*, p. 465.
91 For an account, see F. Jacomoni, *La politica dell'Italia in Albania*, Rocca San Casciano, 1965. For a useful English-language account of the 'exhaustion' of the regime by this time, see A. De Grand, 'Cracks in the facade: the failure of Fascist totalitarianism in Italy 1935–9', *European History Quarterly*, 21, 1991, pp. 515–35.
92 There is also a vast literature on the Axis. For some English-language introduction, see D. Mack Smith, *Mussolini's Roman Empire*, pp. 82–98, 124–68.
93 G. Gafencu, *The Last Days of Europe: A Diplomatic Journey in 1939*, London, 1947, p. 126.
94 For a narration, see M. Toscano, *The Origins of the Pact of Steel*, Baltimore, 1967.
95 See, e.g., B. Mussolini, *Opera omnia*, vol. XXIX, pp. 249–53 (26 March 1939); G. Ciano, *Diario 1937–1943* (ed. R. De Felice), Milan, 1980, pp. 54, 328, 343.
96 For an ironical example, cf. the October 1939 Italo-German 'option' agreement permitting transfer of German speakers in the Alto Adige 'home' to the Reich. Despite a generation of 'fascistisation', 90 per cent of the population opted to go (if only 70,000 actually left). For English-language background, see D.L. Rusinow, *Italy's Austrian Heritage 1919–1946*, Oxford, 1969.
97 Churchill would make this statement in a broadcast by the BBC on 23 December 1940. See R. De Felice, *Lo stato totalitario 1936–1940*, p. 844.
98 For the most detailed accounts of Italian 'public opinion', see S. Colarizi, *L'opinione degli italiani sotto il regime 1929–1943*, pp. 329–39; and P. Melograni, *Rapporti segreti della polizia fascista 1938–1940*, Bari, 1979. The most important matter to note about any comments in this period is exactly when they were made and in what circumstances. Grandi, for example, was in favour of intervention by 20 May (G. Ciano, *Diario 1937–1943*, p. 433); Macgregor Knox dates Mussolini's final decision to 25 May (though he is a little inconsistent in his argument), M. Knox, *Mussolini Unleashed*, p. 107. De Felice says 'probably' 28 May was decisive but avers, accurately, that Mussolini did not set a date to enter the war until virtually forced to do so. The pro-war demonstration of 10 June was only cleared the day before (R. De Felice, *Lo stato totalitario 1936–1940*, pp. 682, 804–5, 824, 839).
99 Ciano is particularly derided by De Feliceans as the obverse of what they see as the cool realism of Grandi. See, e.g., R. De Felice, *Lo stato totalitario 1936–1940*, pp. 338–46, 513.
100 For an account of this meeting and for Ciano's list of supplies needed by the Italian ally, 'enough to kill a bull', see D. Mack Smith, *Mussolini's Roman Empire*, pp. 192–3.
101 G. Ciano, *Diary 1939–1943* (ed. M. Muggeridge), London, 1947, p. 264.
102 In December 1937 Ciano, the young Foreign Minister, who was alleged

to leap to attention whenever Mussolini telephoned him, christened his son Marzio and wondered when it would be Italy's turn to start a war. G. Ciano, *Diario 1937–1943*, pp. 69–70; cf. also G.B. Guerri, *Galeazzo Ciano: una vita*, Milan, 1979, p. 86.

103 Ciano showed much of his character by remarking to Bottai in November 1939 that he hoped Britain would win the war since Britain stood for 'golf, whisky and comforts' (G. Bottai, *Diario 1935–1944*, p. 167). For what Ciano allegedly did in the rough of a golf-course, see G. B. Guerri, *Galeazzo Ciano*, pp. 69–70. Ciano thought his *compaesani*, the Livornese, were a little like 'the Australians of Italy' because of their criminal predilections. O. Vergani, *Ciano: una lunga confessione*, Milan, 1974, p. 38.

104 P. Kennedy, *The Rise and Fall of the Great Powers: Economic and Military Conflict from 1500 to 2000*, Glasgow, 1989, pp. 378, 385.

105 Even De Felice admits that December 1940 did reflect the nadir of Fascism and indeed argues that the attack on Greece was the real turning-point of Mussolini's life (R. De Felice, *L'Italia in guerra 1940–1943*, p. 328). For some nice detail on Italy's position in the Axis by 1942, see S. Trifkovic, 'Rivalry between Germany and Italy in Croatia 1942–1943', *Historical Journal*, 36, 1993, pp. 879–904.

106 Cited by M. Michaelis, *Mussolini and the Jews: German–Italian Relations and the Jewish Question in Italy 1922–1945*, Oxford, 1978, p. 348.

107 J. Goebbels, *Final Entries 1945: Diaries* (ed. H. Trevor-Roper), New York, 1978, p. 78; cf. R. De Felice, *Il problema dell'Alto Adige nei rapporti italo-tedeschi dall'Anschluss alla fine della seconda guerra mondiale*, Bologna, 1973, pp. 70–1.

108 F. Meinecke, *The German Catastrophe: Reflections and Recollections*, Boston, 1963, pp. 6–7.

109 For this point, see R.J.B. Bosworth, 'Mito e linguaggio nella politica estera italiana', in R.J.B. Bosworth and S. Romano (eds), *La politica estera italiana, 1860–1985*, Bologna, 1991, pp. 60–2.

110 L. Villari, *Affari esteri, 1943–1945*, Rome, 1948.

111 A. Tamaro, *La condanna dell'Italia nel trattato di pace*, Rocca San Casciano, 1952, pp. 9–10, 92.

112 For a useful recent documentary collection, see E. Serra (ed.), *L'accordo De Gasperi-Gruber nei documenti diplomatici italiani ed austriaci*, Trento, n.d.

113 For an English-language narration, see R.G. Rabel, *Between East and West: Trieste, the United States, and the Cold War 1941–1954*, Durham, NC, 1988; and, with more of a cultural reference, G. Sluga, 'Trieste: ethnicity and the Cold War, 1945–1954', *Journal of Contemporary History*, 29, 1994, pp. 285–303.

114 See, e.g., P. Cacace, *Venti anni di politica estera italiana (1943–1963)*, Rome, 1986, p. 155. According to one account, Sforza, by contrast, urged Italian diplomats to conduct a great battle to retain their colonies but only with the understanding that it was a battle which they must lose. E. Serra, *La diplomazia in Italia*, Milan, 1984, p. 96. For a useful,

brief, English-language survey, see C. Seton-Watson, 'Italy's imperial hangover', *Journal of Contemporary History*, 15, 1980, pp. 169–79.

115 P. Cacace, *Venti anni*, p. 265; cf., e.g., B. Croce, 'Contro l'approvazione del dettato della pace', *Belfagor*, II, 1947, pp. 514–17.

116 P. Cacace, *Venti anni*, p. 6.

117 But cf. Sforza's approach to the French government in September 1939 saying that, if he became Anti-Fascist Prime Minister, he would be pro-French and look to a cordial solution in Tunis, Djibouti and Suez. French Foreign Minister Georges Bonnet joked in response that, after all, it did not seem worth making a war against Mussolini. D. Bolech Cecchi, *Non bruciare i ponti con Roma*, p. 493.

118 L. Zeno, *Ritratto di Carlo Sforza*, Florence, 1975, p. 95. Churchill, by contrast, defined Sforza as a 'foolish and crooked old man' (Papers of Anthony Eden (PRO, London), FO 954/14B/It/45/55, Churchill to Cadogan, 16 June 1945).

119 Though there is a considerable literature in the journals, there is as yet no full scholarly study of Republican foreign policy. For a patriotic and conservative narrative, see P. Cacace, *Venti anni*.

120 In English see D. Ellwood, *Italy 1943–5*, Leicester, 1985; J.E. Miller, *The United States and Italy 1940–1950: The Politics and Diplomacy of Stabilization*, Chapel Hill, NC, 1986; J.L. Harper, *America and the Reconstruction of Italy, 1945–1948*, Cambridge, 1986, for useful analyses of Italy's disappearance beneath the American umbrella (though each has a largely domestic reference).

121 E. Serra, 'L'unione doganale italo-francese e la conferenza di Santa Margherita (1947–1951)', in J.B. Duroselle and E. Serra (eds), *Italia e Francia 1946–1954*, Milan, 1988, pp. 73–91.

122 None of this meant that Italy would not seek to utilise the EEC for its national benefit. Cf. R.E.M. Irving, 'Italy's Christian Democrats and European integration', *International Affairs*, 52, 1976, pp. 400–16.

123 F.R. Willis, *Italy Chooses Europe*, New York, 1971, p. 37.

124 It found it easiest to commence with 'foreign affairs'. See D.L.M. Blackmer, *Unity in Diversity: Italian Communism and the Communist World*, Cambridge, Mass., 1968.

125 Cited in J.E. Miller, *The United States and Italy*, p. 269.

126 R.E. Osgood, 'The PCI, Italy and NATO', in S. Serfaty and L. Gray (eds), *The Italian Communist Party: Yesterday, Today and Tomorrow*, London, 1980, p. 143.

127 This concept was first developed by the political scientist, Giorgio Galli.

128 For the historiographical context, see R.J.B. Bosworth, *Explaining Auschwitz and Hiroshima*, pp. 129–41.

129 G. Volpe, *Scritti su Casa Savoia*, Rome, 1983, p. 203.

130 For a narrative, again with almost entirely domestic concern, see L. Radi, *Tambroni trent'anni dopo: il luglio 1960 e la nascita del centrosinistra*, Bologna, 1990; and for the MSI see P. Ignazi, *Il polo escluso: profilo del Movimento Sociale Italiano*, Bologna, 1989.

3 THE ITALIAN MILITARY IN WAR AND PEACE 1860–1960

1 S. Butler, *Alps and Sanctuaries of Piedmont and the Canton Ticino*, new edn, Gloucester, 1986 (first published, 1881), p. 19.

2 *Ibid.*, pp. 122–3.

3 *Ibid.*, p. 123.

4 See, e.g., A. Marwick, *War and Social Change in the Twentieth Century*, London, 1974. Marwick's is another of those important general works which, much to the irritation of Italian historians, omits any serious reference to Italy.

5 L. Mondini (ed.), *Un immagine insolita del Risorgimento: dalle memorie del Conte Eugenio De Roussy De Sales*, Rome, 1977, pp. 91, 170.

6 D. Mack Smith, *Italy and Its Monarchy*, New Haven, Conn., 1989, pp. 292, 298.

7 D. Mack Smith, *Cavour*, London, 1985, p. 153.

8 J. Mazzini, *The Duties of Man and Other Essays*, London, 1907, p. 53.

9 *Ibid.*, pp. 143, 147–8.

10 F. Hayez, *L'opera completa*, Milan, 1971, plate 52.

11 See R.J.B. Bosworth, 'Italian history and Australian universities', *Risorgimento*, 4, 1983, p. 197.

12 For the latest English-language biography, see J. Ridley, *Giuseppe Garibaldi*, London, 1974; and cf. the works of D. Mack Smith who, as a historian, has continued to promulgate the Garibaldi legend.

13 D. Beales, 'Garibaldi in England: the politics of Italian enthusiasm', in J.A. Davis and P. Ginsborg (eds), *Society and Politics in the Age of the Risorgimento: Essays in Honour of Denis Mack Smith*, Cambridge, 1991, pp. 184–216.

14 See S. Magliani, 'Giuseppe Garibaldi: bilancio di un centenario', *Rassegna Storica del Risorgimento*, LXXIX, 1992, pp. 185–232 for a remarkable list of contemporary *garibaldiniana*.

15 J. Gooch, *Army, State and Society in Italy, 1870–1915*, London, 1989, p. 176; cf., in English, also J. Whittam, *The Politics of the Italian Army 1861–1918*, London, 1977.

16 P. Del Negro, *Esercito, stato, società*, Bologna, 1979, p. 64.

17 J. Gooch, *Army, State and Society*, p. 59.

18 See, e.g., R. Denicotti, *Delle vicende dell'Arma dei Carabinieri in un secolo dalla fondazione del Corpo*, Rome, 1914.

19 J. Gooch, *Army, State and Society*, p. 119.

20 M. Meriggi, 'L'ufficiale a Milano in età liberale', *Rivista di storia contemporanea*, XVII, 1988, pp. 525, 529, 536.

21 J. Gooch, *Army, State and Society*, p. 62.

22 M. Meriggi, 'L'ufficiale a Milano', p. 539.

23 See R. Bosworth, *Italy and the Approach of the First World War*, London, 1983, pp. 41–6.

24 G. Rochat, 'L'esercito italiano nell'estate 1914', *Nuova Rivista Storica*, XLV, 1961, pp. 295–348.

25 P. Del Negro, *Esercito, stato, società*, p. 227.

26 D. Farini, *Diario di fine secolo* (ed. E. Morelli), Rome, 1961, p. 382 (emphasis in original).

27 In English see a detailed analysis in L.A. Tilly, *Politics and Class in Milan 1881–1901*, Oxford, 1992.

28 In English see, e.g., T.R. Sykes, 'Revolutionary syndicalism in the Italian labor movement: the agrarian strikes of 1907–8 in the province of Parma', *International Review of Social History*, XXI, 1976, pp. 186–211.

29 R. Bosworth, 'The Messina earthquake of 28 December 1908', *European Studies Review*, 11, 1981, pp. 189–206.

30 For a detailed account, see U. Levra, *Il colpo di stato della borghesia: la crisi politica di fine secolo in Italia 1896–1900*, Milan, 1975.

31 P. Melograni, *Storia politica della grande guerra 1915–1918*, Bari, 1969, pp. 131–43. Chaplains had been banned from the Italian army in 1878. They were restored at Cadorna's behest in 1915. For their further history, see M. Franzinelli, *Il riarmo dello spirito: i cappellani militari nella seconda guerra mondiale*, Paese, Treviso, 1991.

32 P.L. Meloni, 'I cattolici e la grande guerra nella pubblicistica perugina', in M.C. Giuntella *et al.* (eds), *Cattolici e società in Umbria tra Ottocento e Novecento*, Rome, 1984, pp. 408, 410–11.

33 F. Minniti, *Esercito e politica da Porta Pia alla Triplice Alleanza*, Rome, 1984, p. 195.

34 N. Labanca, 'Una pedagogia militare per l'Italia liberale. I primi giornali per il soldato', *Rivista di storia contemporanea*, XVII, 1988, pp. 572–3.

35 M. Isnenghi, *Le guerre degli italiani: parole, immagini, ricordi 1848–1945*, Milan, 1989, pp. 212–13.

36 See E. Lussu, *Sardinian Brigade*, New York, 1970, who says that, if anything, the members of his crack regiment 'sardised' themselves through membership of it. Cf. also E. Lussu, *Il cinghiale del diavolo e altri scritti sulla Sardegna*, Turin, 1976; G. Ledda, *Padre Padrone: The Education of a Shepherd*, London, 1979, for the reverse process two generations later.

37 R. Bosworth, *Italy, the Least of the Great Powers: Italian Foreign Policy before the First World War*, Cambridge, 1979, p. 55–7.

38 See, e.g., Admiral Bettolo in *ibid.*, p. 57. In Milan, it was reported before 1914 that the local bourgeoisie was lessening in its traditional mistrust of the military, as it better understood the advantages of winning defence contracts. M. Meriggi, 'L'ufficiale a Milano', pp. 544–5.

39 See, e.g., the memoirs of Susanna Agnelli, *We Always Wore Sailor Suits*, London, 1976; and cf. L. Vannutelli, *Il Mediterraneo e la civiltà mondiale dalle origini all'impero fascista della Nuova Italia*, Bologna, 1936.

40 In English, see C. Seton-Watson, *Italy from Liberalism to Fascism 1870–1925*, London, 1967, pp. 393–4.

41 A. Iachino, *La campagna navale di Lissa 1866*, Milan, 1966, p. 559.

42 B.R. Sullivan, 'A fleet in being: the rise and fall of Italian sea power, 1861–1943', *International History Review*, X, 1988, p. 123.

43 See M. Gabriele, *Le convenzioni navali della Triplice*, Rome, 1969.

44 See M. Mazzetti, *L'esercito italiano nella triplice alleanza*, Naples, 1974, p. 396.

45 F. Minniti, *Esercito e politica*, p. 187.

46 N. Brancaccio, *In Francia durante la guerra*, Milan, 1926, p. 171; J. Gooch, *Army, State and Society*, pp. 156–7. Actually his opponent was probably his fellow Piedmontese, Giolitti.

47 P. Fussell, *The Great War and Modern Memory*, Oxford, 1975.

48 See, e.g., M. Eksteins, *Rites of Spring: The Great War and the Birth of the Modern Age*, New York, 1989.

49 See, e.g., F. Brancaccio, *In Francia durante la guerra*, p. 161.

50 For the context, see R.J.B. Bosworth, *Explaining Auschwitz and Hiroshima: History Writing and the Second World War 1945–1990*, London, 1993, pp. 123–4.

51 P. Pieri, *L'Italia nella prima guerra mondiale (1915–1918)*, Turin, 1965, p. 204.

52 P. Melograni, *Storia politica*, p. v.

53 D. Mack Smith, *Italy, a Modern History*, rev. edn, Ann Arbor, 1969, p. 313.

54 P. Melograni, *Storia politica*, pp. 93, 326. By contrast, Salandra set some sort of prime ministerial example. Each of his three sons was an *imboscato* (draft dodger) (*ibid.*, p. 112).

55 *Ibid.*, p. 114.

56 See E. Forcella and A. Monticone, *Plotone di esecuzione: i processi della prima guerra mondiale*, Bari, 1968.

57 L. Spitzer, *Lettere di prigionieri di guerra italiani 1915–1918*, Turin, 1976, pp. 24–5, 52, 96.

58 G. Corni, 'L'occupazione austro-germanica del Veneto nel 1917–8: sindaci, preti, austriacanti e patrioti', *Rivista di storia contemporanea*, XVIII, 1989, pp. 380–406. It is also worth remembering that some 'Italians' fought in the Habsburg armies. See L. Sondhaus, *In the Service of the Emperor: Italians in the Austrian Armed Forces, 1814–1918*, Boulder, 1992.

59 L. Tosi, 'Romeo A. Gallenga Stuart e la propaganda di guerra all'estero (1917–1918)', *Storia contemporanea*, II, 1971, pp. 519–43.

60 A.J. Mayer, *Wilson vs. Lenin: Political Origins of the New Diplomacy, 1917–1918*, New Haven, Conn., 1959.

61 N. Tranfaglia, *Carlo Rosselli dall'interventismo a Giustizia e Libertà*, Bari, 1968, p. 28.

62 H.S. Harris, *The Social Philosophy of Giovanni Gentile*, Urbana, 1960, p. 162.

63 G.B. Guerri, *Giuseppe Bottai, un fascista critico*, Milan, 1976, provides a lively biographical introduction.

64 G. Bottai, *La carta della scuola*, Milan, 1939, pp. 9, 75, 96, 188. (Bottai also talked about the just separation of Jews and Italians, pp. 209–10.)

65 S. Setta, *Renato Ricci. Dallo squadrismo alla Repubblica Sociale Italiana*, Bologna, 1986, p. 129.

66 *Ibid.*, p. 132.

67 Quoted by T.M. Mazzatosta, *Il regime fascista tra educazione e propaganda (1935–1943)*, Bologna, 1978, p. 10.

68 *Ibid.*, p. 204.

69 S. Cilibrizzi, *Pietro Badoglio rispetto a Mussolini e di fronte alla storia*, Naples, n.d., pp. 15, 59–60, noting that Mussolini had denounced

Badoglio in *Popolo d'Italia* on 14 October 1922 for saying a whiff of grapeshot could disperse the Fascists.

70 G. Rochat, *L'esercito italiano da Vittorio Veneto a Mussolini (1919–1925)*, Bari, 1967, pp. 197–213.

71 G. Rochat and G. Massobrio, *Breve storia dell'esercito italiano dal 1861 al 1943*, Turin, 1978, pp. 208–12.

72 G. Rochat, *L'esercito italiano*, p. 586.

73 M. Knox, *Mussolini Unleashed 1939–1941: Politics and Strategy in Fascist Italy's Last War*, Cambridge, 1982, pp. 30–3 for the figures.

74 G. Rochat and G. Massobrio, *Breve storia*, p. 225.

75 *Ibid.*, p. 283.

76 M. Clark, *Modern Italy 1871–1982*, London, 1984, p. 288.

77 G. Rochat and G. Massobrio, *Breve storia*, pp. 210–11.

78 See *Il 1919: rassegna mensile illustrata della vecchia guardia fascista* (edited by Mario Giampaoli), 1926; and cf., for fine photographic histories of Fascist Italy, R. De Felice and L. Goglia, *Storia fotografica del fascismo*, Bari, 1982, and *Mussolini. Il mito*, Bari, 1983.

79 See G. Rochat, *Italo Balbo: aviatore e ministro dell'aeronautica 1926–1933*, Ferrara, 1979; or, in English, C.G. Segrè, *Italo Balbo: A Fascist Life*, Berkeley, 1987.

80 G. Rochat, *Italo Balbo*, p. 71.

81 *Ibid.*, p. 84.

82 *Ibid.*, p. 85.

83 See, e.g., J.J. Sadkovich, 'Aircraft carriers and the Mediterranean 1940–1943: rethinking the obvious', *Aerospace Historian*, 34, 1987, pp. 263–71; cf. M. Knox, *Mussolini Unleashed*, p. 18, who briefly dismisses Douhet as a 'crackpot'; and note also C.G. Segrè, 'Douhet in Italy: prophet without honour?', *Aerospace Historian*, 26, 1979, pp. 69–80.

84 G. Rochat, *Italo Balbo*, p. 156.

85 P. Kennedy, *The Rise and Fall of the Great Powers*, Glasgow, 1989, p. 422.

86 M. Knox, *Mussolini Unleashed*, p. 256.

87 A.S. Milward, *War, Economy and Society 1939–1945*, Harmondsworth, 1987, p. 97.

88 J.J. Sadkovich, 'The Italo-Greek war in context: Italian priorities and Axis diplomacy', *Journal of Contemporary History*, 28, 1993, p. 439.

89 P. Monelli, *Toes Up*, London, 1930, p. 68.

90 G. Carocci, *Il campo degli ufficiali*, Turin, 1954, p. 13.

91 C. Pavone, *Una guerra civile: saggio storico sulla moralità nella Resistenza*, Turin, 1991, p. 12.

92 See, e.g., R. Graziani, *Ho difesa la patria*, Cernusco sul Naviglio, 1948, pp. 381–8; G. Pansa, *L'esercito di Salò*, Milan, 1970.

93 C. Pavone, *Una guerra civile*, p. 234; cf. J. Goebbels, *Final Entries, 1945* (ed. H. Trevor-Roper), New York, 1978, p. 268.

94 P. Cacace, *Venti anni di politica estera italiana 1943–1963*, Rome, 1989, pp. 312–13 reports Sforza saying that Italy joined to preserve peace and avoid isolation and (pp. 303–4) that Truman was not especially delighted at the news.

95 See, e.g., P. Ignazi, *Il polo escluso: profilo del Movimento Sociale Italiano*,

Bologna, 1989, pp. 110–15 on the party's dealings with returned servicemen's organisations. Despite General De Lorenzo's alleged coup plan in 1964 and subsequent election as an MSI deputy, Ignazi has concluded that the MSI's direct influence on most parts of the armed services was usually weak and that these services were mostly loyal to the Resistance–Republican tradition.

96 R. Absalom, *A Strange Alliance: Aspects of Escape and Survival in Italy, 1943–45*, Florence, 1991, p. 16.

97 *Ibid.*, p. 122.

98 *Ibid.*, p. 146; cf. Eric Newby's memoirs of this time with his emphasis on the skill of Italian peasants in picking up changes in their environment. It was easier 'to hide' in Germany amid a lettered population than to try to conceal oneself in Italy. E. Newby, *Love and War in the Apennines*, London, 1971, p. 31.

99 R. Absalom, *A Strange Alliance*, pp. 21–2; cf. Anna Bravo's revelations about the happier memories held by Piedmontese women of First World War deserters compared with Second World War partisans (A. Bravo, 'Italian peasant women and the First World War', in P. Thompson (ed.), *Our Common History*, London, 1982, pp. 166–8).

100 For a sentimental account, see H. Gordon, *Die Like the Carp*, Maryborough, Queensland, 1980.

4 ITALIAN COMMERCE AND THE WIDER WORLD 1860–1960

1 For example, *L'Espresso*, XXIV, 5 February 1978.

2 In 1988, *The Economist* estimated Italy's GDP at US \$10,490 per head, well ahead of Britain (US \$9,650) and just behind Australia (US \$10,540).

3 J. La Palombara, *Democrazia all'italiana*, Milan, 1988, pp. 347–8. (Also available in English as *Democracy, Italian Style*, New Haven, Conn., 1987).

4 *The Economist* continued to rage against the Republican system. See, e.g., its leader of 20 February 1993.

5 G. Luzzatto, *L'economia italiana dal 1861 al 1894*, Turin, 1968, pp. 40–1, 161–2.

6 *Ibid.*, pp. 54–5, 61–2.

7 R. Romeo, *Risorgimento e capitalismo*, Bari, 1959.

8 Cf., e.g., the less enlightened conservative, R. Moscati, who in the historiographical introduction to his *La fine del Regno di Napoli*, Florence, 1960, pp. 3–14, simply ignores Gramsci.

9 A. Gerschenkron, 'Notes on the rate of industrial growth in Italy, 1881–1913', *Journal of Economic History*, XV, 1955, pp. 360–75, and *Economic Backwardness in Historical Perspective*, Cambridge, Mass., 1962.

10 G. Luzzatto, *L'economia italiana*, p. 116.

11 P.M. Kalla-Bishop, *Italian Railways*, Newton Abbot, 1971, p. 26.

12 *Ibid.*, p. 25.

13 See, e.g., E.E.Y. Hales, *Pio Nono: A Study in European Politics and Religion in the Nineteenth Century*, London, 1956, p. 58.

14 A. Wingate, *Railway Building in Italy Before Unification*, Reading, 1970, p. 42.

15 For some English-language introductions, see S.J. Woolf, *A History of Italy 1700–1860*, London, 1979, pp. 97–8, 213–18; K.R. Greenfield, *Economics and Liberalism in the Risorgimento: A Study of Nationalism in Lombardy, 1814–1848*, rev. edn, Baltimore, 1965, p. 134. Cf. also B. Croce, *A History of the Kingdom of Naples* (ed. H. S. Hughes), Chicago, 1970; H. Acton, *The Last Bourbons of Naples*, London, 1961.

16 H. Acton, *The Last Bourbons of Naples*, p. 140.

17 B. Croce, *A History of the Kingdom of Naples*, p. 223.

18 G. Luzzatto, *L'economia italiana*, p. 85.

19 J.A. Davis, *Merchants, Monopolists and Contractors – A Study of Economic Activity and Society in Bourbon Naples 1815–1860*, New York, 1981, p. 9. In 1860 the kingdom lacked any savings bank. R. Moscati, *La fine del Regno di Napoli*, p. 30.

20 See, in great detail, M. Marmo, *Il proletariato industriale a Napoli in età liberale (1880–1914)*, Naples, 1978.

21 See F.M. Snowden, *Violence and Great Estates in the South of Italy: Apulia, 1900–1922*, Cambridge, 1986, p. 34; cf. also F.M. Snowden, 'Cholera in Barletta 1910', *Past and Present*, 132, 1991, pp. 67–103; L. Masella and B. Salvemini (eds), *La Puglia*, Turin, 1989.

22 G. Cingari, *Brigantaggio, proprietari e contadini nel sud (1799–1900)*, Reggio Calabria, 1976, pp. 135–6.

23 A. Forti Messina, *Società ed epidemia. Il colera a Napoli nel 1836*, Milan, 1979, notes (p. 21) that the 1836–7 epidemic killed almost 20,000 people or 60 per cent of those infected. In 1884 the death toll was some 8,000.

24 *Ibid.*, p. 39.

25 J.A. Davis, *Merchants, Monopolists and Contractors*, p. 337.

26 See, for a highly romantic evocation, R. Trevelyan, *Princes Under the Volcano*, New York, 1973.

27 The hellish working conditions (and social structure) here, which more reflected the time of Spartacus than that of Lord Shaftesbury, have not surprisingly become an object of literary (and film) exposure. See the *novelle* by Sciascia or Verga and, e.g., the film, *La discesa di Aclà a Floristella* (director Aurelio Grimaldi, 1992).

28 For some general listing of foreign investment, see V. Zamagni, 'The rich in a late industrialiser: the case of Italy, 1800–1945', in W.D. Rubinstein (ed.), *Wealth and the Wealthy in the Modern World*, London, 1980.

29 K.R. Greenfield, *Economics and Liberalism*, p. 242.

30 G. Luzzatto, *L'economia italiana*, p. 53.

31 A. Helps, *Life and Labours of Mr. Brassey*, London, 1969, pp. 86–8, for one entrepreneur who thought 'the Piedmontese' were 'very good hands' but the Neapolitans *'would not take any heavy work'* (sic).

32 G. Luzzatto, *L'economia italiana*, pp. 62, 123–4.

33 B. Stringher, *Gli scambii con l'estero e la politica commerciale italiana dal 1860 al 1910*, Rome, 1912, pp. 9–11.

34 G. Luzzatto, *L'economia italiana*, pp. 65–6, 83–4.

35 B. Stringher, *Gli scambii*, p. 19.

36 *Ibid.*, pp. 58–9.

37 In 1900 Britain still led with 21.2 per cent, the USA was now second with 12.8 per cent, Germany 11.7 per cent, Austria 11.3 per cent, France 9.9 per cent; Italian exports then went 16.6 per cent to Germany, 15.5 per cent to Switzerland, 12.6 per cent to France, 11.5 per cent to Britain, 9.1 per cent to the USA. In 1910, by contrast, the list went: imports – Germany 16.2 per cent, Britain 14.7 per cent, USA 11.2 per cent, France 10.3 per cent, Austria 8.9 per cent, Russia 8.2 per cent; exports – Germany 14.1 per cent, USA 12.7 per cent, France 10.5 per cent, Switzerland 10.4 per cent, Britain 10.1 per cent, Austria 7.9 per cent, Russia 2.4 per cent (*Ibid.*, pp. 58–9, 108).

38 But, e.g., see G. Luzzatto, *L'economia italiana*, pp. 118–22 on the frequent waste of what resources Italy did have.

39 See, e.g., FO 371/23798/R 9301, 24 October 1939, F. Rodd to Ministry of Economic Warfare summarising Italy's urgent requirement of raw materials.

40 F.R. Willis, *Italy Chooses Europe*, New York, 1971, pp. 104–5. In 1960, gas gave 11.6 per cent of Italy's energy.

41 G. Luzzatto, *L'economia italiana*, p. 176.

42 B. Stringher, *Gli scambii*, p. 4.

43 Italy suffered much more directly than France from the conflict, and the losses, especially in agrarian traffic, helped to engender the Sicilian *fasci* of 1893–4. See F. Renda, *I fasci siciliani*, Turin, 1977.

44 See E. Vitale, *La riforma degli istituti di emissione e gli 'scandali bancari' in Italia 1892–1896*, Rome, 1972.

45 R. Canosa, *Storia della criminalità 1845–1945*, Turin, 1991, p. 230.

46 For an English-language analysis, see S.B. Clough, *The Economic History of Modern Italy*, New York, 1964, pp. 124–32; G. Toniolo, *An Economic History of Liberal Italy 1850–1918*, London, 1990, pp. 113–17.

47 G. Toniolo, *An Economic History*, p. 140.

48 For an early, optimistic, English-language introduction, see A.W. Salomone, *Italy in the Giolittian Era: Italian Democracy in the Making, 1900–1914*, Philadelphia, 1960. For a more critical account, see R.A. Webster, *Industrial Imperialism in Italy, 1908–1915*, Berkeley, 1975.

49 See, e.g., E.M. Gray, *The Bloodless War*, New York, 1916, p. 57, who defined Joel as Germany's 'real pro-Consul in Italy'.

50 See R.A. Webster, *L'imperialismo industriale italiano 1908–1915*, Turin, 1974, pp. 116–54.

51 *Ibid.*, p. 4.

52 R.J.B. Bosworth, *Italy, the Least of the Great Powers: Italian Foreign Policy before the First World War*, Cambridge, 1979, pp. 139–41.

53 For a rather propagandist English-language introduction, see M. Sedgwick, *Fiat*, New York, 1974; for a far more scholarly Italian account cf. V. Castronovo, *Giovanni Agnelli: la Fiat dal 1899 al 1945*, Turin, 1977.

54 V. Castronovo, *Giovanni Agnelli*, p. 57; P. Melograni, *Gli industriali e Mussolini: rapporti tra Confindustria e Fascismo dal 1919 al 1929*, Milan, 1980, p. 45.

55 A. Lyttelton, 'The middle classes in Liberal Italy', in J. Davis and P. Ginsborg (eds), *Society and Politics in the Age of the Risorgimento: Essays in Honour of Denis Mack Smith*, Cambridge, 1991, p. 219.

56 See P. Farneti, *Sistema politico e società civile: saggi di teoria e ricerca politica*, Turin, 1971.

57 V. Zamagni, 'The rich in a late industrialiser', p. 136. In 1914 it was 14 per cent; it had fallen to 9.5 per cent in 1920; but then rose rapidly to 25 per cent by 1934. For a fine English-language study of Italy's commercial heartland, see J. Morris, *The Political Economy of Shopkeeping in Milan 1886–1922*, Cambridge, 1993.

58 K.R. Greenfield, *Economics and Liberalism*, p. 53.

59 For English-language background, see A.L. Cardoza, *Agrarian Elites and Italian Fascism: The Province of Bologna 1901–1926*, Princeton, 1982; A.A. Kelikian, *Town and Country under Fascism: The Transformation of Brescia 1915–26*, Oxford, 1986.

60 For the most detailed English-language study of such variation, see P. Arlacchi, *Mafia, Peasants and Great Estates: Society in Traditional Calabria*, Cambridge, 1983.

61 S.J. Woolf, *A History of Italy*, p. 479.

62 A. Papa, *Classe politica e intervento pubblico nell'età giolittiana: la nazionalizzazione delle ferrovie*, Naples, 1973.

63 See, generally, M. Abrate, *Ricerche per la storia dell'organizzazione sindacale dell'industria in Italia dalle origini al patto di palazzo Vidoni*, Turin, 1966.

64 In English, see D.J. Forsyth, *The Crisis of Liberal Italy: Monetary and Financial Policy 1914–1922*, Cambridge, 1993.

65 For a splendid evocation, see E. Conti, *Dal taccuino di un borghese*, Cremona, 1946; and cf. R. Bosworth, *Italy and the Approach of the First World War*, London, 1983, pp. 125–7.

66 M. Abrate, *Ricerche per la storia*, pp. 166–7; and cf. L. Villari, *Le avventure di un capitano d'industria*, Turin, 1991, pp. 21–37.

67 See R. Paci, 'Le trasformazioni ed innovazioni nella struttura economica italiana', in A. Caracciolo *et al.*, *Il trauma dell'intervento: 1914–9*, Florence, 1968, p. 42.

68 A. Caracciolo, 'L'ingresso delle masse sulla scena europea', in A. Caracciolo *et al.*, *Il trauma*, p. 17.

69 L. Villari, *Le avventure*, pp. 38–41.

70 For an English-language account of this last event (by a communist Italian historian), see P. Spriano, *The Occupation of the Factories: Italy 1920*, London, 1975.

71 L. Villari, *Il capitalismo italiano del Novecento*, Bari, 1992, p. 58; cf. a similar but more simply nationalist flirtation by the very political entrepreneur Oscar Sinigaglia, L. Villari, *Le avventure*, pp. 104–5.

72 Perhaps the most terrifying event between 1918 and 1922 for economic interest groups had been the collapse of the Banco di Sconto in 1921. P. Grifone, *Il capitale finanziaria in Italia*, Turin, 1971, p. 40.

73 E. Rossi, *Padroni del vapore e fascismo*, Bari, 1966, pp. 53–74.

74 But cf. his advocacy of 'the Japanese model' in 1935. A. De Stefani, *Garanzie di potenza: saggi economici*, Bologna, 1936, p. 17.

75 C. Maier, *Recasting Bourgeois Europe: Stabilization in France, Germany, and Italy in the Decade after World War I*, Princeton, 1975.

76 G. Petracchi, 'Ideology and *realpolitik*: Italo-Soviet relations 1917–1932', *Journal of Italian History*, 2, 1979, pp. 473–519; and cf. M. Pizzigallo, *Mediterraneo e Russia nella politica italiana (1922–1924)*, Milan, 1983.

77 Cited in L. Villari, *Il capitalismo italiano*, p. 37.

78 In 1929 Moody's gave Italy a very favourable rating and in 1940 Italy would still owe $2 billion to the USA. See C. Damiani, *Mussolini e gli Stati Uniti 1922–1935*, Bologna, 1980, pp. 221, 244.

79 G. Carocci, *Italian Fascism*, Harmondsworth, 1974, p. 111, says industrial production rose 60 per cent between 1922 and 1929.

80 For English-language accounts, see R. Sarti, *Fascism and the Industrial Leadership in Italy, 1919–1940: A Study in the Expansion of Private Power under Fascism*, Berkeley, 1971, and 'Mussolini and the Italian industrial leadership in the battle of the lira 1925–1927', *Past and Present*, 47, 1970, pp. 97–112.

81 See, generally, L. Villari, *Il capitalismo italiano*; and, in English, cf. J.S. Cohen, 'The 1927 revaluation of the lira: a study in political economy', *Economic History Review*, XV, 1972, pp. 642–54, and his 'Was Italian fascism a developmental dictatorship? Some evidence to the contrary', *Economic History Review*, XLI, 1988, pp. 95–113.

82 If industrial production is given an index of 100 in 1922, it had risen to 202 in 1929, had fallen to 146 in 1932, and risen again to 195 in 1935. S. La Francesca, *La politica economica del fascismo*, Bari, 1972, pp. 34, 71.

83 V. Zamagni, 'The rich in a late industrialiser', p. 147.

84 For a detailed memoir, full of unconscious irony about union life under Fascism, see T. Cianetti, *Memorie dal carcere di Verona* (ed. R. De Felice), Milan, 1983.

85 Cf. one historian's ironical conclusion: 'Italy became an industrial country during the very years of Fascist ruralisation' (P. Melograni, *Gli industriali e Mussolini*, p. 261). Industrial production did finally surpass agriculture in 1937–9.

86 S. Romano, *Giuseppe Volpi: industria e finanza tra Giolitti e Mussolini*, Milan, 1979, p. 12.

87 See R.J.B. Bosworth, *Italy, the Least of the Great Powers*, pp. 189–92.

88 S. Romano, *Giuseppe Volpi*, p. 48.

89 *Ibid.*, p. 93.

90 *Ibid.*, p. 197.

91 See M. De Marco, *Il Gazzettino: storia di un quotidiano*, Venice, 1976, pp. 99–102; for the *Mostre*, see F. Paulon, *La dogaressa contestata: la favolosa storia della Mostra di Venezia dalle regine alla contestazione*, Venice, 1971.

92 G.G. Migone, *Gli Stati Uniti e il fascismo: alle origini dell'egemonia americana in Italia*, Milan, 1980, pp. 156–60. Migone estimates that, from 1925 to 1928, Fascist Italy secured twenty-three loans in the USA to a value of US $316.5 million.

93 Cf. E. Rossi, *Padroni del vapore e fascismo*, p. 19 for a typical example of Volpi's at least public devotion to his 'tireless and infallible warrior' Duce.

94 A. Pirelli, *Taccuini 1922–1943* (ed. D. Barbone), Bologna, 1984, p. 300 gives a typical example.

95 R. De Felice, *Mussolini l'alleato 1940–1945 1. L'Italia in guerra 1940–1943*, Turin, 1990, p. 415. The Japanese, he said, reminded him of a flight of locusts which he had once seen in Morocco.

96 S. Romano, *Giuseppe Volpi*, pp. 245–6. Bernardino Nogara, Volpi's old colleague in the Libya negotiations, would make another splendid case-study. He survived to set up the Istituto per le opere di religione, of later Marcinkus and Calvi fame, in 1942.

97 V. Castronovo, *Storia di una banca: la Banca Nazionale del Lavoro e lo sviluppo economico italiano 1913–1983*, Turin, 1983, pp. 98–100. The bank actually did not acquire that name until 1927. Before then it was called the Istituto nazionale di credito per la cooperazione.

98 In English, see H. Fornari, *Mussolini's Gadfly: Roberto Farinacci*, Nashville, 1971.

99 For introduction, see G.P. Brunetta, 'The conversion of the Italian cinema to fascism in the 1920s', *Journal of Italian History*, 1, 1978, pp. 432–54, and cf. his *Storia del cinema italiano 1895–1945*, Rome, 1979.

100 V. Castronovo, *Storia di una banca*, pp. 152–3, 168, 188, 190, 215–16.

101 *Ibid.*, pp. 224–5.

102 *Ibid.*, pp. 191–4, 272, 312–13.

103 For a useful, brief, English-language introduction to this period, see A. Aquarone, 'Italy: the crisis and the corporative economy', *Journal of Contemporary History*, 4, 1969, pp. 37–58.

104 See, e.g., P. Melograni, *Rapporti segreti della polizia fascista, 1938–1940*, Bari, 1979, pp. 32–4, 52–4.

105 G. Ciano, *Diario 1937–1943* (ed. R. De Felice), Milan, 1980, p. 343.

106 See R. Bosworth, 'Italy's historians and the myth of Fascism', in R. Langhorne (ed.), *Diplomacy and Intelligence During the Second World War*, Cambridge, 1985, pp. 93–8, for the case of ISPI and Pirelli.

107 J.E. Miller, *The United States and Italy, 1940–1950: The Politics and Diplomacy of Stabilization*, Chapel Hill, NC, 1986, pp. 43–5.

108 See R. Faenza, *Gli americani in Italia*, Milan, 1976, pp. 267–304.

109 For an English-language introduction, see E.A. Carillo, *Alcide De Gasperi: the Long Apprenticeship*, Notre Dame, Ind., 1965, and more generally C.F. Delzell, *Mussolini's Enemies: The Italian Anti-Fascist Resistance*, Princeton, 1961.

110 For an English-language introduction to DC ideology, see G. Poggi, *Catholic Action in Italy: The Sociology of a Sponsored Organization*, Stanford, 1967.

111 C. Daneo, *La politica economica della ricostruzione 1945–1949*, Turin, 1975, p. 5. According to Daneo, industry proper in 1936 still only employed 15.2 per cent of the workforce (p. 41).

112 For an example, see R. Bosworth, 'Official Italy rediscovers Australia 1945–50', *Affari sociali internazionali*, XVI, 1988, pp. 46–8. For an unreconstructed Italian diplomatic historian in this regard, see F. Cataluccio, 'Problemi dell'emigrazione: emigrazione e "porta aperta" in Africa', *Nuova Antologia*, f. 1770, June 1948, pp. 192–7.

113 See S. Turone, *Storia del sindacato in Italia (1943–1969)*, Bari, 1976, pp.

287–8; and cf. G.G. Migone, 'Stati Uniti, Fiat e repressione antioperaia negli anni cinquanta', *Rivista di storia contemporanea*, I, 1974, pp. 232–81.

114 For some English-language introduction, see G. Podbielski, *Italy: Development and Crisis in the Post-War Economy*, Oxford, 1974, pp. 131–44.

115 In English, for a journalistic introduction, see P.H. Frankel, *Mattei, Oil and Power Politics*, London, 1966; and cf. P. Ginsborg, *A History of Contemporary Italy: Society and Politics 1943–1988*, Harmondsworth, 1990, pp. 163–5, and N. Perrone, 'Politica estera dell'ENI e neutralismo italiano', *Rivista di storia contemporanea*, XVI, 1987, pp. 616–29.

116 P.H. Frankel, *Mattei*, p. 51.

117 G. Galli, *La sfida perduta: biografia politica di Enrico Mattei*, Milan, 1976, pp. 141, 175.

118 For a classic English-language example, see M.V. Posner and S.J. Woolf, *Italian Public Enterprise*, London, 1967. Once again, then, Italy seemed a sort of Western Yugoslavia, all the more given similar optimistic views then about the 'diverse' functioning of the Yugoslav economy and society. By the 1980s and 1990s, state capitalism was no longer in such good odour. Rather, to the ruling monetarists, it was the final proof that Italy needed urgent and radical economic, and therefore political, change.

119 For a recent study, see E. Ciconte, *'Ndrangheta dall'Unità a oggi*, Bari, 1992. For English-language background, cf. J. Walston, *The Mafia and Clientelism: Roads to Rome in Post-War Calabria*, London, 1988.

120 For a fine sociological analysis, see P.A. Allum, *Politics and Society in Post-War Naples*, Cambridge, 1973.

121 For a recent general study, which emphasises the lack of any serious documentation of 'crime' before 1860, see R. Canosa, *Storia della criminalità*.

122 See C. Duggan, *Fascism and the Mafia*, New Haven, Conn., 1989. There is a huge further literature on this subject.

123 P. Arlacchi, *Mafia Business: The Mafia Ethic and the Spirit of Capitalism*, London, 1986.

124 E. Ciconte, *'Ndrangheta*, pp. 146, 314–16. One of the nineteenth-century precursors of the *'ndrangheta* at Nicastro had, with apparent harmlessness, called itself the Società nicastrese.

5 THE RISE AND FALL OF THE ITALIAN EMPIRE 1860–1960

1 Quoted by R.H. Rainero, 'Le relazioni italo-francesi e la questione del Fezzan (1948–1949)', in J.B. Duroselle and E. Serra (eds), *Italia e Francia (1946–1954)*, Milan, 1988, p. 63.

2 R. Robinson, 'British imperialism: the Colonial Office and the settler in East–Central Africa, 1919–63', in E. Serra and C. Seton-Watson (eds), *Italia e Inghilterra nell'età dell'imperialismo*, Milan, 1990, pp. 195–6.

3 Cited by M. Isnenghi, *Intellettuali militanti e intellettuali funzionari: appunti sulla cultura fascista*, Turin, 1979, p. 197.

4 On its new Via dell'Impero, now the Via dei Fori Imperiali, opened by the Fascist regime to join the Colosseum to the Victor Emmanuel monument and the Piazza Venezia, four large maps were displayed showing the growth of the empire from its beginning under Romulus to its greatest expanse. Wits were soon saying, however, that the maps' message varied somewhat depending in which direction a passer-by was walking. For urban Rome under Fascism, see A. Cederna, *Mussolini urbanista: lo sventramento di Roma negli anni del consenso*, Bari, 1979.

5 For a lively account, see M. Cagnetta, *Antichisti e impero fascista*, Bari, 1979.

6 M. Petricioli, *L'Italia in Asia Minore: equilibrio mediterraneo e ambizioni imperialiste alla vigilia della prima guerra mondiale*, Florence, 1983 has many vivid examples.

7 See R. Bosworth, 'Italy and the end of the Ottoman Empire', in M. Kent (ed.), *The Great Powers and the End of the Ottoman Empire*, London, 1984, pp. 52–7. Carlo Sforza, among many others, can also be found arguing that Napoleon, with his origin in ex-Genoese Corsica, was 'racially' Italian (C. Sforza, *Diplomatic Europe since the Treaty of Versailles*, New Haven, Conn., 1928, pp. vi–vii).

8 R.A. Vicentini, *Il movimento fascista veneto attraverso il diario di uno squadrista*, Venice, 1935, p. 3.

9 See, e.g., F. Piva, *Lotte contadine e origine del fascismo, Padova–Venezia: 1919–1922*, Venice, 1977, pp. 27–8, 31.

10 See, typically, some of his collected speeches, P. Foscari, *Per l'Italia più grande!* (ed. T. Sillani), Rome, 1928.

11 R.J.B. Bosworth, *Italy, the Least of the Great Powers: Italian Foreign Policy before the First World War*, Cambridge, 1979, p. 44.

12 For a very general introduction, see J.F. Pollard, 'Il Vaticano e la politica estera italiana', in R.J.B. Bosworth and S. Romano (eds), *La politica estera italiana, 1860–1985*, Bologna, 1991, pp. 197–230.

13 J. Boswell, *The Life of Samuel Johnson*, London, 1906, vol. 1, p. 63.

14 See R. Bosworth, *Italy and the Approach of the First World War*, London, 1983, pp. 6–7.

15 F. Crispi, *Memoirs* (ed. T. Palamenghi-Crispi), vol. 2, London, 1912, p. 140.

16 See R. and M. Bosworth, *Fremantle's Italy*, Rome, 1993.

17 Cf. F. Braudel, *The Mediterranean and the Mediterranean World in the Age of Philip* II, 2 vols, London, 1973. Braudel was not interested in that sort of question, but, arguably, geography and history before modern times did give the peoples of the Italian littoral a primacy in the Mediterranean.

18 For a splendid evocation of these feelings, see F. Martini, *Nell'Affrica italiana: impressioni e ricordi*, rev. edn, Milan, 1895. His 'Italic' or Latinate spelling of Africa was appropriate for such an elegant, urbane and belle-lettrist politician.

19 A. Iachino, *La campagna navale di Lissa 1866*, Milan, 1966, pp. 44–5.

20 F.M. Tamagna, *Italy's Interests and Policies in the Far East*, New York, 1941, pp. 3–4.

21 See, for an introduction, G. Cresciani, 'Australia, Italy and Italians, 1845–1945', *Studi Emigrazione*, XX, 1983, pp. 6–18.

22 R. Petrignani, *Neutralità e alleanza: le scelte di politica estera dell'Italia dopo l'Unità*, Bologna, 1987, pp. 132–3.

23 *Ibid.*, p. 137.

24 V. Gayda, *Italia e Francia: problemi aperti*, Rome, 1939, p. 30; cf. B. Pegolotti, *Corsica, Tunis, Gibuti*, Florence, 1939, p. 101, which raised the alleged number of Italians to 120,000.

25 T. Tittoni, *Questioni del giorno*, Milan, 1928, pp. 3–4, 38, 129.

26 R. Petrignani, *Neutralità e alleanza*, p. 259.

27 *Ibid.*, p. 381

28 T. Negash, *Italian Colonialism in Eritrea 1882–1941: Policies, Praxis and Impact*, Uppsala, 1987, p. 43; G. Rochat, *Militari e politici nella preparazione della campagna d'Etiopia: studi e documenti 1932–1936*, Milan, 1971, p. 24.

29 B. Melli, *La Colonia Eritrea dalle sue origini fino al 1 marzo 1900*, rev. edn, Parma, 1900, p. xx.

30 A. Del Boca, *Gli italiani in Africa orientale dall'unità alla marcia su Roma*, Bari, 1976, pp. 756–7; cf. also L. Goglia and F. Grassi, *Il colonialismo italiano da Adua all'impero*, Bari, 1981.

31 Fascist Italy would eventually win this territory in the south of Somalia through an agreement with Britain in 1924. See A. Cassels, *Mussolini's Early Diplomacy*, Princeton, 1970, pp. 217–25.

32 G.A. Rosso, *I diritti d'Italia oltremare*, Rome, 1916, p. 50.

33 R. Sertoli Salis, *Italia Europa Arabia*, Milan, 1940, pp. 78, 154–5, 202–3, 234.

34 See L.V. Cassanelli, *The Shaping of Somali Society: Reconstructing the History of a Pastoral People, 1600–1900*, Philadelphia, 1982, pp. 175, 197–8; and cf. R.L. Hess, *Italian Colonialism in Somalia*, Chicago, 1966; or, more generally, L. Goglia and F. Grassi, *Il colonialismo italiano da Adua all'impero*, Bari, 1981.

35 L.V. Cassanelli, *The Shaping of Somali Society*, p. 160.

36 C.M. De Vecchi di Val Cismon, *Orizzonti d'impero: cinque anni in Somalia*, Milan, 1935, p. 4.

37 A. Bullotta, *La Somalia sotto due bandiere*, Cernusco sul Naviglio, 1949, p. 4.

38 *Ibid.*, p. xxi.

39 R.L. Hess, *Italian Colonialism in Somalia*, p. 209.

40 L.V. Cassanelli, *The Shaping of Somali Society*, p. 54.

41 *Ibid.*, pp. 177–8.

42 T. Negash, *Italian Colonialism in Eritrea*, pp. 48–9; 129.

43 L.V. Cassanelli, *The Shaping of Somali Society*, p. 21.

44 See B. Melli, *La Colonia Eritrea*, appendix, for example, for a long list of *ascari* accorded medals for valour in the various 1890s campaigns in East Africa.

45 See, generally, R.L. Hess, *Ethiopia: The Modernization of Autocracy*, Ithaca, NY, 1970.

46 B. Melli, *La Colonia Eritrea*, p. 3.

47 D. Mack Smith, *Storia di cento anni di vita italiana visti attraverso il Corriere della Sera*, Milan, 1978, p. 39.

48 H.G. Marcus, *The Life and Times of Menelik II: Ethiopia 1844–1913*, Oxford, 1975, p. 86.

49 D. Farini, *Diario di fine secolo* (ed. E. Morelli), Rome, 1961, p. 388.

50 The son of the marriage had allegedly been 'Menelik I'. See H.G. Marcus, *Life and Times*.

51 D. Farini, *Diario*, pp. 928, 980.

52 *Ibid.*, pp. 969, 1089. In fact there was a characteristic or unseemly competition in charity between the Pope and Queen Margherita, the most imperialist of the Savoys.

53 G. Rochat, *Militari e politici*, p. 21; R.J.B. Bosworth, *Italy, the Least of the Great Powers*, pp. 329–35.

54 See, e.g., G. Salvemini, *Come siamo andati in Libia e altri scritti dal 1900 al 1915* (ed. A. Torre), Milan, 1963, which is full of wonderfully accurate demonstrations of the gap between Libyan reality and overblown nationalist rhetoric.

55 Cited by C. Seton-Watson, 'British perceptions of the Italo-Turkish war 1911–1912', in E. Serra and C. Seton-Watson (eds), *Italia e Inghilterra*, p. 114.

56 In English, see especially R.J.B. Bosworth, *Italy, the Least of the Great Powers*, pp. 127–95; T.W. Childs, *Italo-Turkish Diplomacy and the War over Libya 1911–1912*, Leiden, 1990; and, with more general reference, C.G. Segrè, *Fourth Shore: The Italian Colonization of Libya*, Chicago, 1974.

57 C. Moffa, 'I deportati libici della guerra 1911–12', *Rivista di storia contemporanea*, XIX, 1990, p. 45 notes that 31 per cent of those imprisoned in October 1911 and dispatched to the Tremiti Islands were dead by December, with the casualty rate being especially high among children and the old; cf. A. Del Boca, *Gli italiani in Libia: Tripoli bel suol d'amore 1860–1922*, Bari, 1986, pp. 241–9.

58 *Ibid.*, pp. 153–4, 455–6.

59 L. Turba, 'Vestigia romane a Tripoli', *Le Vie d'Italia*, XXVI, August 1920, pp. 389–92. Turba did admit that a lot more work was needed there.

60 *Ibid.*, p. 453.

61 G. Rochat and G. Massobrio, *Breve storia dell'esercito italiano dal 1861 al 1943*, Turin, 1978, p. 243.

62 *Ibid.*, p. 246. The population of Cyrenaica fell from 225,000 (1928) to 142,000 (1931).

63 P. Lanza di Scalea, 'La politica coloniale', in T. Sillani (ed.), *L'Italia di Vittorio Emanuele 1900–1925*, Rome, 1926, p. 173.

64 A. Mussolini, *Tripolitania*, Rome, n.d., p. 16.

65 *Ibid.*, p. 36; A. Lessona, *Scritti e discorsi coloniali*, Milan, 1935, p. 90.

66 A. Lessona, *Scritti*, p. 13.

67 A. Del Boca, *Gli italiani in Libia dal fascismo al Gheddafi*, Bari, 1988, p. 126. An economic journal prophesied that 3 million Italians would eventually settle in Libya.

68 P. Bernasconi, 'Le industrie e i commerci in Libia', in T. Sillani (ed.), *La*

Libia in venti anni di occupazione, studi e documenti, Rome, 1932, p. 141.

69 R. Cantalupo, *L'Italia musulmana*, Rome, 1928, pp. 177, 294.
70 The figure is cited in M. Moore, *Fourth Shore: Italy's Mass Colonization of Libya*, London, 1940, pp. 72–3, a still enthusiastic contemporary account. In 1929 there had been 455 families in Tripolitania and in 1931 429 colonists in total in Cyrenaica.
71 For Balbo, see G.B. Guerri, *Italo Balbo*, Milan, 1984; G. Rochat, *Italo Balbo: aviatore e ministro dell'aeronautica 1926–1933*, Ferrara, 1979; and in English, C.G. Segrè, *Italo Balbo: A Fascist Life*, Berkeley, 1987.
72 C.G. Segrè, 'Italo Balbo: governatore generale e creatore della quarta sponda', *Storia contemporanea*, XVI, 1985, p. 1048.
73 *Ibid.*, p. 1057.
74 For its history see R. De Felice, *Ebrei in un paese arabo*, Bologna, 1978, translated as *Jews in an Arab Land: Libya 1835–1970*, Austin, 1985.
75 A. Del Boca, *Gli italiani in Libia dal fascismo al Gheddafi*, pp. 258–9.
76 D.C. Cummings, 'British stewardship of the Italian colonies: an account rendered', *International Affairs*, XXIX, 1953, p. 11.
77 C. Marongiu Buonaiuti, *La politica religiosa del Fascismo nel Dodecanneso*, Naples, 1979, pp. 39–41, 54, 82–5; in English there is a journalistic and Hellenophile introduction in C.D. and I.B. Booth, *Italy's Aegean Possessions*, London, 1928.
78 In a superb recent thesis, a Dodecano-Australian historian has pointed out, however, that, for a lot of the local populace, post-1945 Greek rule did not much improve things. Indeed, especially among the poorest social groups, Italian administration had left reasonably fond memories. See N. Doumanis, 'Occupiers and occupied in the Dodecanese, 1912–1947: Italian colonialism and Greek popular memory', Ph.D. thesis, University of NSW, 1994.
79 C. Marongiu Buonaiuti, *La politica religiosa*, pp. 95–6, 99–100, 102, 105–6. For De Vecchi's own measure of himself, see C. De Vecchi di Val Cismon, *Il quadrumviro scomodo: il vero Mussolini nelle memorie del più monarchico dei fascisti*, Milan, 1983.
80 See, e.g., P.M. Masotti, *Ricordi d'Etiopia di un funzionario coloniale*, Milan, 1981, pp. 16–23; A. Sbacchi, *Ethiopia under Mussolini: Fascism and the Colonial Experience*, London, 1985, pp. 55, 78; and cf. H.M. Larebo, *The Building of an Empire: Italian Land Policy and its Practice in Ethiopia*, Oxford, 1994.
81 A. Sbacchi, *Ethiopia under Mussolini*, pp. 190–5.
82 *Ibid.*, p. 72.
83 *Ibid.*, p. 111. Sbacchi estimates there were then only forty agricultural companies in Ethiopia against 1,436 commercial and 1,225 industrial firms operating there.
84 L. Calabrò, *Intermezzo africano: ricordi di un Residente di Governo in Etiopia (1937–41)* (ed. R. De Felice), Rome, 1988, pp. 38, 108.
85 Calabrò speaks generically of the *'umanissimo comportamento'* of the Italians in the colonies (*ibid.*, p. 126).
86 For the lyrics, see A.V. Savona and M.L. Straniero (eds), *Canti dell'Italia fascista (1919–1945)*, Milan, 1979, pp. 270–1.

87 The common hostility of Italo-American communities to the black civil rights movement in the 1960s and 1970s USA might confirm this point. For an evocation, see M. De Marco Torgovnick, *Crossing Ocean Parkway: Readings by an Italian American Daughter*, Chicago, 1994, pp. 3–18.

88 F.S. Nitti, *The Decadence of Europe*, London, 1923, pp. 118, 123, 127–9.

89 A. Solmi *et al.*, *Egitto moderno e antico*, Milan, 1941, pp. 10, 17–18, 90, 258; cf. G. Volpe, *Guerra dopoguerra fascismo*, Venice, 1928, pp. 115–35.

90 See especially, R. De Felice, *Il Fascismo e l'Oriente: Arabi, ebrei e indiani nella politica di Mussolini*, Bologna, 1990.

91 L. Goglia, 'Il Mufti e Mussolini: alcuni documenti italiani sui rapporti tra nazionalismo palestinese e fascismo negli anni trenta', *Storia contemporanea*, XVII, 1986, p. 1208.

92 S. Colarizi, *L'opinione degli italiani sotto il regime, 1929–1943*, Bari, 1991, p. 242.

93 S. Zucotti, *The Italians and the Holocaust: Persecution, Rescue and Survival*, New York, 1987, p. 40; cf. M. Michaelis, *Mussolini and the Jews: German–Italian Relations and the Jewish Question in Italy 1922–1945*, Oxford, 1978, who is more inclined to see an ever-present anti-Semitism in Mussolini; and D. Carpi, *Between Mussolini and Hitler: The Jews and the Italian Authorities in France and Tunisia*, Hanover, NH, 1994.

94 V. Mantegazza, *Note e ricordi*, Milan, 1910, pp. 132–3; G. Vannutelli, *Il Mediterraneo e la civiltà mondiale dalle origini all'impero fascista della Nuova Italia*, Bologna, 1936, p. 50.

95 A. Nasalli Rocca, *Memorie di un prefetto*, Rome, 1946, pp. 240, 259.

96 See, e.g., D. Farini, *Diario*, p. 1045; cf. H.S. Hughes, *Prisoners of Hope: The Silver Age of the Italian Jews 1924–1974*, Cambridge, Mass., 1983, who says 8 per cent of university professors in 1911 were Jewish. Rabbis would join Catholic chaplains in servicing Italian soldiers in the First World War.

97 See, e.g., 'Le logge israelitiche segrete pienamente illustrate', *Civiltà Cattolica*, 16th series, VI, 1896, p. 170.

98 A. Gramsci, *Letters from Prison* (ed. L. Lawner), New York, 1975, p. 217.

99 For a fine evocation of the Italian Jew as (super-) patriot, see A. Stille, *Benevolence and Betrayal: Five Italian Jewish Families under Fascism*, Harmondsworth, 1993, especially pp. 17–89, and the characterisation of Ettore Ovazza, editor before 1938 of the anti-Zionist and pro-Fascist paper *La nostra bandiera*.

100 R. De Felice, *Storia degli ebrei italiani sotto il fascismo*, Turin, 1961, p. 85.

101 *Ibid.*, p. 83.

102 R. De Felice, *Il Fascismo e l'Oriente*, p. 161.

103 For a moving exposition of this as Italians in Croatia and France did what they could to block the 'Final Solution', see J. Steinberg, *All or Nothing: The Axis and the Holocaust 1941–1943*, London, 1990.

104 The number of Italian Jews deported then was 7,495; 610 lived. See R. De Felice, *Storia degli ebrei italiani*, p. 524.

105 L. Goglia, 'Sulla politica coloniale fascista', *Storia contemporanea*, XIX, 1988, p. 48.

106 M. Michaelis, *Mussolini and the Jews*, p. 92.

107 I.M. Lewis, *The Modern History of Somaliland from Nation to State*, London, 1965, pp. 141–3, says the Italians did a notably good job in the educational field in a place where the total tax returns in 1950 were still only £1 million. For a fuller account of post-1945 Italian policy in its ex-empire, see A. Del Boca, *Gli italiani in Africa orientale: nostalgie delle colonie*, Bari, 1984.

6 THE RISE AND RISE OF THE EMPIRE OF THE ITALIES: EMIGRATION 1860–1960

1 F. Coletti, 'Dell'emigrazione italiana', in P. Blaserna (ed.), *Cinquanta anni di storia italiana*, Milan, 1911, vol. 3, p. 81.

2 F.S. Nitti, *Scritti di economia e finanza*, Bari, 1966, vol. 3, part 2, p. 383.

3 For a basic economic and demographic history, see E. Sori, *L'emigrazione italiana dall'Unità alla seconda guerra mondiale*, Bologna, 1979; and cf. G. Rosoli (ed.), *Un secolo di emigrazione italiana 1876–1976*, Rome, 1978.

4 G. Fofi, *L'immigrazione meridionale a Torino*, Milan, 1975, p. 9.

5 A. Pirelli, *Taccuini 1922–1943*, Bologna, 1984, p. 365.

6 In his youth Mussolini had emigrated both to Switzerland and to the Austrian Trentino. For a narration of his emigrant experience, see R. De Felice, *Mussolini il rivoluzionario 1883–1920*, Turin, 1965, pp. 23–45, 62–78.

7 For De Felice's own admissions in this regard, see R. De Felice, 'Gli studi sull'emigrazione cinque anni dopo', *Affari sociali internazionali*, 6, 1978, pp. 7–18; cf. also his 'Alcuni temi per la storia dell'emigrazione italiana', *Affari sociali internazionali*, 1, 1973.

8 For fuller readings of the historiography of Italian emigration, see the journal *Altreitalie*, established by the Agnelli foundation in 1989, which has regularly published review articles on the subject; cf. also the foundation's multi-volume (and multi-authored) history of Italians abroad: M. Pacini (ed.), *Euroamericani*, vol. 1: *La popolazione di origine italiana in Argentina*; vol. 2: *La popolazione di origine italiana in Argentina*; vol. 3: *La popolazione di origine italiana in Brasile*, Turin, 1987; and the follow-up volume on Australia, S. Castles, C. Alcorso, G. Rando and E. Vasta, *Australia's Italians: Culture and Community in a Changing Society*, North Sydney, 1992.

9 R.F. Foerster, *The Italian Emigration of Our Times*, Cambridge, Mass., 1919.

10 Apart from the Agnelli foundation, other groups, notably the Scalabrinian Centro Studi Emigrazione in Rome which publishes the valuable journal, *Studi Emigrazione*, and the Fondazione Sella which

continues to investigate emigration from Biella, do much useful work. But it remains typically more microcosmic than macrocosmic.

11 Z. Ciuffoletti and M. Degl'Innocenti, *L'emigrazione nella storia d'Italia 1868–1975*, Florence, 1978, vol. 1, p. 118.

12 F. Coletti, 'Dell'emigrazione italiana', p. 242.

13 B. Stringher, 'Gli scambi con l'estero e la politica commerciale italiana dal 1860 al 1910', in P. Blaserna (ed.), *Cinquanta anni*, vol. 3, pp. 121–2.

14 For an analysis of the debate, see F. Manzotti, *La polemica sull'emigrazione nell'Italia unita fino alla prima guerra mondiale*, Milan, 1962.

15 F. Papafava, *Dieci anni di vita italiana (1899–1909): cronache*, Bari, 1913, vol. 1, p. 29.

16 R. Murri, 'Gl'Italiani nell'America latina – impressioni di viaggio', *Nuova Antologia*, f. 991, 1 April 1913, p. 437.

17 L. Villari, *Gli Stati Uniti d'America e l'emigrazione italiana*, Milan, 1912, pp. 204–5.

18 For an account of such ideas in Liberal Italy, see R.J.B. Bosworth, *Italy, the Least of the Great Powers: Italian Foreign Policy before the First World War*, Cambridge, 1979, pp. 39–67.

19 L. Luzzatti, *Memorie*, Milan, 1966, vol. 3, p. 14.

20 P.J. Gallo, *Old Bread, New Wine: A Portrait of the Italo-Americans*, Chicago, 1981, pp. 114–17.

21 L. Avagliano (ed.), *L'emigrazione italiana: testi e documenti*, Naples, 1976, p. 258, says 9 were killed, 96 severely injured, 2 disappeared and 521 were assaulted; cf. T. Vertone, 'Antécédents et causes des événements d'Aigues-Mortes', in J-B. Duroselle and E. Serra (eds), *L'emigrazione italiana in Francia prima del 1914*, Milan, 1978, pp. 107–38.

22 See B. Pisa, 'Pasquale Villari e la Dante Alighieri: considerazioni su sette anni di mandato presidenziale', *Storia contemporanea*, XXIII, 1992, pp. 445–8, for semi-official patriotic reactions in Italy.

23 L. Avagliano (ed.), *L'emigrazione italiana*, pp. 37–49.

24 E. Corradini, *Il nazionalismo italiano*, Milan, 1911, pp. 53–9.

25 For some introduction, see R.J.B. Bosworth, *Italy, the Least of the Great Powers*, p. 114; and cf. G.B. Scalabrini, *Trent'anni di apostolato: memorie e documenti*, Rome, 1909, p. 363.

26 Z. Ciuffoletti and M. Degl'Innocenti, *L'emigrazione*, vol. 1, pp. 283–4.

27 R. Bauer, *La Società umanitaria 1893–1958*, Milan, n.d.

28 L. Avagliano (ed.), *L'emigrazione italiana*, pp. 53–4.

29 Z. Ciuffoletti and M. Degl'Innocenti, *L'emigrazione*, vol. 1, pp. 332–9.

30 For a classic English-language statement of this thesis, see J.S. MacDonald, 'Agricultural organisation, migration and labour militancy in rural Italy', *Economic History Review*, XVI, 1963, pp. 61–75.

31 Z. Ciuffoletti and M. Degl'Innocenti, *L'emigrazione*, vol. 2, pp. 139–40.

32 A. Lessona, *La missione dell'Italia in Africa*, Rome, 1936, p. 9.

33 P.V. Cannistraro and G. Rosoli, 'Fascist emigration policy in the 1920s: an interpretative framework', *International Migration Review*, XIII, 1979, p. 675, reports that in 1927 the Italian Foreign Ministry estimated 9.2 million Italians lived abroad, of whom 7.7 million were in the Americas.

34 E. Santarelli, *Fascismo e neofascismo: studi e problemi di ricerca*, Rome,

NOTES

1974, pp. 113–33; L. Tosi, *Alle origini della FAO: le relazioni tra l'Istituto Internazionale di Agricoltura e la Società delle Nazioni*, Milan, 1989.

35 For graphic examples, see P.V. Cannistraro, 'Fascism and Italian-Americans in Detroit', *International Migration Review*, IX, 1975, pp. 29–40; R. Bosworth, 'Luigi Mistrorigo and *La Stampa italiana*: the strange story of a Fascist journalist in Perth', in R. Bosworth and M. Melia (eds), *Aspects of Ethnicity: Studies in Western Australian History*, XIII, Nedlands, WA, 1991, pp. 61–70.

36 Z. Ciuffoletti and M. Degl'Innocenti, *L'emigrazione*, Vol. 2, pp. 149–50, 156–63.

37 A. Nobile, 'Politica migratoria e vicende dell'emigrazione durante il fascismo', *Il Ponte*, XXX, 1974, pp. 1325–6.

38 E. Sori, *L'emigrazione italiana*, pp. 405–7, 420–1.

39 G. Volpe, *Guerra dopoguerra fascismo*, Venice, 1928, pp. 165–6, 183–4, 353–76.

40 For case-studies in English, see G. Cresciani, *Fascism, Antifascism and Italians in Australia 1922–1945*, Canberra, 1980; and J.E. Zucchi, *Italians in Toronto: Development of a National Identity, 1875–1935*, Kingston, Ontario, 1988.

41 For another example, see A. Morelli, 'Les tentatives d'implantation fasciste dans l'émigration italienne de Belgique', *Risorgimento*, I, 1980, pp. 47–57.

42 For a fine acount which might have been improved by some investigation of Mussolini's image in emigration, see L. Passerini, *Mussolini immaginario*, Bari, 1991.

43 For some introduction, see R. Bosworth, 'Official Italy rediscovers Australia 1945–50', *Affari sociali internazionali*, XVI, 1988, pp. 51–6.

44 For an English-language summary, see C.F. Delzell, *Mussolini's Enemies: The Italian Anti-Fascist Resistance*, Princeton, 1961.

45 For a biography of Salvemini, see M.L. Salvadori, *Gaetano Salvemini*, Turin, 1963; for typical examples of Villari's propaganda, see, e.g., L. Villari, *The Fascist Experiment*, London, 1926, and *The Expansion of Italy*, London, 1930.

46 G. Cresciani, *Fascism, Antifascism*, pp. 223–43.

47 R. Pascoe, *Buongiorno Australia: An Italian Heritage*, Melbourne, 1987, p. 88.

48 Notoriously, the Ethiopian War would tempt some Anti-Fascists to rally to the national cause. The Ribbentrop–Molotov pact would also lower Anti-Fascist morale.

49 C.F. Delzell, *Mussolini's Enemies*, pp. 158–61. Alberto Moravia's novel *The Conformist* and the Bertolucci movie are very roughly based on this event. See A. Moravia, *The Conformist*, London, 1952.

50 G. Pintor, *Doppio diario 1936–1943* (ed. M. Serri), Turin, 1987, p. xxii.

51 Z. Ciuffoletti and M. Degl'Innocenti, *L'emigrazione*, vol. 2, p. 232; cf. a charitable explanation of De Gasperi's reaction to seeing the South in M.R. Catti De Gasperi, *De Gasperi, uomo solo*, Milan, 1964, p. 279.

52 P. Cinanni, 'La scelta del governo italiano nel secondo dopoguerra', *Il Ponte*, XXX, 1974, p. 1348.

53 G. De Luna, *Storia del Partito d'Azione 1942–1947*, Milan, 1982, p. 233.

54 P. Cinanni, 'La scelta', pp. 1348–9.

55 L. Avagliano (ed.), *L'emigrazione italiana*, pp. 327–34.

56 See, e.g., M. Gianturco's commentary in *Nuova Antologia*, f. 1801, January 1951, pp. 95–100; f. 1804, April 1951, pp. 431–2; f. 1808, August 1951, pp. 421–2; f. 1811, November 1951, pp. 310–11; f. 1812, December 1951, pp. 423–7.

57 For a typical example, see G. Andreotti, 'Discorso di apertura alla conferenza nazionale dell'emigrazione "gli italiani nel mondo"', *Affari sociali internazionali*, XVII, 1989, pp. 5–13.

58 See, e.g., S.L. Baily, 'The Italians and the development of organised labor in Argentina, Brazil, and the United States: 1880–1914', *Journal of Social History*, 3, 1969, pp. 123–34, 'Chain migration of Italians to Argentina: case studies of the Agnonesi and the Sirolesi', *Studi emigrazione*, XIX, 1982, pp. 73–90, 'The adjustment of Italian immigrants in Buenos Aires and New York, 1870–1914', *American Historical Review*, 88, 1983, pp. 281–305, 'The Italian migrant experience: understanding continuity and change', *Journal of Urban History*, 11, 1985, pp. 503–13; cf. also H.S. Klein, 'The integration of Italian immigrants into the United States and Argentina: a comparative analysis', *American Historical Review*, 88, 1983, pp. 300–42.

59 M.C. Nascimbene, 'Origini e destinazioni degli italiani in Argentina', in M. Pacini (ed.), *Euroamericani*, vol. 2, p. 70.

60 R. Murri, 'Gl' Italiani', p. 85.

61 F. Korn and L. de la Torre, 'Gli italiani a Buenos Aires: le professioni, l'inserimento sociale (1869–1914)', J.F. Bullrich, 'Presenza italiana nell'architettura rioplatense', R.D. Halperin, 'L'influenza italiana nella letteratura argentina', R. Arizaga, 'L'Italia e la musica del Rio de la Plata', M. Montserrat, 'L'influenza italiana nell'attività scientifica argentina del diciannovesimo secolo', A. Korn, 'Contribuiti scientifici degli italiani in Argentina nel ventesimo secolo', all in M. Pacini (ed.), *Euroamericani*, vol. 2.

62 M.C. Nascimbene, 'Origini e destinazioni', p. 344.

63 R. Murri, 'Gl' Italiani', p. 86.

64 G. Dore, *La democrazia italiana e l'emigrazione in America*, Brescia, 1964, p. 190; cf. G. Bernardi, *Un patriota italiano nella Repubblica Argentina: Silvino Olivieri* (ed. B. Croce), Bari, 1946.

65 G. Rosoli, 'Chiesa ed emigrati italiani in Brasile 1880–1940', *Studi Emigrazione*, XIX, 1982, p. 250.

66 Cited in L. Sponza, *Italian Immigrants in Nineteenth Century Britain: Realities and Images*, Leicester, 1988, pp. 24, 217.

67 C. Hughes, *Lime, Lemon and Sarsaparilla: The Italian Community in South Wales, 1881–1945*, Bridgend, 1991, pp. 52–7.

68 As cited in L. Sponza, *Italian Immigrants*, p. 60. In regard to another part of the entertainment industry, it has been estimated that in 1900 20 per cent of Marseilles prostitutes were Italian. E. Serra, 'L'emigrazione italiana in Francia durante il secondo governo Crispi (1893–1896)', in J-B. Duroselle and E. Serra (eds), *L'emigrazione italiana in Francia*, p. 163.

69 E.A. Millar, '*La Scozia*, 1908', unpublished paper, History Department University of Glasgow, n.d., p. 334.

70 *Ibid.*, p. 333.
71 L. Sponza, *Italian Immigrants*, p. 260.
72 *Ibid.*, p. 257.
73 *Ibid.*, pp. 105–8.
74 *Voices from Ellis Island: An Oral History of American Immigration*, Frederick, MD, 1988, 1/009.
75 But cf. G.R. Mormino and G.E. Pozzetta, *The Immigrant World of Ybor City: Italians and Their Latin Neighbors in Tampa, 1885–1985*, Urbana, 1990, for a tale of extended working-class unity.
76 D. Cinel, 'Dall'Italia a San Francisco: l'esperienza dell'immigrazione', in M. Pacini (ed.), *Euroamericani*, vol. 1, p. 350.
77 D. Cinel, *The National Integration of Italian Return Migration 1870–1929*, Cambridge, 1991, p. 164.
78 See F.L. Auerbach, *Immigration Laws of the United States*, Indianapolis, 1955.
79 A. Cornelisen, *Flight from Torregreca*, London, 1980, p. 94.
80 For an introduction to this Australian world, see J. Wilton and R. Bosworth, *Old Worlds and New Australia: The Post-War Migrant Experience*, Ringwood, Victoria, 1984, pp. 1–37.
81 Cited in E. Franzina, 'Frammenti di cultura contadina nelle lettere degli emigranti', *Movimento operaio e socialista*, IV, 1981, p. 53.
82 C. Tilly, 'Migration in modern European history', in W.H. McNeill and R.S. Adams (eds), *Human Migration: Patterns and Policies*, Bloomington, 1978, p. 68.
83 D. Gabaccia, *Militants and Migrants: Rural Sicilians Become American Workers*, New Brunswick, NJ, 1988, p. 4; cf. her more general piece, 'Worker internationalism and Italian labor migration, 1870–1914', *International Labor and Working-Class History*, 45, 1994, pp. 63–79.
84 D. Gabaccia, *Militants and Migrants*, p. 12.
85 See E. Banfield, *The Moral Basis of a Backward Society*, New York, 1958, and the subsequent massive controversy.
86 D. Gabaccia, *Militants and Migrants*, pp. 79–80.
87 *Ibid.*, p. 171.
88 G.R. Mormino and G.E. Pozzetta, *Immigrant World*.
89 For some introduction, see W.A. Douglass, 'Images and adages: Anglo-Australian perceptions of Italians in Queensland', in R. Bosworth and R. Ugolini (eds), *War, Internment and Mass Migration: The Italo-Australian Experience 1940–1990*, Rome, 1992, pp. 33–59; and cf. his *Emigration in a South Italian Town: An Anthropological History*, New Brunswick, NJ, 1984.
90 B. Bottignolo, *Without a Bell Tower: A Study of the Italian Immigrants in South West England*, Rome, 1985, pp. 87–8.
91 M. Triaca, *Amelia: A Long Journey*, Richmond, Victoria, 1985, p. 35.
92 G.R. Mormino and G.E. Pozzetta, *Immigrant World*, pp. 192–5.
93 D. Cinel, *From Italy to San Francisco: The Immigrant Experience*, Stanford, 1982; cf. also J.W. Briggs, *An Italian Passage: Immigrants to Three American Cities, 1890–1930*, New Haven, Conn., 1978.
94 D. Cinel, *From Italy to San Francisco*, p. 13.

95 D. Cinel, *The National Integration of Italian Return Migration*, pp. 7–9.
96 D. Cinel, *From Italy to San Francisco*, p. 250.
97 J.E. Zucchi, *Italians in Toronto*, p. 8.
98 See, generally, R.F. Harney, *Dalla frontiera alle Little Italies: gli italiani in Canada 1800–1945*, Rome, 1984; and cf. Harney's important article, 'Italophobia: English-speaking malady?', *Studi Emigrazione*, XXII, 1985, pp. 6–43; also published in the posthumous collection, R.F. Harney, *From the Shores of Hardship: Italians in Canada*, Welland, Ontario, 1993.
99 See, generally, R. Bosworth and R. Ugolini (eds), *War, Internment and Mass Migration*.
100 Quoted by P. Fussell, *Wartime: Understanding and Behavior in the Second World War*, New York, 1989, p. 124.
101 R.F. Harney, *Dalla frontiera alle Little Italies*, p. 56.
102 L.W. Levine, 'The unpredictable past: reflections on recent American historiography', *American Historical Review*, 94, 1989, p. 678.

7 CULTURES AND IDEOLOGY FOR EXPORT: ITALY AND THE ITALIES 1860–1960

1 Cited by R.J. Vecoli, 'La ricerca di un'identità italo-americana: continuità e cambiamento', in M. Pacini (ed.), *Euroamericani*, vol. 1: *La popolazione italiana negli Stati Uniti*, Turin, 1987, p. 221.
2 E.J. Hobsbawm, *Nations and Nationalism since 1780: Programme, Myth, Reality*, Cambridge, 1990, p. 118.
3 C. Belgiojoso, 'Della presente condizione delle donne e del loro avvenire', *Nuova Antologia*, f. 1, 1866, pp. 96, 111.
4 For an English-language introduction, see D. Pick, 'The faces of anarchy: Lombroso and the politics of criminal science in post-unification Italy', *History Workshop*, 21, 1986, pp. 60–86; cf. M. Gibson, *Prostitution and the State in Italy, 1860–1915*, New Brunswick, NJ, 1986; or, for a fuller Italian account, M. De Giorgio, *Le italiane dall'Unità a oggi: modelli culturali e comportamenti sociali*, Bari, 1992.
5 See P. Meldini, *Sposa e madre esemplare: ideologia e politica della donna e della famiglia durante il fascismo*, Florence, 1975.
6 See R. and M. Bosworth, *Fremantle's Italy*, Rome, 1993, for an evocation of its usage in one of the most distant emigrant Italian communities in the world.
7 L. Passerini, *Fascism in Popular Memory: The Cultural Experience of the Turin Working Class*, Cambridge, 1987.
8 For a very fine analysis, see V. De Grazia, *How Fascism Ruled Women: Italy 1922–1945*, Berkeley, 1992.
9 M. Warner, *Alone of all Her Sex: The Myth and Cult of the Virgin Mary*, London, 1985, p. 71. Santa Maria Goretti was beatified in 1947 and made a saint in 'Holy Year', 1950.
10 See, e.g., as English-language examples, J. Boissevain, *Friends of Friends: Networks, Manipulations and Coalitions*, Oxford, 1974; J. Brögger,

Montevarese: A Study of Peasant Society and Culture in Southern Italy, Bergen, 1971; J. Chubb, *Patronage, Power, and Poverty, in Southern Italy: A Tale of Two Cities*, Cambridge, 1982; J. Davis, *Land and Family in Pisticci*, London, 1973; A.H. Galt, *Far From the Church Bells: Settlement and Society in an Apulian Town*, Cambridge, 1991; F.J. Kjellberg, *Political Institutionalization: A Study of Two Sardinian Communities*, London, 1975; F. Gross, *Il Paese: Values and Social Change in an Italian Village*, New York, 1973; A.L. Maraspini, *The Study of an Italian Village*, Paris, 1968; D.S. Pitkin, *The House that Giacomo Built: History of an Italian Family, 1898–1978*, Cambridge, 1985; F. Sabetti, *Political Authority in a Sicilian Village*, New Brunswick, NJ, 1984; J. and P. Schneider, *Culture and Political Economy in Western Sicily*, New York, 1976; C. White, *Patrons and Partisans: A Study of Politics in Two Southern Italian 'Comuni'*, Cambridge, 1980; cf. also D.I. Kertzer, *Family Life in Central Italy 1880–1910: Sharecropping, Wage Labor and Coresidence*, New Brunswick, NJ, 1984.

11 A. Blok, 'Rams and billy-goats: a key to the Mediterranean code of honour', *Man: The Journal of the Royal Anthropological Institute*, 16, 1981, pp. 427–40; cf. in the same volume, M.J. Giovannini, 'Woman: a dominant symbol within the cultural system of a Sicilian town', pp. 408–26.

12 For a splendid evocation in the post-1945 era, see A. Cornelisen, *Torregreca: Life, Death, Miracles*, New York, 1969, and *Women of the Shadows*, London, 1976.

13 J. Haycraft, *Italian Labyrinth: Italy in the 1980s*, Harmondsworth, 1987, p. 132.

14 A. Macdonell, *In the Abruzzi*, London, 1908, pp. 19–20.

15 *Ibid.*, pp. 20–1.

16 *Ibid.*, p. 22. One local woman did gain a certain revenge on decades of Anglo-Saxon racial slights by remarking to the visitor: 'I am glad to see the English before I die. I always thought they were black' (p. 214).

17 D.R. Gabaccia, *From Sicily to Elizabeth St. Housing and Social Change Among Italian Migrants, 1880–1930*, Albany, NY, 1984, p. 49.

18 E. Ciccotosto and M. Bosworth, *Emma: A Translated Life*, Fremantle, 1990; cf. M. Hall Ets, *Rosa: The Life of an Italian Immigrant*, Minneapolis, 1970.

19 E. Ciccotosto and M. Bosworth, *Emma*, p. 38.

20 R.M. Bell, *Fate and Honor, Family and Village: Demographic and Cultural Change in Rural Italy since 1800*, Chicago, 1979, pp. 72–3.

21 D.R. Gabaccia, *From Sicily to Elizabeth St.*, pp. xv–xvi; for an introduction to the problem of the Italian family in Italy, see M. Barbagli, 'Marriage and the family in Italy in the early nineteenth century', in J.A. Davis and P. Ginsborg (eds), *Society and Politics in the Age of the Risorgimento: Essays in Honour of Denis Mack Smith*, Cambridge, 1991.

22 *Ibid.*, p. 115.

23 F. Piselli, *Parentela ed emigrazione: mutamenti e continuità in una comunità calabrese*, Turin, 1981, p. 26.

24 *Ibid.*, p. 50.

25 *Ibid.*, p. 310.

26 J. Walston, *The Mafia and Clientelism: Roads to Rome in Post-War Calabria*, London, 1988, p. 35.

27 For a naive example, see R. Pascoe, 'Place and community: the construction of an Italo-Australian space', in S. Castles, C. Alcorso, G. Rando and E. Vasta, *Australia's Italians: Culture and Community in a Changing Society*, North Sydney, 1992, pp. 85–97.

28 For important explorations of this concept, see J.E. Zucchi, *Italians in Toronto: Development of a National Identity, 1875–1935*, Kingston, Ontario, 1988; W.A. Douglass, *Emigration in a South Italian Town: An Anthropological History*, New Brunswick, NJ, 1984.

29 R.M. Bell, *Fate and Honor*, pp. 30–2.

30 For the great introduction to the problematics of this subject, see D. Lowenthal, *The Past is a Foreign Country*, Cambridge, 1985.

31 For a splendid evocation, see U. Eco, *Faith in Fakes*, London, 1986.

32 P. Ortoleva, 'Tradition and abundance. Reflections on Italian-American foodways', *Altreitalie*, 7, 1992, pp. 56, 67.

33 *Corriere d'Australia*, 11 October 1960.

34 R. Harney, 'Toronto's people', *Polyphony*, 6, 1984, p. 11.

35 D.E. Byrne, 'The race of the saints: an Italian religious festival in Jessup, Pennsylvania', *Journal of Popular Culture*, 19, 1985, pp. 119–30.

36 R. Bosworth and M. Melia, 'The Italian *feste* of Western Australia and the myth of the universal church', in R. Bosworth and M. Melia (eds), *Aspects of Ethnicity: Studies in Western Australian History*, XII, Nedlands, WA, 1991, pp. 71–84.

37 P. Fortini, 'Gli italiani a Marsiglia: vita e lavoro dei pescatori italiani nel grande porto francese', *Le Vie d'Italia*, XXX, January 1924, p. 39.

38 R.A. Orsi, *The Madonna of 115th Street: Faith and Community in Italian Harlem, 1880–1950*, New Haven, Conn., 1985; cf. his 'The religious boundaries of an inbetween people: street *feste* and the problem of the dark-skinned other in Italian Harlem, 1920–1990', *American Quarterly*, 44, 1992, pp. 313–47, in which Orsi alleges that Italians perceived French-speaking 'Latin' Haitians as more 'like them' than American blacks.

39 R.A. Orsi, *The Madonna of 115th Street*, pp. 50, 172, 197, 218–19; cf. also D.I. Kertzer, *Comrades and Christians: Religion and Political Struggle in Communist Italy*, Cambridge, 1980, for Italian background.

40 A. Zerafa, 'San Pellegrino comes to Norwood: an Italo-Australian religious feast', *CIRC Papers*, 29, 1981, pp. 1–8.

41 The Federation of the Associations of Campanian Emigrants in South Australia, *I Campani in Sud Australia: A History of the Settlement of the People of the Italian Region of Campania in South Australia*, Adelaide, 1989, pp. 39–40.

42 *25mo anniversario della festa di San Nicola 1963–88*, Osborne Park, WA, 1988, pp. 1, 3, 5.

43 For some explanation, see R. Bosworth, 'L'Italia d'Australia: 1988', in R. Ugolini (ed.), *Italia-Australia 1788–1988*, Rome, 1991, pp. 27–43.

44 For a now somewhat dated, English-language biography, see E.E.Y. Hales, *Pio Nono*, London, 1954.

45 *Civiltà Cattolica*, 8th series, I, 1871, pp. 8, 13.

46 *Civiltà Cattolica*, 16th series, VI, 1896, article entitled 'Lezioni della Provvidenza agl'Italiani', pp. 13–14.

47 Again, there is a useful if rather dated English-languge study, L.P. Wallace, *Leo XIII and the Rise of Socialism*, Durham, NC, 1966.

48 For some introduction, see L. Ganapini, *Il nazionalismo cattolico: i cattolici e la politica estera in Italia dal 1871 al 1914*, Bari, 1970.

49 P. Melograni, *Storia politica della grande guerra*, Bari, 1969, pp. 131–40.

50 For an English-language narrative, see J.N. Molony, *The Emergence of Political Catholicism in Italy: Partito Popolare 1919–1926*, London, 1977.

51 For some English narrative, see J.F. Pollard, *The Vatican and Italian Fascism 1929–32: A Study in Conflict*, Cambridge, 1985; P.C. Kent, *The Pope and the Duce: The International Impact of the Lateran Agreements*, London, 1981. Also still useful is the more detailed D.A. Binchy, *Church and State in Fascist Italy*, Oxford, 1941.

52 E. Fouilloux, 'Straordinario ambasciatore? Parigi 1944–1953', in G. Alberigo (ed.), *Papa Giovanni*, Bari, 1987, p. 85.

53 J. Cornwell, *A Thief in the Night: The Death of Pope John Paul I*, Harmondsworth, 1990, pp. 182–3.

54 See, e.g., R.J. Vecoli, 'Prelates and peasants: Italian immigrants and the Catholic Church', *Journal of Social History*, 2, 1969, pp. 217–68, and 'Italian religious organizations in Minnesota', *Studi Emigrazione*, XIX, 1982, pp. 191–201.

55 E. Neill, 'Note sull'emigrazione nella canzone popolare', *Movimento operaio e socialista*, IV, 1981, p. 109.

56 R.J. Vecoli, 'Prelates and peasants', p. 239.

57 F.W. Lewins, *The Myth of the Universal Church: Catholic Migrants in Australia*, Canberra, 1978, p. 99; cf. Centro Studi Emigrazione, *La religiosità meridionale*, n.p., 1972.

58 F.W. Lewins, *Myth of the Universal Church*, p. 59.

59 For Australian examples see, e.g., P. O'Farrell, *The Catholic Church and Community in Australia: A History*, Sydney, 1977, pp. 215–17; F. Lewins, *Myth of the Universal Church*. The Vatican's policy of the 'Australian Church for the Australians', announced by Apostolic Delegate Cerretti in 1916 and pursued thereafter, notably by G.B. Montini (the later Paul VI), had as one purpose the circumventing of the resident 'Irish' hierarchy. It looks like a classic case of 'the enemy of my enemy is my friend'.

60 R. Bosworth, 'Official Italy rediscovers Australia 1945–50', *Affari sociali internazionali*, XVI, 1988, p. 58.

61 For the text, see Z. Ciuffoletti and M. Degl'Innocenti (eds), *L'emigrazione nella storia d'Italia 1868–1975*, Florence, 1978, pp. 356–61.

62 For a study of this 'national populism', not always enthusiastic about its subject, see A. Asor Rosa, *Scrittori e popolo: il populismo nella letteratura italiana*, Rome, 1972.

63 J.V. Femia, *Gramsci's Political Thought: Hegemony, Consciousness and the Revolutionary Process*, Oxford, 1981, p. 151.

64 See, e.g., D. Betti, 'Il partito editore: libri e lettori nella politica culturale del PCI 1945–53', *Italia contemporanea*, 175, 1989, pp. 53–74.

65 A. Gramsci, *Selections from the Cultural Writings* (eds D. Forgacs and G. Nowell-Smith), London, 1985, p. 247.

66 In English, see, e.g., R.H. Evans, *Coexistence: Communism and its Practice in Bologna 1945–1965*, Notre Dame, Ind., 1967; M. Jäggi, R. Müller and S. Schmid, *Red Bologna*, London, 1976; D.I. Kertzer, *Comrades and Christians: Religion and Political Struggle in Communist Italy*, Cambridge, 1980.

67 B. Mussolini, *Opera omnia* (eds E. and D. Susmel), Florence, 1951–80, vol. XX, pp. 227–30 (10 April 1924).

68 For a characteristic statement by a leading Anti-Fascist and patriotic historian of the Risorgimento, see L. Salvatorelli, *The Risorgimento: Thought and Action*, New York, 1970.

69 The still definitive English-language study is K.R. Greenfield, *Economics and Liberalism in the Risorgimento: A Study of Nationalism in Lombardy, 1814–1848*, rev. edn, Baltimore, 1965.

70 B. Croce, *History of the Kingdom of Naples* (ed. H.S. Hughes), Chicago, 1970, pp. 33, 195–6.

71 F. Protonotari, 'La Nuova Antologia', *Nuova Antologia*, f. 1, 1866, p. 6.

72 T. Mamiani, 'Roma', *Nuova Antologia*, f. 1, 1866, p. 94; D. Comparetti, 'Virgilio nella tradizione letteraria fino a Dante', *Nuova Antologia* f. 1, 1866, pp. 9–55.

73 C. De Vecchi di Val Cismon, 'Esame di coscienza', *Rassegna Storica del Risorgimento*, XXIII, 1936, p. 13.

74 J. Mazzini, *The Duties of Man and Other Essays*, London, 1907, p. xxxv.

75 R.J.B. Bosworth, *Italy, the Least of the Great Powers: Italian Foreign Policy before the First World War*, Cambridge, 1979, pp. 49–52.

76 *Rivista Mensile del Touring Club Italiano*, May 1910.

77 A. Cippico, *Italy: The Central Problem of the Mediterranean*, New Haven, Conn., 1926, p. 4.

78 L. Rava, *Per la 'Dante Alighieri' (trent'anni di propaganda): discorsi e ricordi 1900–1931*, Rome, 1932, pp. 63–4.

79 See text in A.V. Savona and M.L. Straniero (eds), *Canti dell'Italia fascista (1919–1945)*, Milan, 1979, pp. 205–6. There were a number of variant lyrics to this song. Dante appeared, typically, in the most official version.

80 *Le Vie d'Italia*, XXXVIII, August 1932, p. xiv.

81 M.E. Lacy, *With Dante in Modern Florence*, London, 1912, p. 161 (though Dante Olive Oil is produced in Spain).

82 For an introduction, see J. Kinder, 'Italian in Australia 1940–1990', in R. Bosworth and R. Ugolini (eds), *War, Internment and Mass Migration: The Italo-Australian Experience 1940–1990*, Rome, 1992, pp. 279–90; and, more generally, T. De Mauro, *Storia linguistica dell'Italia unita*, Bari, 1965.

83 L.W. Levine, *Highbrow/Lowbrow: The Emergence of Cultural Hierarchy in America*, Cambridge, Mass., 1988, p. 220.

84 E.R. Vincent, 'Lo sviluppo degli studi italiani in Gran Bretagna durante il '900', in *Inghilterra e Italia nel '900: atti di convegno di Bagni di Lucca, ottobre 1972*, Florence, 1973, p. 63.

85 H.M. Moran, *In My Fashion: An Autobiography of the Last Ten Years*, London, 1946, pp. 1–19.

86 See, e.g., the account by L. Goglia, 'La propaganda italiana a sostegno della guerra contro l'Etiopia svolta in Gran Bretagna nel 1935–36', *Storia contemporanea*, XV, 1984, pp. 845–906.

87 See, e.g., R. Bosworth, 'Conspiracy of the consuls? Official Italy and the Bonegilla riot of 1952', *Historical Studies*, 22, 1987, p. 564.

88 See R. Joseph, 'The Martignoni affair: how a Swiss politician deceived Mussolini', *Journal of Contemporary History*, 9, 1974, pp. 77–90.

89 For an English-language study, see M. Ledeen, *Universal Fascism: The Theory and Practice of the Fascist International, 1928–1936*, New York, 1972.

90 For a rapidly ageing defence, see J. La Palombara, *Democracy, Italian Style*, New Haven, Conn., 1987.

91 See, e.g., L. Barzini, *The Italians*, Harmondsworth, 1964 and *From Caesar to the Mafia*, New York, 1971; and the novels of Giovanni Guareschi. The far right-wing politics of each author were not much noticed outside Italy.

8 VISITING ITALY: TOURISM AND LEISURE 1860–1960

1 R. Douglas, *Between the Wars 1919–1939: The Cartoonists' Vision*, London, 1992, p. 56. Perhaps not all Australians would have seen the joke. In the 1880s, it was suggested that gondolas might look nice on Lake Ballarat. One town councillor thriftily opined that the cheapest way forward was to import two such animals from Italy and encourage them to breed. E.M. La Meslée, *The New Australia* (ed. R. Ward), London, 1979, p. 33.

2 M. McCarthy, *Birds of America*, Harmondsworth, 1972, p. 247; but cf. her own presumably rewarded career as a tourist commentator on Venice. T. Cole (ed.), *Venice: A Portable Reader*, New York, 1979, pp. 23–5.

3 The use of the word '*turismo*' (and its current spelling) did not become completely accepted in Italy until after the First World War and even then 'tourist experts' remained defensive about their nomenclature and discipline. See, e.g., A. Mariotti, *L'importanza economica del turismo*, Florence, 1931, p. 4; A. Niceforo, *Il movimento dei forestieri in Italia*, Rome, 1923.

4 C. Dickens, *Pictures from Italy*, London, n.d., p. 377.

5 J. Boswell, *The Life of Samuel Johnson*, London, 1906, vol. II, pp. 25–6.

6 C. Dickens, *Pictures from Italy*, pp. 207–8, 315. Dickens did agree that the collection of buildings in the Campo Santo was 'perhaps the most remarkable and beautiful in the whole world'.

7 *Ibid.*, p. 366.

8 *Ibid.*, p. 258.

9 *Ibid.*, p. 318.

10 J. Pemble, *The Mediterranean Passion*, Oxford, 1987, pp. 39, 172.

11 P. Brendon, *Thomas Cook: 150 Years of Popular Tourism*, London, 1991, pp. 12, 96. Brendon does point out (p. 8) that the first modern tourist

agent was a fifteenth-century Venetian, Agostino Contarino, who proffered a package to the Holy Land for 60 gold ducats. It included travel and two hot meals a day.

12 C. Dickens, *Pictures from Italy*, pp. 208, 428.

13 M. Scattarreggia, *San Remo 1815–1915: turismo e trasformazioni territoriali*, Milan, 1986, pp. 11, 36.

14 For an introduction to the history of Salso, see M. Bonatti, *Nascita e sviluppo di una città termale: Salsomaggiore*, Parma, 1981; L. Pavia, *Guida illustrata di Salsomaggiore, sue acque, suoi dintorni*, Milan, 1898; F.M. Ricci, *Salsomaggiore: art dèco termale*, Milan, 1989.

15 In 1876, Antonio Stoppani denominated Italy '*Il Bel Paese*' and urged that its natural beauties were second to none. A. Stoppani, *Il Bel Paese: conversazioni sulle bellezze naturali, la geologia e la geografia fisica d'Italia*, Milan, 1876.

16 G. Paravicini, 'Di una società per accrescere il numero dei "Touristes" in Italia', *Rassegna Nazionale*, XX, 16 October 1898, pp. 809–21; cf. his earlier article 'Sul lavoro italiano', *Rassegna Nazionale*, XX, 16 July 1898, pp. 246–69.

17 B. Stringher, *Gli scambii con l'estero e la politica commerciale italiana dal 1860 al 1910*, Rome, 1912, pp. 122–5. Later economists were troubled by Stringher's mathematics and reduced the 900,000 to about 550,000.

18 M. Ferraris, 'Il movimento dei forestieri in Italia', *Nuova Antologia*, f. 650, 16 January 1899, p. 325.

19 M. Ferraris, 'Vetture, automobili e tassametri nelle grandi città', *Nuova Antologia*, f. 987, 1 February 1913, pp. 526–7.

20 M. Ferraris, 'Il movimento dei forestieri in Italia', p. 325.

21 M. Ferraris, 'Per il movimento dei forestieri in Italia', *Nuova Antologia*, f. 682, 16 May 1900, p. 351. Ferraris claimed hoteliers thought Bodio had underestimated the number of tourists and the profits drawn from them.

22 M. Ferraris, 'Di un ufficio di stato per il movimento dei forestieri', *Nuova Antologia*, f. 985, 1 January 1913, p. 147.

23 M. Ferraris, 'Il movimento dei forestieri in Italia', p. 326.

24 M. Ferraris, 'Per il movimento dei forestieri in Italia', *Nuova Antologia*, f. 770, 16 January 1904, p. 338.

25 See, e.g., M. Ferraris, 'Le terze classi nei treni diretti', *Nuova Antologia*, f. 986, 16 January 1913, pp. 320–9.

26 M. Ferraris, 'Per le industrie termali e climatiche d'Italia', *Nuova Antologia*, f. 968, 16 April 1912.

27 M. Ferraris, 'Vetture, automobili e tassametri nelle grandi città', p. 531.

28 M. Ferraris, 'Di un ufficio di stato per il movimento dei forestieri', p. 151.

29 M. Ferraris, 'Per il movimento dei forestieri in Italia' (1900), pp. 353–4.

30 M. Ferraris, 'Per il movimento dei forestieri in Italia' (1904), p. 336.

31 M. Ferraris, 'Per il movimento dei forestieri in Italia' (1900), p. 357.

32 *Ibid.*, p. 360.

33 M. Ferraris, 'Il movimento dei forestieri in Italia', pp. 329–330.

34 See, e.g., *Rivista Mensile del Touring Club Ciclistico Italiano* which commenced publication in January/February 1897.

35 See his obituary, *Le Vie d'Italia*, XXXII, March 1926, which occupies

virtually the whole issue, and especially therein A. Gerelli, 'L.V. Bertarelli nella vita privata', pp. 252–62; and cf. the memorial volume of his own writings, Touring Club Italiano, *L'Italia e il Touring negli scritti di Luigi Vittorio Bertarelli*, Milan, 1927; and L.V. Bertarelli and E. Boegan, *Duemila grotte: quarant'anni di esplorazioni nella Venezia Giulia*, Milan, 1926.

36 *Enciclopedia italiana*, 34, pp. 118–19, entry on 'Touring Club Italiano'.

37 *Ibid.*, p. 118; *Le Vie d'Italia*, XXIX, 1923, pp. 479–82, for 1922 financial statement.

38 Cf. also the characteristic L.V. Bertarelli, 'La Guida d'Italia per gli stranieri', *Le Vie d'Italia*, XXIX, February 1923, pp. 117–22, where he explained that foreigners needed a simplified product since there were places in Italy to which they would not want to go. The two-volume Guide to Libya, by contrast, was already available in 1923. See L.V. Bertarelli, 'La Guida della Libia del TCI', *Le Vie d'Italia*, XXIX, 1923, pp. 425–32.

39 See D. Mack Smith, *Italy: A Modern History*, rev. edn, Ann Arbor, 1969, pp. 85–7 for his character and (austere) policies.

40 See, e.g., A. Cuzzi, 'Un precursore', *Il 1919*, III, July 1927.

41 *Enciclopedia italiana*, 2, entry on 'Alpinismo', pp. 656, 659.

42 G. Rossi-Osmida, *1872–1972. Cento anni di sport a Venezia*, Venice, 1971 (unnumbered pages); cf. also L. Ferretti, *Il libro dello sport*, Rome, 1928.

43 G. Rossi-Osmida, *1872–1972*.

44 Genoa's team was founded in 1893 under the name of the Genoa Football and Cricket Club. See annual editions of the *Annuario illustrato del calcio*; and A. Ghirelli, *Storia del calcio in Italia*, Turin, 1967.

45 For Scalea, see R.J.B. Bosworth, *Italy, the Least of the Great Powers: Italian Foreign Policy before the First World War*, Cambridge, 1979, pp. 110–11; and R. Cantalupo, *Ritratto di Pietro Lanza di Scalea*, Rome, 1939.

46 See, e.g., F.M. Snowden, *The Fascist Revolution in Tuscany 1919–1922*, Cambridge, 1989, pp. 23–4, 58, on the limits of 'enlightened paternalism'.

47 See, e.g., A. Mosso, *L'uomo sulle alpi*, Milan, 1909.

48 A. Mosso, *Mens sana in corpore sano*, Milan [1903], p. 257.

49 *Ibid.*, p. 73. Mosso, on the other hand, was emphatic in his belief that the 'Latin race' should find its own way to physical education; German-style gymnastics, he feared, carried 'within itself the fatal germ of athleticism' (p. 72), i.e. a specialised rather than mass form of exercise. Running, Mosso urged, was the simplest and best way to train both the male and female body (p. 74).

50 By the 1920s, it was certainly out-paced by the German–Austrian one (which was in *Anschluss* well before the event). The German club had a membership of 197,497 in 1927, five times that of the CAI.

51 See 'Ciclismo', *Enciclopedia italiana*, 10, p. 208; A.G. Bianchi, 'L.V. Bertarelli nei primi anni del Touring', *Le Vie d'Italia*, XXXII, 1926, p. 230. The great cycle race, the Giro d'Italia, was inaugurated in 1909, but on the model of the Tour de France, 1903. For the French Touring Club,

see *Rivista Mensile del Touring Club Ciclistico Italiano*, February/March 1897, pp. 44–7.

52 A. Mosso, *Mens sana in corpore sano*, p. 151. In 1909, Sonnino's Minister of Education, Camillo Daneo, did produce a law for compulsory physical education. It was bracketed with compulsory choral singing (another activity imported from the North). See L. Ferretti, *Il libro dello sport*, pp. 82–3.

53 A. Mosso, *Mens sana in corpore sano*, pp. 275–6.

54 F.H. Hinsley, *Power and the Pursuit of Peace*, Cambridge, 1963; from 1925, the various Touring Clubs were also united in their own International. See also C. Moldenhauer, 'La costituzione del consiglio centrale del turismo internazionale', *Le Vie d'Italia*, XXXI, 1925, pp. 427–9.

55 V. De Grazia, *How Fascism Ruled Women: Italy, 1922–1945*, Berkeley, 1992, p. 21. Beauty contests also came late to Italy; the first fully organised one coincided with the *Cinquantennio* celebrations. The magazine, *Scena illustrata*, had, in 1901, run a 'Cinderella' contest for which female entrants were invited to send their foot measurements. See M. De Giorgio, *Le italiane dall'Unità a oggi*, Bari, 1992, pp. 159–60.

56 M. Ferraris, 'Per il movimento dei forestieri in Italia' (1900), p. 352; cf. also the TCI's nationalist enthusiasms in the Libyan War, e.g., *Rivista Mensile del Touring*, XVII, 1911.

57 Touring Club Italiano, *L'Italia e il Touring*, p. 6.

58 See, e.g., A. Mariotti, *L'industria del forestiero in Italia*, Bologna, 1923, pp. 6–7. An economist, for example, remarked that in wartime a lot of hotels closed and recalled sadly that then tourists, if they arrived in the later afternoon, could not always rely upon finding accommodation.

59 *Rivista Mensile del Touring*, January 1915. This comment was all the more paradoxical given the Club's enthusiastic backing both of irredentism and of Italian imperialism, for example, in Libya, before 1914.

60 C. Dickens, *Pictures from Italy*, p. 277.

61 J. Ruskin, *The Stones of Venice*, London, 1851, vol. 1, p. 17.

62 T. Cole (ed.), *Venice*, p. 277.

63 See, e.g., G. Damerini, *D'Annunzio a Venezia*, Verona, 1943, p. 95.

64 See, e.g., G. Greene (ed.), *An Impossible Woman: The Memories of Dottoressa Moor of Capri*, London, 1975, p. 146.

65 See, e.g., N. Douglas, *Old Calabria*, London, 1975.

66 Taormina as a tourist resort rose with the Baron whose work was, for example, exhibited in Rome during the grandiose *Cinquantennio* celebrations of 1911. See, e.g., S. Porretta, 'La fotografia all'esposizione universale di Roma 1911', in G. Piantoni (ed.), *Roma 1911*, Rome, 1980, pp. 215–22; P. Quennell, *Spring in Sicily*, London, 1952, p. 88. For a more general analysis, see R. Aldrich, *The Seduction of the Mediterranean: Writing, Art and Homosexual Fantasy*, London, 1993.

67 Cited in T. Cole (ed.), *Venice*, pp. xi–xii.

68 See generally G. Damerini, *D'Annunzio*; and cf. also the recent conference, the papers of which were published as E. Mariano (ed.), *D'Annunzio e Venezia*, Rome, 1991. They prove, unwittingly, that in time an Italian intellectual can get away with anything. D'Annunzio had first seen Venice in 1887 when he attended the inauguration ceremonies

of the equestrian statue of Victor Emmanuel II on the Riva degli Schiavoni. (It is a curious statue since the King seems to be racing away from enemies in the north-east.) D'Annunzio, who was rescued by the Italian navy on an adventurous yachting trip through which he had aimed to reach Venice, allegedly then discovered navalism. He was struck by the arrogant superiority of British sailors under the Duke of Edinburgh who were also in Venice for the opening ceremonies.

69 The most famous raid, of course, would be the one against Italian parliamentarism in 1919. See M. Ledeen, *The First Duce: D'Annunzio at Fiume*, Baltimore, 1977.

70 E.M. Gray, *L'invasione tedesca in Italia (Professori, commercianti, spie)*, Florence [1915], pp. 12, 258–9. For Le Queux's character and prose style, see C. Andrew, *Secret Service: The Making of the British Intelligence Community*, London, 1985, pp. 37–56.

71 *Il Popolo d'Italia*, 8 May 1915; E.M. Gray, *L'invasione*, pp. 63, 244–8. Gray also objected to the alleged German dominance of large sections of the Italian cultural, academic and economic worlds and was especially appalled (p. 11) that some German writers should claim Dante was a German. An Australian might find it equally alarming that Gray regarded the wartime Australian Prime Minister, Billy Hughes, as a perceptive student of the German peril. E.M. Gray, *The Bloodless War*, New York, 1916, p. 34.

72 E.M. Gray, *Venezia in armi*, Milan, 1917, pp. 3–4, 24–6.

73 *Ibid.*, pp. 66, 131, 150. In fact, in April 1918, the city's population had fallen from the pre-war 154,000 to only 40,263. See R. Gallo, 'Il VI censimento della popolazione', *Rivista Mensile della Città di Venezia*, I, 1922, pp. 12–23.

74 E.M. Gray, *L'invasione*, p. 129.

75 See, e.g., D. Nash, 'Tourism as a form of imperialism', and D.J. Greenwood, 'Culture by the pound: an anthropologial perspective on tourism as cultural commoditisation', both in V.L. Smith (ed.), *Hosts and Guests: The Anthropology of Tourism*, Oxford, 1978. For further comment on Gray's career, see R.J.B. Bosworth, 'International tourism and bureaucracy in Fascist Italy' (forthcoming).

76 He had already favoured this idea in 1913. See M. Ferraris, 'Di un ufficio di stato per il movimento dei forestieri', p. 147.

77 See, e.g., A. Mariotti, *L'industria del forestiero in Italia*, and his *L'importanza economica del turismo*, Florence, 1931, *Corso di economia turistica*, Rome, 1933, *L'enseignement du tourisme*, Montreux, 1956. There is an interesting and typical fascistisation and then de-fascistisation of Mariotti's discourse.

78 M. Avancini, *Entità e svolgimento del traffico turistico in Italia: dati e congetture*, Rome, 1925, and 'Statistica turistica', in C. Gini (ed.), *Trattato elementare di statistica*, Milan, 1935.

79 For a splendidly redolent example, see F.W. Ogilvie, *The Tourist Movement: An Economic Study*, London, 1933, p. 7. This economist still felt it necessary to explain that tourists and emigrants could be distinguished: 'Holiday visitors to Yarmouth are tourists: Aberdeen fisher-girls in Yarmouth for herring-packing are not' (p. 5).

80 R.A. Vicentini, *Il movimento fascista veneto attraverso il diario di uno squadrista*, Venice, 1935, pp. 12, 62.

81 A. Niceforo, *Il movimento dei forestieri in Italia*, Rome, 1923, pp. 43, 48, 52, 54–6, 58, 62.

82 *Ibid.*, p. 11. Niceforo, a somewhat humourless statistician, was troubled in his reckoning by the fact that Italian border guards only tallied the number of cars and not their complement of passengers.

83 As was perhaps only appropriate for a war in which the soldiers seem often to have viewed themselves, at least partially, as 'tourists'. For some innovative work in this regard, see R. White, 'The soldier as tourist: the Australian experience of the Great War', *War and Society*, 5, 1987, pp. 63–77. The Touring Club eventually published a lengthy guide to the battlefields.

84 A. Mariotti, *L'industria del forestiero in Italia*, pp. 12–13.

85 See, e.g., 'Italiani, visitate il Pasubio', *Le Vie d'Italia*, XXIX, July 1923, p. 732; or G. Bertarelli, 'Le Gallerie di guerra nei ghiaccai dell'Ortler (osservazioni sul movimento dei ghiacciai)', *Le Vie d'Italia*, XXIX, July 1923, pp. 760–74 which, with wonderful photos, enthused about the wartime tunnelling in the glaciers of the region.

86 A. Mariotti, *L'industria del forestiero in Italia*, p. 81.

87 *Ibid.*, p. 56.

88 *Ibid.*, pp. 57–60.

89 See, e.g., *Il Popolo d'Italia*, 21 February 1931; A. Mariotti, *Corso di economia turistica*, p. 37; cf. also Mussolini's invitation in 1935 to 'as many foreigners as possible' to visit Italy (*Le Vie d'Italia*, XLII, 1935, p. 320).

90 *Le Vie d'Italia*, XXIX, May 1923, pp. 551–3; *Le Vie d'Italia*, XXXII, April 1926, p. 338.

91 A. Mariotti, *Corso di economia turistica*, p. 14.

92 For much detail of administrative in-fighting, see R.J.B. Bosworth, 'International tourism and bureaucracy in Fascist Italy'.

93 *Italian Bulletin of Commerce: Official Organ of the Italian Chamber of Commerce in Australia*, 13, October 1935.

94 *Ibid.*, June 1936; cf. *Le Vie d'Italia*, XLII, May 1936. For evidence that Fascism had not entirely eliminated the 'corruption' that easily went with tourism, see M. Stone, 'Staging Fascism: the Exhibition of the Fascist Revolution', *Journal of Contemporary History*, 28, 1993, p. 234.

95 A. Del Boca, *Gli italiani in Libia dal fascismo a Gheddafi*, Bari, 1988, p. 278.

96 *Italian Bulletin of Commerce: Official Organ of the Italian Chamber of Commerce in Australia*, 15, February 1937.

97 See article 'Convegno dei giornalisti degli Stati del Tripartico e degli Stati aderenti', *Le Tre Venezie*, April 1942, p. 129.

98 The scheduled *Biennali* of 1940 and 1942 occurred in the normal way. Volpi endorsed the first in *Le Tre Venezie*, whose art critic was later curiously dismissive of the German display in 1942. See D. Valeri, 'La XXIII Biennale Veneziana: gli stranieri', *Le Tre Venezie*, August 1942, p. 301. He found German exhibitions arid and scholastic. For a general history of the art exhibition see F. Paulon, *La dogaressa contestata. La*

favolosa storia della Mostra di Venezia, Mestre, 1971. Similarly, in the 1920s, it had been perfectly possible to celebrate Soviet art. See, e.g., V. Paladini, *Arte nella Russia dei Soviets: il padiglione dell'URSS a Venezia*, Rome, 1925.

99 'Fasin e Pendini alla Galleria "Le Tre Venezie"', *Le Tre Venezie*, January/February 1944, pp. 73–4.

100 E. Pagliari, *Ferrovie e alberghi d'Italia nell'industria turistica*, Rome, 1931, p. 15.

101 Touring Club Italiano, *Manuale del turismo*, Milan, 1934, p. 19; A. Mariotti, *L'importanza economica del turismo*, 1931, p. 26.

102 The Touring Club was ill-advised enough to criticise the damaging effects of this policy and then had to explain away the temerity of the criticism. See *Le Vie d'Italia*, XXXIII, October 1927; XXXIV, March 1928.

103 TCI, *Manuale*, p. 19; A. Mariotti, *L'importanza economica del turismo*, pp. 55–6, noted that, after Venice and the big cities, foreigners went to Merano, Abbazia, San Remo, Rapallo and Capri in order of preference. Italians, by contrast, opted for Montecatini, Viareggio, Salsomaggiore and then San Remo. On holiday there was a curious, if predictable, segregation of the two groups.

104 *Il Popolo d'Italia*, 8 August 1929; A. Mariotti, *Corso di economia turistica*, pp. 52, 57–8, 74–82. Mariotti claimed that trains did indeed now run on time whereas in 1921 37 per cent of the Milan–Rome line and 53 per cent on the Naples–Foggia one did not. Tourism was another of those areas of Italian business where there was much enthusiasm for emulating United States expertise.

105 TCI, *Manuale*, p. 19.

106 Italy changed its method of counting in 1931 in a way which greatly increased the alleged number of tourists but did not alter their expenditure. See 'Turismo', *Enciclopedia italiana*, 34, p. 559.

107 Fascist Italy was anxious to claim that, in its state organisation of tourism, it had at last bested France. See A. Mariotti, *Corso di economia turistica*, p. 26.

108 Rotary International, *Terza conferenza regionale Europa–Africa–Asia Minore Venezia settembre 1935*, Venice, 1936. Delegates may have been calmed by the invitation of the German representative to them to attend the coming Berlin Olympics. Given its Venetian site it was inevitable that Giuseppe Volpi should give the official welcome speech to the conference. Arnaldo Mussolini had been a well publicised member of the Milan branch of Rotary in the 1920s. See *Le Vie d'Italia*, XXXIV, February 1928.

109 *Ibid.*, p. 37.

110 For a fine study, see V. De Grazia, *The Culture of Consent: Mass Organization of Leisure in Fascist Italy*, Cambridge, 1981.

111 One black American writer, remembering Carnera's nickname 'the Ambling Alp', noted: 'What had started out as an Alp looked about the altitude of a chicken croquet by the time Joe [Louis] got through with him' (J.T. Sammons, *Beyond the Ring: The Role of Boxing in American Society*, Urbana, 1988, p. 102).

112 See article by L. Ferretti, 'Olimpici Giuochi', *Enciclopedia italiana*, 25,

p. 280. In this and his *Libro dello sport* Ferretti was naturally anxious to acknowledge that Mussolini was the First Sportsman of Italy.

113 TCI, *Manuale*, pp. 43–5; but cf. earlier enthusiasms for 'dynamic' rather than safely bourgeois tourism. F. Valsecchi, 'Il bilancio della vista estiva', *Rivista Mensile del Touring*, XVII, 1911, pp. 607–9.

114 *Le Vie d'Italia*, XLVIII, 1942, pp. 145–7 (editoral). The TCI had also rapidly published a series of *Guide* on Greece, Albania and Croatia, for use by Italian troops and 'at the urgent request of the Ministry for Foreign Affairs'.

115 C. Graves, *Italy Revisited*, London, n.d., p. 61. In 1932 the Dante Alighieri Society had, at its XXVIIth congress, already led an attack on shamefully 'un-Italian' names like the Hotel Grand. *Il Popolo d'Italia* had campaigned against foreign hotel names as early as 29 July 1923.

116 Ministero del Turismo e dello Spettacolo, *Lo Stato e le Olimpiadi di Roma*, Rome [1960], p. 115.

117 *Ibid.*, pp. 115, 125.

118 ENIT, *Turisti stranieri in Italia: sondaggio di opinione 1965*, Rome, 1966, p. 93. Taking hotels and other accommodation together, Venice was still the most popular site with more than 1.3 million visitors. Rome had 1.25 million, Florence 740,000, Naples 530,000. Potenza had only 4,251 foreign visitors to its hotels that year, Nuoro 3,662 and Cosenza 2,934. ENIT, *Il turismo in Italia nel 1965*, Rome, 1966, pp. 127, 181, 230, 254, 276, 282, 312.

119 ENIT, *Turisti stranieri in Italia*, pp. 13–14.

120 F.W. Ogilvie, *The Tourist Movement*, p. 140.

121 ENIT, *Turisti stranieri in Italia*, p. 101.

122 P. Brendon, *Thomas Cook*, p. 312.

123 R. King, 'Italy: multi-faceted tourism', in A.M. Williams and G. Shaw (eds), *Tourism and Economic Development*, London, 1988, p. 58.

124 A.M. Williams and G. Shaw, 'Western European tourism in perspective', in *ibid.*, p. 31, placed Italy second behind Spain in Europe as a tourist earner but from far fewer tourists.

125 N. Douglas, *Siren Land*, Harmondsworth, 1948, p. 99.

126 Cf. Bordighera of which Linda Villari would remark: 'it is amazing to behold how English respectability and cleanliness, English solidity and order have seized on this southern [sic] fishing [sic] and planted the Union Jack firmly in its midst' (L. Villari, *Here and There in Italy and Over the Borders*, London, 1893, p. 39).

127 For some period comment, see A.M. Rebucci, 'Per l'industria termale italiana', *Nuova Antologia*, f. 1205, 1 June 1922, pp. 253–6.

128 For example, see A.L. Maraspini, *The Study of an Italian Village*, Paris, 1968, p. 15.

129 For a splendid example, see A. Arbasino's attack on '*gente in mutande*' ('people in their undies') who, he says, now throng Italy's historic centres and are so different from the genteel millionaires of long ago (*La Repubblica*, 6 September 1992).

130 For a French introduction to the pre-history of the beach, couched in very intellectual terms, see A. Corbin, *L'invenzione del mare: l'Occidente e il fascino della spiaggia 1750–1840*, Venice, 1990.

131 J. Ruskin, *The Stones of Venice*, vol. 1, p. 346.
132 See, e.g., C.M. Young, 'Migration and mortality: the experience of birthplace groups in Australia', *International Migration Review*, XXI, 1987, pp. 531–54. Somewhere in the middle of the fall and rise of garlic can be found James Joyce's Leopold Bloom. He meditated

> on the contrary that stab in the back touch was quite in keeping with those italianos [in Dublin] though candidly he was none the less free to admit those icecreamers and friers in the fish way not to mention the chip potato variety and so forth in little Italy there near the Coombe were sober thrifty hardworking fellows except perhaps a bit too given to puthunting the harmless necessary animal of the feline persuasion of others at night so as to have a good old succulent tuckin with garlic *de rigeur* off him or her next day on the quiet and, he added, on the cheap.
>
> (J. Joyce, *Ulysses*, Harmondsworth, 1986, p. 520)

The use and prestige of mineral water might be another instructive topic to investigate.
133 The classic examples were the great neo-realist films of the immediate post-war period. Venice, meanwhile, from 1932 staged Italy's major international film festival. After the Second World War, the Cannes Festival, which only started in 1939, was generally regarded as superior to that of Venice. See F. Bono, 'Le Mostre del cinema di Venezia: nascita e sviluppo nell'anteguerra (1932–1939)', *Storia contemporanea*, XXII, 1991, pp. 513–49.
134 R. King, 'Italy', p. 74.

CONCLUSION

1 *The Economist*, 3 April 1993.
2 *Ibid.*, 20 February 1993.
3 A.M. dell'Oso, 'The sewing machine', in F. Arena (ed.), *Growing Up Italian in Australia*, Sydney, 1993, p. 59 (emphasis in original). M. Melia assures me, from her knowledge of Italo-Western Australia, that the 'facts' that there are no road accidents in Italy, no cholesterol and no lung cancer, should be added to this list.
4 For this classic definition, see E.J. Hobsbawm, *Nations and Nationalism Since 1780: Programme, Myth, Reality*, Cambridge, 1990, p. 118.
5 J. Winterson, *The Passion*, Harmondsworth, 1988, pp. 49, 58, 76, 122.
6 See C.E. Gadda, *That Awful Mess on the Via Merulana*, London, 1985, and its wonderful and scabrous overturning of the Victorian and mathematical norms of detective writing. The book was first published in Italy in 1957. Gadda had commenced writing it in 1946 and set it in 1927.
7 U. Eco, *Faith in Fakes*, London, 1986, p. 222.
8 A. Bernardini, 'Industrializzazione e classi sociali nel primo cinema italiano', *Risorgimento*, II, 1981, p. 159.
9 G.P. Brunetta, *Storia del cinema italiano 1895–1945*, Rome, 1979, p. 153.

10 *Ibid.*, p. 248.
11 *Ibid.*, p. 285.
12 For English-language introduction, see, e.g., D. Overbey (ed.), *Springtime in Italy: A Reader on Neo-Realism*, London, 1978.
13 C. Zavattini, *Neorealismo ecc.*, Milan, 1979, p. 16.
14 C. Zavattini, 'Some ideas on the cinema', *Sight and Sound*, 23, 1953, p. 67.
15 For a useful general history of Italian cinema, see P. Leprohon, *The Italian Cinema*, London, 1972. On audiences, cf. V. Spinazzola, *Cinema e pubblico: lo spettacolo filmico in Italia 1945–1965*, Milan, 1974.
16 E. Murray, *Fellini the Artist*, Bembridge, 1977, pp. 84, 237.
17 D. Malouf, *12 Edmonstone St.*, Ringwood, Victoria, 1986, p. 78.

INDEX

Abba, Giuseppe 19
Abbazia 173
abortion 139
Abruzzi ix, 119, 131, 139–41, 147
Absalom, Roger ix, 73–4
Addis Ababa 9, 48–50, 69, 101, 107
Adelaide 147
Adowa, Battle of 20, 47, 87, 102, 148
Adriatic Sea 23, 33, 46, 95, 139, 171
Aegean Sea 33
Africa 20, 24, 26, 43–4, 49–50, 54, 80, 97–103, 105–9, 112–14, 127, 156
AGIP (Azienda Generale Italiana Petroli) 77, 91
Agnelli, Giovanni 31, 83–4, 86
Agordat, Battle of 101
Agrigento 163
Aigues Mortes 120
Air Force 49, 69–70, 122, 170
Albania 3, 12, 22–3, 41, 44, 51, 94, 97, 113, 149, 160
Alexandria 96
Algeciras 46
Alighieri, Dante 2, 125, 153–5, 168, 177
Alitalia 77
Alleanza Nazionale 182
Alsace 80
Altavilla Irpina 147
Alto Adige 22, 32, 34, 43, 46, 54, 194
Amalfi 146
Amendola, Giovanni 67, 87, 104

American Express 161
Ancona 65
Andrássy von Csik-Szent-Király, Gyula 97
Andreotti, Giulio 90, 185–6
Anglo-German Naval Pact 47
Annales 2, 6, 180
Ansaldo 80, 85
Anschluss 46–7
anthropology 1, 139, 142
anti-fascism 50, 56, 66–7, 91, 124–5
anti-Semitism 54, 89, 106–7, 110–12, 124–6, 149
AOI (Africa Orientale Italiana) 108
Aosta, Duke Amedeo of 108
Arabs 106, 110, 156
archaeology 104–5, 153
Aretino, Pietro 150
Argentina 122, 129
Arlacchi, Pino 93
ascari 101
Asia Minor 3, 42, 43, 87, 94–5, 107
Asmara 88, 98–9
Aspromonte 60
Assab 98
Assisi 152, 163, 180
Associazione nazionale per il movimento dei forestieri 165–6, 168
Associazione nazionalista italiana (ANI) 21, 42–4, 46–7, 54, 64, 68, 83, 87, 95, 105–6, 111, 123–4
Assyria 160
Athens 42, 88
atomic weapons 54

Augustus, Emperor 3, 110
Auschwitz 54, 112
Australia ix–x, 1, 3, 71, 93, 97,
    123–5, 132, 134, 136, 147–8, 151,
    155–6, 166, 179, 182, 187
Austria 46–7
Austria–Hungary 22–5, 31–2, 44,
    53, 55, 61, 65, 67, 69, 78, 80–2,
    85, 95–6, 154, 168
Avancini, Marco 172
Avanti! 102
Axis 12, 39, 42, 89, 149, 174

Bachi, Riccardo 85
Baden Baden 162
Badoglio, Pietro 63, 69–70, 72–3
Baedeker guides 161–2
Bahamas 149
Baily, Samuel 129
Baird, a footballer 167
Balbo, Cesare 153
Balbo, Italo 69–70, 105–6, 174
Balilla 69, 176
Banca Commerciale Italiana 77, 83,
    87–8
Banca d'Italia 82, 163
Banca Nazionale del Lavoro 77,
    88–9
Banca Romana 25, 82
Banco di Roma 77, 83, 86, 148
bandits 20, 59, 61, 79, 103, 141
Bangkok 162
Baratieri, Oreste 102, 104
Bardia 71
Barilla 77
Barrès, Maurice 170
Barzini, Luigi (jun.) 157
Basilicata 119
Basques 134
Bassani, Giorgio 13
Bavaria 80
Beatles, the 182
Bedford 130
Beethoven, Ludwig van 177
Belgiojoso, Cristina 138–9, 153
Belgium 9, 48, 78, 80, 82, 122, 165,
    178
Bell, Rudolf 142
'Benadir coasts' 99

Benedict XV, Pope 31, 148–9
Benetton 77
Berlin 43, 46, 157
Berlusconi, Silvio 182
Bernini, Gian Lorenzo 149
Bertarelli, Luigi Vittorio 166–7,
    169, 180
Bielefeld school 6–8
Bigliari di Viarigi, Agostino 168
Birmingham 156
Bismarck, Otto von 18, 20, 46, 97
Bizerta 24–5
Boccaccio, Giovanni 2, 150
Bodio, Luigi 163–4
Bologna 19, 53, 64, 152
Bolzano 22
Bonomelli, Geremia 121
Borgese, Giuseppe Antonio 67
Bosnia 23, 97
Bossi, Umberto 182
Bottai, Giuseppe 68, 185
Bourbon dynasty 61, 79
Brancati, Vitaliano 13
Brassey, Thomas 16
Brazil 4, 69, 123, 129
Brenner Pass 46, 173
Brescia 149
Brigata di Sassari 64
Bristol 130
Britain 15, 55, 57–8, 65, 72, 76, 79,
    94, 113, 144, 156, 161, 168,
    183; and Fascist Italy 12, 36,
    38–9, 41–3, 45–8, 71, 108, 110,
    136, 157, 174; and Liberal Italy
    20, 25–6, 81–4, 97–101, 103, 114,
    117, 129–31, 140–1, 164–6, 172;
    and Republican Italy 126, 134,
    149, 178; and the Risorgimento
    18, 60, 78, 80
Browning, Robert 161
Brzezinski, Zbigniew 38
Budapest 172
Buenos Aires 3, 129, 175
Buitoni 100
Bulgaria 44
Burgos 88
Butler, Samuel 57–8, 74

Cadorna, Luigi 66

Caesar, Caius Julius 100
Cafaro, Filippo 130
Cagoulards 126
Calabria 84, 92, 119, 143–5, 170, 179
Calabrò, Lino 108
Calvino, Italo 13
Calwell, Arthur 124, 151
Cambridge University 156
camorra 92
Campania 119, 147
Canada 93, 123, 128, 135–6, 175
Cantalupo, Roberto 105
Capone, Al 2
Capo d'Orlando 5
Caporetto, Battle of 33, 51, 63, 66–7, 69, 76, 171
Capri 163, 170
Capuchin order 147
carabinieri 61
Caracalla, Emperor 148
Carducci, Giosuè 177
Carlo Emanuele of Piedmont 167
Carnera, Primo 176
Carocci, Giampiero 38
Carone, Giuseppe 176
Carso 66, 173
Carthage 95, 97, 111
Caruso, Michele 20
Casa Italiana 137
Casalbordino 141–2
Casana, Severino 62
Cassa per il Mezzogiorno 90
Catania 28, 79
Catholicism 4–5, 16, 21–2, 24–5, 31, 50, 63, 72, 90–1, 96, 99–103, 111, 120–1, 124, 127, 129, 135–6, 138, 143, 145–51, 154, 157, 174, 177, 179, 184
Cattaneo, Carlo 153
Caucasus 33, 95
Cavour, Camille Benso de 11, 16, 18–9, 24, 27–9, 31, 34, 39, 45, 53, 59, 80, 101, 153
Cento 19
Chabod, Federico 7–10, 48
Chad, Lake 25
Chamberlain, Neville 48
Chambery 24

Charles Albert, King of Piedmont-Sardinia 16
Chicago 92, 134
Chicopee, Kansas 151
Chieti 147
China 95, 110, 156
Chini, Galileo 162
Christian Democracy 54–6, 89–90, 113, 124–7, 139, 150, 157, 185
Churchill, Winston 52
Ciano, Galeazzo 50–2,
Ciccotosto, Emma ix, 141–2
Cinel, Dino 117, 135
Cinzano 77
CIT (Compagnia Italiana Turismo) 173–5
Civiltà Cattolica 111, 148
Civitavecchia 112
Clausewitz, Carl von 18
Club Alpino Italiano 167–8
Club Automobile d'Italia 168
coal 26, 82
Colarizi, Simona 37, 40
Cold War 55, 89
Colle della Maddalena 173
Colombus, Christopher 95
Comitato italiano contro le insidie straniere 171
Commisariato dell'Emigrazione 120, 122
Commissione permanente per il rimpatrio 122
Como 165
Confindustria 85, 88
Congress of Historical Sciences 9
Congresso Ginnastico Italiano 167
Connecticut 2
Constantinople 43, 95, 104
Cook, Thomas 161
Corfu 3, 41–3, 159
Corradini, Enrico 121
Corriere della Sera 101
Corsica 3, 6, 19, 60
Cortemaggiore 91
Cortina d'Ampezzo 179
'Corvo, Baron' (Frederick Rolfe) 170
Cosenz, Enrico 62
Credito Italiano 77

Cremona 88, 121
Cricket Club Italiano 131
Crimea 95
Crispi, Francesco 20–1, 27, 29, 39,
    42, 45, 47, 82, 102, 107, 120–1
Critica Sociale 121
Croatia 3, 44, 156, 164
Croce, Benedetto 25, 48, 54, 56,
    137, 153
Cuba 134
Custozza, Battle of 61
Cyprus 3
Cyrenaica 103–5
Czechoslovakia 44

Dalmatia 2, 19, 33, 54
Danakils 2
Danieli family 167
D'Annunzio, Gabriele 13, 33–4,
    95, 155, 170–1, 177
Danzig 51
Dapples (footballer) 167
Davis, John 79
D'Azeglio, Massimo 92, 94
De Amicis, Edmondo 64
De Bosdari, Alessandro 106
Decennale 45, 156
De Felice, Renzo 8–9, 12, 37–40,
    43, 48–9, 110, 135
De Gasperi, Alcide 54–5, 90–1,
    126–7
De Gaulle, Charles 55
Del Balzo, Giulio 151
Del Boca, Angelo 106
De Mauro, Tullio 155
De Michaelis, Giuseppe 122
Depero, Fortunato 49
Depretis, Agostino 27, 29, 45, 98
Derby, Fifteenth Earl of 97
De Sica, Vittorio 185
Dessie, Lake 49
De' Stefani, Alberto 86
Detroit 44, 122
De Vecchi, Cesare Maria 100,
    106–7, 153–4
Dickens, Charles 160–1, 170
Di Nolfo, Ennio 10, 40
Di San Giuliano, Antonino 28, 34,

39, 85, 103, 130
Direzione Generale degli Italiani
    all'estero 122
Direzione Generale per il Turismo
    174
Disarmament Conference 45
divorce 139
Djibouti 3, 25, 99
Dodecanese Islands 3, 28, 42, 94,
    106–7, 113
Dogali 101
Dollfuss, Engelbert 46
Domitian, Emperor 148
Dorso, Guido 18
Douglas, Norman 179
Douhet, Giulio 71
Drumont, Edouard 111
Duccio di Buoninsegna 180
Durack family 174
Durazzo 22–3, 54

Eco, Umberto 184
Economist, The 103, 182–3
Eden, Anthony 71
EEC 55, 91
Eire 95, 100, 131, 151, 179, 184
Egypt 25, 91, 98, 110, 114, 148, 165
Einaudi, Luigi 18, 129
Ellis Island 131
emigration ix, 4–5, 7, 13, 25, 62,
    86, 89–90, 92–3, 97, 104, 107–8,
    114–48, 150, 155, 160, 163, 169,
    175, 179, 182–4
ENI (Ente Nazionale Idrocarburi)
    77, 91
ENIT (Ente Nazionale per le
    Industrie Turistiche) 172–3, 175,
    178
Ente Provinciale per il Turismo
    174
Entente Cordiale 25
Eritrea 50, 94, 98–9, 101, 103,
    113–4, 160
Esposizione Internazionale d'Arte
    171
Esposizione Universale 156
Ethiopia 3, 12, 20, 42, 44, 47–50,
    94, 100–3, 107–9, 112–3, 116,
    122, 149, 174–5

Facey, Albert ix
Falklands War 48
family, 'the Italian' 3–5, 133–6,
    142–6, 186
Fanfani, Amintore 90
Farinacci, Roberto 49, 88
Farini, Domenico 21, 23, 102
Farneti, Paolo 18
fasci all'estero 122–3
fascism 2–3, 5–7, 9–13, 15–6, 18,
    20–1. 34–54, 56, 58, 60, 66–74,
    76, 86–9, 92–5, 97–102, 104–7,
    110–12, 116–17, 122–7, 130, 132,
    134–5, 137–9, 143, 146, 149,
    152–4, 156–9, 163, 168–9, 172–7,
    183–5
Federazione Nazionale Fascista
    Alberghi e Turismo 173
Federzoni, Luigi 42, 64, 67
Fellini, Federico 13, 186
Ferdinand II, King of Naples–
    Sicily 78
Ferrara 19, 161
Ferrari 2
Ferraris, Maggiorino 164–6, 169,
    179
feste 145–7, 150
Fezzan 25, 103
Fiat 1, 31, 57, 77, 83–6, 124
film 91, 158, 180, 184–6
Fini, Gianfranco 182
Finland 179
Finzi, Aldo 111
First World War 22, 24, 26, 28–33,
    51–2, 56, 62–4, 66–7, 70–2, 81,
    83, 85, 87, 95, 104, 107, 111, 114,
    118–20, 130, 148, 156, 169–70, 173
Fischer, Fritz 6, 8, 11–2
Fiume 3, 33, 54,
Flanders 66
Florence 2, 142, 145, 147, 161, 163,
    171, 173, 177, 179–80
Florida 134
Florio, Ignazio 165
Flotta Lauro 179
Foerster, Robert 117
food 2, 4, 7, 84, 93, 96, 135, 144–5,
    147, 159, 164, 180
Forza Italia 182

Foscari, Piero 95, 167
'Four Power Pact' 46
France 9, 10, 15, 19, 57, 78, 95, 111,
    156, 161, 162, 183; and Fascist
    Italy 3, 36, 44, 46–8, 101, 108–9,
    126, 157, 159, 175, 185; and
    Liberal Italy 20, 23–5, 62, 65,
    81–2, 84–5, 97–8, 100, 102–3,
    109, 130, 155, 165, 168–9, 172;
    and Republican Italy 76, 113,
    179; and the Risorgimento 80
Francis Ferdinand, Archduke 65–6
Francis Joseph, Emperor of
    Austria 22
Franco y Bahamonde, Francisco 51
Freemasonry 30–1, 66
Fremantle 122, 142, 146–7
Friedrich, Carl 38
Friuli 119
Fussell, Paul 66
futurism 49, 138, 155, 170

Gabaccia, Donna 117, 133–4, 136,
    142–4
Gadafi, Mummar 113
Gaeta 146
Gafencu, Grigore 51
Galla 103
Gallenga Stuart, Romeo 67
Gandhi, Mahatma 44
Garibaldi, Giuseppe 2, 11, 19, 22,
    24, 32, 60, 153–4, 162
Gautier, Théophile 170
Gazzettino 88
Gedda, Luigi 90
Genoa 26, 61, 78, 80, 95, 161, 165,
    167
Gentile, Emilio 37, 40
Gentile, Giovanni 68
Germany 4, 15, 53, 57, 131, 156,
    161–2, 168; and Fascist Italy 12,
    36, 38, 40–1, 43–4, 46–8, 51, 53,
    72–4, 87, 89, 97, 103, 109–10,
    112, 116, 157, 175, 183–4; and
    Liberal Italy 14, 20–3, 25–6,
    31–3, 62, 65, 68, 81–3, 85, 109,
    154–5, 164–5, 170–1; and
    Republican Italy 6, 8–11, 132,
    173, 178; and the Risorgimento

59, 78
Germino, Dante 37
Gerschenkron, Alexander 77
Ginzburg, Carlo 7
Gioberti, Vincenzo 15, 153, 183
Giolitti, Antonio 127
Giolitti, Giovanni 26–31, 33–4, 45, 50, 54, 61–3, 83–7, 103–4, 109, 120, 164, 169, 171
giornale del soldato, Il 64
Giorno, Il 91
Giustizia e Libertà 125–6
Gladstone, William 96
Glasgow 130–1
Gloeden, Wilhelm von 170
Gobetti, Piero 18
Goebbels, Josef 53, 73
Goglia, Luigi x, 110
Gooch, John 60
Goretti, Maria (Saint) 139
Gramsci, Antonio 2, 11, 18, 38, 75, 77, 111, 121, 152
Grandi, Dino 39, 44–5, 122–3, 130
Gray, Ezio Maria 171–2, 174, 180
Graziani, Rodolfo 73, 107–8
Grazioli, Francesco Saverio 69
Greece 22, 41–2, 44, 53, 70, 106–7, 160
Greenwich time 5
Gregory XVI, Pope 78
Guadalajara, Battle of 51, 110
Guariglia, Raffaele 47
Gubbio 145, 163
Guicciardini, Francesco 85, 168

Hafun 154
Hague, The 169
Haile Selassie 107–8
Harlem 146
Harney, Robert 117, 135–6, 145
Hayez, Francesco 59–60
Herder, Johann Gottfried von 58
Herzegovina 23, 97
Hillgruber, Andreas 8
Hitler, Adolf 2, 8, 12, 37–9, 45, 47, 52–3,
Hoare, Samuel 50
Hoboken 146
Hollywood 185

Holy Year 174, 177
homosexuality 170
Hotel Anglo-Americano 177
Hungary 14, 44, 172
Hurst, Michael ix
hydroelectricity 26, 82

imperialism 6, 12, 23–4, 26, 31, 47–9, 55, 70, 80, 83, 89, 94–113, 120
India 109–110, 156
intervento 30–1, 52, 66, 85
Iran 116
Iraq 48, 91, 110
IRI (Istituto per la Ricostruzione industriale) 89
irredentism 22–3, 55, 95
Isonzo 34
Israel 112
Istituto di Credito per il lavoro italiano all'estero 122
Istituti Coloniali Italiani 123, 168
Istria 2, 19, 32
Italia Libera 126

Jacini, Stefano 133
James, Henry 170
Japan 8, 36, 46, 74, 76, 103, 157, 183
Jeddah 99
Jeserum, Michelangelo 166–7
Jesuit order 148
Jews 14, 66, 106–7, 111–12, 116, 124, 172
Joel, Otto 83
John XXIII, Pope 149, 158
John Paul I, Pope 149
John Paul II, Pope 149–50
Johnson, Federigo 166
Johnson, Samuel 96, 160
Joll, James 7
Joyce, James 13–14
Jubaland 99
Jung, Guido 111

Kehr, Eckart 6
Keitel, Wilhelm 73
Kellogg–Briand Pact 45
Kennedy, Paul 53
Kenya 3

Kern, Stephen 32
Knox, Macgregor 39–40

La Scozia 130
La Spezia 65
Lago, Mario 106–7
Lancet 130
language questions 3, 96, 137, 155–7
Lanza di Scalea, Pietro 165, 167
Las Vegas 145
Lateran Pacts 149
Laurel and Hardy 185
Lausanne, Treaty of 104
Laval, Pierre 50
Lazio 119
Le Figaro 155
Le Goff, Jacques 6
Le Queux, William 171
Le Vie d'Italia 167
League of Nations 41–2, 45, 112, 122
Lebanon 179
Lega Navale 65, 168
Lega Nord 60, 93, 113, 182
Lenin, Vladimir 33, 67
Leo XIII, Pope 21, 121
Leptis Magna 95, 107
Lerici 163
Lessona, Alessandro 122–3
Levine, Larry 136
Libro e Moschetto 69
Libya 3, 26–7, 30, 50, 62, 71, 87, 94, 103–7, 109, 112–13, 116, 121, 148, 164, 174, 184
L'Idea Nazionale 87
Lido 172
Liguria 19, 97, 119
Lindsay, Dr. 165
lira, value of 49, 86, 174
Lissa, Battle of 61, 65
Little St. Bernard Pass 173
Liverpool 161
Livorno 161
Lloyd George, David 51
Lloyd Triestino 179
Lo Monaco Aprile, Captain 64
Locarno, Treaty of 45
Lombardy 78, 119
Lombroso, Cesare 82, 138

London 16, 39, 78, 130–1
Louisiana 134
Loyola, Ignatius (Saint) 79
Lucca 173
L'Unione Italiana 135
Luzzatti, Luigi 120, 172
Luzzatto, Gino 78
Lyttelton, Adrian 84

Macdonell, Anne 139–40
Machiavelli, Niccolò 2, 15
Mack Smith, Denis 11–12, 27, 49
'Madonna' (pop singer) 156
Madonna, The 4, 146–7
Mafia 2, 33, 77, 92–3, 120, 141, 144, 146, 168
Magnaghi, Giuseppe 162
Maier, Charles 86
'Malaparte, Curzio' (Erich Suckert) 13
malaria 79
Malta 3, 19, 26, 134, 149
Mancini, Pasquale Stanislao 98
Manin, Daniele 27
Manjimup 114
Mann, Thomas 170
Manzoni, Alessandro 153
Marano Lagunare 74
Marche 119
Marinetti, Filippo Tommaso 170
Mariotti, Angelo 172–3
Marseilles 24, 114, 146
Martin, Dean 156
Martini, Ferdinando 99
Marwick, Arthur 58
Marxism 6–9, 11, 18, 38, 44, 152
Massawa 50, 88, 98–9, 101
Mattei, Enrico 91–2, 113
Matteotti, Giacomo 111
Mayer, Arno 67
Mazzini, Giuseppe 19, 59–60, 153–4
McCarran–Walter Act 132
McCarthy, Mary 159–60
Mediterranean 3, 24, 26, 38–9, 41, 43, 45, 71, 78, 95–6, 98, 102, 110–11, 114, 132, 159–60, 180
Meinecke, Friedrich 53
Melbourne 125, 134
Menabrea, Luigi 23–4

Menelik II, Emperor of Ethiopia 20, 47, 100, 102–3
Mesopotamia 26
Messina 78–9, 184
Mestre 172, 180
Metternich, Clemens von 46,
Michelin 51
Milan 34, 61, 63, 92, 101–2, 121, 166, 181
Milward, Alan 71
Mogadishu 54, 99–101
Molfetta 5, 96, 146–7
Molise 119, 134
Moltke, Helmuth von 25
Montagna, Giulio Cesare 42
Montanelli, Indro 7
Monte Carlo 18
Monte Grappa 66, 173
Montecatini 173, 179
Monza 138
'Moravia, Alberto' (Alberto Pincherle) 13
Morea 95
Morgan, J.P. 86
Mosca, Gaetano 18
Moscow 42, 125, 133, 152, 184
Mosso, Angelo 168
Mozart, Wolfgang 96
MSI (Movimento Sociale Italiano, Italian neo-fascist party) 56, 73
Muhammad Abdullah Hassan 100
multiculturalism 5, 151
Munich 89
Murri, Romolo 120, 129
Mussolini, Benito 2, 8–9, 12, 15, 21, 29, 31, 34–6, 38–42, 44–53, 67–70, 72–3, 82, 86, 88–9, 105–12, 116, 123–4, 126, 138–9, 153, 156–7, 173–5, 177, 185–6

Naples 26, 28, 62, 78–80, 92, 137, 151, 159, 164–5, 173
Napoleon I, Emperor of France 25, 57, 60–1
Napoleon III, Emperor of France 24
nationalism 6, 11, 15–8, 23, 27, 31–3, 38, 41, 48, 56, 58, 63–4, 69, 85, 99, 108–10, 112, 116, 127,

139, 153, 156–7, 173–5, 177, 185–6; see Associazione nazionalista italiana (ANI)
NATO 54–5, 73, 91
Navy 25–6, 41–2, 62, 64, 68, 83, 159
Nazism 12, 38–40, 43–4, 46–8, 51–3, 87, 89, 108, 110, 112, 132, 157, 183
'ndrangheta 92–3, 144
Nenni, Pietro 55
Nero, Emperor 148
Netherlands 178
New Guinea 97
New South Wales 74
New Orleans 120, 134
New York 3, 86, 92, 134, 137, 142, 146, 175
New Zealand 74
Nicastro 93
Nice 3, 19, 24
Nicolson, Harold 15–16
Nietzsche, Friedrich 177
Nile 59
Nitti, Francesco Saverio 18, 34, 42, 109, 114, 172
Nuoro 179
Nuova Antologia 7, 138, 153, 164

oil 26, 91, 105, 113
Ojetti, Ugo 67
Olivetti 77
Olympic Games 157–8, 176–7
Oneglia 19
Opera Bonomelli 121–2
Operation Barbarossa 69
Orlando, Vittorio Emanuele 33, 67
Oromo 103
Orsi, R. A. 146
Osio, Arturo 88–9, 91
Ouchy, Treaty of 87
Oxford University 156

'Pact of Steel' 51–2
Paestum 180
Palermo 26, 79, 92, 108, 165
Palestine 43, 110
Palmerston, Third Viscount 18
Pan German League 154
Pantaleoni, Maffeo 104

Paravicini, Guido 163–4
Pareto, Vilfredo 18, 86
Parma 130, 161–2
Parini, Piero 122
Paris 9, 16, 18–19, 33, 44, 65, 78, 83, 88, 125, 155, 171
Parri, Ferruccio 126
Partito d'Azione (Action Party) 126
Partito Popolare (Popular Party) 88, 149
Pascoli, Giovanni 177
Passerini, Luisa x, 7, 138
Patagonia 114
Paul VI, Pope 151
Pavone, Claudio 72
PCI (Partito Comunista Italiano, Italian Communist Party) 7, 38, 42, 54–5, 60, 122, 124, 127, 152, 157, 184
Pellagra 79
Pelloux, Luigi 63, 72
Peron, Juan 129
Persia 95, 160
Perth x, 1, 44, 142
Petacci family 89
Petrarch, Francesco 177
Philippines 116
Piacenza 121, 161
Piedmont 19, 22, 24, 27, 58–63, 66, 69, 78, 83–4, 97, 113, 119, 164, 167
Pieri, Piero 66
Pini, Giorgio 94, 112
Pirelli 77
Pisa 145, 161
Piselli, Fortunata 143–4
Pittsburgh 114, 145–6
Pius IX, Pope 148, 177
Pius XI, Pope 149
Pius XII, Pope 127, 139, 149, 177
Platì 93
Po Valley 34, 74, 84
Poland 46, 109, 111, 149, 184
Polla 146
Pollio, Alberto 62, 65
Pollutri 147–8
Polo, Marco 95
Pompei 163

Ponza 146
Popolo d'Italia, Il 41
Port Pirie 146
Porto Marghera 87, 172
Portugal 48, 128, 156
Potenza 173, 179
Preziosi, Giovanni 111
Prezzolini, Giuseppe 137, 155
Prinetti, Giulio 85
Prussia 59
Puccini, Giacomo 155–6
Puglia 5, 79, 119
Pugliese, Emanuele 111

Quarnaro 34, 154
Quartararo, Rosaria 38–9, 46
Queensland 4, 134

'Race Manifesto' 110, 112
racism 56, 72, 92, 109–12, 120, 132, 168
railways 16, 25–6, 62, 77–8, 80, 85, 161, 163–5, 175–6
ralliement 22, 121
Rankeanism 8, 37, 46, 117
Rapallo 163
Rapallo, Treaty of 34
Rassegna Storica del Risorgimento 153
Rattazzi, Urbano 20
Ravenna 91, 180
Red Cross 169
Red Sea 98–9
Republican Party (PRI) 7
Resistance, the 8, 54, 56, 126, 152, 185
Rhodes 107
Ribbentrop, Joachim von 52
Ricci, Renato 69
Ricotti Magnani, Cesare 61
Risorgimento 2, 5, 8–9, 11, 15, 18, 20–2, 24, 27–9, 32, 37, 47, 51, 53, 55–7, 59–60, 77, 80–1, 85, 96, 111, 138, 148–9, 153, 155, 161–2, 183
Riviera 162–3
Robinson, Ronald 94
Rochat, Giorgio 69
Rodolico, Niccolò 7

Romania 51
Romano, Sergio x, 7,
Rome 2, 19, 27, 33, 40, 47, 55, 67–9,
    72, 77–8, 88, 94, 96, 101–2,
    106–7, 109, 118, 120, 123, 141–2,
    145, 152, 155–61, 163, 166,
    173–4, 179–80, 184; empire 22,
    95, 100, 103, 110–11, 114, 153,
    157; 'Myth of Rome' 8–9, 23, 41,
    64, 77, 97, 153, 184; Treaty of 55
Romeo, Rosario 7, 11, 26, 32, 77–8
Roosevelt, Franklin 136
Roosevelt, Theodore 45
Rosmini, Antonio 153
Rosselli, Carlo 67–8, 125–6
Rosselli, Nello 125–6
Rossellini, Roberto 185
Rotary International 175
Rubattino shipping company 98
Ruini, Meuccio 172
Rumi, Giorgio 38
Rumor, Mariano 126
Ruskin, John 170, 180
Russia, Imperial 2, 33, 65, 82–3,
    102, 156, 161, 172
Russia, post-Communist 113

Saar 47
Sadkovich, James 72
St Petersburg 2
saints 4, 146–7, 152
Salamanca 88
Salandra, Antonio 29–30, 32–3, 39,
    42, 52, 172
Salento 180
Salerno 146
Saletta, Tancredi 62
Salò Republic 53, 73, 112
Salsomaggiore 162–3, 179
Salvemini, Gaetano 18, 50, 103, 125
Salzburg 52
Sambuca 133–4
San'a 99
San Francisco 135
San Gimignano 163
San Remo 162–3, 179
Santoro, Carlo 10
Sardinia 64, 97, 118–19, 180
Saseno 23

Sassari 64, 173
Savoy 3, 24, 59, 97
Scalabrini, Giovanni Battista 121
Scalabrinian order 121, 137, 150–1
Scattarreggia, Massimo 162
Schiassi, Omero 125
Schoenberg, Arnold 156
Sciascia, Leonardo 13
Scotland 114, 130
Second World War 3, 6, 8, 15,
    26, 32, 34, 36, 39–40, 42, 52–3,
    55, 59, 70–2, 88–90, 100, 106–7,
    113–14, 125, 135, 142–3, 149, 151,
    177
Sella, Quintino 167
Serbia 22
Serra, Enrico x, 10
Seville 88
Sforza, Carlo 34, 54, 56, 125
Shakespeare, William 155
Sheba, Queen of 102
Shelley, Percy 177
Sherman, Tecumseh 104
Sicily 5, 19, 25, 28, 32, 62–3, 78–80,
    84, 91–3, 108, 113, 119, 133–5,
    139, 141, 143, 151, 163–5, 168
Siena 163
Simplon tunnel 120
Sinatra, Frank 156
Singapore 88
Sinigaglia, Oscar 111
Sistine Chapel 159–60
Slovenia 3, 14
Snia Viscosa 124
socialism 21, 31, 34, 55, 60–1, 72,
    88, 92, 102, 121–2, 125, 184
Società delle Strade Ferrate
    dell'Alta Italia 80
Società italiana degli albergatori
    165–6, 173
Società italiana di mutuo soccorso
    131
Solomon, King 102
Somalia 94, 99–101, 103, 113–14,
    116
Sonnino, Sidney 28–30, 32–3, 42,
    52, 98, 117, 164, 168
South Africa 114
South America 24, 128–9

South Australia 146–7
'Southern Question' 2, 18, 20, 24, 34, 67, 90, 92–3, 118, 120, 126, 131, 133, 138–9
Spadolini, Giovanni 7, 9
Spain 12, 30, 36, 51, 70, 101, 110, 128, 149, 178–9, 183
Spensley (footballer) 167
Sponza, Lucio 130–1
Sri Lanka 116
Stalin, Joseph 42, 55, 125
Statius 97
Steinberg, Jonathan 13
Stravinsky, Igor 156
Stringher, Bonaldo 82, 163–4
Sturzo, Luigi 125
Sudan 98
Suez 26, 97
Susa 57, 74, 179
'Svevo, Italo' (Ettore Schmitz) 13–14, 186
Sweden 30, 165, 178–9
Switzerland 36, 65, 80–1, 83, 101, 114, 120, 132, 157, 163, 165, 168–9, 171
Sydney 145
Syria 25, 43, 95

Taiwan 97
Tamaro, Attilio 54
Tambroni, Ferdinando 56
Tampa 134–5
Taormina 163, 170–1
Taylor, A.J.P. 11, 27–8, 32, 37
Tempo 94, 109
Thaon di Revel, Paolo 42
Thompson, E.P. 5, 133
Ticino 19, 157
Tigray 103
Tilly, Charles 133
Times, The 130
Tittoni, Tommaso 23, 97–8
Tobruk 106
Toeplitz, Giuseppe 83
Togliatti, Palmiro 42, 55, 121, 125
Toronto 135, 145
Tosi, Luciano x, 10
'totalitarianism' 36–8, 42, 52, 68, 71, 94, 123–5, 149

Touring Club Ciclistico Italiano 166
Touring Club Italiano 166–70, 173, 175, 180
tourism 7, 13, 77, 158–81
Trajan, Emperor 3
Treitschke, Heinrich von 26
Trentino 2, 19, 97, 119
Trento 22, 24, 68, 154
Trento and Trieste Society 22
Trieste 2, 13–14, 19, 22, 24, 32, 43, 46, 53–4, 68, 73, 97
Triple Alliance 23, 28, 62, 65, 83
Triple Entente 28, 82
Tripoli 30, 83, 87, 97, 103–5, 113
Tunis 3, 24–5, 43, 94, 97–8, 102, 116, 171
Turati, Filippo 31
Turin 16, 78, 83, 102, 138, 168
Turkey 95, 97–8, 104
Tuscany 34, 78, 84, 99, 119, 151, 154, 163, 168, 179, 187

Ugolini, Romano x
Umanitaria 121–2
Umberto I, King of Italy 20, 23, 29, 72, 101–2
Umberto II, King of Italy 59
Umbria 34, 63, 119, 163
Unione Velocipedistica Italiana 168
USA 2, 4, 39, 83, 117, 145, 146, 157, 161, 183; and Fascist Italy 12, 36, 44–6, 70–4, 86, 88–9, 92, 105, 123, 125–6, 128, 132, 135–7, 141, 173, 175, 185; and Liberal Italy 81–3, 92, 123, 128–9, 131, 133–5, 140, 143, 146, 151, 156, 166, 168; and Republican Italy 55, 89–91, 128, 132, 149, 178–9
USSR 12, 36, 41, 45–6, 55, 69, 72, 86, 91, 109, 125, 149, 152, 157, 183–4

Vaccari, Gualtiero 124–5
Val d'Aosta 3, 9
Val di Tenda 3
Valentino 77
Valle del Pasubio 66
Valona 23, 88

Valsecchi, Franco 9
Valtaro 130
Varese 77
Vasto 141
Vatican (Papacy) 21–4, 28, 31,
    51–2, 72, 78, 83, 90, 96, 101–2,
    121, 126, 148–51, 159
Vecoli, Rudi 117
Veloce Club 166
Veloce Club Veneziano 167
Veneto 2, 78, 119
Venice 19, 27, 33, 65, 87, 95, 111,
    142, 145, 159, 161, 163–4, 166–7,
    170–5, 179–80, 184
Venturi, Franco 7
Verdi, Giuseppe 153, 155–6
Verona 80
Versailles, peacemaking at 15, 33
Vesuvius 79, 164
Viareggio 179
Vichy 162
Victor Emmanuel II, King of Italy
    16, 29, 59, 72, 78
Victor Emmanuel III, King of Italy
    6, 22, 29, 31, 35–6, 50, 52, 72,
    106, 111
Victoria, Queen 58
Vienna 18, 155
Vienna, Congress of 97
Vietnam 72
Vigezzi, Brunello 10
Villari, Lucio 32
Villari, Luigi 54, 120, 125
Villari, Pasquale 18, 120

Virgil 153, 177
Visconti, Luchino 13, 185
Visconti Venosta, Emilio 29, 45
Vittorio Veneto 34–5, 68
Volpe, Gioacchino 6–7, 10, 56, 67,
    123
Volpi, Giuseppe 87–9, 91, 95, 104,
    172

Wagner, Richard 155
Wales 114, 130
Webster, Richard 83
Weimar 43–4, 156
Weizmann, Chaim 44, 111
Western Australia ix–x, 1, 5, 44, 96,
    141–2, 147, 174
whist 17
Whitaker family 165
William II, Emperor of Germany
    26, 171
Wilson, Woodrow 33, 67
women 1, 3–5, 69, 73, 79, 109, 118,
    129, 133, 136, 138–44, 146, 162,
    168–9, 177, 179, 182–3
Woolf, Stuart 85
World Cup 176

Yemen 3, 94, 99
Yugoslavia 3, 34, 44, 55

Zanzibar, Sultan of 99
Zavattini, Cesare 185
Zionism 111–12
Zucchi, John 135

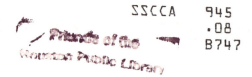